The Present State of Scholarship
in the History of Rhetoric

The Present State of Scholarship in the History of Rhetoric

A Twenty-First Century Guide

EDITED BY

Lynée Lewis Gaillet

WITH

Winifred Bryan Horner

UNIVERSITY OF MISSOURI PRESS

COLUMBIA AND LONDON

Cataloging-in-Publication data available from the Library of Congress
ISBN 978-0-8262-1868-1 (cloth), 978-0-8262-1893-3 (paper)

∞™ This paper meets the requirements of the
American National Standard for Permanence of Paper
for Printed Library Materials, Z39.48, 1984.

Designer and typesetter: Kristie Lee
Printer and binder: Integrated Book Technologies, Inc.
Typefaces: Minion and Gloucester MT Extra Condensed

Contents

Preface to the 2010 Edition

Lynée Lewis Gaillet

First published in 1983 and revised in 1990, *The Present State of Scholarship in Historical and Contemporary Rhetoric* has become a standard research tool in a variety of disciplines. In our early e-mail correspondence discussing the need for a new edition, Professor Winifred B. Horner, editor of the two earlier volumes, explains the early impetus for this work:

> The first edition of *The Present State of Scholarship in the History of Rhetoric* (1983) grew out of an annotated bibliography of rhetoric published by G. K. Hall (1980) and was part of a University of Missouri series outlining the scholarship in a number of literary genres. For authors in the G. K. Hall book, I drew on my colleagues in graduate school who shared my interest in rhetoric. It seemed a simple matter to ask these same authors to follow up their original G. K. Hall bibliographies with a bibliographic essay for the first edition of *The Present State*, reviewing the scholarship and suggesting possibilities for future research. Both of these books were my effort to define the field of rhetoric for myself, since at the time I did my graduate work there was no rhetoric program in the English discipline at a university where I could attend. At the University of Michigan, my professors, who understood my interest in language and rhetoric, allowed me to design an interdisciplinary program that combined courses in the Speech department, the English Language program, and courses in Linguistics. I was still lacking grounding in rhetoric, and I found the book tremendously helpful in my own subsequent research. Apparently, so did many other graduate students and scholars in rhetoric, to the great delight of the contributors and the press. As the study of rhetoric gained programs and students, the book filled a need.

After nineteen years, this reference work (although dated) is still in demand. Like earlier editions, the new volume, entitled *The Present State of Scholarship in the History of Rhetoric,* includes bibliographical essays with lists of both primary and secondary works addressing traditional periods within the history of rhetoric, written by contributors familiar with interdisciplinary approaches to the study of their historical fields: classical (Lois Agnew), medieval (Denise Stodola), Renaissance (Don Abbott), eighteenth century (Linda Ferreira-Buckley), nineteenth century (Lynée Lewis Gaillet), and twentieth and twenty-first centuries (Krista Ratcliffe). Since all the authors from the previous editions, with the exception of Don Abbott, were retired or unable to update their essays, we searched for new contributors who were conversant with new and interdisciplinary trends in rhetoric. Of note, we chose to retain the temporal divisions of historical periods for this volume rather than adopting a purely thematic approach to the study of rhetoric that is now in vogue. In part, this decision is in keeping with earlier versions of this text, but more importantly, we find this organizational schema useful for scholars who are teaching and taking courses grounded in chronological periods and those interested in comparative historical study. However, the recurring subdivisions and areas addressed (such as women rhetors, non-Western rhetoric, educational practices, alternative venues, electronic resources, and so on) across chapters ensure that scholars interested in researching thematic issues across time and place will have no trouble doing so.

The state of scholarship has altered drastically since 1990, to the point that the essays in this edition do not, indeed cannot, simply update, but rather recast the condition of study in the history of rhetoric. The need for a new edition of *The Present State of Scholarship in the History of Rhetoric* stems primarily from the emergence of twin research methodologies: revision and recovery. Discussing his initial plan for updating his chapter published in the revised edition, Don Abbott explains that "[i]t was soon obvious that a revision would not allow me to include a significant portion of the new scholarship on Renaissance rhetoric. Therefore, I decided it was essential to write an entirely new essay to assess the present state of scholarship specifically from 1990" to the present (82); many contributors share this stance in their efforts to update current scholarship. In discussing the revision rationale for the chapter on nineteenth-century rhetoric, I explain that the chapter for the new edition "neither restates nor eclipses Stewart's chapter [in the previous edition], but rather extends and updates the information found there" (154). Early on, the contributors realized that space constraints and burgeoning research required them to fully augment existing scholarship rather than simply repeat or update studies conducted in traditional research veins of the periods under review. The field has matured in the intervening years since the publication of the two previous editions; no longer can one volume encapsulate pertinent scholarly methodologies and research. As Ratcliffe explains in the chapter on twentieth- and twenty-first centuries rhetoric, "[R]hetoric and cultural studies scholars interrogate cultural discourses, such as gender, race, class, sexual orientation, age, region, nationality, religion, and so on. Wedding rhetoric and

cultural studies enables scholars to take 'high' and 'low' cultures as their subject matters and use rhetorical analyses as methods. The results are critiques
not just of culture but of rhetoric theory" (192). This claim holds true for each
essay in this edition and, we hope, suggests a multitude of ways for using this
text. Each contributor addresses the globalization and expansion of rhetoric,
seen clearly in the inclusion of more female rhetors, and revealed in the examination of rhetorical practices outside the academy and in discussions of
nonwhite and non-Western rhetorical practices.

Traditional conceptions of the landscape of "the" history of rhetoric have
been transformed in the wake of scholars' examinations of new venues of rhetorical engagement, recovery of figures heretofore not included in the canon,
and analysis of varying methods of civic discourse. Once scholars interested in
the history of rhetorical practices began searching for more nuanced, layered
interpretations of rhetorical action, their work naturally became more interdisciplinary; in many ways, these changes reflect the tone of scholarship characterizing communication studies rather than traditional research in the history
of rhetoric. In "A Century after the Divorce: Challenges to a Rapprochement
between Speech Communication and English," published in the cutting-edge
Sage Handbook of Rhetorical Studies (2009), Roxanne Mountford analyzes the
fragmentation and splintering that rhetoric studies experienced over the course
of the twentieth century. Calling for a renewed sense of collaboration between
communication and English, Mountford seeks reunification of the estranged
disciplines: "feminist rhetoricians in English studies and speech communication have a history of reading one another's work—and citing it, because their
object of study so frequently overlaps, and because their subaltern position
makes interdisciplinary alliances more attractive. They offer a model for rhetoricians looking for greater rapprochement between speech and English." Our
work takes that model as a guide, striving to bridge twentieth-century divides
between rhetoric and communication while encouraging scholars to join members of the newly formed Alliance of Rhetoric Societies (2001) in seeking "joint
territories shared by rhetoricians in English and speech communication and to
begin anew to define cross-disciplinary coalitions."*

This edition of *The Present State*, then, is less "philosophical" than earlier
versions, in part because emerging scholarship analyzes training of rhetors,
cultural circumstances, and exigencies motivating rhetorical action, along with
focused studies of communities. Although the framework and organization of
the chapters vary within this volume according to individual author's dictates,

---

*Mountford, "A Century after the Divorce: Challenges to a Rapprochement between Speech
Communication and English," in *The Sage Handbook of Rhetorical Studies*, ed. Andrea A. Luns-
ford (Thousand Oaks, Calif.: Sage, 2009), 419, 408. For more information, visit "ARS: Alliance of
Rhetoric Societies," http://www .rhetoricalliance.org/.

each contributor addresses scholarly trends and products emerging since the publication of the revised edition (1990), repeatedly employing metaphors of mapping, photography, and geography. Influenced by the recovery and revision research methodologies that characterize much of the scholarship they are summarizing, the contributors collectively expand the traditional scope of rhetorical studies in their attempts to describe the shifting terrain of the field. The chapters share basic premises, and the resulting characterizations of emerging scholarship are familiar across the centuries, illustrated in repeated refrains. For example, Lois Agnew in the chapter on classical rhetoric challenges scholars to seek new primary sources, traverse disciplinary boundaries, and address issues of historiography and methodology in an effort not only to increase the rigor of our scholarship, but also to breathe new life into our discipline. In her survey of the medieval era, Denise Stodola examines how scholars of the last two decades build "admirably upon the 'shoulders of the giants' who preceded them" and looks to "areas for further research" (a section that is included in each chapter of this volume) as an indicator of "how much progress has been made in more effectively painting the complex picture of medieval rhetoric" (63). Agnew's and Stodola's claims hold true throughout the volume, as each period moves "beyond the outmoded constraints of the monolithic perceptive genres" in predicting future trends of research.

Linda Ferreira-Buckley explains that "the last two decades have seen significant new scholarship. This scholarship crosses continents, expands what we know about gender and class, broadens earlier definitions of rhetoric, and deepens our understanding of established figures. Some of it uses traditional methodologies to mine archives previously unstudied by scholars, and some returns to well-known materials with fresh perspectives. Some of it focuses on one or more primary theorists; others on social and political movements or on institutions and groups" (114). This characterization of current eighteenth-century scholarship joins a chorus repeated often by contributors throughout the pages of this volume, seen clearly in the repeated themes and subheadings.

Readers of earlier editions will find other changes as well. This new volume (particularly the last two sections) incorporates a greater emphasis on composition studies. In an e-mail, Professor Horner explained to me, "Early on, I visualized the study of rhetoric as naturally allied with the field's contemporary composition courses, giving it a history and rich source materials. Even as rhetoric was being abandoned by communications departments, it found a home in English departments and became associated with composition. This marriage resulted in the designation of rhetoric/comp, which has been adopted by most English departments today." Rhetorical education has been a focus of study in every historical period, but pedagogical implications shift toward composition instruction with the advent of the industrial revolution, the emergence of middle classes, the subsequent blending of education in oral and written communicative practice, and the twentieth-century development of a modern field of rhetoric/composition. In particular, the nineteenth century has long been considered an era of composition instruction; the present edition acknowledges that tradition and then expands existing notions to include a wide range of interdisciplinary scholarship addressing rhetors, venues of engagement, and rhetorical practices—both inside and outside of the classroom.

Philosophers and rhetors fully addressed in earlier volumes of this work and in myriad other encyclopedia entries and reference books are not the focus of this edition of *The Present State of the History of Rhetoric.* The contributors detail where readers can find that information and direct them to it; to slavishly repeat information found in earlier editions would negate our purposes of describing the "present state of scholarship in the history of rhetoric" and deny the field's growth and change. We hope, then, that this edition of *The Present State* will invite new scholars to the field, challenge existing scholars to reexamine connections across the disciplines and historical periods, promote interdisciplinary collaboration, and suggest areas for further research.

Acknowledgments

We wish to thank Beverly Jarrett, Clair Willcox, and Sara Davis at the University of Missouri Press for shepherding this project to publication, and Julianna Schroeder for copyediting the manuscript. We are also grateful to Georgia State University for providing research and editorial assistance: Giovanna Micconi helped prepare the first manuscript for submission; and Alice Myatt, through her thorough editing skills, close readings of the chapters, and dedication to the project, improved the quality of this work and ensured that we got the final draft to the press on time. Of course, this project would not be possible without the expertise of the contributors, who worked tirelessly to recast this project in ways that best describe the shifting terrain of rhetorical studies while welcoming new scholars to the field. We also thank the myriad "consulting experts," who were willing to share their specialized knowledge with individual contributors; this volume is richer and truer because of their generosity. As always, we thank our families for their patience and support, for feigning interest in the details of the history of rhetoric, for keeping us grounded.

The Present State of Scholarship
in the History of Rhetoric

From the Foreword to the 1990 Edition

Walter J. Ong, S.J.

The emergence and continued presence of rhetoric as a subject of academic study and as a focal point for academic and para-academic life is one of the central features of Western civilization. Although verbal performance in all cultures across the globe can be highly sophisticated and effective, nothing quite like the rhetoric worked up by the ancient Greeks and their successors developed anyplace else in the world.

Apart from its present specialized reference in the United States to courses in effective writing, the term *rhetoric* commonly suggests to the modern mind, in the United States as elsewhere, verbal profusion calculated to manipulate an audience, an operation whose aims are suspect and whose typical procedures are mostly trivializing. Yet in centuries past *rhetoric* was commonly used in the West to refer to one of the most consequential and serious of all academic subjects and of all human activities. As the art of persuasion, the art of producing genuine conviction in an audience, rhetoric affected the entire range of human action as nothing else in theory or in practice quite did. The study and use of rhetoric enabled one to move others, to get things done.

To many Renaissance humanists, as Jerrold E. Seigel has shown in *Rhetoric and Philosophy in Renaissance Humanism*, by contrast with rhetoric most if not all other academic subjects were trivializing: philosophical and scientific theorizing was utterly inconsequential because it had no effect on events, on the way people actually behaved. The study of rhetoric required engagement

Editors' note: Walter Ong's foreword for the first edition had been repeated in the previous revision. It is such a brilliant definition of rhetoric and an overview of its historical significance through the ages that there seemed little to add or change. It was appropriate for the 1983 first edition and 1990 revision and still speaks eloquently to our time. We decided, therefore, to reprint Father Ong's work in this volume. His words in this section seem even more relevant for the enlarged scope of this edition: "The study of rhetoric required engagement in the totality of human affairs, in politics and other decision-making fields, in real life."

in the totality of human affairs, in politics and other decision-making fields, in real life, as the ancient Greeks and Romans had already appreciated. Rhetoric conferred power, and admirably humane power, for its power depended on producing conviction in others, on giving others grounds to act on out of free human decision resulting from deliberation. Such power befitted human beings. It was radically different from the brute power exerted by war and other uses of physical force. Compared to knowledge of rhetoric, with its power to determine the course of history, the rest of knowledge in itself was ineffectual twaddle, unless it could be put to rhetorical use—as any or all of it might be, for, as Cicero insisted, it is the business of the orator or practicing rhetorician, who is the leader in public affairs, to know everything. The demands of rhetoric defined for Cicero what liberal education was.

Yet the ancient and Renaissance worlds also had some misgivings about rhetoric. Socrates and Plato and Aristotle professed to believe that the Sophists of their day generally were dishonest rhetoricians, using their intellectual and verbal skill to trick their audiences and teaching their disciples to do the same. This charge illustrates in another way the power of rhetoric. There are dangers of deception at many levels inherent in its use: if the charge is true, the Sophists were rhetorical deceivers; if it is not, their accusers were guilty of the rhetorical deception of which they accused the Sophists. It seems that honors here were in fact somewhat even. Much modern scholarship has shown that the Sophists were in fact often brilliant and learned men, though more concerned with training for practical life than with theories of "philosophy," and that they did not all profess or teach intellectual or verbal irresponsibility or chicanery.

Aristotle defined the art of rhetoric as the faculty of finding in any given case the available means of persuasion. As this definition astutely indicates, one who wants to persuade needs skills that are essentially heuristic, an art of finding. Rhetoric starts with the conclusion, the position it wants to convince others to take, for which it must find supporting reasons. In this it contrasts with logic. Logic lets premises lead to whatever conclusion they lead to. Rhetoric knows its conclusions in advance, and clings to them. This heuristic nature of rhetorics is what makes it open to charges of opportunism. With its end in view, it will use any means, moral or immoral, that work to achieve that end.

Aristotle notes that the practice of rhetoric grows at first from a natural ability. Most people attempt to support or assess or attack one or another opinion verbally or to defend or attack other persons verbally, and through hit-and-miss experience many eventually develop a certain knack for highly effective procedures. Presumably such was the case from the beginning of humankind in all cultures. Rhetoric remained pretty much in this relatively unreflective state in the West until the effective interiorization of alphabetic writing among the ancient Greeks by the fifth century B.C. Such writing made possible the lengthy, analytic linear organization of thought that we call scientific and that, once it had become more or less a habit of mind, could transform orally composed thought itself into a new literate orality, using thought processes unavailable before writing. Like Plato, Aristotle felt the new drive to the more abstract, logically sequential thought and undertook to investigate and state in abstract scientific form, among other things, how successful speakers in his milieu gained their ends and why. The result was the book we know as his *Art of Rhetoric.* In Pope's words, Aristotle "methodized" what had previously been a "natural" rhetoric into a consciously reflective, analytic "art." Of course, as Pope had perhaps not been entirely aware, developing "nature" into an "art" changes nature a bit. Reflection always entails creation.

Like all developments deeply embedded in human existence, the new "art" of rhetoric faced into the past as well as into the future. On the one hand, its development into a scientized "art" depended on the mind's having interiorized writing, which was the wave of the future leading quickly not only to abstractly organized science but also to the foundation of empires. But on the other hand, the subject matter of rhetoric among the ancient Greeks belonged to the past: in Aristotle and elsewhere rhetoric was in fact concerned not with written discourse primarily but with oral discourse, the earlier mode of verbal expression, of course still very much alive. *Rhētōr* in Greek means orator, public speaker, and *technē rhētorikē,* or, more simply, *rhētorikē,* means public speaking. To Aristotle's world, teaching students rhetoric meant teaching them to become orators. Deflection of rhetoric from oral performance to written argumentation as such, vaguely incipient at best in Aristotle, would occur only very slowly and imperceptibly over the centuries. Yet it must be remembered that the oral speeches were already being shaped by the chirographic milieu to post-oral thought forms. The mental processes of academically educated Greeks in Plato's day and later, as Eric Havelock has shown in *The Greek Concept of Justice,* differed considerably from those of Homer's age, and these processes, though grounded in literacy, showed clearly not only in written treatises such as *The Art of Rhetoric* but also in the oral performance of literates.

Its long-standing commitment to orality over the centuries, a commitment not consciously designed or even adverted to, suggests that the deepest roots of rhetoric are archaic, though now covered by a centuries-old tangle of academic and other cultural growth. Rhetoric plays an important part in the growth of consciousness that marks human psychic and cultural history and that is accelerated vastly as verbal discourse is technologized through writing, then print, and now electronics and as thought processes are transformed while greater and greater stores of knowledge are accumulated. In its overall effect, rhetoric raises consciousness, as Gilbert Durand has shown in *Les Structures anthropologiques de l'imaginaire,* moving thought from the older, more purely imaging stages toward the greater abstractions of logic. Rhetorical antitheses are negotiable: *yes, more or less; no, more or less.* The antitheses of formal logic are typically nonnegotiable, absolute—setting up irreducible binarism that ultimately makes its way into the computer. *It is, or it isn't.*

The patterns whereby consciousness grows out of the unconscious of course differ from culture to culture—indeed, such patterns in the last analysis may constitute the most basic differences between cultures. And rhetoric is, of course, not the only factor that determines and registers the patterns of growth. But certainly in the West rhetoric is a central determinant and indicator. In other parts of the world, rhetoric was managed differently. In *Polarity and Analogy,* G. E. R. Lloyd has shown how ancient Greek thought generally specialized in differences (polarities) as against likenesses (analogies) more than any of the many other cultures that he examines from across the globe. Greek rhetoric, specifically, certainly specialized in antitheses, and out of this specialization, as I. M. Bochenski has shown in *A History of Formal Logic,* grew the logic that underlay Greek analytic thinking and that underlies modern science and the changes in human life that science has wrought. In *Communication and Culture in Ancient India and China,* where of course rhetoric was practiced, as it has been everywhere, Robert T. Oliver reports no interest in formalized rhetoric comparable to that of ancient Greece. (Formal logic came into being also in India, as Bochenski points out—perhaps independently of the Greek invention—but some five hundred years later than in Greece.)

The centrality of rhetoric in the West is tied in largely with its conspicuous academic and para-academic presence. But academic rhetoric has led no eremitical existence. From the ancient Greeks to the present, the teaching of rhetoric has affected and been affected by political and other institutions, philosophical theories (themselves often partly rhetorical in origin), educational practices and aims, the growth of science, and much else.

From patristic times and earlier, rhetoric has also much affected and been much affected by the Judeo-Christian ethos—a fact more taken for granted than discussed by historians of rhetoric. Judeo-Christian teaching sets up a kind of rhetorical situation between human beings and God. Job argued with God. He argued with utter reverence—observed decorum, as a later rhetoric would put it—but unabashedly, for the relationship of each human being to God in faith is personal and personally interactive. Christian teaching regarding the Incarnation intensified the interaction. The Word himself became flesh, the Word who is also the Son, the Second Person of the Trinity of Father, Son, and Holy Spirit. The Word or Son is the communication of the Father—Son inasmuch as he is Word, and Word inasmuch as he is Son (*eo verbum quo filius,* as the succinct Latin logion puts it), and he came as a human being to announce the Good News, the Gospel, the *kerygma.* Human speaking and persuasion are of the essence of Christianity, though Christian faith as such transcends the human action with which it meshes. *Pistis,* the Greek term for faith among the early Christians, which Paul says "comes from hearing" (Romans 10:17), is the same word that occurs in rhetoric texts for the conviction that the public speaker undertakes to establish in his hearers. Moreover, the Word, the Son, brings human beings to the Father, and Christians plead rhetorically with the Father "through him, with him, and in him." The Holy Spirit, who enables the faithful to pray, is identified by Jesus as the *Paraklētos*, the "advocate," one who pleads another's case as in court. In this prophetic milieu, it is little wonder that the liturgy of the Christian Church, Eastern and Western, is shot through with highly self-conscious rhetoric: the hundreds of opening prayers at Mass in the Latin Liturgy, for example, and comparable prayers in other liturgies, Protestant as well as Catholic, are rhetorical showpieces, as are also countless homilies.

As the studies in this book make abundantly clear, rhetoric as an academic subject persisted, with varied fortunes and intensities, from classical antiquity through the Middle Ages, the Renaissance, and intervening centuries down to the present. Drilled into students in the earlier years of the curriculum, rhetoric inevitably extended itself with greater or lesser force far beyond the classroom, for rhetorical skills were supposed to be applied everywhere: in law and politics, in public celebrations marked by the florid oratory that into the present century bears the mark of academic rhetorical (oratorical) training, in preaching, in medicine (before the present century, physician-patient relationships often depended more upon vocal exchange promoting trust than on precisely targeted pharmaceuticals), in letter-writing and in poetry and fiction (novelists such as Hawthorne and Melville clearly show speechifying tendencies in their prose), and in general, through all affective human relations.

The persistent presence of rhetoric as a recognized force in Western culture can be seen in the number of major intellectual figures known today chiefly for their work in a variety of other subjects who at one time or another taught rhetoric or wrote about it. In the recent English-speaking world alone, one finds, for example, the scientist Joseph Priestley, the economist Adam Smith, the political scientist and diplomat and sixth president of the United States of America John Quincy Adams, who became professor of rhetoric and belles-lettres at Harvard after being in the Unites States Senate, the physician James Rush, the litterateur Thomas De Quincey, and the engineer cum physical scientist cum philosopher Herbert Spencer—all noted, along with others, in the present book.

Perhaps partly because of the very pervasiveness of rhetoric, the history of rhetoric has only begun to shape up effectively in recent times. Early histories of the subject, even as late as John Quincy Adams's brief account, could not achieve the distance required for historical effectiveness.

In recent times rhetoric has become more vigorous and more protean than ever before. The modern world has found new ways of exercising the persuasion that used to be practiced chiefly through verbal performance. Rhetoric has spread from its original habitat in the world of direct vocal exchange into newly created arenas, first to the written page, then to the printed page, with its charts and diagrams and illustrations—presenting the reader with what William M. Ivans, Jr., in *Prints and Visual Communication*, has called "exactly repeatable visual statements"—then to display advertising, a quite new development that utilizes dramatic arrangements of variously printed words as well as illustrations, on to skywriting, television, and all the rest. The present human lifeworld is saturated with rhetoric. Concern with various kinds of human interaction has alerted the present age, perhaps more in the United States than elsewhere, to the precise rhetorical elements in business transactions, in storytelling, in professedly objective reporting, in documentary films, and in philosophy and science, to name only a few of rhetoric's domains. Suddenly, rhetoric, the art of persuasion originally connected chiefly with oratory, has become totally amoeban, surrounding and consuming our entire lifeworld. The reason for this is essentially simple, although it is unfashionable to note it: paradoxically, in our technological world interpersonal relations have become more frequent and more complex in many ways than before.

In the historiography of rhetoric in the West, it appears that a disproportionate amount of work has been done by United States scholars. The reasons for this are various, but the fact itself suggests that rhetoric relates to social structures and to psychic life in the United States somewhat differently than it does in other parts of the Western world. It is sometimes said that Europeans and Latin Americans learn how to practice rhetoric and United States scholars study it. The rhetorical heritage is a part of the ethos of Europe. It is less familiar, more distanced, and more intellectually interesting to scholars in the United States. Whatever the case, this book should be of great practical value to scholars around the world and of special value to those teaching writing as well as to those interested in many areas of literary study not often associated with rhetoric, such as reader-oriented criticism and speech-act theory, structuralism, textualism, deconstructionism, and much else. It is a book for all seasons.

1

The Classical Period

Lois Agnew

The 1990 edition of *The Present State of Scholarship in Historical and Contemporary Rhetoric* emerged at a transitional moment in the production of scholarship in classical rhetoric. Of course, it would be an exaggeration to depict any particular moment as a unique turning point in historical scholarship; after all, each scholarly era must inevitably seek to distinguish itself from the work that has been done before. Such distinctions involve disciplinary transformation that occurs gradually as scholars introduce new questions that engage with ideas that have circulated before and further develop them over time through conversation with others.

As the chapter and bibliography on classical rhetoric written by Richard Leo Enos and Anne Blakeslee for the previous edition of this publication demonstrate, many strands of today's scholarship in classical rhetoric can be found in the body of work that had been done before 1990. Earlier work also anticipated the interest in revisionary histories that has been so important in recent scholarship. The 1988 CCCC panel "Octalog: The Politics of Historiography," which Enos and Blakeslee mention at the end of their essay, highlights this fact, as eight prominent scholars came together to discuss the purpose and methods of historical research, what "counts" as evidence, and the relationship between rhetoric and history writing. Their stimulating exchange and the attention focused on its 1988 publication in *Rhetoric Review* illustrate the interest in historiography and alternative histories of rhetoric that were present before the period of scholarship taken up in this volume.

Many of the questions raised in the 1988 panel have maintained an ongoing presence in subsequent scholarship. Yet, although the outlines for new lines of research can be found in scholarship before 1990, it is important to note that a marked increase in revisionary histories of rhetoric has been evident since then. This essay reflects ways in which these revisionary accounts have offered new conceptions of classical rhetoric's history.

Primary Works

Greek Rhetorics

Key primary texts reveal the varying perspectives on rhetoric's scope and civic function that emerged in Greece during the fifth to fourth centuries BCE. Attention to language's epistemic and persuasive function is evident in pre-Socratic and sophistic writings as early as the fifth century BCE. The rise of democracy during this period also serves as a catalyst for exploring the civic possibilities for persuasive oratory—an interest also reflected in pre-Socratic and sophistic texts. Unfortunately, primary texts representing this group of thinkers are relatively scarce. Several important compilations of pre-Socratic and sophistic fragments are available: *Die Fragmente der Vorsokratiker* (ed. Hermann Diels and Walther Kranz, 1972) and *Artium scriptores: Reste der voraristotelischen Rhetorik* (ed. Ludwig Radermacher, 1951) provide collections of fragments printed in Greek; Kathleen Freeman's *Ancilla to the Pre-Socratic Philosophers* (1983) provides summary and translations of pre-Socratic fragments; Rosamond Kent Sprague's *The Older Sophists* (1972) provides a translation of fragments found in *Die Fragmente der Vorsokratiker;* and a commentary with fragments presented in both Greek and English is found in G. S. Kirk, J. E. Raven, and M. Schofield's *The Presocratic Philosophers: A Critical History with a Selection of Texts* (1995). T. M. Robinson's translation of *Dissoi Logoi* is available in his 1979 publication *Contrasting Arguments,* listed in the bibliography, and is also excerpted in the second edition of Bizzell and Herzberg's *The Rhetorical Tradition* (2001).

One of the important changes in the representation of classical rhetoric's history since 1990 is greater attention to Isocrates' significance in conversations about rhetoric's role in the political life of Athens. Isocrates, who opened a school emphasizing rhetorical education in Athens in 393 BCE, emphasizes pedagogy that guides students to learn how to respond to urgent civic matters through imitation and practice. His exposition of this approach and its ethical implications can be found in *Against the Sophists* (ca. 389 BCE), a text written early in his career to foster interest in his school, and in *Antidosis* (ca. 354–353 BCE), a later text that defends Isocrates' pedagogical methods. Isocrates' works are compiled in three volumes and translated by George Norlin and La Rue Van Hook for the Loeb Classical Library series (1928, 1929, 1945); translations by David Mirhady and Yun Lee Too (2000) and Terry Papillon (2004) have recently been published by the University of Texas Press as part of the Oratory of Classical Greece Series, edited by Michael Gagarin.

Isocrates' emphasis on the connection between instruction in public discourse and the development of civic responsibility provides an interesting response to Plato's questions about rhetoric's identity. In his dialogues, Plato uses the sophists to represent rhetoric's negative potential. Through his constructions of the sophists, Plato depicts rhetoric as inherently superficial and geared toward the pursuit of immediate gratification and self-interest, as opposed to the pursuit of truth through dialectic. In *Gorgias* (ca. 387 BCE), he highlights the danger surrounding rhetorical training that is not firmly grounded in knowledge of the good. Plato's *Phaedrus* (ca. 370 BCE) again denounces the potential abuse of language's power by rhetoricians but goes on to define a "true rhetoric" through which the enlightened rhetor guides others to truth through a carefully defined dialectical process. These dialogues are available in the translations and editions listed in the bibliography. The Lamb translation of *Gorgias* and the Fowler translation of *Phaedrus* are also printed in their entirety in Bizzell and Herzberg.

Another major contribution to developments in Greek rhetoric came from Aristotle, whose *Rhetoric* (ca. 330 BCE) provides a thorough explication of principles of rhetoric he identified based on his observation of the rhetorical practices of his day. Many of Aristotle's precepts for rhetoric, including his description of the three categories of artistic proof (*pathos, ethos,* and *logos*) and his identification of rhetorical genres (deliberative, forensic, and epideictic), have maintained a consistent presence in the subsequent development of rhetoric, both through their elaboration in Latin rhetorical treatises and through their appropriation in the work of twentieth-century rhetoricians. George Kennedy has produced *On Rhetoric,* the most recent complete translation, including extensive notes and commentary, published by Oxford University Press and issued as a second edition in 2006.

Revisionary scholarship has placed new emphasis on the study of figures who have been featured less prominently in previous histories, rhetorical practices, and the cultural contexts in which rhetoric emerged. The bibliography lists translations of several significant Greek orators, including those available through the Oratory of Classical Greece Series mentioned above. The 2006 edition of Kennedy's translation of *On Rhetoric* includes the addition of appendices containing speeches such as Gorgias's "Encomium of Helen," Lysias's "Against the Grain Dealers," and Demosthenes' "Third Philippic" and excerpts from the earliest available example of a rhetoric manual, *Rhetorica ad Alexandrum* (ca. 340 BCE). The complete treatise of *Rhetorica ad Alexandrum* is available in the Loeb series (1938). In 2003, Kennedy published a translation of four Greek progymnasmata exercises attributed to Theon, Hermogenes, Aphthonius, and Nicolaus. Kennedy also published a translation of two texts attributed to Hermogenes, *On Invention* and *On the Method of Forcefulness,* in 2005. This publication includes Hugo Rabe's 1913 version of the Greek texts.

While the writings of classical historians such as Thucydides, Herodotus, and Plutarch have always provided valuable information about rhetoric's historical contexts, they have achieved new importance for scholars determined to recover the voices of those who were not given the opportunity to theorize or practice rhetoric in ways that have traditionally been recognized. The recognition that the writings of ancient historians can provide contemporary scholars with useful information about classical rhetoric's development has expanded the range of sources beyond the traditional canon.

The bibliography provides additional listings for translations of primary texts representing Greek rhetorical pedagogy, theories, and practices. Much current scholarship notes that an awareness of the power of language can be seen in the Greek poetic tradition long before the formal emergence of rhetoric as a discipline. Discussions of rhetoric's stylistic and literary qualities can also be found in the writings of later Greeks, including Dionysius of Halicarnassus, Demetrius, and Longinus. The elaboration of theories of *stasis,* a central principle in Latin rhetorical treatises, can be found in the writings of Hermagoras (second century BCE) and Hermogenes (ca. 150 CE)

Latin Rhetorics

The transmission of rhetoric from Greek to Latin culture led to new developments in rhetoric's identity and civic function. The *Rhetorica ad Herennium* (ca. 84 BCE) provides a complete rhetoric manual, including a thorough discussion of the five canons of rhetoric (invention, arrangement, style, memory, and delivery), with particular attention to style. The author of the text is unknown; although it was originally attributed to Cicero, most scholars now believe that this is not accurate. While the text probably comprises lecture notes and may contain little original material, it provides an excellent example of the Roman development of Greek rhetorical principles. Harry Caplan's translation and introduction (1954) are available in the Loeb series.

Cicero was unquestionably a dominant figure in rhetoric's evolution in Europe from the Medieval period through the eighteenth century. His earliest treatise, *De inventione* (ca. 86 BCE), provides a systematic treatment of the canon of invention, including an extensive treatment of forensic rhetoric and stasis theory. Although Cicero subsequently discounted the significance of *De inventione,* this treatise shared with *Rhetorica ad Herennium* a prominent position in rhetoric's development in the Latin West. Cicero's famous rhetorical work *De oratore* (ca. 55 BCE) presents his argument for rhetoric as the premier discipline that requires breadth of knowledge, the development of a keen ethical sense, and a strong civic consciousness. The bibliography notes several fine translations, including the most recent, a 2001 translation by James M. May and Jakob Wisse. Cicero's other major rhetorical works, *De Optimo Genere Oratorum, Topica, Brutus, Orator,* and *De Partitione Oratoria,* are also included in the bibliography.

Quintilian's educational treatise, *Institutes of Oratory,* applies Cicero's assessment of rhetoric's ethical potential to the cultural demands of the Roman Empire. These twelve books provide a valuable resource in understanding principles of the Roman educational system during the first century CE, particularly as they related to rhetorical pedagogy. The twelfth volume of this treatise presents an exposition of Quintilian's famous notion that rhetorical training should encourage the development of "the good man skilled in speaking," a crystallization of centuries of conversation about rhetoric's ethical mission—and a statement that maintains a presence in rhetoric's evolution for centuries to come. A 2002 translation by Donald A. Russell is now available in five volumes through the Loeb series.

Secondary Scholarship

A vast array of fine scholarship in classical rhetoric has been produced in the years between 1990 and the present. The limited space available for this essay and bibliography does not allow for a full discussion and listing of that scholarship. The essay and the bibliography that follows are intended to identify important recent trends in classical rhetorical scholarship and to offer a sampling of publications since 1990 that represent the wide range of perspectives that are currently enhancing and expanding scholarly conversations about ancient rhetorics.

Historiography

The 1988 Octalog discussion exemplifies the self-conscious engagement with the aims and methods of history writing that has characterized scholarship in classical rhetoric during the last decade and a half. Many scholars have contributed to this conversation through offering alternative ways of reading canonical historical texts. In *The Art of Wondering: A Revisionist Return to the History of Rhetoric* (1988), William Covino offers a reading of Plato, Aristotle, and Cicero that highlights the ambiguity and complexity found in these texts. Victor Vitanza's *Negation, Subjectivity, and the History of Rhetoric* (1997) suggests the possibility of revising rhetorical history through initiating a Third Sophistic that challenges the Aristotelian foundationalism that has dominated rhetoric. Jasper Neel (1994) also encourages resistance to Aristotle's domination of rhetorical studies through a sophistic perspective that can reinvigorate writing instruction. James Berlin (1992) calls for scholars to allow for multiple interpretations of Aristotle, rather than searching for "the true Aristotle." Kathleen E. Welch (1994) explores ways in which issues of race shape constructions of classical rhetoric. In *Seduction, Sophistry, and the Woman with the Rhetorical Figure* (2001), Michelle Ballif argues that an Aristotelian emphasis on dialectical truth has consistently suppressed sophistic possibility, a pattern that can be reversed through the seductive alternative of a Third Sophistic Woman who denies the binary structures embedded in oppositional rhetoric. *Classical Rhetoric and Rhetoricians* (2005), a reference volume edited by Ballif and Michael G. Moran, reflects the turn toward alternative versions of history, as it includes bibliographies and entries on figures traditionally represented in the classical canon, such as Aristotle, Cicero, and Quintilian, alongside those whose contributions have not been featured as prominently in accounts of rhetoric's history, including Anaximenes, Antiphon, Aelius Aristides, Cornelia, and Philodemus. The bibliography also includes several anthologized essays addressing issues of historiography that include explicit discussion of classical rhetorics. Robert Gaines's "De-Canonizing Ancient Rhetoric" (2005), published in *The Viability of the Rhetorical Tradition*, holds particular relevance for issues of historiography in classical rhetoric, as Gaines argues that ancient rhetoric should be conceived not as a body of canonical texts, but as a rich array of rhetorical practices and contexts that provide opportunities for creative scholarship.

Women and Classical Rhetoric

Gaines's call to extend research in ancient rhetoric beyond the boundaries of canonical texts implicitly supports efforts to address the long-standing exclusion of women from discussions of ancient rhetoric. A number of feminist historians have articulated the need to acquire new conceptions of historiography and research methods that challenge narrow conceptions of rhetoric that have historically excluded women from rhetoric's history. Robert Connors's 1992 "The Exclusion of Women from Classical Rhetoric" identifies classical rhetoric's historic connection with agonistic public displays as the cause of women's exclusion from accounts of classical rhetoric's history. Many scholars have accordingly sought to challenge definitions that limit classical rhetoric in various ways in order to develop an understanding of how women engaged rhetorically within the world they inhabited. Because women in the classical world were typically denied opportunities to document their own rhetorical practices, the enterprise of creating women's rhetorical histories benefits from interdisciplinary scholarship that provides an awareness of the cultural circumstances surrounding women in antiquity. It also frequently involves interpreting men's reports of women's activities, which has broader implications for historiography. Susan Blundell's *Women in Ancient Greece* (1995) examines representations of women in art, literature, and legal documents, offering a valuable resource for understanding the status of women in the ancient world. In "Women: The Unrecognized Teachers of the Platonic Socrates," Elena Duverges Blair (1996) examines Plato's emphasis on women as the only teachers from whom Socrates is able to learn, concluding that this framework both reflects Plato's conception of Socrates' mystical intelligence and captures Socrates' appreciation for women's intellectual abilities.

Scholars in rhetoric have drawn upon their expertise in working with rhetorical texts in order to illuminate the intersections between women, language, and power in antiquity. Susan Biesecker (1992) argues that oratory provides an important site for understanding how women's social roles were negotiated; she examines Gorgias's and Isocrates' encomia to Helen within the cultural milieu of Pericles' law expanding citizenship requirements to both parents in order to illuminate ways in which rhetoricians both reinscribe and resist expanded social roles for women in democratic Athens. Jan Swearingen's "A Lover's Discourse: Diotima, Logos, and Desire" (1995) similarly focuses on women's public roles in antiquity as neither fixed nor stable; she maintains that Plato's representation of Diotima and Aspasia provides evidence of women's participation in public life in classical Athens and argues that those who dismiss the value of literary sources and lament the lack of "concrete" evidence concerning women's roles are implicitly supporting earlier eras in which women's contributions have been effaced. Other scholars share Swearingen's interest in recovering the rhetorical achievements of Aspasia, who is described by a number of classical sources as a remarkable rhetorician and teacher. Of particular note are Cheryl Glenn's (1997, 1994, 1997) extensive examinations of classical sources that form the basis for a more complete understanding of Aspasia and her contribution to rhetoric's history ("Locating Aspasia"; "Sex, Lies, and Manuscript"; *Rhetoric Retold*) and Susan Jarratt and Rory Ong's (1995) discussion of how the study of Aspasia contributes to an understanding of not only who she was, but also of cultural assumptions that contributed to varying constructions of her identity ("Aspasia: Rhetoric, Gender"). Madeleine Henry's *Prisoner of History: Aspasia of Miletus and Her Biographical Tradition* (1995) also offers a valuable resource in understanding the character of Aspasia as she has been rhetorically constructed at different points in history.

Robert W. Cape (1997) notes that Roman women's rhetorical practices have not been studied as extensively as those of Greek women. Cape argues that rhetorical historians should devote more attention to Roman women, on the grounds that they were less restricted in their public roles than Greek women. He also maintains that Romans would have been more likely to acknowledge women as engaged in rhetoric due to Roman awareness of the rhetoricity of private discourse.

The project of recovering women's voices for the history of rhetoric is challenging and complex. It offers opportunities for productive conversations about the nature of historical evidence and interpretation, as demonstrated in the 2000 exchange by Xin Liu Gale, Cheryl Glenn, and Susan Jarratt, printed in *College English*. Gale's article raises questions about the methodologies used in historical interpretation; the responses from Glenn and Jarratt articulate their visions of the role of feminist historiography in creating new readings of history and creative possibilities for reimagining the place of women in rhetorical history.

Sophistic Rhetoric

Questions of historiography have also been central in conversations surrounding the Sophists' place in rhetoric's history, which has continued to build on the recovery of the Sophists that was discussed in Enos and Blakeslee's 1990 essay. In *Rereading the Sophists* (1991), Susan Jarratt argues against the centrality of Plato and Aristotle in representations of rhetoric's history. She maintains that carefully studying the Sophists and assigning them a more prominent place in the history of rhetoric can provide a valuable lens for adopting a more progressive approach to contemporary issues of scholarship and pedagogy in rhetoric and composition. In the introduction to *Rhetoric, Sophistry, and Pragmatism* (1995), a collection of essays edited by Steven Mailloux, Mailloux depicts the Sophists of ancient Greece as the founders of the pragmatist tradition. Jacqueline de Romilly's *The Great Sophists in Periclean Athens* (1988; trans. 1992) provides a useful overview of the influence of the Sophists on Greek culture. John Poulakos's work also combines the study of the Sophists with an exploration of the relevance of sophistic thought to contemporary issues. His identification of the sophistic notions of *kairos*, appropriateness, and possibility defines parameters that have contemporary implications for rhetorical theory and pedagogy. Poulakos's 1995 monograph, *Sophistical Rhetoric in Classical Greece*, offers a study of the Sophists in their cultural context, including an exposition of general principles that defined their rhetorical practices and an examination of their early reception.

Among the scholars who have made major contributions to our understanding of the cultural contexts in which the Sophists lived and worked is Richard Leo Enos, whose methodology features an examination of a wide range of archaeological and textual sources; his 1992 article titled "Why Gorgias of Leontini Traveled to Athens: A Study of Recent Epigraphical Evidence" examines the historical forces that fostered Gorgias's reputation and facilitated the spread of rhetoric. Andrew Ford (2001) also seeks an understanding of the Sophists within their own cultural environment, as he suggests that the Sophists would have seen themselves not as teachers of rhetoric, but as pursuing knowledge more broadly conceived through the convergence of a number of liberal arts. Michael Gagarin's examination (2001) of the Sophists leads him to argue that

Gorgias emphasizes the pleasure of language use rather than persuasion as the primary objective of his rhetorical activity.

Much scholarship on the Sophists has focused on Gorgias. Bruce McComiskey's *Gorgias and the New Sophistic Rhetoric* (2002) carefully examines Gorgias's techne within its historical moment and challenges the Platonic assumptions that have often affected subsequent interpretations of Gorgias's texts. Scott Consigny (2001) argues that Gorgias's antifoundational philosophy contains a serious challenge to Platonic idealism.

Edward Schiappa's extensive research in the rhetorical practices of figures associated with sophistic rhetoric, including Gorgias and Protagoras, exemplifies a sustained effort to provide a more complete understanding of the contributions of particular individuals to Greek culture, philosophy, and language use. His *Protagoras and Logos: A Study in Greek Philosophy and Rhetoric* (1991) provides an example of the thorough exploration of one individual's contributions to Greek culture and philosophy. Schiappa's work consistently reflects a meticulous effort to understand the evolution in the perspectives of Greeks at particular cultural moments, which often involves attention to philological issues. In "Did Plato Coin Rhetorike?" (1990) Schiappa argues for the likelihood that Plato originated the term *rhetorike,* and he maintains that the prior absence of that term suggests that people had no formal conception of rhetoric as a discipline until the fourth century BCE. He elaborates this idea more fully in *The Beginnings of Rhetorical Theory in Greece* (1999), as he distinguishes what he describes as predisciplinary language practices and the later development of conscious theories of rhetoric. Schiappa's concern about interpretations that appropriate historical figures to serve contemporary purposes leads him to question histories that in his view lead to generalizations about groups of individuals who might not have seen themselves as members of a group with common characteristics.

Schiappa's forceful critique of contemporary readings of the Sophists has generated an extensive conversation about historiography that in some respects parallels discussions surrounding feminist historiography. The extended conversations among Schiappa, John Poulakos, and Scott Consigny highlight questions concerning evidence, interpretation, and historiography that have surrounded the growing interest in sophistic rhetoric over the past two decades.* The questions that are raised in this exchange, which is documented in

---

* See John Poulakos, "Rhetoric, the Sophists, and the Possible"; Edward Schiappa, "Neo-Sophistic Rhetorical Criticism or the Historical Reconstruction of Sophistic Doctrines?"; John Poulakos, "Interpreting Sophistical Rhetoric: A Response to Schiappa"; Edward Schiappa, "History and Neo-Sophistic Criticism: A Reply to Poulakos"; Edward Schiappa, "Sophistic Rhetoric: Oasis or Mirage?"; Scott Consigny, "Edward Schiappa's Reading of the Sophists"; Edward Schiappa, "Some of My Best Friends Are Neosophists: A Reply to Scott Consigny."

the bibliography, will no doubt continue to be a feature of future conversations as rhetorical historians continue to grapple with the implications of their efforts to enact creatively the project of revisionary history.

Ancient Rhetorics beyond the West

Questions about the assumptions that shape scholarly representations of rhetoric's history have contributed to one of the major changes in ancient rhetorical studies over the past two decades—expanding the parameters of ancient rhetorics to include non-Western texts and practices. Martin Bernal's argument (1987, 1991, 2006) that black African Egyptian culture formed the basis for Greek civilization provides one example of contemporary scholars' willingness to question the assumptions that have historically shaped conceptions of our disciplinary identity. George Kennedy's *Comparative Rhetoric: An Historical and Cross-Cultural Introduction* (1998) provides an early example of an effort to create a cross-cultural study of ancient rhetorics in non-Western cultures, including Mesopotamia, Egypt, Palestine, China, and India.

Conversations about Egyptian rhetoric began as early as 1983, with Michael Fox's identification of characteristics of rhetoric found in Egyptian didactic treatises. Barbara Lesko maintains that her 1997 study of the letters and court testimony of Egyptian women complicates Fox's assessment, as it suggests that women's rhetorical practices in Egypt include bold persuasive activities that deviate from the characteristics that Fox describes as the Egyptian ideal. In 1998's "Epideictic and Ethos in the Amarna Letters: The Withholding of Argument," William Harpine notes that letters found in the ruin of Amarna exemplify language use that avoids the presentation of an overt argument, even in a deliberative situation; this analysis leads him to draw broader conclusions about ways in which unequal power relations affect rhetorical interactions. David Hutto (2002) emphasizes the significance of silence in Egyptian rhetoric, as he argues that the emphasis on social stability that underlies Egyptian rhetoric places a value both on eloquence and on the strategic use of silence. Carol Lipson's "Recovering the Multimedia History of Writing in the Public Texts of Ancient Egypt" (2005) examines the relationship between language and visual images in Egyptian monuments. Lipson examines the rhetorical deployment of the Egyptian concept of *Maat* in "Ancient Egyptian Rhetoric: It All Comes Down to *Maat*," published in *Rhetoric before and beyond the Greeks* (2004), a collection of essays edited by Lipson and Roberta A. Binkley dealing with ancient rhetorical practices across a variety of ancient cultures.

Other scholars have focused on the rhetoric of ancient cultures as revealed in biblical texts. Robert S. Reid (2005) argues that Paul deliberately uses the *Ad Herennium*'s Complete Argument in constructing his epistolary arguments. However, C. Joachim Classen (1992) raises questions about the use of categories from Greco-Roman rhetoric in interpreting Paul's letters in "St. Paul's Epistles and Ancient Greek and Roman Rhetoric." In *Ancient Rhetoric and Paul's Apology: The Compositional Unity of 2 Corinthians,* Fredrick J. Long (2004) draws upon the tradition of ancient apology found in Andocides, Socrates, Isocrates, and Demosthenes in support of his contention about the essential unity of 2 Corinthians. Margaret Zulick (1992) identifies the active verb form of "to hear" as a central term in notions of rhetoric found in the Hebrew Bible, which in her view assigns much responsibility for rhetorical interactions to the listener.

Several scholars explore how global ancient rhetorics can provide alternatives to Western patterns of thought. In "The Multiple Dimensions of Nubian/Egyptian Rhetoric and Its Implications for Contemporary Classroom Instruction," Clinton N. Crawford (2004) argues that the rhetorical traditions of Africa have been erased from rhetoric's history; he discusses how restoring an African worldview to our notion of our discipline's history can provide an African consciousness that makes justice more central to our educational system. Kermit E. Campbell (2006) argues that scholars need to learn more about the history of rhetoric in ancient Africa in order to enhance their understanding of contemporary African cultures; he examines a variety of sources in supporting his claim that the rhetorical complexity of ancient Africa has not been fully recognized and deserves further study. Xing Lu's *Rhetoric in Ancient China, Fifth to Third Century BCE: A Comparison with Classical Greek Rhetoric* (1998) meticulously studies ancient Chinese rhetoric in its own cultural context and juxtaposes it with classical Greek rhetorics. François Julien's *Detour and Access: Strategies of Meaning in China and Greece* (2000) explores the indirection at the heart of Chinese thought and language, with the goal of appreciating the "otherness" of Chinese culture and promoting an awareness of the particularity and conditioned nature of Western practices. Xiaoye You (2006) examines Confucius's rhetoric as a model of ritual as persuasion that contrasts with Greco-Roman assumptions concerning verbal proficiency as the chief mode of persuasion.

Revisiting the Canon

Even as the scope of ancient rhetoric has expanded, scholarship on canonical texts has continued to flourish. The Landmark Essays series, originally published by Hermagoras Press and continued by Lawrence Erlbaum, has made important early contributions to classical scholarship more readily accessible. Volumes in this series pertaining to classical rhetoric include *Landmark Essays on Classical Greek Rhetoric,* edited by Edward Schiappa (1994), and *Landmark Essays on Aristotelian Rhetoric,* edited by Richard Leo Enos and Lois Agnew (1998). A large amount of fine scholarship produced in recent years has provided valuable insights into classical rhetorical theories and practices. Anthologies produced during recent decades include *Re-Reading Aristotle's Rhetoric*, edited by Alan Gross and Arthur E. Walzer (2000), a collection of essays by scholars in rhetoric and composition and speech communication who emphasize the *Rhetoric*'s particular significance when examined through a rhetorical lens; *Essays on Aristotle's Rhetoric*, edited by Amelie Oksenberg Rorty (1980), a collection that examines *Rhetoric* through a philosophical lens; *Aristotle's "Rhetoric": Philosophical Essays: Proceedings of the 12th Symposium Aristotelicum*, edited by David J. Furley and Alexander Nehamas (1994), another collection that examines philosophical aspects of Aristotle's *Rhetoric; Isocrates and Civic Education*, edited by Takis Poulakos and David J. Depew (2004), an interdisciplinary collection that the editors describe as reflecting Isocrates' emphasis on flexibility in moving across genres and disciplines; and from 1998, *Quintiliano: Historia y actualidad de la retorica*, an ambitious three-volume collection on Quintilian by international scholars, edited by Tomas Albaladejo, Emmilio Del Rio, and Jose Antonio Caballero.

Much classical rhetorical scholarship depends upon careful textual analysis, which illuminates nuances in the text and highlights useful connections among theorists. Brad McAdon's prolific body of work (2004, 2006) offers meticulous readings of classical rhetorical texts; he provocatively argues that the inconsistencies he identifies across Aristotle's *Rhetoric* can be accounted for by a complicated editorial history and that the responsibility for the text that we now have may rest with Andronicus rather than Aristotle. In "Cicero as a Reporter of Aristotle and Theophrastean Rhetorical Doctrine," William W. Fortenbaugh (2005) checks Cicero's statements about Aristotle against the text of the *Rhetoric* in order to determine Cicero's reliability as a source in describing Theophrastean fragments. Lawrence Green's "Aristotle's Enthymeme and the Imperfect Syllogism" (1995) argues against the common view that Aristotle's enthymeme is simply an incomplete syllogism, maintaining that this interpretation involves reading the *Rhetoric* through a distorted Stoic and Peripatetic lens. James J. Murphy's study *On Memory and Recollection* (2002) demonstrates his notion that other Aristotelian texts can shed light on the *Rhetoric*. Sarah Newman (2002) analyzes Aristotle's image of "bringing before the eyes" in order to support her interpretation of Aristotle as endorsing a notion of style that connects with sensory experience. Terry L. Papillon's *Rhetorical Studies in the Aristocratea of Demosthenes* (1998) provides a thorough analysis of Demosthenes' *Against Aristocrates* in order to arrive at a more complete understanding of Demosthenes' persuasive strategies. Carol Poster's "Plato's Unwritten Doctrines: A Hermeneutic Problem in Rhetorical Historiography" (1993) considers textual and doxographical evidence for the existence of Plato's unwritten doctrines, leading to the intriguing conclusion that Plato's philosophical ideas are not explicitly articulated but are instead revealed to people through their active engagement with the text. Nathan Crick and John Poulakos consider how a close study of

Plato's artistic performance in the *Symposium* can illuminate his perspective on rhetoric in their article, "Go Tell Alcibiades: Tragedy, Comedy, and Rhetoric in Plato's *Symposium*" (2008).

Many scholars have focused on acquiring an enhanced understanding of the thought of ancient rhetoricians through examining the cultural assumptions and philosophical perspectives that shape the production and deployment of their rhetorical theories. Janet Atwill's *Rhetoric Reclaimed: Aristotle and the Liberal Arts Tradition* (1998) carefully examines the Greek *logon techne* tradition against Western liberal arts humanism, as she argues that productive knowledge emphasizes rhetoric as a capacity rather than fixed content available for wholesale transmission to passive recipients. Several recent books offer strong support for Isocrates' importance in rhetoric's evolution. Ekaterina Haskins (2004) argues that Isocrates should be assigned a more prominent position in histories of ancient rhetoric; her comparison of the theories of Isocrates and Aristotle depicts Isocrates' rhetoric as dynamic, performative, and social, while Aristotle emphasizes stability and neutrality, an approach that implicitly leads to rhetoric's detachment from the culture that surrounds its production. Takis Poulakos (1997) examines Isocrates' orientation toward ethics and practical wisdom as the basis for a strong relationship between rhetorical education and Athenian political life. Yun Lee Too (1995) also emphasizes the political nature of Isocrates' deployment of a literary rhetoric, as she takes special note of Isocrates' reformulation of the rhetoric teacher as an important public figure. William Benoit (1990, 1991) offers comparisons between Plato and Isocrates and Isocrates and Aristotle with the goal of demonstrating the unique positions these figures occupy in Greek rhetoric's development. Michael Leff (1994) examines the rhetorical function of Cicero's exaggerated account of the Catiline conspiracy, suggesting that an analysis of political discourse offers insight into the surrounding cultural environment beyond the basic information about the conflicts that they seem to document. Elaine Fantham's thorough exploration of Cicero's life and career and careful explication of *De Oratore* in *The Roman World of Cicero's De Oratore* (2004) are situated in a careful discussion of the political conditions that surrounded Cicero. Arthur Walzer (2003) argues that Quintilian's fusion of philosophy and rhetoric in the famous ideal of *vir bonus* is heavily indebted to Stoic thought and contributes to rhetoric's vitality in addressing the political demands of his age.

A number of scholars have contributed to earlier conversations about the complex relationship between orality and literacy in the ancient world. In "The Emergence of a Literate Rhetoric in Greece," Richard Leo Enos (2006) presents an examination of early uses of the paragraph, including examples of paragraph divisions found on stone tablets as early as the Bronze Age. Enos maintains that these paragraph markings provided interpretive guidance to speakers and audiences, which underscores the complex relationship between oral and written communication in antiquity. Kevin Robb's *Literacy and Paideia in Ancient Greece* (1994) also highlights the intricate relationship between orality and literacy in ancient Greece; Robb argues that the origins of the Greek alphabet reflect careful attention to acoustics, with dependency on alphabetic literacy evolving as a gradual process. *Voice into Text: Orality and Literacy in Ancient Greece* (1995), a collection of essays edited by Ian Worthington, examines the complex implications of the interplay between orality and literacy for Greek society. Jan Swearingen's *Rhetoric and Irony: Western Literacy and Western Lies* (1991) provides a thoughtful examination of the Western convergence of rhetoric, irony, and literacy, as the apparent alliance between language and deception assumes new force with rhetoric's alliance with literacy. Jerzy Axer's "Cicero's Court Speeches: The Spoken Text Versus the Published Text" (1995) explores how the distinct contexts surrounding Cicero's spoken and published speeches affect their reception. Richard Graff (2001) identifies a bias toward writing in Aristotle's prescription for style in *Rhetoric* 3.1–12 and explores the complicated interplay between prose and poetry in "Prose versus Poetry in Early Greek Theories of Style."

Embodying Ancient Rhetorics

In addition to studying the cultural contexts that shaped the work of central figures in the rhetorical traditions of Greece and Rome, scholars have devoted much effort to understanding more fully rhetoric as performative, embodied, and located in a specific material environment. The resulting scholarship examines rhetorical practices and physical conditions that affected rhetoric's disciplinary identity, use, reception, and relation to power.

Anthologies that have explored the connection between rhetoric, performance, and ancient cultures include *Persuasion: Greek Rhetoric in Action* (1994), edited by Ian Worthington, an anthology comprising essays about Greek rhetoric written by scholars in classics and history; *Theory, Text, Context: Issues in Greek Rhetoric and Oratory* (1996), edited by Christopher Johnstone; and *Performance Culture and Athenian Democracy* (1999), edited by Simon Goldhill and Robin Osborne. Thomas Cole's *The Origins of Rhetoric in Ancient Greece* (1991) also explores ancient Greek rhetoric as embedded in a particular cultural system, as Cole maintains that contemporary views of rhetoric as inherently opposed to philosophy are not fully in tune with the assumptions that guided rhetoric's early development. He views rhetoric as beginning with an unsystematic awareness of varied forms of language use and only gradually evolving into a distinct discipline.

Enos's *Greek Rhetorics before Aristotle* (1993) also traces the cultural circumstances that shaped the gradual evolution of Greek rhetorics, and his *Roman Rhetoric: Revolution and the Greek Influence* (1995) examines the complicated

cultural interactions that brought rhetoric from Greece to Rome. Laurent Pernot's *Rhetoric in Antiquity* (2005) examines the complex interactions between
theory and practice in rhetoric's early development.

Questions about rhetoric's relationship to poetics provide an intriguing point
of entry for considering rhetoric's civic function and identity. Jeffrey Walker's
Rhetoric and Poetics in Antiquity (2000) persuasively challenges traditional views
of rhetoric as oriented toward resolving the practical issues that arise in civic life; Walker presents a revisionary history that demonstrates how rhetoric's
grounding in the poetic tradition creates an emphasis on public discourse that
performs the epideictic function of shaping cultural identity that has not been
adequately recognized in previous accounts of rhetoric's history.

Rhetoric's role in political life has been another important concern of recent scholarship. Josiah Ober's *Mass and Elite in Democratic Athens* (1989)
considers how different forms of communication contributed to the stability
of Athenian democracy. Robert Morstein-Marx (2004) considers the role of
public discourse in maintaining power relations in the late Roman Republic.
Raphael Sealey's *Demosthenes and His Time: A Study in Defeat* (1993) examines
the intersection between Demosthenes' oratorical career and Athenian political
life. Andrew Riggsby (1997) explores the connection between rhetorical performance and forensics as he considers the extent to which speakers were able to
influence the verdicts of Roman juries.

Rhetoric's participation in cultural ritual practices has also been the subject
of a number of intriguing studies. Nicole Loraux's *The Invention of Athens: The
Funeral Oration in the Classical City* (1986) provides a thoughtful examination
of the social and political impact of funeral speeches, developing Loraux's claim
that funeral orations served an integral function in the formation of citizenship. Takis Poulakos's "Historiographies of the Tradition of Rhetoric: A Brief
History of Classical Funeral Orations" (1990) focuses on ways in which political change is reflected in Athenian funeral orations; although all of the extant
funeral orations share an imperialist message, Poulakos maintains that the contours of that message alter over time. Donovan J. Ochs's *Consolatory Rhetoric:
Grief, Symbol, and Ritual in the Roman Era* (1993) examines a wide array of
sources, including written texts, visual images, and archaeological evidence, in
interpreting ways in which the rituals surrounding funerals provided comfort
to ancient mourners.

The emphasis on rhetoric's cultural position coincides with the notion of
rhetoric as physically embodied, delivered by particular people at particular
times and in particular places. The effort to breathe life into the practices of
people who lived over two thousand years ago has involved remarkable scholarly creativity. It also effectively challenges apparent binaries that have often
characterized conversations about rhetoric, such as theory/practice, mind/
body, and reason/emotion. Debra Hawhee (2006) argues for recapturing the

connection between rhetoric and athletics in order better to understand the union between mind and body that permeated the entire Greek educational system. *Constructions of the Classical Body* (1999), an essay anthology edited by James I. Porter, also points toward the need to acknowledge the significance of the body in antiquity and draws upon a wide range of sources and disciplines in exploring this topic.

Scholars have also identified delivery as an important topic in the study of classical rhetoric. The recognition that rhetoric is embedded in particular cultures has drawn attention not only to the embodied presence of the rhetor, but also to the physical interactions between rhetor and audience. Christopher Johnstone's work (1996) has led him to consider the ramifications of the Pnyx's poor acoustical system for the rhetors and audiences who attempted to communicate there. James Fredal (2001) also demonstrates the importance of delivery in classical experiences of rhetoric. In "The Language of Delivery and the Presentation of Character: Rhetorical Action in Demosthenes' *Against Meidias*," he argues for the central role of delivery in the presentation of character, and his *Rhetorical Action in Ancient Athens: Persuasive Artistry from Solon to Demosthenes* (2006) systematically examines how the physical aspects of rhetorical performance affected communication in the ancient world. Anne Duncan's "Demosthenes versus Aeschines: The Rhetoric of Sincerity" (2006) connects the self-presentation of Demosthenes and Aeschines to theater, as she argues that both orators drew upon theatrical discourse in depicting their own sincerity and raising questions about the integrity of their opponents. Gregory S. Aldrete's *Gestures and Acclamations in Ancient Rome* (1999) describes the intricate communication between speakers and audiences in ancient Rome, including the physical gestures used by speakers and the crowd acclamations that clearly demonstrated the audience's response. Anthony Corbeill's *Nature Embodied: Gesture in Ancient Rome* (2004) provides a fine study of the importance of gesture and physical appearance in ancient Roman culture.

Awareness of the connections between physical presence and the orator's reception has promoted attention to the gendered implications of delivery. Joseph Roisman's *The Rhetoric of Manhood: Masculinity in the Attic Orators* (2006) explores the complexity that surrounds cultural assumptions concerning masculinity in ancient Greece. In "Delivering Delivery: Theatricality and the Emasculation of Eloquence," Jody Enders (1997) considers the relationship between Roman standards for delivery and the marginalization of women and homosexuals. Maud Gleason's study (1995) of the rhetorical career of two Sophists points toward the complexity of precisely defining a masculine ideal in ancient Roman society. Jay Dolmage (2006) also questions the definition of a physical ideal in Greek society; for Dolmage, the figure of Hephaestus provides an ancient model of cunning that establishes a historical precedent for imagining a rhetoric that embraces physical difference and disability.

The importance of revisionary approaches in the study of classical rhetoric was highlighted in a special 2006 issue of *Rhetoric Society Quarterly* titled *Performing Ancient Rhetorics*. Edited by Debra Hawhee and based on a classical rhetoric symposium held at the University of Pittsburgh, this series of articles provides a useful overview of a range of contemporary approaches to revisionary histories offered by a number of scholars in classical rhetoric.

Classical Rhetoric and Pedagogy—Then and Now

An awareness of the material circumstances that surround rhetoric contributes to a sense of rhetoric as practiced and taught. This recognition fosters attention to rhetoric's pedagogical mission, which Michael Leff and Richard Graff (2005) perceive as enhancing the vitality and coherence of rhetorical history. Current scholarship in contemporary rhetoric both seeks a stronger understanding of ancient teaching practices and suggests strategies for adapting ancient pedagogical insights for use in contemporary classrooms. In her 2001 introduction to *Education in Greek and Roman Antiquity,* classical scholar Yun Lee Too describes the collection as one that revises Marrou's account of ancient pedagogy, not by locating new material for study, but by asking new questions. The essays that follow devote attention to both Greek and Roman educational practices and examine the relationship between pedagogy, politics, and cultural values. James J. Murphy's edited volume, *A Short History of Writing Instruction from Ancient Greece to Modern America* (2001), contains two essays about ancient education: Richard Leo Enos writes about Greece; Murphy writes about Rome.

Examinations of classical rhetoric's potential connections to contemporary classrooms are also significant in current scholarship on classical rhetoric. Several textbooks provide immediate examples of how teachers might apply insights from ancient rhetorics in responding to the needs of contemporary students. The fourth edition of Edward P. J. Corbett's *Classical Rhetoric for the Modern Student,* coedited by Robert J. Connors, appeared in 1998. *Ancient Rhetorics for Contemporary Students* (2003), coauthored by Sharon Crowley and Debra Hawhee, also adapts classical theories to suit the needs of contemporary classrooms. Marvin Diogenes' "An Honors Course in Freshman Composition: Classical Rhetoric and Contemporary Writing" (2002) offers a detailed discussion of how classical rhetoric can provide a foundation for first-year writing students, as they come to recognize how classical ideas about language change over time and use this knowledge to shape their interactions with their own environments. Melissa Ianetta (2004) explores ways in which engaging with classical rhetorical theories might offer alternatives to the theory/practice binary that at times has characterized writing center administration and scholarship. Too's monograph, *The Pedagogical Contract: The Economics of Teaching and Learning in the Ancient World* (2000), considers how reflecting upon ancient pedagogical practices can contribute to new insights about contemporary teaching and learning. Walter Jost (1995) identifies the value of classical topics for contemporary work with invention that furthers the aims of liberal education. Thomas Miller (1991) argues for the potential of classical rhetoric to enhance instruction in professional writing, as it provides a context for exploring ethical questions that are normally left out of instruction in those courses. A 1993 survey conducted by Gerald Nelms and Maureen Daly Goggins examines several areas in which the revival of classical rhetoric has had an impact on modern approaches to writing instruction.

In addition to exploring classical rhetoric's potential for addressing contemporary pedagogical issues, numerous scholars are identifying connections between classical rhetoric and other contemporary questions about communication and public life. Enos and Janice Lauer (1992) argue that Aristotle's heuristics represent an inventional strategy that could potentially offer contemporary theorists a new understanding of how invention brings rhetor and audience together. Alan Gross (2004) discusses the potential use of Hermagoras's theory of stasis for questions of incommensurability, which can only be solved through cooperation across disciplines. James Kastely's *Rethinking the Rhetorical Tradition: From Plato to Postmodernism* (1997) draws upon classical thought as a resource for exploring rhetoric's potential responses to contemporary concerns. Eugene Garver's *Aristotle's Rhetoric: An Art of Character* (1994) and *For the Sake of Argument: Practical Reasoning, Character, and the Ethics of Belief* (2004) draw upon Aristotle's integration of practical reasoning and character in order to provide new insights into contemporary issues. Kathleen E. Welch (1999) adapts sophistic approaches to rhetoric in order to provide new ways of understanding contemporary transformations of literacy brought about by technological change.

Suggestions for Future Scholarship

The intriguing new avenues for scholarship that have evolved since 1990 reveal multiple productive directions for future scholarship. The exploration of the rhetorical practices of ancient women and global ancient cultures has just begun. As feminist historiographers can attest, the recovery and recuperation of rhetorics that have been erased from previous accounts of rhetoric's history will require patience, painstaking effort, and new methodologies that can account for conceptions of rhetoric that fall outside the boundaries that have defined it in the past. These methodologies should include attention to Richard Leo Enos's repeated call for the diligent search for new primary sources that can provide a more complete understanding of how rhetoric developed in particular cultures. They should also attend to Susan Jarratt's insistence that scholarship in rhetoric must cross disciplinary boundaries in order to consider the varied texts and practices that have historically been part of rhetoric's dynamic cultural activity. They will also benefit from ongoing conversations about issues of historiography, including questions about evidence, interpretation, disciplinary goals, and how we can responsibly seek to understand the cultural forces that have contributed to rhetoric's evolution in an era very different from our own. Such conversations will not only contribute to the rigor of our scholarship, but will also enhance the vitality of our discipline.

BIBLIOGRAPHY
Primary Works

Greek Rhetorics

Aeschines. *Aeschines.* Trans. Chris Carey. Vol. 3 of The Oratory of Classical Greece Series, ed. Michael Gagarin. Austin: University of Texas Press, 2000.
——. *Speeches.* Trans. Charles Darwin Adams. The Loeb Classical Library. Cambridge: Harvard University Press, 1958.
Antiphon. *Antiphon the Sophist: The Fragments.* Ed. and trans. Gerard J. Pendrick. Cambridge: Cambridge University Press, 2002.
Antiphon and Andocides. Trans. Michael Gagarin and Douglas M. MacDowell. Vol. 1 of The Oratory of Classical Greece Series, ed. Michael Gagarin. Austin: University of Texas Press, 1998.
Antiphon and Lysias. Trans. Michael Edwards and Stephen Usher. Warminster, England: Aris and Phillips, 1985.
Antiphon-Andocides. *Minor Attic Orators.* Trans. K. J. Maidment. Vol. 1, The Loeb Classical Library. Cambridge: Harvard University Press, 1941.
Aristotle. *The "Art" of Rhetoric.* Trans. J. H. Freese. Aristotle vol. 22, The Loeb Classical Library. Cambridge: Harvard University Press. 1926.
——. *On Rhetoric.* Trans. George A. Kennedy. 2nd ed. Oxford: Oxford University Press, 2006.
——. *The Poetics.* Trans. Stephen Halliwell. Longinus. *On the Sublime.* Trans. W. Hamilton Fyfe, revised by Donald A. Russell. Demetrius. *On Style.* Trans. Doreen C. Innes, based on W. Rhys Roberts. Aristotle vol. 23, The Loeb Classical Library. Cambridge: Harvard University Press, 1996.
——. *Rhetorica ad Alexandrum.* Trans. H. Rackham. Aristotle vol. 16, The Loeb Classical Library. Cambridge: Harvard University Press, 1938.
Demosthenes. (Orations and Letters.) 7 vols. Trans. J. H. Vince, C. A. Vince, A. T. Murray, N. W. DeWitt, and N. J. DeWitt. The Loeb Classical Library. Cambridge: Harvard University Press, 1926–1949.
——. *Speeches 50–59.* Trans. Victor Bers. The Oratory of Classical Greece Series, ed. Michael Gagarin. Austin: University of Texas Press, 2003.

——. *Speeches 27–38.* Trans. Douglas M. MacDowell. The Oratory of Classical Greece Series, ed. Michael Gagarin. Austin: University of Texas Press, 2004.

——. *Speeches 18–19.* Trans. Harvey Yunis. The Oratory of Classical Greece Series, ed. Michael Gagarin. Austin: University of Texas Press, 2005.

——. *Speeches 60–61, Prologues, Letters.* Trans. Ian Worthington. The Oratory of Classical Greece Series, ed. Michael Gagarin. Austin: University of Texas Press, 2006.

Diels, Hermann, and Walther Kranz, eds. *Die Fragmente der Vorsokratiker.* Zurich: Weidman, 1985.

Dinarchus, Hyperides, and Lycurgus. Trans. Ian Worthington, Craig Cooper, and Edward M. Harris. Vol. 5 of The Oratory of Classical Greece Series, ed. Michael Gagarin. Austin: University of Texas Press, 2001.

Dionysius of Halicarnassus. *Critical Essays I* (Ancient Orators). Dionysius of Halicarnassus, Vol. 8. Trans. Stephen Usher. The Loeb Classical Library. Cambridge: Harvard University Press, 1974.

Freeman, Kathleen, ed. *Ancilla to the Pre-Socratic Philosophers, A Complete Translation of the Fragments in Diels, Fragmente der Vosokratiker.* Cambridge: Harvard University Press, 1983.

Hermogenes. *On Types of Style.* Trans. Cecil W. Wooten. Chapel Hill: University of North Carolina Press, 1987.

Isocrates. *Isocrates I.* Trans. David Mirhady and Yun Lee Too. The Oratory of Classical Greece Series, ed. Michael Gagarin. Austin: University of Texas Press, 2000.

——. *Isocrates II.* Trans. Terry L. Papillon. The Oratory of Classical Greece Series, ed. Michael Gagarin. Austin: University of Texas Press, 2004.

——. *Isocrates,* Vol. I. Trans. George Norlin. The Loeb Classical Library. Cambridge: Harvard University Press, 1928.

——. *Isocrates,* Vol. II. Trans. George Norlin. The Loeb Classical Library. Cambridge: Harvard University Press, 1929.

——. *Isocrates.* Vol. III. Trans. La Rue Van Hook. The Loeb Classical Library. Cambridge: Harvard University Press, 1945.

Jebb, R. C., P. E. Easterling, and Michael Edwards, trans. *Selections from the Attic Orators: Antiphon, Andocides, Lysias, Isocrates, Isaeus.* Exeter, U.K.: Bristol Phoenix Press, 2005.

Kennedy, George A., trans. *Invention and Method: Two Rhetorical Treatises from the Hermogenic Corpus,* based on Hugo Rabe's Greek text. Atlanta, GA: Society of Biblical Literature, 2005.

——. *Progymnasmata: Greek Textbooks of Prose Composition and Rhetoric.* Atlanta, GA: Society of Biblical Literature, 2003.

Kirk, G. S., J. E. Raven, and M. Schofield, eds. *The Presocratic Philosophers: A Critical History with a Selection of Texts.* 2nd ed. Cambridge: Cambridge University Press, 1983.

Lysias. *Lysias.* Trans. W. R. M. Lamb. The Loeb Classical Library. Cambridge: Harvard University Press, 1930.

——. *Lysias.* Trans. S. C. Todd. The Oratory of Classical Greece Series, ed. Michael Gagarin. Austin: University of Texas Press, 2000.

Meador, Prentice A., Jr. "Minucian, On Epicheiremes: An Introduction and Translation." *Speech Monographs* 31 (March 1964): 54–63.

Nadeau, Ray. "Hermogenes' *On Stasis:* A Translation with an Introduction and Notes." *Speech Monographs* 31 (November 1964): 361–424.

Plato. *Euthyphro—Apology—Crito—Phaedo—Phaedrus.* Trans. H. N. Fowler. Plato I, The Loeb Classical Library. Cambridge: Harvard University Press, 1914.

——. *Gorgias—A Revised Text with Introduction and Commentary, by E. R. Dodds.* Ed. E. R. Dodds. Oxford: Clarendon, 1959.

——. *Lysis—Symposium—Gorgias.* Trans. W. R. M. Lamb. Plato III, The Loeb Classical Library. Cambridge: Harvard University Press, 1925.

——. *Plato's Phaedrus.* Trans. R. Hackforth. Cambridge: Cambridge University Press, 1972.

——. *Theaetetus—Sophist.* Trans. H. N. Fowler. Plato VII, The Loeb Classical Library. Cambridge: Harvard University Press, 1921.

——. *Timaeus, Critias, Cleitophon, Menexenus, Epistles.* Trans. R. G. Bury. Plato IX, The Loeb Classical Library. Cambridge: Harvard University Press, 1929.

Radermacher, Ludwig, ed. *Artium Scriptores: Reste Der Voraristotelischen Rhetorik.* Vienna: Rudolf M. Rohrer, 1951.

Robinson, T. M. *Contrasting Arguments: An Edition of the Dissoi Logoi.* Salem, NH: Ayer, 1979.

Sprague, Rosamond K., ed. *The Older Sophists: A Complete Translation by Several Hands of the Fragments in Die Fragmente Der Vorsokratiker, Edited by Diels-Kranz with a New Edition of Antiphon and of Euthydemus.* Indianapolis: Hackett, 2001.

Latin Rhetorics

[Cicero.] *Ad C. Herennium de Ratione Dicendi (Rhetorica ad Herennium).* Trans. Harry Caplan. Cicero I, Rhetorical Treatises, The Loeb Classical Library. Cambridge: Harvard University Press, 1954.

——. *Brutus.* Trans. G. L. Hendrickson. *Orator.* Trans. H. M. Hubbell. Cicero V, Rhetorical Treatises, The Loeb Classical Library. Cambridge: Harvard University Press, 1939.

——. *Cicero: On the Ideal Orator.* Trans. James M. May and Jakob Wisse. Oxford: Oxford University Press, 2001.

——. *Cicero on Oratory and Orators.* Trans. and ed. by J. S. Watson. Introduction by Ralph A. Micken. Foreword by David Potter. Preface by Richard Leo

Enos. Landmarks in Rhetoric and Public Address Series. Carbondale: Southern Illinois University Press, 1986.

———. *On Invention. The Best Kind of Orator. Topics.* Trans. H. M. Hubbell. Cicero II, Rhetorical Treatises, The Loeb Classical Library. Cambridge: Harvard University Press, 1949.

———. *On the Orator, Books I and II.* Trans. E. W. Sutton and H. Rackham. Cicero III, Rhetorical Treatises, The Loeb Classical Library. Cambridge: Harvard University Press, 1942.

———. *On the Orator, Book III. On Fate. Stoic Paradoxes. On the Divisions of Oratory.* Trans. H. Rackham. Cicero IV, Rhetorical Treatises, The Loeb Classical Library. Cambridge: Harvard University Press, 1942.

Horace. *Satires, Epistles, The Art of Poetry.* Trans. H. Rushton Fairclough. Horace II, The Loeb Classical Library. Cambridge: Harvard University Press, 1926.

Quintilian. *The Institutio Oratoria of Quintilian.* Ed. and trans. Donald A. Russell. 5 vols. The Loeb Classical Library. Cambridge: Harvard University Press, 2002.

Seneca the Elder. *Controversiae, I–VI.* Trans. Michael Winterbottom. Declamations I, The Loeb Classical Library. Cambridge: Harvard University Press, 1974.

———. *Controversiae, VII–X. Suasoriae. Fragments.* Trans. Michael Winterbottom. Declamations II, The Loeb Classical Library. Cambridge: Harvard University Press, 1974.

Commentators and Historians of Rhetoric

Appian. *Roman History.* 4 vols. Trans. Horace White. Cambridge: Harvard University Press, 1972–1979.

Diogenes Laertius. *Lives of Eminent Philosophers.* 2 vols. Trans. R. D. Hicks. The Loeb Classical Library. Cambridge: Harvard University Press, 1925.

Enos, Richard Leo. "When Rhetoric Was Outlawed in Rome: A Translation and Commentary of Suetonius's Treatise on Early Roman Rhetoricians." *Speech Monographs* 39 (March 1972): 37–45.

Herodotus. *The Persian Wars.* 4 vols. Trans. A. D. Godley. The Loeb Classical Library. Cambridge: Harvard University Press, 1920–1925.

Philostratus. *Lives of the Sophists. Eunapius: Lives of the Philosophers and Sophists.* Trans. Wilmer C. Wright. Philostratus IV, The Loeb Classical Library. Cambridge: Harvard University Press, 1921.

Plutarch. *Lives of the Ten Orators.* Trans. H. N. Fowler. Moralia X, The Loeb Classical Library. Cambridge: Harvard University Press, 1936.

———. *Parallel Lives.* 11 vols. Trans. Bernadette Perrin. The Loeb Classical Library. Cambridge: Harvard University Press, 1914–1926.

Suetonius. *The Lives of the Caesars.* Trans. J. C. Rolfe. Suetonius I, The Loeb Classical Library. Cambridge: Harvard University Press, 1914.

——. *The Lives of the Caesars. The Lives of Illustrious Men: Grammarians and Rhetoricians. Poets.* Trans. J. C. Rolfe. Suetonius II, The Loeb Classical Library. Cambridge: Harvard University Press, 1914.

Thucydides. *History of the Peloponnesian War.* 4 vols. Trans. C. F. Smith. The Loeb Classical Library. Cambridge: Harvard University Press, 1919–1923.

——. *History of the Peloponnesian War.* Trans. Rex Warner, notes M. I. Finley. London: Penguin, 1954.

Anthologies

Bizzell, Patricia, and Bruce Herzberg, eds. *The Rhetorical Tradition.* 2nd ed. Boston: Bedford, 2001.

Donawerth, Jane, ed. *Rhetorical Theory by Women before 1900.* Lanham, MD: Rowman and Littlefield, 2002.

Ritchie, Joy, and Kate Ronald, eds. *Available Means: An Anthology of Women's Rhetoric(s).* Pittsburgh: University of Pittsburgh Press, 2001.

Secondary Scholarship

Albaladejo, Tomas, Emilio Del Rio, and Jose Antonio Caballero, eds. *Quintiliano: Historia y actualidad de la retorica, I–III.* Logrono, Spain: Ayuntamiento de Calahorra, 1998.

Aldrete, Gregory S. *Gestures and Acclamations in Ancient Rome.* Baltimore: Johns Hopkins University Press, 1999.

Anderson, Graham. *The Second Sophistic: A Cultural Phenomenon in the Roman Empire.* New York: Routledge, 1993.

Atwill, Janet. *Rhetoric Reclaimed: Aristotle and the Liberal Arts Tradition.* Ithaca: Cornell University Press, 1998.

——. "The Uses of Deception: Epistemological and Axiological Measurement in Aristotle and Ancient Thought." *Pre/Text: A Journal of Rhetorical Theory* 14, no. 3/4 (1993): 343–72.

Axer, Jerzy. "Cicero's Court Speeches: The Spoken Text versus the Published Text: Some Remarks from the Point of View of the Communication Theory of Text." In Horner and Leff, *Rhetoric as Pedagogy,* 7–63.

Ballif, Michelle. *Seduction, Sophistry, and the Woman with the Rhetorical Figure.* Carbondale: Southern Illinois University Press, 2001.

Ballif, Michelle, and Michael G. Moran, eds. *Classical Rhetorics and Rhetoricians.* Westport, CT: Greenwood Publishing, 2005.

Barrett, Harold. *The Sophists: Rhetoric, Democracy, and Plato's Idea of Sophistry.* Novato, CA: Chandler and Sharp, 1987.

Benoit, William L. "Isocrates and Aristotle on Rhetoric." *Rhetoric Society Quarterly* 20, no. 3 (1990): 251–60.

———. "Isocrates and Plato on Rhetoric and Rhetorical Education." *Rhetoric Society Quarterly* 21, no. 1 (1991): 60–71.

Berlin, James. "Aristotle's Rhetoric in Context: Interpreting Historically." In Witte, Nakadate, and Cherry, *Rhetoric of Doing*, 55–64.

Berlin, James A., Robert J. Connors, Sharon Crowley, Richard Leo Enos, Victor J. Vitanza, Susan C. Jarratt, Nan Johnson, and Jan Swearingen, moderated by James J. Murphy. "Octalog: The Politics of Historiography." *Rhetoric Review* 7, no. 1 (Fall 1988): 5–49.

Bernal, Martin. *Black Athena: The Afroasiatic Roots of Classical Civilization.* 3 vols. New Brunswick, NJ: Rutgers University Press, 1987, 1991, 2006.

Biesecker, Susan. "Rhetoric, Possibility, and Women's Status in Ancient Athens: Gorgias' and Isocrates' Encomiums of Helen." *Rhetoric Society Quarterly* 22, no. 1 (1992): 99–108.

Bizzell, Patricia. "Opportunities for Feminist Research in the History of Rhetoric." *Rhetoric Review* 11, no. 1 (1992–1993): 50–58.

Bizzell, Patricia, ed. *Feminist Historiography in Rhetoric* [special issue]. *Rhetoric Society Quarterly* 32, no. 1 (2002).

Bizzell, Patricia, and Susan Jarratt. "Rhetorical Traditions, Pluralized Canons, Relevant History, and Other Disputed Terms: A Report from the History of Rhetoric Discussion Groups at the ARS Conference." *The Alliance of Rhetoric Societies Conference, 2003: Conversations in Evanston* [special issue]. *Rhetoric Society Quarterly* 34, no. 3 (2004): 19–25.

Blair, Elena Duverges. "Women: The Unrecognized Teachers of the Platonic Socrates." *Ancient Philosophy* 16 (1996): 333–50.

Blundell, Susan. *Women in Ancient Greece.* Cambridge: Harvard University Press, 1995.

Bonner, Stanley F. *Education in Ancient Rome.* Berkeley: University of California Press, 1977.

Brinton, Alan. "Outmoded Psychology of Aristotle's Rhetoric." *Western Journal of Speech* 54 (1990): 204–18.

Campbell, Kermit E. "Rhetoric from the Ruins of African Antiquity." *Rhetorica* 24, no. 3 (2006): 255–74.

Cape, Robert W. "Roman Women in the History of Rhetoric and Oratory." In Wertheimer, *Listening to Their Voices*, 112–32.

Caplan, Harry. "The Classical Tradition: Rhetoric and Oratory." Ed. and reconstructed by Richard Leo Enos, Mark James, Harold Barrett, and Lois Agnew; foreword by Edward P. J. Corbett. *Rhetoric Society Quarterly* 27, no. 2 (1997): 7–38.

Classen, C. Joachim. "St. Paul's Epistles and Ancient Greek and Roman Rhetoric." *Rhetorica* 10, no. 4 (1992): 319–44.

Cole, Thomas. *The Origins of Rhetoric in Ancient Greece.* Baltimore: Johns Hopkins University Press, 1991.

Conley, Thomas M. *Rhetoric in the European Tradition.* New York: Longman's, 1990.

Connors, Robert J. "The Exclusion of Women from Classical Rhetoric." In Witte, Nakadate, and Cherry, *Rhetoric of Doing*, 65–78.

——. "Greek Rhetoric and the Transition from Orality." *Philosophy and Rhetoric* 19, no. 1 (1986): 38–65.

Consigny, Scott. "Edward Schiappa's Reading of the Sophists." *Rhetoric Review* 14 (1996): 253–69.

——. *Gorgias: Sophist and Artist.* Columbia: University of South Carolina Press, 2001.

——. "Sophistic Freedom: Gorgias and the Subversion of *Logos*." *PreText* 12, no. 3/4 (1991): 226–35.

Corbeill, Anthony. *Controlling Laughter: Political Humor in the Late Roman Republic.* Princeton: Princeton University Press, 1996.

——. *Nature Embodied: Gesture in Ancient Rome.* Princeton: Princeton University Press, 2004.

Corbett, Edward P. J., and Robert J. Connors. *Classical Rhetoric for the Modern Student.* 4th ed. Oxford: Oxford University Press, 1998.

Covino, William. *The Art of Wondering: A Revisionist Return to the History of Rhetoric.* Portsmouth, NH: Boynton/Cook, 1988.

Crawford, Clinton N. "The Multiple Dimensions of Nubian/Egyptian Rhetoric and Its Implications for Contemporary Classroom Instructions." In *African American Rhetoric(s): Interdisciplinary Perspectives,* ed. Elaine B. Richardson and Ronald L. Jackson II, 111–35. Carbondale: Southern Illinois University Press, 2004.

Crick, Nathan, and John Poulakos. "Go Tell Alcibiades: Tragedy, Comedy, and Rhetoric in Plato's *Symposium*." *Quarterly Journal of Speech* 94, no. 1 (2008): 1–22.

Crowley, Sharon. "A Plea for the Revival of Sophistry." *Rhetoric Review* 7, no. 2 (1989): 318–34.

Crowley, Sharon, and Debra Hawhee. *Ancient Rhetorics for Contemporary Students.* 3rd ed. White Plains, NY: Longman, 2003.

Davis, Janet B. "Translating Gorgias in [Aristotle] 980 A 10." *Philosophy and Rhetoric* 30 (1997): 31–37.

de Romilly, Jacqueline. *Great Sophists in Periclean Athens.* Trans. Janet Lloyd. Oxford: Oxford University Press, 1988.

——. *Magic and Rhetoric in Ancient Greece.* Cambridge: Harvard University Press, 1975.

Diogenes, Marvin. "An Honors Course in Freshman Composition: Classical Rhetoric and Contemporary Writing." In *Strategies for Teaching First-Year Composition,* ed. Duane Roen, Veronica Pantoja, Lauren Yena, Susan K. Miller, and Eric Waggoner, 114–32. Urbana: NCTE, 2002.

Dolmage, Jay. "Breathe upon Us an Even Flame: Hephaestus, History, and the Body of Rhetoric." *Rhetoric Review* 25, no. 2 (2006): 119–40.

Dominik, William J., ed. *Roman Eloquence: Rhetoric in Society and Literature.* London: Routledge, 1997.

Duncan, Anne. "Demosthenes versus Aeschines: The Rhetoric of Sincerity." In *Performance and Identity in the Classical World,* 58–89. Cambridge: Cambridge University Press, 2006.

Edwards, Michael. *The Attic Orators.* London: Bristol Classical, 1994.

Enders, Jody. "Delivering Delivery: Theatricality and the Emasculation of Eloquence." *Rhetorica* 15, no. 3 (1997): 253–78.

Enos, Richard Leo. "The Emergence of a Literate Rhetoric in Greece." *Rhetoric Society Quarterly* 36, no. 3 (Summer 2006): 223–41.

——. "The Epistemology of Gorgias' Rhetoric: A Reexamination." *Southern Speech Communication Journal* 42 (1976): 35–51.

——. *Greek Rhetoric before Aristotle.* Prospect Heights, IL: Waveland, 1993.

——. "Literacy in Athens during the Archaic Period: A Prolegomenon to Rhetorical Invention." In *Perspectives on Rhetorical Invention,* ed. Janet M. Atwill and Janice M. Lauer, 176–91. Knoxville: University of Tennessee Press, 2003.

——. *Roman Rhetoric: Revolution and the Greek Influence.* Prospect Heights, IL: Waveland, 1995.

——. "Why Gorgias of Leontini Traveled to Athens: A Study of Recent Epigraphical Evidence." *Rhetoric Review* 11, no. 1 (1992): 1–15.

Enos, Richard Leo, and Lois Peters Agnew. *Landmark Essays on Aristotelian Rhetoric.* Mahwah, NJ: Lawrence Erlbaum, 1998.

Enos, Richard Leo, and Anne M. Blakeslee. "The Classical Period." In *The Present State of Scholarship in Historical and Contemporary Rhetoric,* ed. Winifred Bryan Horner, 9–44. Columbia: University of Missouri Press, 1990.

Enos, Richard Leo, and Margaret Kantz. "A Selected Bibliography on Corax and Tisias." *Rhetoric Society Quarterly* 13 (1983): 71–74.

Enos, Richard Leo, and Janice M. Lauer. "The Meaning of Heuristic in Aristotle's Rhetoric and Its Implications for Contemporary Rhetorical Theory." In Witte, Nakadate, and Cherry, *Rhetoric of Doing,* 79–87.

Fantham, Elaine. *The Roman World of Cicero's "De Oratore."* Oxford: Oxford University Press, 2004.

Fantham, Elaine, Helene P. Foley, Natalie B. Kampen, Sarah B. Pomeroy, and H. Alan Shapiro. *Women in the Classical World: Image and Text.* Oxford: Oxford University Press, 1994.

Farrell, Thomas B. "Philosophy against Rhetoric in Aristotle." *Philosophy and Rhetoric* 28 (1995): 181–98.

——. "Practicing the Arts of Rhetoric: Tradition and Invention." *Philosophy and Rhetoric* 24, no. 3 (1991): 183–212.

Fleming, David. "The Streets of Thurii: Discourse, Democracy, and Design in the Classical Polis." *Rhetoric Society Quarterly* 32, no. 3 (2002): 5–32.

——. "The Very Idea of a *Progymnasmata*." *Rhetoric Review* 22, no. 2 (2003): 105–20.

Ford, Andrew. "Sophists without Rhetoric: The Arts of Speech in Fifth Century Athens." In Too, *Education in Greek and Roman Antiquity*, 85–109.

Fortenbaugh, William W. "Aristotle on Persuasion through Character." *Rhetorica* 10, no. 3 (1992): 207–44.

——. "Cicero as a Reporter of Aristotelian and Theophrastean Rhetorical Doctrine." *Rhetorica* 23, no. 1 (2005): 37–64.

Fortenbaugh, William W., and David C. Mirhady, eds. *Peripatetic Rhetoric after Aristotle*. Rutgers University Studies in Classical History, vol. 6. New Brunswick, NJ: Transaction, 1994.

Fox, Michael V. "Ancient Egyptian Rhetoric." *Rhetorica* 1 (1983): 9–22.

Fredal, James. "The Language of Delivery and the Presentation of Character: Rhetorical Action in Demosthenes' *Against Meidias*." *Rhetoric Review* 20, no. 3–4 (2001): 251–67.

——. *Rhetorical Action in Ancient Athens: Persuasive Artistry from Solon to Demosthenes.* Carbondale: Southern Illinois University Press, 2006.

Furley, David J., and Alexander Nehamas, eds. *Aristotle's Rhetoric: Philosophical Essays.* Princeton: Princeton University Press, 1994.

Gagarin, Michael. *Antiphon the Athenian: Oratory, Law, and Justice in the Age of the Sophists.* Austin: University of Texas Press, 2002.

——. "Did the Sophists Aim to Persuade?" *Rhetorica* 19 (2001): 275–91.

Gaines, Robert N. "De-Canonizing Ancient Rhetoric." In Graff, Walzer, and Atwill, *Viability of the Rhetorical Tradition*, 61–73.

——. "Knowledge and Discourse in Gorgias's *On the Non-Existent or On Nature*." *Philosophy and Rhetoric* 30 (1997): 1–12.

Gale, Xin Liu. "Historical Studies and Postmodernism: Rereading Aspasia of Miletus." *College English* 62 (2000): 361–86.

Garver, Eugene. *Aristotle's Rhetoric: An Art of Character.* Chicago: University of Chicago Press, 1994.

——. *For the Sake of Argument: Practical Reasoning, Character, and the Ethics of Belief.* Chicago: University of Chicago Press, 2004.

Gleason, Maud W. *Making Men: Sophists and Self-Presentation in Ancient Rome.* Princeton: Princeton University Press, 1995.

Glenn, Cheryl. "Locating Aspasia on the Rhetorical Map." In Wertheimer, *Listening to Their Voices*, 19–41.

——. *Rhetoric Retold: Regendering the Tradition from Antiquity through the Renaissance.* Carbondale: Southern Illinois University Press, 1997.

——. "Sex, Lies, and Manuscript: Refiguring Aspasia in the History of Rhetoric." *College Composition and Communication* 45 (1994): 180–99.

——. "Truth, Lies, and Method: Revisiting Feminist Historiography." *College English* 62, no. 3 (2000): 387–89.

Goldhill, Simon, and Robin Osborne, eds. *Performance Culture and Athenian Democracy.* Cambridge: Cambridge University Press, 1999.

Graff, Richard. "Prose versus Poetry in Early Greek Theories of Style." *Rhetorica* 23, no. 4 (2005): 303–35.

——. "Reading and the 'Written Style' in Aristotle's Rhetoric." *Rhetoric Society Quarterly* 31 (2001): 19–44.

Graff, Richard, and Michael Leff. "Revisionist Historiography and Rhetorical Tradition(s)." In Graff, Walzer, and Atwill, *Viability of the Rhetorical Tradition,* 11–30.

Graff, Richard, Arthur E. Walzer, and Janet M. Atwill, eds. *The Viability of the Rhetorical Tradition.* Albany: State University of New York Press, 2005.

Green, Lawrence D. "Aristotle's Enthymeme and the Imperfect Syllogism." In Horner and Leff, *Rhetoric as Pedagogy,* 19–41.

Gronbeck, Bruce E. "Gorgias on Rhetoric and Poetic: A Rehabilitation." *Southern Speech Communication Journal* 38 (1972): 27–38.

Gross, Alan G. "Why Hermagoras Still Matters: The Fourth Stasis and Interdisciplinarity." *Rhetoric Review* 23, no. 2 (2004): 141–55.

Gross, Alan, and Arthur E. Walzer, eds. *Rereading Aristotle's Rhetoric.* Carbondale: Southern Illinois University Press, 2000.

Gunderson, Erik. *Staging Masculinity: The Rhetoric of Performance in the Roman World.* Ann Arbor: University of Michigan Press, 2000.

Hariman, Robert, ed. *Prudence, Classical Virtue, Postmodern Practice.* University Park: Penn State University Press, 2003.

Harpine, William E. "Epideictic and Ethos in the Amarna Letters: The Withholding of Argument." *Rhetoric Society Quarterly* 28, no. 1 (1998): 81–98.

Haskins, Ekaterina. *Logos and Power in Isocrates and Aristotle.* Columbia: University of South Carolina Press, 2004.

——. "Philosophy, Rhetoric, and Cultural Memory: Rereading Plato's Menexenus and Isocrates' Panegyricus." *Rhetoric Society Quarterly* 35, no. 1 (2005): 25–46.

Hauser, Gerard. "Aristotle on Epideictic: The Formation of Public Morality." *Rhetoric Society Quarterly* 29 (1999): 5–23.

Havelock, Eric. *The Muse Learns to Write: Reflections on Orality and Literacy from Antiquity to the Present.* New Haven: Yale University Press, 1986.

——. "Preface to *Plato.*" Cambridge: Harvard University Press, 1963.

Hawhee, Debra. *Bodily Arts: Rhetoric and Athletics in Ancient Greece.* Austin: University of Texas Press, 2004.

Hawhee, Debra, Jeffrey Walker, Janet Atwill, John Poulakos, James Fredal, Ekaterina Haskins, Michael Leff, and Susan C. Jarratt. "Performing Ancient Rhetorics: A Symposium." *Rhetoric Society Quarterly* 36, no. 2 (Spring 2006): 135–219.

Henry, Madeleine M. *Prisoner of History: Aspasia of Miletus and Her Biographical Tradition.* Oxford: Oxford University Press, 1995.

Horner, Winifred Bryan. *Rhetoric in the Classical Tradition.* New York: St. Martin's, 1988.

Horner, Winifred, and Michael C. Leff, eds. *Rhetoric as Pedagogy: Its History, Philosophy, and Practice: Essays in Honor of James J. Murphy.* Mahwah, NJ: Lawrence Erlbaum, 1995.

Hutto, David. "Ancient Egyptian Rhetoric in the Old and Middle Kingdoms." *Rhetorica* 20, no. 3 (2002): 213–33.

Ianetta, Melissa. "If Aristotle Ran the Writing Center: Classical Rhetoric and Writing Center Administration." *Writing Center Journal* 24, no. 2 (2004): 37–59.

Jarratt, Susan. "Comment: Rhetoric and Feminism Together Again." *College English* 62 (2000): 390–93.

——. *Rereading the Sophists: Classical Rhetoric Refigured.* Carbondale: Southern Illinois University Press, 1991.

Jarratt, Susan, and Rory Ong. "Aspasia: Rhetoric, Gender, and Colonial Ideology." In Lunsford, *Reclaiming Rhetorica*, 9–24.

Johnstone, Christopher. "Communicating in Classical Contexts: The Centrality of Delivery." *Quarterly Journal of Speech* 87 (2001): 121–42.

——. "Greek Oratorical Settings and the Problem of the Pnyx: Rethinking the Athenian Political Process." In Johnstone, *Theory, Text, Context*, 97–128.

Johnstone, Christopher, ed. *Theory, Text, Context: Issues in Greek Rhetoric and Oratory.* Albany: State University of New York Press, 1996.

Jost, Walter. "Teaching the Topics: Character, Rhetoric, and Liberal Education." *Rhetoric Society Quarterly* 21, no. 1 (1991): 1–16. Rpt. in *Rhetoric and Pluralism: Legacies of Wayne Booth,* ed. Frederick J. Antczak, 19–39. Columbus: Ohio State University Press, 1995.

Julien, François. *Detour and Access: Strategies of Meaning in China and Greece.* Trans. Sophie Hawkes. Cambridge: Massachusetts Institute of Technology Press, 2000.

Kastely, James L. *Rethinking the Rhetorical Tradition: From Plato to Postmodernism.* New Haven: Yale University Press, 1997.

Kennedy, George A. "Attitudes toward Authority in the Teaching of Rhetoric before 1050." In Horner and Leff, *Rhetoric as Pedagogy*, 65–71.

———. *Comparative Rhetoric: An Historical and Cross-Cultural Introduction.* Oxford: Oxford University Press, 1998.

———. *A New History of Classical Rhetoric.* Princeton: Princeton University Press, 1994.

Kinneavy, James L. "Kairos in Classical and Modern Rhetorical Theory." In *Rhetoric and Kairos: Essays in History, Theory, and Praxis,* ed. Phillip Sipiora and James S. Baumlin, 58–76. Albany: State University of New York Press, 2002.

Kirby, John T. "The 'Great Triangle' in Early Greek Rhetoric and Poetics." *Rhetorica* 8 (1990): 213–28.

Kirkpatrick, Andy. "China's First Systematic Account of Rhetoric: An Introduction to Chen Kui's *Wen Ze.*" *Rhetorica* 23, no. 2 (2005): 103–52.

Lauer, Ilon. "Ritual and Power in Imperial Roman Rhetoric." *Quarterly Journal of Speech* 90 (2004): 422–45.

Leff, Michael C. "Cicero's Redemptive Identification." In *Critical Questions: Invention, Creativity, and the Criticism of Discourse and the Media,* ed. William L. Nothstine, Carole Blair, and Gary A. Copeland, 327–42. New York: St. Martin's, 1994.

Lentz, Tony. *Orality and Literacy in Hellenic Greece.* Carbondale: Southern Illinois University Press, 1989.

Lesko, Barbara S. "The Rhetoric of Women in Pharaonic Egypt." In Wertheimer, *Listening to Their Voices,* 89–111.

Lipson, Carol S. "Ancient Egyptian Rhetoric: It All Comes Down to *Maat.*" In Lipson and Binkley, *Rhetoric before and beyond the Greeks,* 79–97.

———. "Recovering the Multimedia History of Writing in the Public Texts of Ancient Egypt." In *Eloquent Images: Word and Image in the Age of New Media,* ed. Mary E. Hocks and Michelle R. Kendrick, 89–115. Cambridge: MIT Press, 2005.

Lipson, Carol, and Roberta A. Binkley, eds. *Rhetoric before and beyond the Greeks.* Albany: State University of New York Press, 2004.

Long, Fredrick J. *Ancient Rhetoric and Paul's Apology: The Compositional Unity of 2 Corinthians.* Cambridge: Cambridge University Press, 2004.

Loraux, Nicole. *The Invention of Athens: The Funeral Oration in the Classical City.* Trans. Alan Sheridan. Cambridge: Harvard University Press, 1986.

Lu, Xing. *Rhetoric in Ancient China, Fifth to Third Century BCE: A Comparison with Classical Greek Rhetoric.* Columbia: University of South Carolina Press, 1998.

Lunsford, Andrea, ed. *Reclaiming Rhetorica: Women in the Rhetorical Tradition.* Pittsburgh: University of Pittsburgh Press, 1995.

Mailloux, Steven, ed. *Rhetoric, Sophistry, Pragmatism.* Cambridge: Cambridge University Press, 1995.

Marback, Richard. *Plato's Dream of Sophistry.* Columbia: University of South Carolina Press, 1999.

Marrou, Henri Irénée. *A History of Education in Antiquity.* Trans. George Lamb. Madison: University of Wisconsin Press, 1982.

May, James M., ed. *Brill's Companion to Cicero: Oratory and Rhetoric.* Leiden, Netherlands: Brill, 2002.

———. *Trials of Character: The Eloquence of Ciceronian Ethos.* Chapel Hill: University of North Carolina Press, 1988.

McAdon, Brad. "Reconsidering the Intention or Purpose of Aristotle's *Rhetoric.*" *Rhetoric Review* 23, no. 3 (2004): 216–34.

———. "The 'Special Topics' in the Rhetoric: A Reconsideration." *Rhetoric Society Quarterly* 36, no. 4 (2006): 399–424.

———. "Two Irreconcilable Conceptions of Rhetorical Proofs in Aristotle's Rhetoric." *Rhetorica* 22, no. 4 (2004): 307–25.

McComiskey, Bruce. *Gorgias and the New Sophistic Rhetoric.* Carbondale: Southern Illinois University Press, 2002.

Miller, Carolyn R. "The Polis as Rhetorical Community." *Rhetorica* 11, no. 3 (1993): 211–40.

Miller, Thomas P. "Treating Professional Writing as Social Praxis." *JAC: A Journal of Composition Theory* 11, no. 1 (1991): 57–72.

Mitchell, Thomas N. *Cicero: The Senior Statesman.* New Haven: Yale University Press, 1991.

Morstein-Marx, Robert. *Mass Oratory and Political Power in the Late Roman Republic.* Cambridge: Cambridge University Press, 2004.

Murphy, James J. "The Historiography of Rhetoric: Challenges and Opportunities." *Rhetorica* 1, no. 1 (1983): 1–8.

———. "The Metarhetoric of Aristotle, with Some Examples from His *On Memory and Recollection.*" *Rhetoric Review* 21, no. 3 (2002): 213–28.

Murphy, James J., ed. *A Short History of Writing Instruction from Ancient Greece to Modern America.* 2nd ed. Mahwah, NJ: Lawrence Erlbaum, 2001.

Murphy, James J., Richard A. Katula, Forbes I. Hill, and Donovan J. Ochs. *A Synoptic History of Classical Rhetoric.* 3rd ed. Mahwah, NJ: Lawrence Erlbaum, 2003.

Neel, Jasper. *Aristotle's Voice: Rhetoric, Theory and Writing in America.* Carbondale: Southern Illinois University Press, 1994.

Nelms, Gerald, and Maureen Daly Goggin. "The Revival of Classical Rhetoric for Modern Composition Studies: A Survey." *Rhetoric Society Quarterly* 23, no. 3–4 (1994): 11–26.

Newman, Sara. "Aristotle's Notion of 'Bringing-before-the-Eyes': Its Contributions to Aristotelian and Contemporary Conceptualizations of Metaphor, Style, and Audience." *Rhetorica* 20 (2002): 1–23.

Nye, Andrea. *Words of Power: A Feminist Reading of the History of Logic.* New York: Routledge, 1990.

Ober, Josiah. *Mass and Elite in Democratic Athens: Rhetoric, Ideology, and the Power of the People.* Princeton: Princeton University Press, 1989.

Ochs, Donovan J. *Consolatory Rhetoric: Grief, Symbol, and Ritual in the Roman Era.* Columbia: University of South Carolina Press, 1993.

O'Gorman, Ned. "Longinus's Sublime Rhetoric, or How Rhetoric Came Into Its Own." *Rhetoric Society Quarterly* 34, no. 2 (2004): 71–89.

Olmsted, Wendy. *Rhetoric: An Historical Introduction.* Malden, MA: Blackwell, 2006.

Papillon, Terry. "Isocrates' *Techne* and Rhetorical Pedagogy." *Rhetoric Society Quarterly* 25(1995): 149–59.

———. *Rhetorical Studies in the Aristocratea of Demosthenes.* New York: Peter Lang, 1998.

Pernot, Laurent. *Rhetoric in Antiquity.* Trans. W. E. Higgins. Washington, D.C.: Catholic University of America Press, 2005.

———. "The Rhetoric of Religion." *Rhetorica* 24, no. 3 (2006): 235–54.

Porter, James I., ed. *Constructions of the Classical Body (The Body, In Theory: Histories of Cultural Materialism).* Ann Arbor: University of Michigan Press, 1999.

Porter, Stanley E., ed. *Handbook of Classical Rhetoric in the Hellenistic Period, 330 BC–AD 400.* Leiden, Netherlands: Brill, 1997.

Poster, Carol. "Being and Becoming: Rhetorical Ontology in Early Greek Thought." *Philosophy and Rhetoric* 29 (1996): 1–14.

———. "Framing *Theaetetus:* Plato and Rhetorical (Mis)representation." *Rhetoric Society Quarterly* 35, no. 3 (2005): 31–73.

———. "Plato's Unwritten Doctrines: A Hermeneutic Problem in Rhetorical Historiography." *Pre/Text: A Journal of Rhetorical Theory* 14, no. 1–2 (1993): 127–38.

Poulakos, John. "Hegel's Reception of the Sophists." *Western Journal of Speech Communication* 54 (1990): 160–71.

———. "Interpreting Sophistical Rhetoric: A Response to Schiappa." *Philosophy and Rhetoric* 23 (1990): 218–28.

———. Rhetoric, the Sophists, and the Possible." *Communication Monographs* 51 (1984): 215–26.

———. *Sophistical Rhetoric in Classical Greece.* Columbia: University of South Carolina Press, 1995.

———. "Toward a Sophistic Definition of Rhetoric." *Philosophy and Rhetoric* 16 (1983): 35–48.

Poulakos, Takis. "Historiographies of the Tradition of Rhetoric: A Brief History of Classical Funeral Orations." *Western Journal of Speech Communication* 54, no. 2 (1990): 172–88.

——. *Speaking for the Polis: Isocrates' Rhetorical Education.* Columbia: University of South Carolina Press, 1997.

Poulakos, Takis, ed. *Rethinking the History of Rhetoric: Multidisciplinary Essays on the Rhetorical Tradition.* Boulder, CO: Westview, 1993.

Poulakos, Takis, and David Depew, eds. *Isocrates and Civic Education.* Austin: University of Texas Press, 2004.

Pullman, George L. "Reconsidering Sophistic Rhetoric in Light of Skeptical Epistemology." *Rhetoric Review* 13 (1994): 50–68.

Reid, Robert S. "Paul's Conscious Use of the *Ad Herennium's* 'Complete Argument.'" *Rhetoric Society Quarterly* 35, no. 2 (2005): 65–92.

Riggsby, Andrew M. "Did the Romans Believe in Their Verdicts?" *Rhetorica* 15, no. 3 (1997): 235–51.

Robb, Kevin. *Literacy and Paideia in Ancient Greece.* Oxford: Oxford University Press, 1994.

Roisman, Joseph. *The Rhetoric of Conspiracy in Ancient Athens.* Berkeley: University of California Press, 2006.

——. *The Rhetoric of Manhood: Masculinity in the Attic Orators.* Berkeley: University of California Press, 2005.

Rorty, Amelie Oksenberg, ed. *Essays on Aristotle's Rhetoric.* Berkeley: University of California Press, 1980.

Schiappa, Edward. *The Beginnings of Rhetorical Theory in Classical Greece.* New Haven: Yale University Press, 1999.

——. "Did Plato Coin *Rhetorike?*" *American Journal of Philology* 111 (1990): 457–70.

——. "An Examination and Exculpation of the Composition Style of Gorgias of Leontini." *Pre/Text* 12, no. 3/4 (1991): 237–57.

——. "History and Neo-Sophistic Criticism: A Reply to Poulakos." *Philosophy and Rhetoric* 23 (1990): 307–15.

——. "Neo-Sophistic Rhetorical Criticism or the Historical Reconstruction of Sophistic Doctrines?" *Philosophy and Rhetoric* 23 (1990): 192–217.

——. *Protagoras and Logos: A Study in Greek Philosophy and Rhetoric.* Columbia: University of South Carolina Press, 1991.

——. "Some of My Best Friends Are Neosophists: A Response to Scott Consigny." *Rhetoric Review* 14 (1996): 270–79.

——. "Sophistic Rhetoric: Oasis or Mirage?" *Rhetoric Review* 10 (1991): 5–18.

Schiappa, Edward, ed. *Landmark Essays on Classical Greek Rhetoric.* Davis, CA: Hermagoras, 1994.

Schildgen, Brenda Deen, ed. *The Rhetoric Canon.* Detroit: Wayne State University Press, 1997.

Sealey, Raphael. *Demosthenes and His Time: A Study in Defeat.* Oxford: Oxford University Press, 1993.

Sipiora, Phillip, and James S. Baumlin, ed. *Rhetoric and Kairos: Essays in History, Theory, and Praxis.* Albany: State University of New York Press, 2002.

Snyder, Jane McIntosh. *The Woman and the Lyre: Women Writers in Classical Greece and Rome.* Carbondale: Southern Illinois University Press, 1989.

Stauffer, Devin. *The Unity of Plato's Gorgias: Rhetoric, Justice, and the Philosophic Life.* Cambridge: Cambridge University Press, 2006.

Sullivan, Robert G. "Eidos/Idea in Isocrates." *Philosophy and Rhetoric* 34 (2001): 79–92.

Swearingen, Jan. "A Lover's Discourse: Diotima, Logos, and Desire." In Lunsford, *Reclaiming Rhetorica,* 25–51.

———. "Plato's Feminine: Appropriation, Impersonation, and Metaphorical Polemic." *Rhetoric Society Quarterly* 22, no. 1 (1992): 109–23.

———. *Rhetoric and Irony: Western Literacy and Western Lies.* Oxford: Oxford University Press, 1991.

Tellegen-Couperus, Olga, ed. *Quintilian and the Law: The Art of Persuasion in Law and Politics.* Leuven, Belgium: Leuven University Press, 2003.

Thomas, Rosalind. *Literacy and Orality in Ancient Greece.* Cambridge: Cambridge University Press, 1992.

Too, Yun Lee. *The Pedagogical Contract: The Economies of Teaching and Learning in the Ancient World.* Ann Arbor: University of Michigan Press, 2000.

———. *The Rhetoric of Identity in Isocrates: Text, Power, Pedagogy.* Cambridge: Cambridge University Press, 1995.

Too, Yun Lee, ed. *Education in Greek and Roman Antiquity.* Leiden, Netherlands: Brill, 2001.

Usher, Stephen. *Greek Oratory: Tradition and Originality.* Oxford: Oxford University Press, 1999.

Vickers, Brian. *In Defence of Rhetoric.* Oxford: Oxford University Press, 1989.

Vitanza, Victor J. *Negation, Subjectivity, and the History of Rhetoric.* Albany: State University of New York Press, 1997.

Vitanza, Victor J., ed. *Writing Histories of Rhetoric.* Carbondale: Southern Illinois University Press, 1994.

Walker, Jeffrey. "Before the Beginnings of 'Poetry' and 'Rhetoric': Hesiod on Eloquence." *Rhetorica* 14, no. 3 (1996): 243–64.

———. *Rhetoric and Poetics in Antiquity.* Oxford: Oxford University Press, 2000.

Walters, Frank D. "Isocrates and the Epistemic Return: Individuality and Community in Classical and Modern Rhetoric." *Journal of Advanced Composition* 13, no. 1 (1993): 155–72.

Walzer, Arthur E. "Aristotle's Rhetoric, Dialogism, and Contemporary Research in Composition." *Rhetoric Review* 16 (1997): 45–58.

———. "Moral Philosophy and Rhetoric in the Institutes: Quintilian on Honor and Expediency." *Rhetoric Society Quarterly* 36, no. 3 (2006): 263–80.

———. "Quintilian's 'Vir Bonus' and the Stoic Wise Man." *Rhetoric Society Quarterly* 33, no. 4 (2003): 25–41.

Wardy, Robert. *The Birth of Rhetoric: Gorgias, Plato, and Their Successors.* New York: Routledge, 1996.

Welch, Kathleen E. *The Contemporary Reception of Classical Rhetoric: Appropriations of Ancient Discourse.* Mahwah, NJ: Lawrence Erlbaum, 1990.

———. *Electric Rhetoric: Classical Rhetoric, Oralism, and a New Literacy.* Cambridge: Massachusetts Institute of Technology Press, 1999.

———. "Interpreting the Silent 'Aryan Model' of Histories of Classical Rhetoric: Martin Bernal, Terry Eagleton, and the Politics of Rhetoric and Composition Studies." In Vitanza, *Writing Histories,* 38–48.

Wertheimer, Molly Meijer. *Listening to Their Voices: The Rhetorical Activities of Historical Women.* Columbia: University of South Carolina Press, 1997.

Witte, Stephen P., Neil Nakadate, and Roger D. Cherry. *A Rhetoric of Doing: Essays on Written Discourse in Honor of James L. Kinneavy.* Carbondale: Southern Illinois University Press, 1992.

Wooten, Cecil W. "Cicero and Quintilian on the Style of Demosthenes." *Rhetorica* 15, no. 2 (1997): 177–92.

Worthington, Ian, ed. *Persuasion: Greek Rhetoric in Action.* London: Routledge, 1994.

———. *Voice into Text: Orality and Literacy in Ancient Greece.* Leiden, Netherlands: Brill, 1995.

You, Xiaoye. "*The Way,* Multimodality of Ritual Symbols and Social Change: Reading Confucius's *Analects* as a Rhetoric." *Rhetoric Society Quarterly* 36, no. 4 (2006): 425–48.

Yunis, Harvey. *Taming Democracy: Models of Political Rhetoric in Classical Athens.* Ithaca: Cornell University Press, 1996.

Zulick, Margaret D. "The Active Force of Hearing the Ancient Hebrew Language of Persuasion." *Rhetorica* 10, no. 4 (1992): 367–80.

2

The Middle Ages

Denise Stodola

In the years since the publication of the 1990 edition of *The Present State of Scholarship in Historical and Contemporary Rhetoric,* medieval rhetoric as a field has seen a period of transformation and potential redefinition. In fact, while the standard preceptive genres—*ars praedicandi, ars dictaminis,* and *ars poetria*—still serve as the basic pillars of the field, scholars of medieval rhetoric are working to fill in some of the conceptual gaps in research and to cut across previously accepted traditional categories, whether those categories are conceptual or chronological. This broadening purview of medieval rhetoric expands our understanding of the larger rhetorical context of the Middle Ages and includes scholarship focusing on education and pedagogy, non-Western rhetoric, and the role of women within this period.

To engage and control my approach to the mass of materials available, I have retained the basic categories that Murphy and Camargo identified in the second edition as areas that were ripe for development. I have reordered those categories in order to create coherence between those sections and the ones addressing gender and non-Western rhetoric, categories just beginning to emerge at the time of the previous edition. Thus, this chapter discusses:

Reference Works and Basic Resources
Texts and Translations
The Educational Background
The Role of *Dictamen*
Sermons and Sermon Theory

The Relation of Rhetoric and Grammar to the *Ars Poetriae*
Definition and Scope of Medieval Rhetoric
Women and Gender
Non-Western Rhetoric
Areas for Further Research
Bibliography

Spatial limitations required me to set additional parameters for works listed in the bibliography; I have included works published from 1990 to 2008 that fit the following criteria:
- Those pieces for which the primary focus lies within the period from the seventh century through the mid-fifteenth century
- Works in which the majority of the piece focuses on a medieval rhetorical treatise/writing manual, and those that address medieval female rhetors, teaching and pedagogy, and/or non-Western rhetoric

Moreover, I have excluded the following:
- Works that focus exclusively on the rhetorical features of literary and historical works
- Certain primary materials (e.g. letters, sermons, poems), with a few necessary exceptions
- Works focusing primarily on continuities between the various chronological periods, with the exception of pedagogy and teaching, and non-Western rhetoric

I have included non-English works only in very specific cases—such as where the work is of substantial length and scope and provides discussion and/or a perspective that is unavailable in English. Given their centrality to this field, I have also included Latin texts. Thus, what follows is a discussion of a small sample representing the very fine work going on in the field, and although the bibliography is somewhat more inclusive, it, too, is limited by spatial constraints.

Reference Works and Basic Resources

Encyclopedic References

Key Texts from the Revised Edition:
- *Dictionary of the Middle Ages,* edited by Joseph R. Strayer (1982–1989)
- Robert Auty, Robert-Henri Bautier, Norbert Angermann, and Charlotte Bretscher-Gisier, *Lexikon des Mittelalters* [Dictionary of the Middle Ages] (1977–1999)

Basic reference materials addressing rhetoric in the Middle Ages are available in both print and electronic formats. The *Dictionary of the Middle Ages,* in thirteen volumes, and the *Lexikon des Mittelalters,* in nine volumes, remain the most thorough and specific references of their kind and are of invaluable aid to those interested in studying medieval rhetoric and its contexts. The *Lexikon des Mittelalters* (*LexMA*), available online, is discussed in the "Online Reference Materials" section below.

Historisches Wörterbuch der Rhetorik, an interdisciplinary, multivolume encyclopedia focusing on rhetorical terms from the classical period—terms arising from the interaction between rhetoric and other fields, and modern rhetorical concepts—is currently available in eight volumes (through Rhe-Sti), with two more volumes scheduled for publication by 2011. Although this work is currently available only in German, the editors intend eventually to provide an English translation of this indispensable resource.

In addition to these standard references are those that treat medieval rhetoric within the context of modern rhetorical studies. In the *Encyclopedia of Rhetoric and Composition: Communication from Ancient Times to the Information Age* (1996), edited by Theresa Enos, Patricia Bizzell provides an entry on "Women Rhetoricians," which includes women working in the Middle Ages, while Aron Morgan authors the entry on the "Medieval Period."

In the Oxford *Encyclopedia of Rhetoric* (2001), edited by Thomas O. Sloane, Martin Camargo authors the entry on the *ars dictaminis,* and Rita Copeland and Jan Ziolkowski each contribute one portion of a two-part entry on "Medieval Rhetoric." Copeland's section, "Medieval Rhetoric: An Overview," discusses the continuity of the classical tradition in the period and outlines the evolution of the preceptive genres, and Ziolkowski's "Medieval Rhetoric: Medieval Grammar" notes the difficulty of separating grammar from rhetoric, particularly where style is concerned. All entries include brief annotated bibliographies. Finally, Matthew T. Bliss, Annemiek Jansen, and David E. Orton provide an English translation of the *Handbook of Literary Rhetoric: A Foundation for Literary Study* (1998) based on the second German edition of Lausberg's *Handbuch der literarischen Rhetorik* published in 1973. The purpose of the original volume (1963), according to Lausberg, was to "attempt an open-ended presentation of ancient rhetoric with the Middle Ages and the modern era in mind" (xxvii). This work impressively cites, assimilates, and integrates information from various classical authors, and while the translation's bibliography is outdated, the thorough index of terms is still useful.

Surveys and General Studies

Key Texts from Revised Edition:
- Thomas M. Conley, *Rhetoric in the European Tradition* (1990)

- Ernst Robert Curtius, *European Literature and the Latin Middle Ages* (1953)
- George A. Kennedy, *Classical Rhetoric and Its Christian and Secular Traditions from Ancient to Modern Times* (1980)
- James J. Murphy, *Medieval Eloquence: Studies in the Theory and Practice of Medieval Rhetoric* (1978)
- ——, *Rhetoric in the Middle Ages: A History of Rhetorical Theory from Saint Augustine to the Renaissance* (1974)

Many of the surveys and general studies featured in the Medieval Rhetoric section in the revised edition retain their value, and no new comprehensive histories like those listed above have been published in the intervening years. Within this category of very broad surveys, Conley's is the most recent treatment. He adopts a chronological, comprehensive approach to chart the ways in which rhetorical models changed from classical through modern times. Murphy and Kennedy still dominate the field in this particular category, and their texts, along with Curtius's, have become the standard classics. Another standard is Murphy's *Rhetoric in the Middle Ages,* first printed in 1974, reprinted in 2001, and now available in Spanish and Polish—a testimony to the work's influence.

There are, however, single-genre studies that have become indispensable, including Siegfried Wenzel's *Latin Sermon Collections from Later Medieval England: Orthodox Preaching in the Age of Wyclif* (2005), which is part of the Cambridge Studies in Medieval Literature series, a single volume containing both Marianne G. Briscoe's *Artes praedicandi* (1992) and Barbara Haye's *Artes orandi* (1992); Douglas Kelly's *The Arts of Poetry and Prose* (1991); Martin Camargo's *Ars dictaminis, Ars dictandi* (1991); John O. Ward's *Ciceronian Rhetoric in Treatise, Scholion, and Commentary* (1995); and *The Book of Memory: A Study of Memory in Medieval Culture* (1990) by Mary Carruthers. The only works from this list not published by Brepols are those by Wenzel and Carruthers; thus, scholars wishing to juxtapose genres for comparison purposes will find consistency in the format of each work, as each Brepols volume addresses "Definition of the Genre," "Evolution of the Genre," "Critical Rules," "Influence," "Editions," and "History." These Brepols volumes are standard sources for the genres and concepts discussed in this section.

The books by Wenzel and Carruthers are similarly valuable. Wenzel's *Latin Sermon Collections from Later Medieval England* includes a section on the manuscript collections, as well as a section on the "Occasions of Preaching" and "Orthodox Preaching," thus providing discussion of the context in which the sermons were used and the performative nature of the sermon as an event. Similarly, in *The Book of Memory: A Study of Memory in Medieval Culture,* Carruthers discusses the "art of memory" and its relationship to the other medieval rhetorical arts while addressing the broader context in which rhetorical performance—whether written or oral—occurs. These works, along with the books from the Brepols series, are integral components for understanding the various facets of medieval rhetoric.

Bibliographies and Inventories

Key Texts from Revised Edition:
- *Medioevo latino: Bolletino bibliographico della cultura europea dal secolo VI al XIII*, edited by Claudio Leonardi (1981–)
- James J. Murphy, *Medieval Rhetoric: A Select Bibliography* (1989)
- Luke Reinsma, "The Middle Ages," in *Historical Rhetoric: An Annotated Bibliography of Selected Sources in English*, edited by Winifred Horner (1980)

Complementing encyclopedic resources, surveys, and general studies are inventories and bibliographies. Of the inventories, volume 1 of *Repertorium der artes dictandi des mittelalters* (1992), compiled by Franz Josef Worstbrock, Monika Klaes, and Jutta Lütten, provides an inventory of a number of *artes dictandi*, along with extensive bibliographic information. This first volume in a planned series provides a descriptive inventory of twenty-six *artes dictandi* and/or fragments, as well as bibliographical information, and the entries identify all known manuscripts of each work. See also Emil Polak's *Medieval and Renaissance Letter Treatises and Form Letters: A Census of Manuscripts Found in Eastern Europe and the Former U.S.S.R.* (1993), and *Medieval and Renaissance Letter Treatises and Form Letters: A Census of Manuscripts Found in Parts of Western Europe, Japan, and the United States of America* (1994).

While the print resources listed at the beginning of this section are valuable, it is currently far more common to find bibliographic material online. Much of the material that was once only accessible in print has been made available electronically; in fact, many new resources are available online exclusively. Searchable databases like JSTOR, Project Muse, and the online MLA bibliography have revolutionized the ways in which scholars locate materials.

Online Reference Materials

Online digitized archives of articles from hundreds of journals are available in full text format on JSTOR and Project Muse. In addition, the MLA bibliography, both in its hard-copy and online forms, provides helpful citation information for articles that may be of interest to those in medieval rhetoric. However, these databases require subscriptions and are currently unavailable to individual subscribers. Moreover, these databases are broad in scope, covering many diverse fields. Thus, online sources focusing more exclusively on the Middle Ages, such as "Iter: Gateway to the Middle Ages and Renaissance" (included in member-ships in several professional organizations), may ultimately be more useful.

Of these, the *International Medieval Bibliography* (*IMB*), a searchable online database, can be found at *Brepolis,* which is, according to its Web site, the "home-town of Brepols' online publications" (http://www.brepolis.net/). The *IMB* contains over 350,000 records, including works from Europe, North Africa, and the Near East. Other databases provided at *Brepolis* include:

- International Medieval Bibliography
- Bibliographie de civilisation médiévale
- International Directory of Medievalists
- Lexikon des Mittelalters
- International Encyclopaedia for the Middle Ages
- Europa Sacra
- In Principio
- Ut per litteras apostolicas
- Vetus Latina Database
- Dictionnaire d'histoire et de géographie ecclésiastiques
- Revue d'Histoire Ecclésiastique: Bibliographie
- Library of Latin Texts
- Monumenta Germaniae Historica
- Aristoteles Latinus Database
- Archive of Celtic-Latin Literature
- Database of Latin Dictionaries

Currently, the most common way to access these databases is through in-stitutional subscriptions, but Brepols offers individual subscriptions to single databases and to "clusters" of databases (*Brepolis Medieval Bibliographies, Brepolis Medieval Encyclopedias, Brepolis Latin Complete,* and *Brepolis Latin Full-Text*), which provide some savings for the user. Access to various data-bases is also available through membership in particular professional orga-nizations. For example, members of the International Medieval Society have access to the *International Medieval Database.* The availability of primary Latin texts, encyclopedic materials, and bibliographies in online databases has greatly altered research methods. For more information on how to access these databases, see http://www.brepolis.net/ BRP_Info_En.html#.

Texts and Translations

Key Texts from Revised Edition:
- Boethius, *De topicis differentiis.* Translated by Eleonore Stump (1978)

- ——, *In Ciceronis topica*. Translated by Eleonore Stump (1988)
- Geoffrey of Vinsauf, *Documentum de modo et arte dictandi et versifi-candi (Instruction in the Method and Art of Speaking and Versifying)*. Translated by Roger P. Parr (1968)
- ——, *The Poetria nova of Geoffrey of Vinsauf*. Translated by Margaret F. Nims (1967)
- John of Garland, *The* Parisiana Poetria *of John of Garland; Edited with Introduction, Translation, and Notes*. Edited and translated by Traugott Lawler (1974)
- Joseph M. Miller et al., *Readings in Medieval Rhetoric* (1973)
- James Murphy, *Three Medieval Rhetorical Arts* (1971)

In the revised edition, Murphy and Camargo pointed to "a need for the publication of the medieval texts that can provide evidence for our assessment of the subject [. . .]. So far we lack that kind of textual control for preaching manuals, or letter-writing treatises and commentaries, or school texts" (56). Fortunately, much progress has been made in this area in the last twenty years. Indeed, access to primary texts is absolutely crucial for the scholar of medieval rhetoric, and we now have noteworthy editions of manuals and treatises in this category, including both translations and original-language editions. For example, reprints of Eleonore Stump's translations of Boethius's *De topicis differentiis* (2004) and *In Ciceronis topica* (2004) have kept these important documents in circulation and accessible even to those who cannot read Latin. Similarly, the edition of Ranulph Higden's *Ars componendi sermones,* originally Margaret Jennings's 1970 thesis at Bryn Mawr that appeared in published form soon thereafter, was reprinted in 1991 by Brill. A translation of *Ars componendi sermons* (2003), undertaken by Jennings and Sally A. Wilson, appeared as part of the Dallas Medieval Texts and Translations series.

Another significant reprint is James Murphy's *Three Medieval Rhetorical Arts* (2001 reprint), which provides translations of the anonymous *The Principles of Letter Writing*, Geoffrey of Vinsauf's *Poetria nova*, and Robert of Basevorn's *The Form of Preaching.* Murphy's general introduction and introductions to each translation outline major concepts of medieval rhetoric: Geoffrey of Vinsauf is translated by Jane Kopp, Robert of Basevorn by Leopold Krul, O.S.B., and the appended material—selections from Aristotle's *Topics* and *On Sophistical Refutations*—is translated by W. A. Pickard-Cambridge.

A number of previously unpublished editions are now available as well. Mary Carruthers and Jan M. Ziolkowski provide an invaluable tool in *The Medieval Craft of Memory: An Anthology of Texts and Pictures* (2002), which provides translations of various authors; among them are Hugh of St. Victor's *The Three Best Memory Aids for Learning History* and *A Little Book about Constructing Noah's Ark; On the Six Wings of the Seraph,* attributed to Alanus de Insulis; Boncompagno da Signa's *On Memory;* the commentaries on Aristotle's *On Memory and Recollection* by Albertus Magnus and Thomas Aquinas; *On Two Kinds of Order That Aid Understanding and Memory,* by Francesc Eiximenis; Thomas Bradwardine's *On Acquiring a Trained Memory;* John of Metz's *The Tower of Wisdom; The Art of Memory* by Jacobius Publicius; the anonymous *A Method for Recollecting the Gospels;* and two classical texts on rhetorical *memoria,* both entitled *On Memory:* one by Consultus Fortunatianus, and the other by C. Julius Victor. Each translated section provides an extraordinarily useful "further reading" section, general bibliographic information, and—in select cases— distinct bibliographies.

Martin Camargo's *Medieval Rhetorics of Prose Composition: Five English "Artes dictandi" and Their Tradition* (1995) presents Latin editions of *Libellus de arte dictandi rhetorice,* attributed to Peter of Blois; *Compilacio de arte dictandi* by John of Briggis; Thomas Merke's *Formula moderni et usitati dictaminis;* Thomas Sampson's *Modus dictandi;* and the anonymous *Regina sedens Rhetorica.* In his introduction to the volume, Camargo addresses "The Earliest English *Dictatores,*" "The *Ars dictaminis* and the English Chancery," and "*Dictamen* at Oxford"; he also provides a bibliography of primary and secondary sources, a glossary of medieval Latin words, and copious notes throughout the entire text.

Also quite thorough is Ann Dalzell's edition and facing-page translation of *Introductiones dictandi* by Transmundus (1995), with an introduction that summarizes the limited scholarship about the author and also discusses sources, style, and syntax of the work. Dalzell also discusses the manuscripts of the *Introductiones dictandi,* a work important because its author was likely the "protonotary of the papal chancery [. . .] giv[ing] his manual an authority that can be claimed by few others" (x), while the work itself "reflect[s] the state of classical learning in the late twelfth century and contemporary attitudes towards it" (x). The notes are quite useful, as is the facing-page format of the text and its translation.

Another volume that will eventually provide at least a portion of a critical edition of the *Tria sunt* is *Medieval Literary Theory: Grammatical and Rhetorical Traditions,* edited by Rita Copeland and Ineke Sluiter (forthcoming, Oxford University Press). This work provides an anthology of primary works on grammar and rhetoric from the classical period through the late Middle Ages. Camargo is currently working on a complete critical edition of the *Tria sunt,* and his contribution to the Copeland and Sluiter collection will provide a first glance at this promised critical edition.

The Educational Background

Key Texts from Revised Edition:
- John W. Baldwin, *Masters, Princes, and Merchants* (1970)

- A. B. Cobban, *The Medieval English Universities: Oxford and Cambridge to c. 1500* (1988)
- ———. *The Medieval Universities: Their Development and Organization* (1970)
- Gordon Leff, *Paris and Oxford Universities in the Thirteenth and Fourteenth Centuries: An Institutional and Intellectual History* (1975)
- Cora E. Lutz, *Schoolmaster of the Tenth Century* (1977)
- James J. Murphy, "Literary Implications of Instruction in the Verbal Arts in Fourteenth Century England" (1967)
- Nicholas I. Orme, *Education in the West of England, 1066–1548* (1976)
- ———. *English Schools in the Middle Ages* (1973)
- Hastings Rashdall, *The Universities of Europe in the Middle Ages* (1936)
- Edith Rickert, "Chaucer at School" (1931)

In the revised edition, Camargo and Murphy cited the need for a "definitive study of the place of rhetoric in both university and nonuniversity education of the middle ages" (57) that they subdivided into two parts: "The History of Education," and "Educational Biographies," which they described as "[s]ystematically investigating the educational biographies of major writers" (57). Scholars have answered the first challenge, but there remains much work to be done to respond to the latter need.

Scholars have addressed various facets of education and the pedagogical context through analysis of the ways models were used for instructional purposes; such is the case with "Quintilian and Medieval Teaching" (1998) by Marjorie Curry Woods, who suggests that medieval teachers used series of exercises similar to those found in Quintilian, but that they adapted and sequenced them for their own particular uses in the classroom. Similarly, Douglas Kelly's "The Medieval Art of Poetry and Prose: The Scope of Instruction and Uses of Models" (2004), which appeared in *Medieval Rhetoric: A Casebook,* edited by Scott D. Troyan, takes a somewhat broader perspective. He asserts that the arts of poetry and prose illustrate a particular notion of invention that was taught during the Middle Ages and that sources were often used as models in the medieval classroom. Kelly also contends that in order to understand the medieval pedagogical context more effectively, we need to consider more fully what Léopold Genicot calls the "contextual environment"—in other words, where a particular work is placed within a manuscript, what other works are associated with it within the manuscript, as well as "sources or analogues that invite intertextual interpretation" (6).

In addition to examining textual contexts, scholarship now considers geographical, institutional, and temporal contexts; such consideration is apparent in two essays in *Rhetoric and Pedagogy: Its History, Philosophy, and Practice: Essays in Honor of James J. Murphy* (1995), edited by Winifred Horner and Michael Leff. One of these is "Between Grammar and Rhetoric: Composition Teaching at Oxford and Bologna in the Late Middle Ages," in which Martin Camargo examines the pedagogical texts and contexts of the schools at Bologna and Oxford. He stresses the necessity of fully analyzing the institutional context when attempting to understand how treatises were used in the classroom, in order to gain a better understanding of audience and purpose. Such is also the case with the second essay, entitled "Teaching the Tropes in the Middle Ages: The Theory of Metaphoric Transference in Commentaries on the *Poetria nova*," by Marjorie Curry Woods, who asserts that the commentaries on the *Poetria* indicate that medieval readers have very similar responses to the work—and that those contrast with the responses of modern readers. In order to move toward overcoming this temporal and cognitive barrier, she states that we need to "focus first on the verbal level of rhetorical pedagogy, that is, on elocution or style before invention and arrangement, which means being as aware as medieval schoolteachers were of the Latin terms for the tropes and the overlapping and slippage of function that these Latin terms and their English cognates indicate" (81).

Due to space constraints, I have here addressed only a small sample of the many worthwhile articles and books examining the educational background of the Middle Ages; thus, I refer readers to the bibliography at the end of the chapter. As previously mentioned, however, we still lack development in works that address the educational biographies of major writers as epitomized by Orme's work and Donald Clark's *John Milton at St. Paul's School.* The bibliography provides a number of resources that treat the history of education in broader terms. See, for example, *Medieval Education,* edited by Begley and Koterski (2005), and *A Short History of Writing Instruction,* by Murphy (1990, 2001).

The Role of *Dictamen*

Key Texts from the Revised Edition:
* Martin Camargo, "Toward a Comprehensive Art of Written Discourse: Geoffrey of Vinsauf and the *Ars dictaminis*" (1988)
* Paul O. Kristeller, "Philosophy and Rhetoric from Antiquity to the Renaissance" (1979)
* James J. Murphy, "Alberic of Montecassino: Father of the Medieval *Ars dictaminis*" (1971)
* ——. *Rhetoric in the Middle Ages: A History of Rhetorical Theory from Saint Augustine to the Renaissance* (1974)
* William Patt, "The Early '*Ars dictaminis*' as Response to a Changing Society" (1978)

Closely allied with research on education is research on *dictamen,* an area dominated by scholars including Ward, Camargo, and Murphy. At the time of the revised edition, scholars were addressing the origins of the *ars dictaminis* as well as its historic repercussions. Nonetheless, the transmission of *ars dictaminis* was often intertwined with education, whether through classroom learning or through access to handbooks and to the commentaries on those handbooks. John O. Ward engages this phenomenon in "Rhetoric and the Art of *Dictamen,*" in which he outlines "three major aspects of didactic method and instruction in the field of rhetoric" (22). These include the "reduction of material to rules [. . .] and terms" (22); the "embodiment" of these rules and terms in treatises and in models used in imitation exercises; and the impartation of these concepts to students in a classroom setting.

Along the same lines, manuscripts and their immediate context, as well as their potential pedagogical usefulness in specific educational frameworks, are at issue in Camargo's "Si Dictare Velis: Versified *Artes dictandi* and Late Medieval Writing Pedagogy" (1996). In this article, Camargo examines the popular works authored by Otto of Lüneburg and Jupiter Monoculus, asserting that these texts, in hexameter, were associated with Geoffrey of Vinsauf's *Poetria nova* and provided the same pedagogical usefulness as embedded versified sections of the *artes dictandi.*

More recently, the scholarly conversation has turned toward the question of why the *ars dictaminis* seemed to disappear towards the end of the Middle Ages; in fact, an entire issue of *Rhetorica* was devoted to this question and included five articles by authors who presented papers in Amsterdam in 1999 at the Twelfth Biennial Conference of the International Society for the History of Rhetoric. Although the articles in the volume display various overlapping concerns and insights as well as differences, Camargo points out in his introduction that "all five scholars agree that in the fourteenth and fifteenth centuries the *ars dictaminis* underwent major transformations that correlate with changes in the societies whose needs it served and in the disciplines with which it was most closely related" ("The Waning of Medieval *Ars dictaminis,*" 137).

For broader discussions of *dictamen* and the historical evolution of letter writing, see *Letter-Writing Manuals and Instruction from Antiquity to the Present,* edited by Poster and Mitchell (2007). Not only does this collection of essays provide a broad historical framework in which one can place *dictamen,* it also provides, in Appendix B, a "Bibliography of Medieval Latin Dictamen," authored by Poster and Utz of note. Emil Polak's two-volume collection represents a monumental effort to publish organized inventories of the extant manuscript evidence relating to the medieval arts of letter writing and secular oratory, the *ars dictaminis* and the *ars arengandi.*

Sermons and Sermon Theory

Key Texts from the Revised Edition:
- Harry Caplan, *Medieval* Artes Praedicandi: *A Hand-List* (1934, 1936)
- Th.-M. Charland, *Artes praedicandi: Contribution à l'histoire de la rhétorique au moyen âge* (1936)
- James J. Murphy, *Rhetoric in the Middle Ages: A History of Rhetorical Theory from Saint Augustine to the Renaissance* (1974; reprint, 2001)
- Woodburn O. Ross, ed. *Middle English Sermons* (1940)
- Charles H. E. Smyth, *The Art of Preaching: A Practical Survey of Preaching in the Church of England, 747–1939* (1940, 1953)

The revised edition encouraged scholars to consider sermons within the context of their delivery—in a holistic sense—keeping in mind issues like purpose, audience, and occasion (61). Much scholarship has emerged toward this end in response to this admonition. In fact, the trend toward addressing the delivery contexts of medieval sermons has also resulted in scholarly discussions of the role of the sermon within various social groups and subgroups. For example, *Medieval Sermons and Society: Cloister, City, University: Proceedings of the International Symposia at Kalamazoo and New York* (1998), edited by Jacqueline Hamesse, Beverly Mayne Kienzle, Debra L. Stoudt, and Anne T. Thayer, emphasizes context by presenting twenty-one essays by various authors, organized according to the three loci named in the title—the cloister, the city, and the university.

The movement between text and context is reflected in volume 1 of the *Disputatio* book series that takes its name from its predecessor, the journal *Disputatio: An International Transdisciplinary Journal of the Late Middle Ages;* the volume is edited by Georgiana Donavin, Cary J. Nederman, and Richard Utz and is entitled *Speculum Sermonis: Interdisciplinary Reflections on the Medieval Sermon* (2004). Reflecting the concern for the relationship between text and society—in this case, how the sermon functions as a *speculum* for society—the book is divided into four major sections: "How Sermons Reflect Their World(s)," "How Sermons Reflect *upon* Their World(s)," "How Sermons Are Reflected in Other Literatures," and "Reflections *upon* Sermons." Each section concludes with a response to the papers within it, further emphasizing the cyclical nature of mutual influence, and thereby embodying the overall structure of the *disputatio* itself. Of particular interest is the article by Leo Carruthers (2004), "The Word Made Flesh: Preaching and Community from the Apostolic to the Late Middle Ages," in which he contextualizes the medieval sermon both synchronically and diachronically.

A more recent collection of essays, edited by Carolyn A. Muessig, entitled *Preacher, Sermon and Audience in the Middle Ages* (2002), contains thirteen essays contributed by eleven different authors and is organized into six sections (excluding the introduction): "Trends in Medieval Sermon Studies," "Rhetoric and Preaching," "Preaching and Performance," "Preaching and Art," "Preacher and Audience," and "Sermons as an Historical Source." Not only does the volume focus on context by embodying Aristotle's rhetorical triangle in its title, but also the sections within the volume move in a cyclical pattern—from the self-conscious emphasis on textuality invoked by the word *sermon* at the beginning of the collection and at the end. Two essays focus on this bridge between sermon as a material text and as an event: "The *Ars praedicandi* and the Medieval Sermon," by Phyllis B. Roberts (2002), and "From Texts to Preaching: Retrieving the Medieval Sermon as an Event," by Augustine Thompson, OP (2002).

The Relation of Rhetoric and Grammar to the *Ars poetriae*

Key Texts from Revised Edition:
- James J. Murphy, "*Ars poetriae:* Preceptive Grammar, or the Rhetoric of Verse-Writing." In *Rhetoric in the Middle Ages* (1974)
- ———. "A New Look at Chaucer and the Rhetoricians" (1964)
- Richard F. Schoeck, "On Rhetoric in Fourteenth-Century Oxford" (1968)

One difficulty in studying the Middle Ages has remained fairly constant since the previous edition of *The Present State* was published. Then, Murphy and Camargo noted that "we need to distinguish between what we wish to call things today, and what medieval writers may or may not have called things" (61). The way to understand the complexity of such a difficulty, however, once again resides in studying the various contexts of the textual artifacts we have from the period. Context is clearly an issue in *Ars poetriae: Rhetorical and Grammatical Invention at the Margins of Literacy* (1996), by William M. Purcell. This monograph compares the *Ars poetriae* in terms of how the manuals blend orality and literacy, as well as grammar and rhetoric, while treating, in depth, Matthew of Vendôme's *Ars versificatoria,* Geoffrey of Vinsauf's *Poetria nova* and *Documentum de modo et arte dictandi et versificandi,* John of Garland's *De arte prosayca, metrica, et rithmica,* Gervasius of Melkley's *Ars poetica,* and Eberhard the German's *Laborintus.* Purcell also provides two appendices that include definitions of the rhetorical and grammatical figures; he takes those definitions from *Rhetorica ad Herennium* and Donatus's *Ars grammatica,* respectively. Significantly, he concludes by asserting that the "*auctores poetriarum* followed the innovative and adaptive impetus of rhetoric to appropriate whatever measures [were] necessary—rhetorical, grammatical, poetic, and otherwise—to influence their world communicatively" (144). Thus, the shift in scholarship embodies the necessity of considering communicative acts in a larger context while it heightens the awareness that communication and any attendant linguistic and extralinguistic contexts actually shape each other in an ongoing process.

More directly confronting medieval literary theory are Martin Irvine's *The Making of Textual Culture: Grammatical and Literary Theory, 350–1100* (1994), and Rita Copeland's "Rhetoric and the Politics of the Literal Sense in Medieval Literary Theory: Aquinas, Wyclif, and the Lollards" (1997), which appears in *Rhetoric and Hermeneutics in Our Time: A Reader,* edited by Walter Jost and Michael J. Hyde. As the title of Irvine's book suggests, he focuses on what many would consider both the classical and the medieval ages. He repeats this transcendence of temporal constraints when he connects for his reader the classical, medieval, and modern appropriations of the principles of *grammatica:* "At a deep, but now historically unconscious, layer in modern uses of writing and texts are the principles of *grammatica,* the discipline that produced the culture of the text in Western societies. All of Western society is thus post-medieval in a significant sense: the grammatical archive continues to shape the understanding of texts, writing, the literary canon, and literacy" (21). Comprehensive and informative, Irvine's text also provides copious notes and a very thorough bibliography, subdivided according to subject.

Like Irvine, Copeland dissolves standard methods of categorization, but instead of transcending chronological restraints, Copeland's essay transcends conceptual ones. She outlines the shifting medieval attitudes toward rhetoric, particularly the role of rhetoric in determining and distinguishing between the literal and the figurative, the basis of the conflict between the scholastic view of rhetoric and the Wycliffite view. She concludes that "rhetoric is precisely what is political about the literal sense. If the literal sense is always the site of control of the text, rhetoric is the means of that control; and it is the regulation of rhetoric, whether through accommodation or resistance, that determines what is literal about the literal sense" (353). In treating attitudes toward rhetoric as intertwined with religious and ideological perspectives within the Middle Ages, her essay effectively underlines the fluidity of rhetoric as a concept, as well as the terms used to describe and discuss it.

Definition and Scope of Medieval Rhetoric

Key Texts from Revised Edition:
- Judson B. Allen, *The Ethical Poetic of the Later Middle Ages* (1981)
- John W. H. Atkins, *English Literary Criticism: The Medieval Phase* (1943, 1952)

- Charles S. Baldwin, *Medieval Rhetoric and Poetic (to 1400) Interpreted from Representative Works* (1928, 1976)
- Marcia L. Colish, *The Mirror of Language: A Study in the Medieval Theory of Knowledge* (1968)
- Peter Dronke, "Medieval Rhetoric" (1973)
- Louis J. Paetow, *The Arts Course at Medieval Universities with Special Reference to Grammar and Rhetoric* (1910)
- Robert O. Payne, *The Key of Remembrance: A Study of Chaucer's Poetics* (1963, 1973)
- Winthrop Wetherbee, *Platonism and Poetry in the Twelfth Century: The Literary Influence of the School of Chartres* (1972)

When changes in social context and terminology that inevitably alter the way rhetoric is understood are included within the historical landscape, an additional conceptual complication arises: where, exactly, does rhetorical theory intersect with practice? The situation becomes further entangled by the intersections between rhetoric and other arts of the *trivium*, as well as by the connections of one author to another. Indeed, as the research complexities multiply, so does the scope of medieval rhetoric as a scholarly field. It would seem that there is an ever-growing appreciation of the complexities inherent in understanding individual contexts, as well as the overlaps among multiple contexts. (See Brian Vickers, *In Defense of Rhetoric.*)

The primary way to address the complexity is to focus on a very specific text to uncover how that text influenced and was influenced by other authors. This focus on the interrelatedness of writing and the societal forces within which it operates is at issue in Camargo's "*Tria sunt:* The Long and the Short of Geoffrey of Vinsauf's *Documentum de modo et arte dictandi et versificandi*" (1999). He makes a strong case as he asserts that Geoffrey of Vinsauf was not the author of the *Tria sunt;* he connects the work to the larger context, in the process emphasizing not merely that the social forces had an impact on the work itself, but also, and importantly, that the work can tell us something of those social forces. In fact, he notes, "[s]o pervasive is the influence of Geoffrey of Vinsauf that, along with the ownership and makeup of the manuscripts, it represents the most promising means of revealing the complex ties that bound the authors of the surviving texts to one another" (952). Along the same lines, *The Rhetoric of Cicero in Its Medieval and Early Renaissance Commentary Tradition* (2006), edited by Virginia Cox and John O. Ward, includes two major sections that move from text to context: "Origins, Definitions, Nature, and Diffusion" and "Influences and Interrelationships: Contexts for the Utilization of the Ciceronian Rhetorical Juvenilia and Their Commentary Tradition." Readers interested in the interrelationships of rhetoric and the other arts of the *trivium* should consult Stephen Gersh's "Dialectical and Rhetorical Space: The

Boethian Theory of Topics and Its Influence during the Middle Ages" (1998) and Carol D. Lanham's *Latin Grammar and Rhetoric: From Classical Theory to Medieval Practice* (2002).

Visual Images

The difficulties faced by the modern scholar engaging medieval texts and contexts have resulted in a broadening of perspective—one that includes ever-increasing interdisciplinarity—illustrated in the focus on visual rhetoric. Rather than focusing on the appearance of a particular text, however, the emphasis is on moving beyond the visual appearance of written texts themselves, or how visuals complement the written texts, in order to consider what visual, physical artifacts "do"—how they enable understanding and encourage cognitive creativity, as well as what they can tell us about texts and textuality itself. One such work is *The Craft of Thought: Meditation, Rhetoric, and the Making of Images, 400–1200* (1998) by Mary Carruthers, who explores the complex role rhetoric has played in its interactions with the interrelated activities of meditation and image making. Monastic meditation involved the conjuration and creation of mental images in the invention and composition processes, the surrounding material constructs, like architecture, serving as a "meditation machine" (254), the structures of which are intricately woven with those of the individual and collective minds during the invention process.

In another vein is Canavesio's mural within Notre-Dame de Fontaines, which, according to Véronique Plesch in "Pictorial *Ars praedicandi* in Late Fifteenth-Century Paintings" (1999), demonstrates how visual texts may serve as sermons, even to the point of following common rhetorical strategies of preaching, as well as demonstrating how art interacts with sermons, both in the minds of the audience and within the mind of the rhetorical agent—in this case, the preacher. As such, in this case, the perspective with which rhetoric is viewed is thus widened to include visual arts and their complex interrelationships with text, audience, and rhetor.

Definition and Redefinition
of the Discipline

With all of the various trends in medieval rhetoric, it is no surprise that some scholars are explicitly questioning the assumptions underlying the ways in which the field of medieval rhetoric has been defined historically, while others are simultaneously venturing into territory that may best be described as "cutting edge" research, which, by its very existence, calls into question the discipline's ostensible identity. Scholarship that addresses the former category includes Martin Camargo's "Defining Medieval Rhetoric" (2003), appearing in

Rhetoric and Renewal in the Latin West, 1100–1540: Essays in Honour of John O. Ward, edited by Constant J. Mews, Cary J. Nederman, and Rodney M. Thomson; Georgiana Donavin's "The Medieval Rhetoric of Identification: A Burkean Reconception" (1996); and Scott D. Troyan's "Unwritten between the Lines: The Unspoken History of Rhetoric" (2004), appearing in *Medieval Rhetoric: A Casebook,* which he also edited. Camargo argues that it is necessary to "abandon [. . .] the narrow conception of rhetoric underlying traditional histories" (34), while Donavin maintains that American professors of rhetorical history have a negative view of medieval rhetoric, a view that they pass along in their classrooms, and that Burke's notions of "identification of" and "identification with" could help medieval rhetoricians to help their students appreciate and understand medieval rhetoric more fully.

Scott Troyan, however, is concerned with encouraging a better understanding of the relationship between rhetoric and hermeneutics in the Middle Ages. Medieval manual writers, he suggests, approached the same material differently, and this can tell us something about the fluidity of rhetoric: as medieval rhetoricians saw a need for readaptation to new social needs for communication, the rhetoric changed, as did the content and means of interpretation. If one wishes to understand interpretive practices, which is undoubtedly difficult to do since the medieval manuals themselves do not explicitly explain them, it is necessary to compare the manuals in order to uncover what remains unspoken "between the lines." Indeed, the shift in focus from the theory of rhetoric to its practice makes understanding the relationships between rhetoric and hermeneutics more difficult, but perhaps even more important, the tendency of modern-day scholars toward codification of medieval rhetoric needlessly distorts our understanding of the forces at work and the role rhetoric played in responding to and shaping those forces.

Richard Glejzer, in critiquing the "New Medievalism" in "The Subject of Invention: Antifoundationalism and Medieval Hermeneutics" (1998), questions the tendency to focus on the contextualization of the Middle Ages, suggesting that while such an emphasis implies that there is a type of foundational knowledge to be gleaned from such efforts, in actuality, studying "the Middle Ages traces how what we know about what we know defines an ontological structuralism, a topology of knowing" (337). As such, medieval scholarship is in a constant state of "becoming" rather than in a state of "being" or "knowing." (Compare with Vickers, *In Defense of Rhetoric.*)

This notion of "becoming" is also clearly apparent in articles that implicitly engage questions about how the discipline defines itself. John M. Connolly's "*Applicatio* and *Explicatio* in Gadamer and Eckhart" (2002), a chapter in *Gadamer's Century: Essays in Honor of Hans-Georg Gadamer,* edited by Jeff Malpas, Ulrich Arnswald, and Jens Kertscher, analyzes the roles of and relationship between *applicatio* and *explicatio* in Meister Eckhart's German sermons. Likewise, Richard McNabb, in "Remapping Medieval Rhetoric: Reading Boethius from a Grassian Perspective" (1998), adopts Ernesto Grassi's notions about epistemic rhetoric to blur the distinctions between rhetoric and philosophy apparent in Boethius and to suggest, ultimately, that the "rhetorical arguments in the Consolation [. . .] are not to disguise the 'bitter taste' of truth, but rather to provide a more effective means of arriving at the truth" (86). As such, McNabb essentially maintains that rhetoric and philosophy are inextricably intertwined and that philosophy requires rhetoric for the attainment of knowledge. Thus, although widely varied, all of these works indicate explicitly or implicitly that scholars are now examining not only how scholars of medieval rhetoric define the terms and categories they use, but also how they define themselves and their field.

Women and Gender

This broadening of viewpoint is also apparent in the increasing amount of scholarship addressing the myriad relationships between women and rhetoric in the Middle Ages. In fact, the focus on women, their contexts, and their approaches to rhetoric is perhaps the fastest growing subcategory within medieval rhetoric. This scholarship covers the traditional array of medieval rhetorical genres, and it is often grounded in studies of individual women rhetors or in the forms that women's rhetoric took. Indeed, the inclusion of women and women's rhetorics within the broader arena of medieval rhetoric is responsible, at least in part, for the ways in which the discipline has begun to re-define itself.

Works Focused on Specific Individuals

When such studies focus on individual women, they address, not surprisingly, women whose names are widely familiar, including Hildegard of Bingen, Margery Kempe, Julian of Norwich, and Christine de Pisan, among others. Significantly, however, such studies tend also to address how the individual female rhetor may have influenced women rhetors in general, thus connecting individual rhetorical acts to the larger social context in which they occurred. In "The Visionary Rhetoric of Hildegard of Bingen" (1997), published in Molly Meijer Wertheimer's edited collection entitled *Listening to Their Voices: The Rhetorical Activities of Historical Women*, Julia Dietrich suggests that Hildegard, a marginalized woman, was able to speak with some rhetorical authority because she asserted that God spoke through her—that she was not, in essence, speaking in her own voice. Nonetheless, as Dietrich asserts, the case of Hildegard paved the way for later female rhetors to speak in their own voices.

One such woman was Margery Kempe, who was able to use what Cheryl Glenn calls a "double ethos" to her advantage. In fact, in her article "Reexamining The Book of Margery Kempe: A Rhetoric of Autobiography" (1995), published in Andrea Lunsford's collection, *Reclaiming Rhetorica: Women in the Rhetorical Tradition,* Glenn suggests that Margery created an ethos for herself as a character within her own autobiography that differed from—and was at times even at odds with—her ethos as author. Ethos is also at issue in Glenn's subsequent work, *Rhetoric Retold: Regendering the Tradition from Antiquity through the Renaissance* (1997). In fact, chapter 3, devoted to medieval rhetoric, is entitled "Pagan Roots, Christian Flowering, or Veiled Voices in the Medieval Rhetorical Tradition," and focuses largely on Julian of Norwich and Margery Kempe, both of whom used the vernacular and specific rhetorical strategies in order to communicate effectively to a medieval audience that was not always receptive to women's voices. In addition to Margery's rhetorical strategies, which Glenn revisits in this chapter, she discusses Julian of Norwich at some length, suggesting that Julian "uses the humility *topos* repeatedly as she invokes God's tenderness, love, and inclusiveness—all to her advantage, the better to secure goodwill and then moralize" (102).

When the audience and context change, however, the rhetorical stance also changes. Thus, when Christine de Pisan addresses female audience members, which she does in a secular context, she speaks directly. For example, Jenny R. Redfern in "Christine de Pisan and *The Treasure of the City of Ladies:* A Medieval Rhetorician and Her Rhetoric" (1995), published in the Lunsford collection, asserts, "Christine directed women to speak and write for the good of society, and to affirm the best of themselves and their accomplishments in the world" (91). The fact that medieval women were using different strategies depending on their audiences, purposes, and contexts is a notion all the more significant because it reminds us that rhetorical precepts, so long the focus in medieval rhetorical scholarship, were not monolithically applicable, and indicates that avoiding the tendency to focus primarily on medieval rhetorical precepts may allow scholars to appreciate more fully the fluidity of rhetoric apparent when they examine the intricacies of the full rhetorical context of which the precepts were merely one part.

Works Focused on Rhetorical Form

Not surprisingly, then, the scholarship focused on rhetorical form in relation to women and rhetoric includes criticism covering women's relationships not only to the traditional medieval genres—*ars dictaminis, ars poetria,* and *ars praedicandi*—but also to the larger context and the attendant complexities that exerted a shaping force on women's rhetoric, just as women rhetors, in their turn, were exerting their own force on that larger context. Malcolm Richard-son addresses these issues in "'A Masterful Woman': Elizabeth Stonor and En-glish Women's Letters, 1399–c.1530" (2005), an essay in *Women's Letters across Europe, 1400–1700: Form and Persuasion,* edited by Jane Couchman and Ann Crabb. Indeed, in discussing the form of Stonor's letters, he suggests that al-though she employed some of the standard dictaminal strategies, she also went beyond the precepts in order to construct a vivid persona, thereby indicating a shrewd rhetorical ability: a concern for audience.

This multifaceted fluidity of medieval rhetoric apparent in the handling of gender-related topics in the Middle Ages has led some scholars not only to rede-fine some of the traditional medieval rhetorical genres, but also to redefine their contexts. For example, Carolyn A. Muessig's "Prophecy and Song: Teaching and Preaching by Medieval Women," and Roberto Rusconi's "Women's Sermons at the End of the Middle Ages: Texts from the Blessed and Images of the Saints" address the notion of how women as rhetors were received: what was socially acceptable for them to do, as well as how expectations and reception affected the shape of their communication. These articles appear in *Women Preachers and Prophets through Two Millennia of Christianity* (1998), edited by Beverly Mayne Kienzle and Pamela J. Walker, which sets out to "challenge [. . .] the narrow definition of preaching that has constricted the study of women's voices and explores how alternative routes for expression such as prophecy and teaching fall within a larger view of what constitutes preaching" (xvi). Part 2, containing six essays, focuses on the Middle Ages.

Similarly, Claire M. Waters's monograph *Angels and Earthly Creatures: Preaching, Performance, and Gender in the Later Middle Ages* (2004) successfully recontextualizes not only the difficulties and challenges encountered by women rhetors, but also the ways in which understanding women's rhetoric can help to shed light on rhetoric in general—including that of male preachers. The book has six sections: the first three discuss the "hybrid" nature of the male preacher as one who possesses the frailty of the human body but is called to divine ser-vice; the second half focuses on women teachers and preachers. The structure mirrors the content, the aim of which is to give a more accurate understanding of preaching in the Middle Ages by "considering theory in the light of practice, the acceptable in juxtaposition with the excluded, and [. . .] the productive and destructive interactions of the preacher's human body with the authoritative message he worked to convey" (11).

Non-Western Rhetoric

In addition to studies that look at the intersections of rhetoric and gender is another growing subcategory within the field of medieval rhetoric: non-Western rhetoric. The foray into this area is just gaining momentum, and much remains to be done. Nonetheless, works focusing on non-Western reception of ancient Greek texts, as well as on Eastern/Asian and Middle-Eastern rhetoric, have emerged. Volume 4 of *Disputatio: An International Transdisciplinary Journal of the Late Middle Ages* (1999), entitled *Discourses of Power: Grammar and Rhetoric in the Middle Ages,* is devoted to a global view of rhetoric rather than to a Western one; it includes two works that address non-Western rhetorics directly: "The Code of Frustrated Desire: Courtly Love Poetry of the European Troubadours and Chinese Southern Dynasties Traditions" by Whitney Crothers Dilley and Lee S. Tesdell's "Greek Rhetoric and Philosophy in Medieval Arabic Culture: The State of the Research." Interestingly, Dilley's article indicates a similarity in the courtly traditions across the traditional East-West divisions, while Tesdell's asserts that there are materials available for scholars to research how Greek texts were received by Arabic culture, and that what Tesdell calls "indigenous Arabic rhetoric" is a field that is ripe for research.

Other articles that engage non-Western rhetoric include Merlin Swartz's "Arabic Rhetoric and the Art of the Homily in Medieval Islam" (1999), which appears in *Religion and Culture in Medieval Islam,* edited by Richard G. Hovannisian and Georges Sabagh, and George Kanazi's "The Literary Theory of Abu Hilal al-'Askari" (1991). In addition, David R. Knechtges and Eugene Vance have edited a volume entitled *Rhetoric and the Discourses of Power in Court Culture: China, Europe, and Japan* (2005), which contains twelve articles by various authors treating rhetorical topics associated with the geographical regions mentioned in the title. The book is divided along the lines of various "rhetorics": the "Rhetoric of Persuasion," as well as of "Taste," "Communication," "Gender," and "Natural Nobility." Interestingly, each article focuses primarily on one geographical region, although the juxtaposition of articles within particular sections may allow for ease of comparison. (See also Kennedy's *Comparative Rhetoric.*)

Areas for Further Development and Research

Although scholars of medieval rhetoric are clearly expanding the field's horizons, there are areas requiring further development:

1. The field still needs educational biographies of major writers and more general research into nontraditional educational practices. This research would shed light not only on the educational contexts, but also on the societal transmission of rhetorical theories and practices. While formal institutions clearly had a role during the Middle Ages, the new focus on women's rhetoric has shown us that learning took place outside those formal institutions to various degrees.

2. Despite Polak's excellent recovery project, large numbers of *artes dictandi*

and *artes praedicandi* texts remain unprinted, and only some of the available texts have been translated into English. Editions of previously unprinted works, as well as translations of those works, would provide scholars with the materials necessary for a greater understanding of medieval rhetoric.

3. Despite the current availability of various primary texts in critical editions and translations, many of those currently in use are in dire need of updating—thus, new editions with updated annotations and bibliographies reflecting recent research would be particularly helpful.

4. Although many scholars have published studies on women's rhetoric in the Middle Ages, more work remains to be done. Of particular importance is scholarship that seeks to move beyond recovery of figures and rhetorical venues toward analysis of the transactional nature of gendered rhetorics—concerning not only how contextual forces shaped the interacting roles, but also how that gendered interaction worked as a shaping force upon the context.

5. Much of the scholarship focuses on the Latin tradition, but, as we have seen, women tended to use the vernacular, and the use of the vernacular eventually superseded that of Latin. This trend needs to be examined within the context of the history of rhetorical practice. Which sorts of rhetorical approaches shifted to the vernacular first? To what extent did women's writings play a role in this shift?

6. We have a relative scarcity of work on non-Western rhetoric. The problem is twofold: physical and linguistic access to primary texts. Although many medievalists are multilingual, most are conversant in particular languages—various historical versions, say, of Latin, Spanish, French, English, and Italian. Thus, although a number of medieval Arabic and Persian primary texts have appeared since 1990, many scholars are unable to read them; we need to continue to make non-Western primary texts accessible through critical editions and translations.

7. Finally, and contingent upon access to non-Western rhetorical texts, research is needed in comparative and intercultural rhetoric. Some work has been done in this category, as we have seen—the work on courtly literature in Europe and China, for example. What other sorts of comparisons can we make? And once we have made those comparisons, can we sketch out ways in which cultural interaction contributed to the similarities and differences we have found? How might those similarities and differences have shaped subsequent cultural interactions?

Within the last two decades, scholars of medieval history of rhetoric have produced works of the highest quality and have built admirably upon the "shoulders of the giants" who preceded them. Indeed, the list of "areas for further research" indicates how much progress has been made in more effectively painting the complex picture of medieval rhetoric.

BIBLIOGRAPHY
Reference Works and Basic Resources

Encyclopedic References

Dictionary of the Middle Ages. 13 volumes. American Council of Learned Societies. Editor-in-chief Joseph R. Strayer. New York: Scribner, 1982–1989.

Enos, Theresa, ed. *Encyclopedia of Rhetoric and Composition: Communication from Ancient Times to the Information Age.* New York: Garland, 1996.

Lausberg, Heinrich. *Handbook of Literary Rhetoric: A Foundation for Literary Study.* Trans. Matthew T. Bliss, Annemiek Jansen, and David E. Orton; ed. David E. Orton and R. Dean Anderson. Leiden, Netherlands: Brill, 1998.

Lexikon des Mittelalters [Dictionary of the Middle Ages]. Stuttgart; Weimar: Metzler. 28 cm. Vols. 1 (1980)–6 (1993) published by Artemis/Artemis & Winkler; vols. 7 (1995)–9 (1998) published by LexMA-Verlag.

Preminger, Alex, and T. V. F. Brogan, eds. *The New Princeton Encyclopedia of Poetry and Poetics.* Princeton: Princeton University Press, 1993.

Sloane, Thomas O., ed. *Encyclopedia of Rhetoric.* Oxford: Oxford University Press, 2001.

Ueding, Gert, Gregor Kalivoda, and Franz-Hubert Robling. *Historisches Wörterbuch der Rhetorik.* 7 vols. Tübingen: M. Niemeyer, 1992.

Surveys and General Studies

Briscoe, Marianne G., and Barbara J. Haye. *Artes praedicandi* and *Artes orandi.* Typologie des sources du Moyen Âge occidental 61. Turnhout, Belgium: Brepols, 1992.

Camargo, Martin. *Ars dictaminis, Ars dictandi.* Typologie des sources du Moyen Âge occidental 60. Turnhout, Belgium: Brepols, 1991.

Carruthers, Mary. *The Book of Memory: A Study of Memory in Medieval Culture.* Cambridge Studies in Medieval Literature 10. Cambridge: Cambridge University Press, 1990.

Conley, Thomas M. *Rhetoric in the European Tradition.* Chicago: University of Chicago Press, 1994. First published 1990 by Longman.

Curtius, Ernst Robert. *European Literature and the Latin Middle Ages.* Princeton: Princeton University Press, 1990. First published 1953 by Routledge and Kegan Paul.

Kelly, Douglas. *The Arts of Poetry and Prose.* Typologie des sources du Moyen Âge occidental 59. Turnhout, Belgium: Brepols, 1991.

Kennedy, George A. *Classical Rhetoric and Its Christian and Secular Traditions from Ancient to Modern Times.* London: Croom Helm (1980); Chapel Hill: University of North Carolina Press, 1980.

Murphy, James J. *Medieval Eloquence: Studies in the Theory and Practice of Medieval Rhetoric.* Berkeley: University of California Press, 1978.

——. *Rhetoric in the Middle Ages: A History of Rhetorical Theory from Saint Augustine to the Renaissance.* Berkeley: University of California Press, 1974. Reprint, Tempe: Arizona Center for Medieval and Renaissance Studies, 2001.

Ward, John O. *Ciceronian Rhetoric in Treatise, Scholion, and Commentary.* Typologies des sources du Moyen Âge occidental 58. Turnhout, Belgium: Brepols, 1995.

Wenzel, Siegfried. *Latin Sermon Collections from Later Medieval England: Orthodox Preaching in the Age of Wyclif.* Cambridge Studies in Medieval Literature 53. Cambridge: Cambridge University Press, 2005.

Bibliographies and Inventories

Brepolis. http://www.brepolis.net/index.html.

Iter. http://www.itergateway.org/.

JSTOR. http://www.jstor.org/.

Medioevo Latino: Bolletino bibliografico della cultura europea dal secolo VI al XIII. Ed. Claudio Leonardi. Appendix to Studi Medievale, 1981–.

Modern Language Association. "Electronic Format of the *MLA Bibliography.*" http://www.mla.org/bib_electronic.

Murphy, James J. *Medieval Rhetoric: A Select Bibliography.* Toronto Medieval Bibliographies 3. Toronto: University of Toronto Press, 1971. 2nd ed., 1989.

——. "Trends in Rhetorical Incunabula." *Rhetorica* 18 (2000): 389–97.

Murphy, James J., and Martin Davies. "Rhetorical Incunabula: A Short-Title Catalogue of Texts Printed to the Year 1500." *Rhetorica* 15, no. 4 (1997): 355–470.

Polak, Emil. *Medieval and Renaissance Letter Treatises and Form Letters: A Census of Manuscripts Found in Eastern Europe and the Former U.S.S.R.* Davis Medieval Texts and Studies 8. Leiden, Netherlands: Brill, 1993.

——. *Medieval and Renaissance Letter Treatises and Form Letters: A Census of Manuscripts Found in Parts of Western Europe, Japan, and the United States of America.* Davis Medieval Texts and Studies 9. Leiden, Netherlands: Brill, 1994.

Reinsma, Luke. "The Middle Ages." In *Historical Rhetoric: An Annotated Bibliography of Selected Sources in English,* ed. Winifred Horner, 45–108. Boston: G. K. Hall, 1980.

Rutherford, David. "A Finding List of Antonio da Rho's Works and Related Primary Sources." *Italia medioevale e umanistica* 33 (1990): 75–108.

Worstbrock, Franz Josef, Monika Klaes, and Jutta Lütten. *Repertorium der artes dictandi des mittelalters.* Part 1: Von den Anfägen bis um 1200. Münstersche Mittelalter-Schriften 66. Munich: Wilhelm Fink, 1992.

Texts and Translations

Agricola, Rudolf. *De inventione dialectica libri tres.* Ed. Lothar Mundt. Tübingen, Germany: M. Niemeyer, 1992.

Bede. *Libri II De arte metrica et de schematibus et tropis.* Ed. and trans. Calvin B. Kendall. Bibliotheca Germanica, n.s. 2. Saarbrücken, Germany, 1991.

Boethius. *De topicis differentiis.* Trans. Eleonore Stump. 1978. Reprint, Ithaca: Cornell University Press, 2004.

——. *In Ciceronis topica.* Trans. Eleonore Stump. 1988. Reprint, Ithaca: Cornell University Press, 2004.

Bonandree, Iohannis. *Brevis introductio ad dictamen.* Ed. Silvana Arcuti. Galatina, Italy: Congedo, 1993.

Camargo, Martin, ed. *Medieval Rhetorics of Prose Composition: Five English "Artes dictandi" and Their Tradition.* Binghamton, NY: Medieval and Renaissance Texts and Studies, 1995.

Carruthers, Mary, and Jan M. Ziolkowski, eds. *The Medieval Craft of Memory: An Anthology of Texts and Pictures.* Philadelphia: University of Pennsylvania Press, 2002.

Copeland, Rita, and Ineke Sluiter, eds. *Medieval Literary Theory: Grammatical and Rhetorical Traditions.* Forthcoming: Oxford University Press.

Eskenasy, Pauline Ellen. "Antony of Tagrit's Rhetoric Book One: Introduction, Partial Translation, and Commentary." Ph.D. diss. Harvard University, 1991.

Geoffrey of Vinsauf. *Documentum de modo et arte dictandi et versificandi (Instruction in the Method and Art of Speaking and Versifying).* Trans. Roger P. Parr. Mediaeval Philosophical Texts in Translation 17. Milwaukee: Marquette University Press, 1968.

——. *The Poetria nova of Geoffrey of Vinsauf.* Trans. Margaret F. Nims. Toronto: Pontifical Institute of Mediaeval Studies, 1967.

George of Trebizond. *Rhetoricorum libri quinque.* Ed. Luc Deitz and Chrestien Wechel. Hildesheim, Germany: Georg Olms, 2006.

Grotans, Anna A. *The St. Gall Tractate: A Medieval Guide to Rhetorical Syntax.* Columbia, SC: Camden House, 1995.

Higden, Ranulph. *Ars componendi sermones.* Trans. Margaret Jennings and Sally A. Wilson. Dallas Medieval Texts and Translations 2. Paris: Peeters, 2003.

——. *"Ars componendi sermons" of Ranulph Higden O.S.B.* Ed. Margaret Jennings. Davis Medieval Texts and Studies 6. Leiden, Netherlands: Brill, 1991.

Hugh of St. Victor. *The Didascalion of Hugh of St. Victor.* Trans. Jerome Taylor. 1961. Records of Western Civilization. New York: Columbia University Press, 1991.

Isidore of Seville. *The Etymologies of Isidore of Seville.* Trans. and ed. Stephen A. Barney, W. J. Lewis, J. A. Beach, and Oliver Berghof. Cambridge: Cambridge University Press, 2006.

John of Garland. *The Parisiana Poetria of John of Garland.* Ed. and trans. Traugott Lawler. Yale Studies in English 182. New Haven: Yale University Press, 1974.

Llull, Ramon. *Raimundi Lulli opera latina. 97–100: In Cypro, alleas in Cilicia deque transmarinis veniente annis MCCCI–MCCCII compilata.* Ed. Jaume Medina. Corpus Christianorum 184. Turnhout, Belgium: Brepols, 2005.

———. *Ramon Llull's New Rhetoric: Text and Translation of Llull's* Rhetorica nova. Ed. Mark D. Johnston. Davis, CA: Hermagoras, 1994.

Mattias. *Testa nucis* and *Poetria.* Ed. and trans. Birger Bergh. Arlöv, Sweden: Berlings, 1996.

Miller, Joseph M., Michael H. Prosser, and Thomas W. Benson. *Readings in Medieval Rhetoric.* Bloomington: Indiana University Press, 1973.

Murphy, James J., ed. *Three Medieval Rhetorical Arts.* 1971. Medieval and Renaissance Texts and Studies 228; MRTS Reprint Series 5. Tempe: Arizona Center for Medieval and Renaissance Studies, 2001.

Ryan, Maureen Binder. "A Study and Critical Edition of the 'Alanus' Commentary on Pseudo-Cicero *Rhetorica Ad Herennium:* Accessus and Book One (with Latin Text)." Ph.D. diss. Ohio State University, 1992.

Transmundus. *Introductiones dictandi.* Ed. and trans. Ann Dalzell. Studies and Texts 123. Toronto: Pontifical Institute of Mediaeval Studies, 1995.

The Educational Background

Baldwin, John W. *Masters, Princes, and Merchants: The Social Views of Peter the Chanter and His Circle.* Princeton: Princeton University Press, 1970.

Begley, Ronald B., and Joseph W. Koterski, eds. *Medieval Education.* Fordham Series in Medieval Studies 4. New York: Fordham University Press, 2005.

Briggs, Charles F. "Aristotle's *Rhetoric* in the Later Medieval Universities: A Reassessment." *Rhetorica* 25, no. 3 (2007): 243–68.

Briscoe, Marianne G. "How Was the *ars praedicandi* Taught in England?" In *The Uses of Manuscripts in Literary Studies: Essays in Memory of Judson Boyce Allen,* 41–58. Studies in Medieval Culture 31. Kalamazoo, MI: Medieval Institute Publications, 1992.

Camargo, Martin. "Between Grammar and Rhetoric: Composition Teaching at Oxford and Bologna in the Late Middle Ages." In *Rhetoric and Pedagogy: Its History, Philosophy, and Practice: Essays in Honor of James J. Murphy,* ed. Winifred Bryan Horner and Michael Leff, 83–94. Mahwah, NJ: Erlbaum, 1995.

———. "Beyond the *Libri Catoniani:* Models of Latin Prose Style at Oxford University ca. 1400." *Mediaeval Studies* 56 (1994): 165–87.

———. "If You Can't Join Them, Beat Them, or When Grammar Met Business Writing (in Fifteenth-Century Oxford)." In *Letter-Writing Manuals from Antiquity to the Present,* ed. Carol Poster and Linda Mitchell, 67–87. Columbia: University of South Carolina Press, 2007.

——. "The Pedagogy of the *Dictatores*." In *Papers on Rhetoric V: Atti del Convegno Internazionale* "Dictamen, Poetria and Cicero: Coherence and Diversification," Bologna, 10–11 May 2002, ed. Lucia Calboli Montefusco, 65–94. Rome: Herder, 2003.

Cobban, A. B. *The Medieval English Universities: Oxford and Cambridge to c. 1500.* Berkeley: University of California Press; Aldershot: Scolar, 1988.

——. *The Medieval Universities: Their Development and Organization.* London: Methuen, 1970.

Coleman, Joyce. *Public Reading and the Reading Public in Late Medieval England and France.* Cambridge: Cambridge University Press, 1996.

Fraker, Charles F. "*Oppositio* in Geoffrey of Vinsauf and Its Background." *Rhetorica* 11, no. 1 (1993): 63–85.

Fredborg, Karin Margareta. "Abelard on Rhetoric." In *Rhetoric and Renewal in the Latin West 1100–1540: Essays in Honour of John O. Ward,* ed. Constant J. Mews, Cary J. Nederman, and Rodney M. Thomson, 55–80. *Disputatio* 2. Turnhout, Belgium: Brepols, 2003.

Friis-Jensen, Karsten. "The *Ars Poetica* in Twelfth-Century France: The Horace of Matthew of Vendôme, Geoffrey of Vinsauf, and John of Garland." *Cahier de l'Institut du Moyen-Age Grec et Latin* 60 (1990): 319–88.

Gersh, Stephen. "Eriugena's *Ars Rhetorica*—Theory and Practice." In *Iohannes Scottus Eriugena: The Bible and Hermeneutics. Proceedings of the Ninth International Colloquium of the Society for the Promotion of Eriugenian Studies Held at Leuven and Louvain-la-Neuve, June 7–10, 1995,* ed. Gerd van Riel, Carlos Steel, and Michael Richter, 261–78. Ancient and Medieval Philosophy, De Wulf-Mansion Centre, Ser. 1, 20. Leuven, Belgium: Leuven University Press, 1996.

Grotans, Anna A. *The St. Gall Tractate: A Medieval Guide to Rhetorical Syntax.* Columbia, SC: Camden House, 1995.

Hackett, Jeremiah. "Roger Bacon on Rhetoric and Poetics." In *Roger Bacon and the Sciences: Commemorative Essays,* ed. Jeremiah Hackett, 133–49. Studien und Texte zur Geistesgeschichte des Mittelalters 57. Leiden, Netherlands: Brill, 1997.

Hintz, Ernst Ralf. *Learning and Persuasion in the German Middle Ages.* New York: Garland, 1997.

Horner, Winifred Bryan, and Michael Leff, eds. *Rhetoric and Pedagogy: Its History, Philosophy, and Practice: Essays in Honor of James J. Murphy.* Mahwah, NJ: Erlbaum, 1995.

Johnston, Mark D. *The Evangelical Rhetoric of Ramon Llull: Lay Learning and Piety in the Christian West around 1300.* New York: Oxford University Press, 1996.

Kelly, Douglas. "The Medieval Art of Poetry and Prose: The Scope of Instruction and Uses of Models." In *Medieval Rhetoric: A Casebook,* ed. Scott D.

Troyan, 1–24. New York: Routledge, 2004.

Knappe, Gabriele. "The Rhetorical Aspect of Grammar Teaching in Anglo-Saxon England." *Rhetorica* 17, no. 1 (1999): 1–35.

Lanham, Carol Dana. "Freshman Composition in the Early Middle Ages: Epistolography and Rhetoric before the *Ars dictaminis*." *Viator* 12 (1992): 115–34.

Leff, Gordon. *Paris and Oxford Universities in the Thirteenth and Fourteenth Centuries: An Institutional and Intellectual History.* New Dimensions in History: Essays in Comparative History. 1968. Reprint, Huntington, N.Y.: R. E. Krieger, 1975.

Lehman, Jennifer Shootman. "Haimo's Book: Rhetorical Pedagogy in a Medieval Clerical Miscellany" (Munich, Bayerische Staatsbibliothek CLM 14062, ff. 56r–119v). Ph.D. diss. University of Texas at Austin, 2001.

Lutz, Cora E. *Schoolmasters of the Tenth Century.* Hamden, Conn.: Archon Books, 1977.

Mack, Peter. "Theory and Practice in Rudolph Agricola." In *Rhetoric—Rhétoriqueurs—Rederijkers,* ed. Jelle Koopmans et al., 39–51. Verhandelingen van de Koninklijke Nederlandse Akademie van Wetenschappen, Afd. Letterkunde, Nieuwe Reeks 162. Amsterdam: North-Holland, 1995.

Minnis, Alastair. "Absent Glosses: A Crisis of Vernacular Commentary in Late-Medieval England?" *Essays in Medieval Studies* 20 (2003): 1–17.

Murphy, James J. *Kristeller and Renaissance Rhetoric.* Adobe e-books.

——. *Latin Rhetoric and Education in the Middle Ages and Renaissance.* Variorum Collected Studies Series. Aldershot, U.K.: Ashgate, 2005.

——. "Literary Implications of Instruction in the Verbal Arts in Fourteenth Century England." *LSE,* n.s. 1 (1967): 119–35.

——. "Quintilian's Influence on the Teaching of Speaking and Writing in the Middle Ages and Renaissance." In *Oral and Written Communication: Historical Approaches,* ed. Richard Leo Enos, 158–83. Written Communication Annual: An International Survey of Research and Theory 4. Newbury Park, CA: 1990.

——. "Rhetoric in the Fifteenth Century: From Manuscript to Print." In *Rhetoric and Renewal in the Latin West, 1100–1540: Essays in Honour of John O. Ward,* ed. Constant J. Mews, Cary J. Nederman, and Rodney M. Thomson, 227–41. Disputatio 2. Turnhout, Belgium: Brepols, 2003.

——. *A Short History of Writing Instruction from Ancient Greece to Twentieth-Century America.* Davis, CA: Hermagoras, 1990.

——. *A Short History of Writing Instruction: From Ancient Greece to Modern America.* Mahwah, NJ: Erlbaum, 2001.

Orme, Nicholas I. *Education in the West of England, 1066–1548.* Exeter: University of Exeter Press, 1976.

——. *English Schools in the Middle Ages.* London: Methuen, 1973.

———. *Medieval Schools: From Roman Britain to Tudor England*. New Haven: Yale University Press, 2006.

Peterson, Janine Larmon. "Defining a Textbook: Gloss versus Gloss in a Medieval Schoolbook." *Essays in Medieval Studies* 20 (2003): 18–30.

Purcell, William M. "Eberhard the German and the Labyrinth of Learning: Grammar, Poesy, Rhetoric, and Pedagogy in *Laborintus*." *Rhetorica* 11 (1993): 95–118.

———. "*Identitas, similitudo,* and *contrarietas* in Gervasius of Melkley's *Ars poetica:* A *Stasis* of Style." *Rhetorica* 9 (1991): 67–91.

Rashdall, Hastings. *The Universities of Europe in the Middle Ages*. 3 vols. 2nd ed., rev. by F. M. Powicke and A. B. Emden. Oxford: Clarendon Press, 1936.

Rickert, Edith. "Chaucer at School." *Modern Philology* 29, no. 3 (1932): 257–74.

Roberts, Phyllis B. "Sermons and Preaching in/and the Medieval University." In *Medieval Education*, ed. Ronald B. Begley and Joseph W. Koterski, 83–98. Fordham Series in Medieval Studies 4. New York: Fordham University Press, 2005.

Tilliette, Jean-Yves. *Des mots à la parole: Une lecture de la* Poetria nova *de Geoffroy de Vinsauf*. Geneva: Librairie Droz, 2000.

Van Engen, John. "Letters, Schools, and Written Culture in the Eleventh and Twelfth Centuries." In *Dialektik und Rhetorik im frühen und hohen Mittelalter: Rezeption, Überlieferung und gesellschaftliche Wirkung antiker Gelehrsamkeit vornehmlich im 9. und 12. Jahrhundert*, ed. Johannes Fried, 97–132. Schriften des historischen Kollegs. Kolloquien 27. Munich: Oldenbourg, 1997.

Van Engen, John, ed. *Learning Institutionalized: Teaching in the Medieval University*. Notre Dame Conferences in Medieval Studies 9. Notre Dame: University of Notre Dame Press, 2000.

Ward, John O. "The *Catena* Commentaries on the Rhetoric of Cicero and Their Implications for Development of a Teaching Tradition in Rhetoric." *Studies in Medieval and Renaissance Teaching* 6, no. 2 (1998): 79–95.

———. *Ciceronian Rhetoric in Treatise, Scholion, and Commentary*. Typologies des sources du Moyen Âge occidental 58. Turnhout, Belgium: Brepols, 1995.

———. "From Marginal Gloss to *Catena* Commentary: The Eleventh-Century Origins of a Rhetorical Teaching Tradition in the Medieval West." *Parergon: Bulletin of the Australian and New Zealand Association for Medieval and Renaissance Studies* 13, no. 2 (1996): 109–20.

———. "Rhetoric in the Faculty of Arts at the Universities of Paris and Oxford in the Middle Ages: A Summary of the Evidence." *Bulletin du Cange: Archivum Latinitatis Medii Aevi* 54 (1996): 159–231.

Weijers, Olga. "The Evolution of the *Trivium* in University Teaching: The Example of the Topics." In *Learning Institutionalized: Teaching in the Medieval University*, ed. John Van Engen, 43–67. Notre Dame Conferences in Medieval Studies 9. Notre Dame: University of Notre Dame Press, 2000.

Wenzel, Siegfried. "Academic Sermons at Oxford in the Early Fifteenth Century." *Speculum* 70 (1995): 305–29.

Woods, Marjorie Curry. "Among Men—Not Boys: Histories of Rhetoric and the Exclusion of Pedagogy." *Rhetoric Society Quarterly* 22, no. 1 (1992): 18–26.

——. "A Medieval Rhetoric Goes to School—and to the University: The Commentaries on the *Poetria nova.*" *Rhetorica* 9 (1991): 55–65.

——. "Quintilian and Medieval Teaching." In *Quintiliano: Historia y actualidad de la rétorica, I–III,* ed. Tomás Albaladejo et al., 1531–40. Colección Quintiliano de Rétorica y Comunicación 2. Logroño, Spain: Instituto de Estudios Riojanos, 1998.

——. "Teaching the Tropes in the Middle Ages: The Theory of Metaphoric Transference in Commentaries on the *Poetria nova.*" In *Rhetoric and Pedagogy: Its History, Philosophy, and Practice: Essays in Honor of James J. Murphy,* ed. Winifred Bryan Horner and Michael Leff, 73–82. Mahwah, NJ: Erlbaum, 1995.

The Role of *Dictamen*

Calboli, Gualtiero. "The Knowledge of the *Rhetorica ad Herennium* as 'Prerequisite for Training in *dictamen*'" *Papers on Rhetoric V: Atti del Convegno Internazionale* "Dictamen, Poetria, and Cicero: Coherence and Diversification," Bologna, 10–11 May 2002, ed. Lucia Calboli Montefusco, 43–64. Rome: Herder, 2003.

Camargo, Martin. "*Si dictare velis:* Versified *Artes dictandi* and Late Medieval Writing Pedagogy." *Rhetorica* 14 (1996): 265–88.

——. "Toward a Comprehensive Art of Written Discourse: Geoffrey of Vinsauf and the *Ars dictaminis.*" *Rhetorica* 6, no. 2 (1988): 167–94.

——. "A Twelfth-Century Treatise on *Dictamen* and Metaphor." *Traditio* 47 (1992): 161–213.

——. "The Waning of Medieval *Ars dictaminis.*" *Rhetorica* 19, no. 2 (2001): 135–274.

——. "Where's the Brief? The *Ars dictaminis* and Reading/Writing between the Lines." *Disputatio: An Interdisciplinary Journal of the Late Middle Ages* 1 (1996): 1–17.

Kristeller, Paul O. "Philosophy and Rhetoric from Antiquity to the Renaissance." Part 5 in *Renaissance Thought and Its Sources,* ed. Michael Mooney, 211–60 (notes 312–27). New York: Columbia University Press, 1979.

McNabb, Richard. "Innovations and Compilations: Juan Gil de Zamora's *Dictaminis epithalamium.*" *Rhetorica* 21 (2003): 225–54.

——. "To Father Juan, with Love, Bishop Alexander: Juan Gil de Zamora's Medieval Art of Letters." *Rhetoric Review* 23 (2004): 103–20.

Murphy, James J. "Alberic of Montecassino: Father of the Medieval *Ars dictaminis.*" *ABR* 22 (1971): 129–46.

Patt, William D. "The Early *Ars dictaminis* as Response to a Changing Society." *Viator* 9 (1978): 133–35.

Poster, Carol, and Linda Mitchell, eds. *Letter-Writing Manuals from Antiquity to the Present.* Columbia: University of South Carolina Press, 2007.

Ward, John O. "Rhetoric and the Art of *Dictamen.*" In *Méthodes et instruments du travail intellectuel au Moyen Âge. Etudes sur le vocabulaire,* ed. Olga Weijers, 20–61. Etudes sur le vocabulaire intellectuel du Moyen Âge 3. Turnhout, Belgium: Brepols, 1990.

——. "Rhetorical Theory and the Rise and Decline of *Dictamen* in the Middle Ages and Early Renaissance." *Rhetorica* 19 (2001): 175–223.

Sermons and Sermon Theory

Anderson, Roger, ed. *Constructing the Medieval Sermon.* Turnhout, Belgium: Brepols, 2007.

Briscoe, Marianne G., and Barbara J. Haye. *Artes praedicandi* and *Artes orandi.* Typologie des sources du Moyen Âge occidental 61. Turnhout, Belgium: Brepols, 1992.

Caplan, Harry. *Medieval* Artes praedicandi: *A Hand-List.* Cornell Studies in Classical Philology, 24. Ithaca: Cornell University Press, 1934. *Supplement,* 1936.

Carruthers, Leo. "The Word Made Flesh: Preaching and Community from the Apostolic to the Late Middle Ages." In *Speculum Sermonis: Interdisciplinary Reflections on the Medieval Sermon,* ed. Georgiana Donavin et al., 3–27. Coll. Disputatio. Turnhout, Belgium: Brepols, 2004.

Charland, Th.-M. *Artes praedicandi: Contribution à l'histoire de la rhétorique au Moyen Âge.* Publications de l'Institut d'Études Médiévales, 1936.

Donavin, Georgiana. "'*De sermone sermonem fecimus*': Alexander of Ashby's *De artificioso modo predicandi.*" *Rhetorica* 15 (1997): 279–96.

Donavin, Georgiana, Cary J. Nederman, and Richard Utz, eds. Speculum Sermonis: *Interdisciplinary Reflections on the Medieval Sermon. Disputatio* ser.1. Turnhout, Belgium: Brepols, 2004.

Emery, Kent, Jr. "Denys the Carthusian and the Invention of Preaching Materials." *Viator* 25 (1994): 377–409.

Hamesse, Jacqueline, Beverly Mayne Kienzle, Debra L. Stoudt, and Anne T. Thayer, eds. *Medieval Sermons and Society: Cloister, City, University: Proceedings of International Symposia at Kalamazoo and New York.* Louvain-La-Neuve, Belgium: Fédération internationale des Instituts d'études médiévales, 1998.

Kinneavy, James L. "A Sophistic Strain in the Medieval *Ars praedicandi* and the Scholastic Method." In *Oral and Written Communication: Historical Approaches,* ed. Richard Leo Enos, 82–95. Written Communication Annual: An International Survey of Research and Theory 4. Newbury Park, CA: 1990.

Menache, Sophia, and Jeannine Horowitz. "Rhetoric and Its Practice in Medieval Sermons." *Historical Reflections/Réflexions Historiques* 22 (1996): 321–50.

Muessig, Carolyn A., ed. *Preacher, Sermon, and Audience in the Middle Ages.* A New History of the Sermon 3. Leiden, Netherlands: Brill, 2002.

O'Mara, Veronica, and Suzanne Park, eds. *Repertorium of Middle English Prose Sermons.* 4 vols. Turnhout, Belgium: Brepols, 2007.

Roberts, Phyllis B. "The *Ars praedicandi* and the Medieval Sermon." In *Preacher, Sermon, and Audience in the Middle Ages,* ed. Carolyn A. Muessig, 41–62. A New History of the Sermon 3. Leiden, Netherlands: Brill, 2002.

Ross, Woodburn O., ed. *Middle English Sermons.* Early English Text Society 209. London: Early English Text Society, 1940.

Smyth, Charles H. E. *The Art of Preaching: A Practical Survey of Preaching in the Church of England, 747–1939.* 1940. Reprint, London: S.P.C.K., 1953.

Thompson, Augustine. "From Texts to Preaching: Retrieving the Medieval Sermon as an Event." In *Preacher, Sermon, and Audience in the Middle Ages,* ed. Carolyn Muessig, 13–37. Leiden, Netherlands: Brill, 2002.

Wenzel, Siegfried. *Latin Sermon Collections from Later Medieval England: Orthodox Preaching in the Age of Wyclif.* Cambridge Studies in Medieval Literature 53. Cambridge: Cambridge University Press, 2005.

The Relation of Rhetoric and Grammar to the *Ars poetriae*

Bland, Dave L. "The Use of Proverbs in Two Medieval Genres of Discourse: 'The Art of Poetry' and 'The Art of Preaching.'" *Proverbium: Yearbook of International Proverb Scholarship* 14 (1997): 1–21.

Bursill-Hall, G. L., Sten Ebbesen, and Konrad Koerner, eds. De ortu grammaticae: *Studies in Medieval Grammar and Linguistic Theory in Memory of Jan Pinborg.* Amsterdam Studies in the Theory and History of Linguistic Science III: Studies in the History of the Language Sciences 43. Amsterdam: Benjamins, 1990.

Copeland, Rita. "Rhetoric and the Politics of the Literal Sense in Medieval Literary Theory: Aquinas, Wyclif, and the Lollards." In *Rhetoric and Hermeneutics in Our Time: A Reader,* ed. Walter Jost and Michael J. Hyde, 335–57. Yale Studies in Hermeneutics. New Haven: Yale University Press, 1997.

Irvine, Martin. *The Making of Textual Culture: Grammatical and Literary Theory, 350–1100.* Cambridge Studies in Medieval Literature 19. Cambridge: Cambridge University Press, 1994.

Luscombe, David E. "Dialectic and Rhetoric in the Ninth and Twelfth Centuries: Continuity and Change." In *Dialektik und Rhetorik im frühen und hohen Mittelalter: Rezeption, Überlieferung und gesellschaftliche Wirkung antiker*

Gelehrsamkeit vornehmlich im 9. und 12. Jahrhundert, ed. Johannes Fried, 1–
20. Schriften des historischen Kollegs. Kolloquien 27. Munich: Oldenbourg,
1997.

Mack, Peter. "Agricola's Dialectic and the Tradition of Rhetoric." In *Wessel
Gansfort (1419–1489) and Northern Humanism,* ed. F. Akkerman, G. C. Huis-
man, and A. J. Vanderjagt, 272–89. Brill's Studies in Intellectual History 40.
Leiden, Netherlands: Brill, 1993.

———. *Renaissance Argument: Valla and Agricola in the Traditions of Rhetoric and
Dialectic.* Brill's Studies in Intellectual History 43. Leiden, Netherlands: Brill,
1993.

Mews, Constant J. "Peter Abelard on Dialectic, Rhetoric, and the Principles of
Argument." In *Rhetoric and Renewal in the Latin West, 1100–1540: Essays
in Honour of John O. Ward,* ed. Constant J. Mews, Cary J. Nederman, and
Rodney M. Thomson, 37–53. *Disputatio* ser. 2. Turnhout, Belgium: Brepols,
2003.

Murphy, James J. "A New Look at Chaucer and the Rhetoricians." *Review of
English Studies* n.s. 15 (1964): 1–20.

———. *Rhetoric in the Middle Ages: A History of Rhetorical Theory from Saint
Augustine to the Renaissance.* 1974. Reprint, Tempe: Arizona Center for Medieval and Renaissance Studies, 2001.

Poster, Carol, and Richard Utz, eds. *Discourses of Power: Grammar and Rhetoric
in the Middle Ages. Disputatio: An International Transdisciplinary Journal of
the Late Middle Ages* 4, 1999.

Purcell, William M. *"Ars poetriae": Rhetorical and Grammatical Invention at the
Margins of Literacy.* Columbia: University of South Carolina Press, 1996.

Reynolds, Suzanne. *Medieval Reading: Grammar, Rhetoric, and the Classical Text.*
Cambridge: Cambridge University Press, 1996.

Schoeck, Richard F. "On Rhetoric in Fourteenth-Century Oxford." *Mediaeval
Studies* 30 (1968), no. 214–25.

Definition and Scope of Medieval Rhetoric

Allen, Judson B. *The Ethical Poetic of the Later Middle Ages.* Toronto: University
of Toronto Press, 1981.

Astell, Ann. "On the Usefulness and Use Value of Books: A Medieval and Modern Inquiry." In *Medieval Rhetoric: A Casebook,* ed. Scott D. Troyan, 41–62.
New York: Routledge, 2004.

Atkins, John W. H. *English Literary Criticism: The Medieval Phase.* 1943. Reprint, London: Methuen; New York: Peter Smith, 1952.

Baldwin, Charles S. *Medieval Rhetoric and Poetic (to 1400) Interpreted from
Representative Works.* 1928, 1959. Reprint, St. Clair Shores, Mich.: Scholarly
Press, 1983.

Camargo, Martin. "Defining Medieval Rhetoric." In *Rhetoric and Renewal in the Latin West, 1100–1540: Essays in Honour of John O. Ward,* ed. Constant J. Mews, Cary J. Nederman, and Rodney M. Thomson, 21–34. Turnhout, Belgium: Brepols, 2003.

———. "*Tria sunt:* The Long and the Short of Geoffrey of Vinsauf's *Documentum de modo et arte dictandi et versificandi.*" *Speculum* 74 (1999): 935–55.

Carruthers, Mary. "Boncompagno at the Cutting-Edge of Rhetoric: Rhetorical *Memoria* and the Craft of Memory." *Journal of Medieval Latin: A Publication of the North American Association of Medieval Latin* 6 (1996): 44–64.

———. *The Craft of Thought: Meditation, Rhetoric, and the Making of Images, 400–1200.* Cambridge Studies in Medieval Literature 34. Cambridge: Cambridge University Press, 1998.

Chavannes-Mazel, Claudine A. "The Twelve Ladies of Rhetoric in Cambridge (CUL MS Nn.3.2)." *Transactions of the Cambridge Bibliographical Society* 10, no. 2 (1991): 139–55.

Colish, Marcia L. *The Mirror of Language: A Study in the Medieval Theory of Knowledge.* New Haven: Yale University Press, 1968.

Connolly, John M. "*Applicatio* and *Explicatio* in Gadamer and Eckhart." In *Gadamer's Century: Essays in Honor of Hans-Georg Gadamer,* ed. Jeff Malpas, Ulrich Arnswald, and Jens Kertscher, 77–96. Studies in Contemporary German Social Thought. Cambridge, MA: MIT Press, 2002.

Copeland, Rita. "The History of Rhetoric and the *Longue Durée:* Ciceronian Myth and Its Medieval Afterlives." *Journal of English and Germanic Philology* 106, no. 2 (2007): 176–202.

———. "Lydgate, Hawes, and the Science of Rhetoric in the Late Middle Ages." *Modern Language Quarterly: A Journal of Literary History* 53, no. 1 (1992): 57–82.

———. *Rhetoric, Hermeneutics, and Translation in the Middle Ages: Academic Traditions and Vernacular Texts.* Cambridge: Cambridge University Press, 1991.

Copeland, Rita, and Stephen Melville. "Allegory and Allegoresis, Rhetoric and Hermeneutics." *Reflections in the Frame: New Perspectives on the Study of Medieval Literature.* Special issue of *Exemplaria* 3, no. 1 (1991): 159–88.

Cox, Virginia, and John O. Ward. *The Rhetoric of Cicero in Its Medieval and Early Renaissance Commentary Tradition.* Brill's Companions to the Christian Tradition, vol. 2. Leiden, Netherlands: Brill, 2006.

Donavin, Georgiana. "The Medieval Rhetoric of Identification: A Burkean Reconception." *Rhetoric Society Quarterly* 26, no. 2 (1996): 51–66.

Donavin, Georgiana, Carol Poster, and Richard Utz, eds. *Medieval Forms of Argument: Disputation and Debate. Disputatio: An International Transdisciplinary Journal of the Late Middle Ages* 5. Eugene, OR: Wipf and Stock, 2002.

Dronke, Peter. "Mediaeval Rhetoric." In *Literature and Western Civilization,* ed. David Daiches and A. Thorlby, 2:315–45. London: Aldus, 1973.

Edwards, Robert R. "Poetic Invention and the Medieval *Causae.*" *Mediaeval Studies* 55 (1993): 183–217.

Enders, Jody. *Rhetoric and the Origins of Medieval Drama.* Ithaca: Cornell University Press, 1992.

Gehl, Paul F. "Preachers, Teachers, and Translators: The Social Meaning of Language Study in Trecento Tuscany." *Viator: Medieval and Renaissance Studies* 25 (1994): 289–323.

Gersh, Stephen. "Dialectical and Rhetorical Space: The Boethian Theory of Topics and Its Influence during the Middle Ages." In *Raum und Raumvorstellungen im Mittelalter,* ed. Jan A. Aertsen and Andreas Speer, 391–401. Berlin: de Gruyter, 1998.

Glejzer, Richard R. "The Subject of Invention: Antifoundationalism and Medieval Hermeneutics." In *Rhetoric in an Antifoundational World: Language, Culture, and Pedagogy,* ed. Michael F. Bernard-Donals and Richard R. Glejzer, 318–40. New Haven: Yale University Press, 1998.

Heusser, Martin, Michèle Hannoosh, Leo Hoek, Charlotte Schoell-Glass, and David Scott, eds. *Text and Visuality: Word and Image Interactions III.* Studies in Comparative Literature 22. Amsterdam: Rodopi, 1999.

Kirtley, Susan. "Medieval Diglossia and Modern Academic Discourse." *Rhetoric Review* 26, no. 3 (2007): 253–67.

Lanham, Carol Dana, ed. *Latin Grammar and Rhetoric: From Classical Theory to Medieval Practice.* London: Continuum, 2002.

Mack, Peter. "Agricola's Use of the Comparison between Writing and the Visual Arts." *Journal of the Warburg and Courtald Institutes* 55 (1992): 169–79.

McNabb, Richard. "Remapping Medieval Rhetoric: Reading Boethius from a Grassian Perspective." *Rhetoric Society Quarterly* 28, no. 3 (1998): 75–90.

Minnis, A. J., and A. B. Scott, eds., with the assistance of David Wallace. *Medieval Literary Theory and Criticism, c.1100–c.1375: The Commentary Tradition.* 1988. Oxford: Clarendon, 1991.

Morse, Ruth. *Truth and Convention in the Middle Ages: Rhetoric, Representation, and Reality.* Cambridge: Cambridge University Press, 1991.

Oosterman, Johan. "Imprint on Your Memory: An Exploration of Mnemonics in the Work of Anthonis de Roovere." In *Medieval Memory: Image and Text,* ed. Frank Willaert, Herman Braet, Thom Mertens and Theo Venckeleer, 161–75. Fédération Internationale des Instituts d'Etudes Médiévales: Textes et Etudes du Moyen Âge 27. Turnhout, Belgium: Brepols, 2004.

Paetow, Louis J. *The Arts Course at Medieval Universities with Special Reference to Grammar and Rhetoric.* University Studies of the University of Illinois, nos. 3, 7. 1910. Reprint, Dubuque, IA: Wm. C. Brown Reprint Library, n.d.

Payne, Robert O. *The Key of Remembrance: A Study of Chaucer's Poetics.* 1963. Reprint, Westport, Conn.: Greenwood Press, 1973.

Plesch, Véronique. "Pictorial *Ars praedicandi* in Late Fifteenth-Century Paintings." In *Text and Visuality: Word and Image Interactions III,* ed. Martin Heusser, Michèle Hannoosh, Leo Hoek, Charlotte Schoell-Glass, and David Scott, 173–86. Studies in Comparative Literature 22. Amsterdam: Rodopi, 1999.

Sears, Elizabeth. "Visual Rhetoric." In *Reading Medieval Images: The Art Historian and the Object,* ed. Elizabeth Sears and Thelma K. Thomas, 36–37. Ann Arbor: University of Michigan Press, 2002.

Troyan, Scott D. "Rhetoric without Genre: Orality, Textuality, and the Shifting Scene of the Rhetorical Situation in the Middle Ages." *Romanic Review* 82 (1990): 377–95.

———. "Unwritten between the Lines: The Unspoken History of Rhetoric." In *Medieval Rhetoric: A Casebook,* ed. Scott D. Troyan, 217–45. New York: Routledge, 2004.

Vickers, Brian. *In Defence of Rhetoric.* New York: Oxford University Press, 1989.

Ward, John O. "Rhetoric, Truth, and Literacy in the Renaissance of the Twelfth Century." In *Oral and Written Communication: Historical Approaches,* ed. Richard Leo Enos, 126–57. Written Communication Annual: An International Survey of Research and Theory 4. Newbury Park, CA: 1990.

Wetherbee, Winthrop. *Platonism and Poetry in the Twelfth Century: The Literary Influence of the School of Chartres.* Princeton: Princeton University Press, 1972.

Witt, Ronald G. *Italian Humanism and Medieval Rhetoric.* Aldershot, U.K.: Ashgate/Variorum, 2001.

Woods, Marjorie Curry. "In a Nutshell: *Verba* and *sententia* and Matter and Form in Medieval Composition Theory." In *The Uses of Manuscripts in Literary Studies: Essays in Memory of Judson Boyce Allen,* ed. Charlotte Cook Morse, Penelope Reed Doob, and Marjorie Curry Woods, 19–39. Studies in Medieval Culture 31. Kalamazoo, MI: Medieval Institute Publications, 1992.

Zumthor, Paul. *Toward a Medieval Poetics.* Trans. Philip Bennett. Minneapolis: University of Minnesota Press, 1992.

Women and Gender

Arden, Heather. "Women's History and the Rhetoric of Persuasion in Christine de Pizan's *Cité des Dames.*" In *Autour de Jacques Monfrin: Néologie et création verbale. Actes du colloque international, Université McGill, Montréal, 7–8–9 Octobre 1996,* ed. Guiseppe di Stefano and Rose M. Bidler, 7–17. Le Moyen Français 39–41. Montreal: Editions Ceres, 1997.

Birky, Robin Hass. "'The Word Was Made Flesh': Gendered Bodies and Anti-Bodies in Twelfth- and Thirteenth-Century Arts of Poetry." In *Medieval Rhetoric: A Casebook,* ed. Scott D. Troyan, 161–216. New York: Routledge, 2004.

Brownlee, Kevin. "Structures of Authority in Christine de Pizan's 'Ditié de Jehanne d'Arc.'" In *The Selected Writings of Christine de Pizan,* trans. Renate Blumenfeld-Kosinski and Kevin Brownlee, ed. Renate Blumenfeld-Kosinski, 371–90. New York: Norton, 1997.

Couchman, Jane, and Ann Crabb, eds. *Women's Letters across Europe, 1400–1700: Form and Persuasion.* Aldershot, U.K.: Ashgate, 2005.

Dietrich, Julia. "The Visionary Rhetoric of Hildegard of Bingen." In *Listening to Their Voices: The Rhetorical Activities of Historical Women,* ed. Molly Meijer Wertheimer, 199–214. Studies in Rhetoric/Communication. Columbia: University of South Carolina Press, 1997.

———. "Women and Authority in the Rhetorical Economy of the Late Middle Ages." In *Rhetorical Women: Roles and Representations,* ed. Hildy Miller and Lillian Bridwell-Bowles, 17–43. Tuscaloosa: University of Alabama Press, 2005.

Erler, Mary Carpenter, and Maryanne Kowaleski, eds. *Gendering the Master Narrative: Women and Power in the Middle Ages.* Ithaca: Cornell University Press, 2003.

Glenn, Cheryl. "Reexamining the Book of Margery Kempe: A Rhetoric of Autobiography." In *Reclaiming Rhetorica: Women in the Rhetorical Tradition,* ed. Andrea A. Lunsford, 53–71. Pitt Series in Composition, Literacy, and Culture. Pittsburgh: University of Pittsburgh Press, 1995.

———. *Rhetoric Retold: Regendering the Tradition from Antiquity through the Renaissance.* Carbondale: Southern Illinois University Press, 1997.

Holderness, Julia Simms. "*Compilatio,* Commentary, and Conversation in Christine de Pizan." *Essays in Medieval Studies* 20 (2003): 47–55.

Kempton, Daniel. "Christine de Pizan's *Cité des Dames* and *Trésor de la Cité:* Toward a Feminist Scriptural Practice." In *Political Rhetoric, Power, and Renaissance Women,* ed. Carole Levin and Patricia A. Sullivan, 15–37. Albany: SUNY Press, 1995.

Kienzle, Beverly Mayne, and Pamela J. Walker. *Women Preachers and Prophets through Two Millennia of Christianity.* Berkeley: University of California Press, 1998.

Lunsford, Andrea. *Reclaiming Rhetorica: Women in the Rhetorical Tradition.* Pittsburgh: University of Pittsburgh Press, 1995.

Masson, Cynthea. "The Point of Coincidence: Rhetoric and the Apophatic in Julian of Norwich's *Showings.*" In *Julian of Norwich: A Book of Essays,* ed. Sandra J. McEntire, 153–81. Garland Medieval Casebooks 21. New York: Garland, 1998.

McCormick, Betsy. "Building the Ideal City: Female Memorial Praxis in Christine de Pizan's *Cité des Dames.*" *Studies in the Literary Imagination* 36, no. 1 (2003): 149–71.

Muessig, Carolyn A. "Prophecy and Song: Teaching and Preaching by Medieval Women." In *Women Preachers and Prophets through Two Millennia of Christianity,* ed. Beverly Mayne Kienzle and Pamela J. Walker, 146–58. Berkeley: University of California Press, 1998.

Redfern, Jenny R. "Christine de Pisan and *The Treasure of the City of Ladies:* A Medieval Rhetorician and Her Rhetoric." In *Reclaiming Rhetorica: Women in the Rhetorical Tradition,* ed. Andrea A. Lunsford, 73–92. Pittsburgh: University of Pittsburgh Press, 1995.

Richardson, Malcolm. "'A Masterful Woman': Elizabeth Stonor and English Women's Letters, 1399–c.1530." In *Women's Letters across Europe, 1400–1700: Form and Persuasion,* ed. Jane Couchman and Ann Crabb, 43–62. Aldershot, U.K.: Ashgate, 2005.

———. "Women, Commerce, and Rhetoric in Medieval England." In *Listening to Their Voices: The Rhetorical Activities of Historical Women,* ed. Molly Meijer Wertheimer, 133–49. Studies in Rhetoric/Communication. Columbia: University of South Carolina Press, 1997.

Roest, Bert. "Female Preaching in the Late Medieval Franciscan Tradition." *Franciscan Studies* 62 (2004): 119–54.

Rusconi, Roberto. "Women's Sermons at the End of the Middle Ages: Texts from the Blessed and Images of the Saints." In *Women Preachers and Prophets through Two Millennia of Christianity,* ed. Beverly Mayne Kienzle and Pamela J. Walker, 173–95. Berkeley: University of California Press, 1998.

Ruys, Juanita Feros. "Playing Alterity: Heloise, Rhetoric, and *Memoria.*" In *Maistresse of My Wit: Medieval Women, Modern Scholars,* ed. Louise D'Arcens and Juanita Feros Ruys, 211–43. Making the Middle Ages 7. Turnhout, Belgium: Brepols, 2004.

Somerset, Fiona. "Excitative Speech: Theories of Emotive Response from Richard Fitzralph to Margery Kempe." In *The Vernacular Spirit: Essays on Medieval Religious Literature,* ed. Renate Blumenfeld-Kosinski, Duncan Robertson, and Nancy Bradley Warren, 59–79. New York: Palgrave, 2002.

Tarvers, Josephine Koster. "'Thys ys my mystrys boke': English Women as Readers and Writers in Late Medieval England." In *The Uses of Manuscripts in Literary Studies: Essays in Memory of Judson Boyce Allen,* 305–27. Studies in Medieval Culture 31. Kalamazoo, MI: Medieval Institute Publications, 1992.

Ward, John. "Women and Latin Rhetoric from Hrotsvit to Hildegard." In *The Changing Tradition: Women in the History of Rhetoric,* ed. Christine Mason Sutherland and Rebecca Sutcliffe, 121–32. Calgary: University of Calgary Press, 1999.

Waters, Claire M. *Angels and Earthly Creatures: Preaching, Performance, and Gender in the Later Middle Ages.* Philadelphia: University of Pennsylvania Press, 2004.

Wertheimer, Molly Meijer, ed. *Listening to Their Voices: The Rhetorical Activities of Historical Women.* Studies in Rhetoric/Communication. Columbia: University of South Carolina Press, 1997.

Non-Western Rhetoric

Borrowman, Shane. "The Islamization of Rhetoric: Ibn Rushd and the Reintroduction of Aristotle into Medieval Europe." *Rhetoric Review* 27, no. 4 (2008): 341–60.

Browning, Robert. "Teachers." In *The Byzantines,* ed. Guglielmo Cavallo, 95–116. Chicago: University of Chicago Press, 1997.

Conley, Thomas M. "John Italos' *Methodos Rhetorikê:* Text and Commentary." *Greek, Roman, and Byzantine Studies* 44 (2004): 411–37.

———. "Notes on the Byzantine Reception of the Peripatetic Tradition in Rhetoric." In *Peripatetic Rhetoric after Aristotle,* ed. William W. Fortenbaugh and David C. Mirhady, 217–42. Rutgers University Studies in Classical Humanities 6. New Brunswick, NJ: Transaction Publishers, 1994.

———. "Revisiting 'Zonaios': More on the Byzantine Tradition περι σχηματων." *Rhetorica* 22 (2004): 257–68.

———. "Rummaging in Walz's Attic: Two Anonymous *Opuscula* in *Rhetores Graeci.*" *Greek, Roman, and Byzantine Studies* 46 (2006): 101–22.

Dilley, Whitney Crothers. "The Code of Frustrated Desire: Courtly Love Poetry of the European Troubadours and Chinese Southern Dynasties Traditions." *Disputatio: An International Transdisciplinary Journal of the Late Middle Ages* 4 (1999): 1–21.

Ezzaher, Lahcen E. "Alfarabi's Book of Rhetoric: An Arabic-English Translation of Alfarabi's Commentary on Aristotle's Rhetoric. *Rhetorica.* 26 (2008): 347–93.

———. "Aristotle's Rhetoric in the Commentary Tradition of Averroes." *Disputatio: An International Transdisciplinary Journal of the Late Middle Ages* 4 (1999): 33–50.

Fisher, Elizabeth A. "Michael Psellos on the Rhetoric of Hagiography and the *Life of St. Auxentius.*" *Byzantine and Modern Greek Studies* 17 (1993): 43–55.

———. "Planoudes, Holobolos, and the Motivation for Translation." *Greek, Roman, and Byzantine Studies* 43 (2003): 77–104.

Gully, Adrian. "*Tadmīn.* 'Implication of meaning,' in Medieval Arabic." *Journal of the American Oriental Society* 117, no. 3 (1997): 466–80.

Halldén, Philip. "What Is Arab Islamic Rhetoric? Rethinking the History of Muslim Oratory Arts and Homiletics." *International Journal of Middle East Studies* 37 (2005): 19–38.

Jeffreys, Elizabeth. *Rhetoric in Byzantium: Papers from the Thirty-fifth Spring Symposium of Byzantine Studies, Exeter College, University of Oxford, March 2001.* Aldershot, U.K.: Ashgate Variorum, 2003.

Kanazi, George. "The Literary Theory of Abu Hilal al-'Askari." In *Studies in Medieval Arabic and Hebrew Poetics,* ed. Sasson Somekh, 21–36. Israel Oriental Studies 11. Leiden, Netherlands: Brill, 1991.

Kennedy, George A. *Comparative Rhetoric: An Historical and Cross Cultural Introduction.* New York: Oxford University Press, 1997.

Knechtges, David R., and Eugene Vance, eds. *Rhetoric and the Discourses of Power in Court Culture: China, Europe, and Japan.* Seattle: University of Washington Press, 2005.

Simidchieva, Marta. "Imitation and Innovation in Timurid Poetics: Kashifi's *Badāyi' al-afkār* and Its Predecessors, *al-Mu'jam and Hadā'iq al-sihr.*" *Iranian Studies: The Journal of the Society for Iranian Studies* 36 (2003): 509–30.

Somekh, Sasson, ed. *Studies in Medieval Arabic and Hebrew Poetics.* Leiden, Netherlands: Brill, 1991.

Swartz, Merlin. "Arabic Rhetoric and the Art of the Homily in Medieval Islam." In *Religion and Culture in Medieval Islam,* ed. Richard Hovannisian and Georges Sabagh, 36–65. Giorgio Levi della Vida conferences 14. Cambridge: Cambridge University Press, 1999.

Tesdell, Lee S. "Greek Rhetoric and Philosophy in Medieval Arabic Culture: The State of the Research." *Disputatio: An International Transdisciplinary Journal of the Late Middle Ages* 4 (1999): 51–58.

Theodore. *Opuscula rhetorica.* Ed. Aloysius Tartaglia. Bibliotheca Scriptorum Graecorum et Romanorum Teubneriana. Munich: Saur, 2000.

Walker, Jeffrey. "Michael Psellos on Rhetoric: A Translation and Commentary on Psellos' Synopsis of Hermogenes." *Rhetoric Society Quarterly* 31 (2001): 5–40.

———. "The Things I Have Not Betrayed: Michael Psellos' Encomium of His Mother as a Defence of Rhetoric." *Rhetorica* 22 (2004): 49–101.

Wansbrough, John. "*Majāz al-Qu'an:* Periphrastic Exegesis." In *The Qur'an: Formative Interpretations,* ed. Andrew Rippin, 243–62. The Formation of the Classical Islamic World 25. Aldershot, U.K.: Ashgate, 1999.

Watt, John W. "Syriac Rhetorical Theory and the Syriac Tradition of Aristotle's Rhetoric." In *Peripatetic Rhetoric after Aristotle,* ed. W. Fortenbaugh and David C. Mirhady, 243–60. Rutgers University Studies in Classical Humanities 6. New Brunswick, NJ: Transaction, 1994.

3

The Renaissance

Don Paul Abbott

Nearly twenty-five years ago, James J. Murphy wrote that "Renaissance rhetoric must surely be one of the most-mentioned and least-studied subjects in modern scholarship" (*Renaissance Eloquence,* 29). In the quarter century since Murphy made that claim, things have certainly changed. And in the seventeen years that have passed since the previous edition of this book, even the process of determining the "present state of scholarship" has itself changed very much since those earlier surveys. I began my revision by conducting a Google keyword search of "Renaissance rhetoric." When, in 0.12 seconds, the search engine returned 1,780,000 results, I began to suspect that Renaissance rhetoric had perhaps become the most-studied subject in modern scholarship.

Whatever the imprecision of a Google search, the astounding number of "hits" did indicate the challenges that I might encounter in revising a seventeen-year-old essay. When more refined searches of library online catalogs returned hundreds of works relevant to Renaissance rhetoric published since 1990, it became apparent that I needed to rethink my original plan to revise the earlier chapter by simply adding significant new works where necessary. It was soon obvious that a revision would not allow me to include a significant portion of the new scholarship on Renaissance rhetoric. Therefore, I decided it was essential to write an entirely new essay to assess the present state of scholarship specifically from 1990 to the middle of 2007.

The study of rhetoric onward from the early twentieth century has, of necessity, been interdisciplinary. In the last seventeen years, as the awareness of the extent to which rhetoric influenced and guided so many intellectual efforts in the Renaissance, that interdisciplinarity has only increased. This chapter reflects the interdisciplinary direction of rhetorical scholarship. I begin with a review of bibliographic and other reference resources, considering the availability of primary texts. I then examine comprehensive studies of rhetoric and Renaissance culture. The remainder of the chapter is organized by sections devoted to rhetoric and its relations with humanism, logic and philosophy, literature, preaching, education, and science. I conclude by addressing two issues that have emerged since the previous edition: women and rhetoric and rhetoric and the New World.

In an effort to maintain continuity with the previous editions, I have included at the beginning of each section a brief list of "Key Texts from the Revised Edition." If no "key texts" are designated, this indicates that the section did not appear in the previous edition. These key texts appear in the bibliography at the end of the chapter. However, only a sample of the scholarship presented in the previous editions is represented by the key texts. Therefore, for a wider view of the scholarship of Renaissance rhetoric from about mid-twentieth century, I suggest that readers consult the second edition. Despite the need to be selective, I hope that what follows will convey a sense of the remarkable record of scholarship that has been accomplished in the preceding seventeen years.

Bibliographies and Other Reference Works

Key Texts from the Revised Edition:
- R. C. Alston, *A Bibliography of the English Language from the Invention of Printing to the Year 1800*. 20 vols. Vol. 6, *Rhetoric, Style, Elocution, Prosody, Rhyme, Pronunciation, Spelling Reform* (1974)
- James J. Murphy, *Renaissance Rhetoric: A Short-Title Catalogue of Works on Rhetorical Theory from the Beginning of Printing to A.D. 1700* (1981)

In *Renaissance Eloquence,* James J. Murphy declared that "the 'infrastructure' —or basic equipment" necessary for the scholarly examination of Renaissance rhetoric—was not yet fully available to investigators (29). In the two and a half decades since that observation, the infrastructure has increased significantly, if not exponentially. Of course, Murphy himself has had a great deal to do with the improvements in the basic equipment available to students of rhetoric. The long-awaited second edition of *Renaissance Rhetoric: Short-Title Catalogue, 1460–1700* (1981) by Murphy and Lawrence D. Green appeared in 2006. This revised and expanded bibliography "now presents 1,717 authors and 3,842 rhetorical titles in 12,325 printings, published in 310 towns and cities by 3,340 printers and publishers from Finland to Mexico" (xi). The more than 1,700 authors cataloged in this bibliography are almost double the already remarkable 867 authors cataloged in the previous edition. If there are any lingering doubts about the extraordinary scope of Renaissance rhetoric, the *Short Title Catalogue* has surely eliminated it. As Murphy and Green observe, with considerable understatement, the bibliography "demonstrates the breadth and depth of rhetorical inquiry during the Renaissance, the centrality of rhetoric to cultural studies, and the opportunities for research" (xi).

The *Renaissance Rhetoric Short-Title Catalogue* presents an alphabetical list of authors, from "A., D." to "Wynuntius, Christianus," some 462 pages later. For each author, the editors include life dates, if available, aliases, if used, and short titles of works in chronological order, together with publishers and places of publication. The *Renaissance Rhetoric Short-Title Catalogue, 1460–1700* is a remarkable accomplishment and an exceptional tool for researchers.

A second important bibliography is Heinrich F. Plett, *English Renaissance Rhetoric and Poetics: A Systematic Bibliography of Primary and Secondary Sources* (1995). Plett's bibliography contains virtually all rhetorical and poetical works printed in England from 1479 to 1660. Plett divides his work into three broad categories: bibliographies, primary sources, and secondary sources. Rather than employing a chronological listing, Plett's organization is based on "generic concepts which evolve from standardized communicative situations and find their ultimate expression in normative theories" (4). Thus there are categories for humanist rhetorics, ecclesiastical rhetorics, Ramistic rhetorics, and the like.

Each entry contains basic bibliographical details, including author with life dates, if available, and aliases, if used, together with the date of the *princeps editio* and subsequent editions. Unlike Green and Murphy, Plett includes modern editions and reprints of early modern texts in his bibliography. Also unlike the *RRSTC*, Plett's bibliography contains a listing of secondary sources. These are grouped into the categories of "General Studies," "Rhetorical Genres," "Poetical Subjects," "Rhetoric/Poetics and Related Fields of Research," and "Rhetoric/Poetics and Individual Authors."

One obvious change from the previous edition of *The Present State* is the appearance of electronic databases that have begun to alter the way scholars conduct research. Many of these databases are primarily bibliographic in nature and therefore supplement the bibliographies cited above. These include such sites as the MLA International Bibliography (Modern Language Association), Iter: Gateway to the Middle Ages and Renaissance, LION (Literature Online), Project Muse, FRANCIS (International Humanities and Social Studies), JSTOR, and many others. One of the advantages of these databases is that many of them make available abstracts, outlines, and summaries of the index material, essential elements for deciding if the material deserves further perusal. All of these bibliographies list works on rhetoric among many other subjects. Online bibliographies devoted to rhetoric may be found at the Rhetoric and Composition Web site (rhetoric.eserver.org). For the student of Renaissance rhetoric, however, none of the online databases can approach the comprehensiveness of Green and Murphy or Plett.

In addition to the bibliographies noted above, two "bio-bibliographies" have appeared recently: *British Rhetoricians and Logicians, 1500–1660, First Series* (2001) and *British Rhetoricians and Logicians, 1500–1660, Second Series* (2003), both edited by Edward A. Malone. These two works, part of the ongoing *Dictionary of Literary Biography,* provide both biographies and bibliographies of some sixty writers on rhetoric and logic. These two volumes were inspired by Wilbur S. Howell's *Logic and Rhetoric in England, 1500–1700* (1956) but, as the editor notes, *British Rhetoricians and Logicians* places greater emphasis on rhetoric and less on logic than does Howell's history. The first series includes bio-bibliographies of twenty-five rhetoricians including Roger Ascham, Francis Bacon, Abraham Fraunce, Henry Peacham, and Richard Sherry. The second series includes a group of names that are less familiar than those in the first volume, in part because the second series includes Scottish, Irish, and Welsh writers. Thus, while many of the entries, like George Puttenham, are familiar, others are less so. For example, William Salesbury's unpublished "Llyfr Rhetoreg" (book of rhetoric), the first rhetorical treatise in the Welsh language, is included. Each entry begins with a primary bibliography, including full titles whenever possible. This bibliography is followed by a biography that stresses the subject's literary career and concludes with a bibliography of secondary sources. Thus *British Rhetoricians and Logicians* offers a useful combination of biography and bibliography about many Renaissance rhetoricians.

Just as bibliographic resources have greatly improved since the previous edition of the *Present State,* so too has the availability of other reference resources. Two encyclopedias of rhetoric have been published since 1990. These are *The Encyclopedia of Rhetoric and Composition: Communication from Ancient Times to the Information Age,* edited by Theresa Enos (1996), and *The Encyclopedia of Rhetoric,* edited by Thomas Sloane (2001). Both encyclopedias are comparable in scope and coverage and are organized similarly, though not identically. Both are about eight hundred pages in length and include major entries on each of the standard historical periods from rhetoric's classical origins to its present orientation. Thus the Enos volume includes my entry "Renaissance Rhetoric" together with separate entries on major English and continental rhetoricians of the Renaissance.

It is here that the organization of the Sloane volume diverges from that of Enos. Sloane's work contains no entries for individual rhetoricians. Rather, it is arranged entirely by concepts, principles, elements, and historical periods. The Renaissance is represented by a four-part entry consisting of "An Overview," by Heinrich Plett; a discussion of the Dutch "Rederijkers," by Marijke Spies; "Rhetoric in Renaissance language and literature," by Jean Dietz Moss; and "Rhetoric in the Age of Reformation and Counter-Reformation," by Gregory Kneidel. Taken together, these two encyclopedias offer an excellent starting point for investigations into virtually any aspect of rhetoric including, of course, the Renaissance.

Finally, I want to call attention to the publication of the English translation of Heinrich Lausberg's *Handbook of Literary Rhetoric: A Foundation for Literary Study* (1998), originally published in German in 1960. Lausberg's *Handbook* has achieved the status of a standard reference work. His systematic and synthetic descriptive catalog of ancient rhetoric remains unique. Of particular value for students of the Renaissance is Lausberg's thorough description of *elocutio*, including what remains the most complete catalogs of schemes and tropes ever compiled. The *Handbook* concludes with a three-hundred-page index of key terms in Latin, Greek, and French.

Old Texts and New Databases

Key Texts from the Revised Edition:
- *British and Continental Rhetoric and Elocution.* Sixteen microfilm reels (1953)
- Leonard Cox, *The Arte or Craft of Rhetorike* [1530?] (1899, 1969, 1975, 1977)
- Abraham Fraunce, *The Arcadian Rhetorike* [1588] (1950)
- James J. Murphy, ed., *Renaissance Rhetoric: A Microfiche Collection of Key Texts, A.D. 1472–1602* (1987)
- George Puttenham, *The Art of English Poesie* [1589] (1936, 1968)
- Richard Sherry, *A Treatise of Schemes and Tropes* [1550] (1961)
- Thomas Wilson, *The Arte of Rhetorique* [1553] (1909, 1962, 1969)

In 1990, in the second edition of *The Present State*, I lamented, as I had in the first edition, the shortage of both modern critical editions and English translations of important texts. While the availability of key texts has improved in recent years, there remains a notable shortage of modern, critical, and scholarly editions of Renaissance rhetorics, although new editions of important works continue to appear regularly, if not rapidly. New editions include Izora Scott, *Controversies over the Imitation of Cicero in the Renaissance, with Translations of Letters between Pietro Bembo and Gianfrancesco Pico "On Imitation" and A Translation of Desiderius Erasmus, "The Ciceronian (Ciceronianus)"* (1991); Peter Ramus, *Peter Ramus's Attack on Cicero: Text and Translation of Ramus's "Brutinae Quaestiones,"* edited by James J. Murphy and translated by Carole Newlands (1992); Thomas Wilson, *The Arte of Rhetorique,* edited by Peter E. Medine (1994); Justus Lipsius, *Principles of Letter-Writing: A Bilingual Text of Justi Lipsi Epistolica Institutio,* edited and translated by R. V. Young and M. Thomas Hester (1996); and *A Reformation Rhetoric: Thomas Swynnerton's "The Tropes and Figures,"* edited by Richard Rex (1999).

The availability of original works has been considerably augmented by the publication of several anthologies. Particularly notable is *Renaissance Debates on Rhetoric,* edited and translated by Wayne Rebhorn (2000). Rebhorn includes excerpts from the works of rhetoricians who "present the widest possible range of views about rhetoric" (2). This volume includes selections from twenty-four writers, arranged chronologically, from the fourteenth century (Petrarch, for example) to the seventeenth century (Bary). Included among the selections are the famous (Erasmus), the familiar (Ramus), and the relatively obscure (de' Conti). The writers represent manifestations of the rhetorical tradition in Italy (Patrizi), France (du Vair), Spain (Guzman), the Netherlands (Agricola), Germany (Melancthon), and England (Jewel). While a few of the authors are well-known and their work generally available, many of the texts included in this volume are not easily obtainable, and many have never before been translated into English. Moreover, no other collection assembles so many Renaissance views of rhetoric in a single volume. Rebhorn, as translator, has rendered the texts into readable and idiomatic English and has accompanied each selection with extensive annotations. Those texts written originally in English (Wilson, Puttenham, Peacham) have been modernized where possible, and, where necessary, the intricacies of Elizabethan English have been clarified in extensive notes. Rebhorn's goal in preparing this collection was to give "a host of Renaissance writers on rhetoric, including both its defenders and its critics, the opportunity to speak for themselves and to show us why rhetoric mattered so much for them and their culture" (2–3).

Another important anthology is Brian Vickers, *English Literary Criticism in the Renaissance* (1999). This is a valuable collection because of its great comprehensiveness combined with the excellent introductions and headnotes provided by Vickers. This work contains thirty-six selections arranged chronologically, beginning with Sir Thomas Elyot in 1531 and concluding with Thomas Hobbes in 1675. This anthology is also valuable because, rather than containing snippets, Vickers has elected to include substantial portions from the works selected. Thus the work includes the entirety of Philip Sidney's *A Defence of Poetry* and George Puttenham's *The Arte of English Poesie.* Vickers also includes a substantial portion of Thomas Wilson's *The Arte of Rhetorique.* Because of this completeness, *English Renaissance Literary Criticism* gives an excellent introduction to the primary sources in English.

Yet another anthology is *The Rhetorical Tradition: Readings from Classical Times to the Present,* edited by Patricia Bizzell and Bruce Herzberg (second edition, 2001). The Renaissance section of this collection includes excerpts from Erasmus, Castiglione, Ramus, Thomas Wilson, and Francis Bacon. For the second edition, the editors have increased the selections from women writers, which now include Margaret Fell, Madeleine de Scudéry, and Sor Juana Inés de la Cruz.

The rich rhetorical heritage of Spain is now much more accessible to scholars than at the time of previous editions of *The Present State. Antología de textos retóricos españoles del siglo XVI,* edited by Elena Artaza (1997), includes selections from eleven Spanish rhetoricians whose works were written originally in Latin or Spanish (Latin texts have been translated into Spanish). The selections are organized under the headings of *progymnasmata, inventio, dispositio, elocution,* and *memoria.*

A remarkably complete collection of Renaissance texts is available on the compact disc *Retóricas españoles del siglo xvi escritas en latín, edición digital,* edited by Miguel Ángel Garrido Gallardo (2004). This digital edition contains an astounding 2,500 pages of Latin texts and 2,500 pages of Spanish translation, together with 500 pages of notes and commentaries. Writers represented in this collection include Antonio de Nebrija, Alfonso García Matamoros, Antonio Llull, Sebastián Fox Morcillo, Francisco Sánchez de las Brozas, and Cipriano Suárez.

One of the most dramatic changes since the 1990 edition of *The Present State* is the effect the Internet has had on the accessibility of once-rare texts. Increasingly, online databases offer ready access to complete texts of rhetorical treatises. The best database for rhetorics in English is *Early English Books Online (EEBO).* A work in progress, this collection intends to provide digital images of every book printed in England from the beginning of English printing through the end of the Renaissance. *EEBO* now contains about 100,000 of over 125,000 titles listed in Pollard and Redgrave's *Short-Title Catalogue (1475–1640)* and Wing's *Short-Title Catalogue (1641–1700)* and their revised editions, as well as the *Thomason Tracts (1640–1661)* collection, and the *Early English Books Tract Supplement.* A keyword search of "rhetoric" yields 193 records (including many duplicate holdings) of rhetorical treatises printed in England in various languages up to 1700. English rhetorical texts include titles by Thomas Blount, Leonard Cox, Abraham Fraunce, Angel Day, Dudley Fenner, Richard Sherry, and Thomas Wilson. *EEBO* is usually accessible through the online catalogs of major research libraries.

Another useful database is *Renascence Editions,* a publicly accessible repository of works printed in English between 1477 and 1799. *Renascence Editions* offers a small number of rhetorical texts including Roger Ascham, *Scholemaster;* Thomas Elyot, *The Boke Named the Governour;* Philip Sidney, *A Defence of Poesie;* and Thomas Wilson, *The Arte of Rhetorique.* Unlike *EEBO,* these works are not facsimile images but are texts that have been transcribed and are available in both PDFG and HTML formats that permit text to be imported into word processing files.

Comprehensive Studies

Key Texts from the Revised Edition:
  • Marc Fumaroli, *L'âge de l'éloquence: Rhétorique et "res literaria" de la Renaissance au seuil de l'époque classique* (1980)

- Wilbur S. Howell, *Logic and Rhetoric in England, 1500–1700* (1956)
- James J. Murphy, ed., *Renaissance Eloquence* (1983)
- Brian Vickers, *In Defence of Rhetoric* (1988)

The obvious place to begin a study of Renaissance rhetoric is Marc Fumaroli's *Histoire de la rhétorique dans l'Europe moderne, 1450–1950* (1999). This is a volume that can only be described as monumental—a work of over 1,300 pages with contributions from twenty-four distinguished European historians of rhetoric. Although this book traces the development of rhetoric from the middle of the fifteenth century through the middle twentieth century, well over half of the work is devoted to the Renaissance. The Renaissance section of *Histoire de la rhétorique* comprises six chapters on various aspects of rhetoric in the sixteenth century and an additional six chapters on the seventeenth century. The essays in this work are arranged both chronologically and conceptually and include the complete range of rhetorical concerns including humanism, Protestant reform, the post-Tridentine response, conceptism, Ramism, and many other issues. Although there is a focus on France and Italy, the essays include the entire range of geographical and intellectual issues affecting the Renaissance of rhetoric. The *Histoire de la rhétorique* must be considered a comprehensive history of Renaissance rhetoric in Europe.

Another comprehensive study of Renaissance rhetoric, by a leading German scholar, is Heinrich F. Plett's *Rhetoric and Renaissance Culture* (2004). Plett begins with a survey, "The Scope and Genres of Renaissance Rhetoric," which provides a clear overview of the subject and an orientation for the analysis that follows. Next Plett addresses "Poetica Rhetorica," in which he examines in detail what he calls the "rhetoricization" of poetic theory in the Renaissance. A later section, "Poeta Orator: Shakespeare as Orator Poet," serves to illustrate the theoretical discussion of poetics and rhetoric.

A comprehensive study of rhetoric in sixteenth-century England is Peter Mack's *Elizabethan Rhetoric: Theory and Practice* (2002). In *Elizabethan Rhetoric*, Mack sets out to demonstrate the influence of humanist rhetoric on Elizabethan life. Others have done this before, particularly with respect to drama and poetry, but probably no one has attempted to demonstrate the breadth of rhetoric's influence as does Mack. Studies of Shakespeare, Sidney, Milton, and other writers have clearly documented the indebtedness of English poets to classical rhetoricians. While Mack acknowledges that understanding rhetoric helps us appreciate Shakespeare, his interest is primarily in forms of discourse other than the poetic. Indeed, his intent is to show just how pervasively rhetoric influenced virtually all of Elizabethan public life—or at least the public life of the Elizabethan elite. Thus he extends his analysis beyond poetry and drama to look at all kinds of expression, formal and informal, public and private, in his effort to document rhetoric's impact on early modern England.

Mack considers Elizabethan manuals of rhetoric and dialectic and asserts that English-language texts have received perhaps more attention from scholars than they deserve. Mack says that only four such works were printed more than once in the sixteenth century: Wilson's *Rule of Reason* and *Art of Rhetoric,* Fulwood's *Enemie of Idelness,* and Day's *The English Secretary.* Therefore, says Mack, any "educationally based account of English manuals must concentrate on Wilson, Fulwood, and Day" combined with what he calls "the English style manual" (76). This "manual," a composite of Sherry's *A Treatise of Scheme and Tropes,* Peacham's *Garden of Eloquence,* and Puttenham's *Arte of English Poesie,* together with the treatments of figures and tropes in Day and Wilson, constitutes "a single archetext: the Renaissance English style manual" (84). However, Mack argues that rhetoric supplied the Elizabethans with more than simply compositional techniques. He concludes that "[r]hetorical education provided Elizabethan writers, statesmen and priests with content as well as techniques. Reflections on humanist moral topics are found across a wide range of texts and genres. Moral themes and axioms at times constituted the subject matter of a chapter or sermon, or they were used in a letter, speech or treatise to provide grounding principles to support an argument" (301).

In *The Emperor of Men's Minds: Literature and the Renaissance Discourse of Rhetoric* (1995), Wayne Rebhorn offers a history of Renaissance rhetoric— albeit, he says, not a diachronic one. Despite the differences, ambiguities, and contradictions apparent in the rhetorical treatises of various authors, Rebhorn argues that there is a unified discourse of Renaissance rhetoric that is essentially consistent over time and across borders. This is a discourse that has little to do with debate and dialogue, and everything to do with power and control. Power is central to this discourse because rhetoric is the art of persuasion, and that persuasion is used both to maintain the status and to alter the social order. Rebhorn assembles an impressive variety of material from rhetorical treatises and literary texts to support his argument that rhetoric is, above all else, "the emperor of men's minds."

Rhetoric and Humanism

Key Texts from the Revised Edition:
- Hanna H. Gray, "Renaissance Humanism: The Pursuit of Eloquence" (1968)
- Victoria Kahn, *Rhetoric, Prudence, and Skepticism in the Renaissance* (1985)
- Paul Oskar Kristeller, *Renaissance Thought and Its Sources* (1979)
- John Monfasani, "Humanism and Rhetoric" (1988)

A convenient overview of rhetoric and its place in Renaissance humanism is Peter Mack, "Humanist Rhetoric and Dialectic," in *The Cambridge Compan-*

ion to Renaissance Humanism (1996). Mack argues that Renaissance humanism differed from its medieval predecessors by having rhetoric and dialectic work together to explain ancient texts. Mack selects seven great teachers to represent the course of humanism from the late fourteenth to late sixteenth century: Antonio Loschi, George of Trebizond, Lorenzo Valla, Rudolph Agricola, Desiderius Erasmus, Philip Melancthon, and Peter Ramus. Mack jointly examines the textbooks these men wrote and the education practices they inspired. Many of the themes in this essay are developed more fully by Mack in *Renaissance Argument: Valla and Agricola in the Traditions of Rhetoric and Dialectic* (1993). The centerpiece of Mack's analysis is Agricola's *De inventione dialectica,* and this analysis makes *Renaissance Argument* probably the most complete discussion available on Agricola's influence on rhetoric.

The early development of humanism is traced by Ronald G. Witt, *In the Footsteps of the Ancients: The Origins of Humanism from Lovato to Bruni* (2000). Witt argues that the first century and a half of humanism's development has been "misconceived." In particular, he maintains that humanism derived initially not from rhetoric and notaries and lawyers but from poetics and grammarians. That does not necessarily mean a diminished role for rhetoric in the development of humanism, however. Witt sees much of that development explained by tension between the "oratorical rhetoric" of lawyers and politicians and the "literary rhetoric" of writers and poets. From its very beginnings, then, the development of humanism was shaped by competing conceptions of rhetoric.

One of the great practitioners of rhetoric is examined by Victoria Kahn in *Machiavellian Rhetoric from the Counter-Reformation to Milton* (1994). Machiavelli, claims Kahn, "was more a humanist than he would have his readers believe" (15). Kahn examines several Renaissance figures who read and interpreted Machiavelli rhetorically. Many of Machiavelli's readers that she examines are sixteenth- and seventeenth-century Englishmen. Most surprising, perhaps, is that Kahn finds that John Milton was "one of Machiavelli's best readers" and concludes her work with an examination of Machiavellian rhetoric in the work of Milton (15).

Kahn notes that one strain of Renaissance humanism held that "dialogue and argument on both sides of a question were assumed to foster social and political consensus" (ix). Thomas O. Sloane, in *On the Contrary: The Protocol of Traditional Rhetoric* (1997), claims that this arguing pro and con on any question was the very essence of rhetoric and of humanism. In support of his proposition, Sloane draws evidence especially from Desiderius Erasmus and Thomas Wilson. In fact, the last one-third of *On the Contrary* is a "case study" of Wilson as a rhetorician. Sloane admits that his book was not written for Renaissance specialists but for "humanists of all stripes" (3). And as such, much of Sloane's work serves as a call for the restoration of rhetoric, and especially contrarian rhetoric, to the curriculum of contemporary education.

The humanist's belief in the desirability of arguing both sides of any proposition had significant consequences. One of those consequences is explored by Gary Remer in *Humanism and the Rhetoric of Toleration* (1996). While the later Renaissance was a time of great religious intolerance, Remer maintains that there were "voices of moderation" who developed arguments in favor of toleration in response to the proponents of religious repression (6). These voices were those of the Renaissance humanists. Remer claims that while these arguments are well-known, the dominant source of this toleration has been overlooked. He argues that it is the tradition of classical rhetoric that best explains the humanist defense of toleration: "the humanists' preference for persuasion over force; their skepticism and toleration in nonessentials; and their emphasis on ethical living over dogma. The rhetorician's commitment to *decorum*, his ability to argue both sides of an issue, and his search for an acceptable epistemological standard in probability and consensus influenced the humanist's arguments" (6).

Rhetoric, Logic, and Philosophy

Key Texts from the Revised Edition:
- Marc Cogan, "Rodolphus Agricola and the Semantic Revolutions of the History of Invention" (1984)
- Sister Joan Marie Lechner, O.S.U., *Renaissance Concepts of the Commonplaces* (1962)
- Kees Meerhof, *Rhétorique et poétique au XVIe siècle en France: Du Bellay, Ramus et les autres* (1986)
- Walter Ong, S.J., *Ramus, Method, and the Decay of Dialogue* (1958)

The relations between rhetoric and philosophy have often been strained, and that strain was especially great in the Renaissance. Both rhetoricians and philosophers sought to assert the superiority of their art over that of the other. One of the great controversialists was Peter Ramus. Ramus is mentioned above in the section on humanism, but, given his antipathy toward his classical forebears, some scholars deny that Ramus was a humanist, though few would deny that he was a master of disputation. One example of such disputation is *Peter Ramus's Attack on Cicero*, a translation of Ramus's *Brutinae Quaestiones* by Carole Newlands with an introduction by James J. Murphy (1992). Ramus and Ramism continue to be subjects of great scholarly interest, and, happily, much of this recent scholarship has been surveyed by Peter Sharret in "Ramus 2000" (2000). Sharret examines studies of Ramist views of grammar, rhetoric, logic, and science. He also looks at studies of the reception and influence of Ramus in Britain and New England, France, Spain, Italy, Germany, and, indeed, most of Europe. Thus Sharret's inventory is an excellent overview of recent interpretations of Ramism.

Thomas Hobbes is another philosopher with a complicated relationship to rhetoric. In Quentin Skinner's *Rhetoric and Reason in the Philosophy of Hobbes* (1996), this relationship is addressed with an admirable combination of clarity and thoroughness. Skinner examines Hobbes's early training and career as a humanist, his subsequent rejection of eloquence and its replacement by science, and finally his return to rhetoric in the *Leviathan*. Skinner concludes by asking, "Why did Hobbes change his mind?" (436) The answer, in part, lies in Hobbes's attempt to reach a broader audience in *Leviathan* than he did in previous works. But the answer to this profound reappraisal may also be found in Hobbes's exile in France during the *âge de l'éloquence* and his concern about the rhetorical efficacy of his opponents in the English civil war. All of these factors served to persuade Hobbes that rhetoric had its place, and an important one, in the pursuit of civil science.

The question of Hobbes's relationship with rhetoric is also addressed by Bryan Garsten in "The Rhetoric against Rhetoric: Hobbes," in *Saving Persuasion: A Defense of Rhetoric and Judgment* (2006). Garsten, however, challenges Skinner's view of Hobbesian rhetoric by denying that *Leviathan* can be construed as part of the humanist tradition. Garsten concedes that "Hobbes believed that eloquence would make his arguments more attractive, but that fact alone is not enough to make *Leviathan* a 'contribution to' or an 'endorsement of' the Renaissance rhetorical tradition" (29). Rather, "the new function of Hobbesian rhetoric was to minimize uncertainty and controversy. The new rhetoric moved men to act according to the dictates of science. It motivated and managed, but it did not invent arguments of its own" (28). Thus, in Garsten's view, Hobbes turns rhetoric into merely "a servant of science" (28).

Much like Hobbes, René Descartes is one of rhetoric's most notable detractors. Thomas M. Carr Jr., in *Descartes and the Resilience of Rhetoric: Varieties of Cartesian Rhetorical Theory* (1990), finds that, despite Descartes's hostility to traditional rhetoric, there is nonetheless a rhetorical theory implicit in Cartesian thought. He traces this theory in the works of Descartes and writers deeply influenced by Cartesianism: the Port-Royalists Antoine Arnauld and Pierre Nichole, Nicholas Malebranche, and Bernard Lamy. Carr discovers "a theoretical justification for persuasive discourse even within the systems of such detractors of traditional rhetoric as Descartes or Malebranche" (3). This, then, is the resilience of rhetoric: "its ability to reappear in new guises just when it appears to have been discounted" (3).

Rhetoric and Literature

Key Texts from the Revised Edition:
* Joel B. Altman, *The Tudor Play of the Mind: Rhetorical Inquiry and the Development of Elizabethan Drama* (1978)

- O. B. Hardison Jr., *The Enduring Monument: A Study of the Idea of Praise in Renaissance Literary Theory and Practice* (1962)
- Sister Miriam Joseph, C.S.C., *Rhetoric in Shakespeare's Time: Literary Theory of Renaissance Europe* (1947; reprint, 1962)
- Wesley Trimpi, *Ben Jonson's Poems: A Study of the Plain Style* (1962)
- Marion Trousdale, *Shakespeare and the Rhetoricians* (1982)
- Rosemond Tuve, *Elizabethan and Metaphysical Imagery: Renaissance Poetic and Twentieth-Century Critics* (1947)

The deep debt that Renaissance literature owes to the rhetorical tradition is now no longer seriously disputed. Thus where it was once difficult to find studies that adequately investigated this debt, the problem has become rather the opposite—how to select from among so many studies exploring rhetoric and literature. Fortunately, there are a number of concise introductions to literary rhetoric. In his essay "Rhetoric," in *The Cambridge Companion to English Poetry—Donne to Marvel* (1993), Brian Vickers provides an excellent introduction to rhetoric's history and its role in early modern English literature. As he has done before, Vickers includes a clear explanation and justification for the Renaissance interest in the rhetorical figures. Another useful overview of literary rhetoric in the Renaissance is Marion Trousdale, "Rhetoric," in *A Companion to English Renaissance Literature and Culture* (2001).

Scholars have continued to investigate the already widely acknowledged influence that rhetoric exerted on Shakespeare and his art. While the rhetorical nature of Shakespeare's work has been well studied, recent scholarship portrays rhetoric's influence on Shakespeare the writer as more profound than previously recognized. Trevor McNeely is a leading proponent of this approach. His study, *Proteus Unmasked: Sixteenth-Century Rhetoric and the Art of Shakespeare* (2004), considers the role of rhetoric in sixteenth-century culture, in the rise of Elizabethan drama, and finally in its application in Shakespeare's plays. To McNeely, however, rhetoric is not simply an important intellectual development, but rather, as the art of persuasion, rhetoric "is *the* integrating principle behind the Renaissance revolution in both Italy and England, the essential element that holds tenuously together a universe threatening momentarily to lapse into incoherence and chaos" (9). And to McNeely, Shakespeare is the master rhetorician of the age, conscious of rhetoric's role in Elizabethan life and intentionally applying its precepts in his plays. That Shakespeare has not always been recognized as a rhetorician is due only to his ability to achieve "the rhetorician's ideal of making his *art* invisible, of separating his speech from his own personality, as if he himself did not exist" (11).

In *Shakespeare's Proverbial Themes: A Rhetorical Context for the "Sententia" as "Res"* (1992), Marjorie Donker argues that the very premises of Shakespeare's plays originate in the rhetorical tradition. According to her, Shakespeare's themes are derived directly from the *sententia,* the maxim, and the adages, so central to rhetorical education. In her chapters "The Rhetorical Context" and "Tudor Schools," she traces the importance of the *sententiae* in Renaissance England and concludes that "it has been generally unremarked that the *sententiae* occupied a key position in *inventio* (invention), the rhetorical operation which 'discovers' the *res,* the subject matter of discourse" (39). Thus, for Donker, Shakespeare's *inventio,* no less than his *elocutio,* is derived from the rhetorical tradition. Particularly striking, she argues, with some surprise, is the influence of Erasmus. Shakespeare, she concludes, was Erasmus's greatest pupil.

While Donker and others argue that the rhetorical analysis of style has often mistakenly overshadowed invention, style remains a significant object of scholarly scrutiny. The classical context of Renaissance *elocutio* is nicely summarized by Lawrence D. Green in "Aristotelian *Lexis* and Renaissance *Elocutio,*" in *Rereading Aristotle's Rhetoric* (2000). While Renaissance rhetoric was dominated by Cicero and Quintilian, the third book of Aristotle's rhetoric was important as well. Green concludes that when Renaissance writers "began to think about the newly discovered text of Aristotle's *Rhetoric,* they would see Book 3 as being far more central to the entire rhetorical enterprise than we are apt to see it today" (149).

James Beister, in *Lyric Wonder: Rhetoric and Wit in English Renaissance Poetry* (1997), explores what he calls the "wonderful" or "admirable" style: a kind of style that—because the meanings of these words have changed greatly since the time of the Renaissance—has become difficult for modern readers to understand. Beister seeks to understand why "poets in the late sixteenth and early seventeenth adopted witty, difficult, rough, and obscure styles" (3).

Rhetoric and Preaching

Key Texts from the Revised Edition:
- J. W. Blench, *Preaching in England in the Late Fifteenth and Sixteenth Centuries: A Study of English Sermons, 1450–c. 1600* (1964)
- Alan F. Herr, *The Elizabethan Sermon: A Survey and a Bibliography* (1969)
- W. Fraser Mitchell, *English Pulpit Oratory from Andrewes to Tillotson* (1932; reprint, 1962)
- Debora K. Shuger, *Sacred Rhetoric: The Christian Grand Style in the English Renaissance* (1988)

The importance of preaching in the Renaissance, and indeed the importance of preaching in Western culture, is addressed by O. C. Edwards Jr., in *A History of Preaching* (2004). Edwards devoted eight years to writing this history of preaching from the beginnings of Christianity to the end of the twentieth century. At the beginning of this ambitious project, Edwards was reminded that "all the great preachers of the early church had been trained as professional rhetoricians before their ordination. That drove me to Aristotle, Cicero, and Quintilian" (xix). And Edwards is always mindful of the role of traditional rhetoric in the preaching arts. Early modern preaching is discussed in part 3, "From the Renaissance and Reformation to the Enlightenment." This section includes chapters on Erasmus, Luther and Melancthon, Calvin, Catholic reform, and "Upheaval in Britain."

Edwards was also convinced from the outset of his study that "the historical survey had to be accompanied by a collection of documents—both sermons and theoretical treatments—that illustrated the development being traced. To do anything else would have been as senseless as a history of painting in which there were no pictures" (xxi). This necessary collection of documents is contained in the second volume of *A History of Preaching* as a compact disc affixed to the inside cover. The CD collection parallels exactly the order of the chapters in the first (print) volume. The Renaissance is represented by two theoretical documents: a résumé of the *Ecclesiastes* of Erasmus and a portion of the *Elementorum rhetorices libri duo* of Melanchton. The other documents accompanying the Renaissance chapters are all sermons, including texts by Luther, Calvin, Latimer, and Andrews.

The influence of preaching on the poetry of John Milton is demonstrated by Jameela Lares in *Milton and the Preaching Arts* (2001). Her intent is to "not only demonstrate how Milton's age understood the role of the preacher but also demonstrate the degree to which Milton does in fact appropriate into his own works the forms and procedures that shaped sermons" (2). Lares claims that Milton's appropriation of preaching has been neglected "in spite of numerous studies showing how Milton's Christianity influences and directs his work" (10–11). She notes that "one problem with the term 'rhetoric' for literary scholars is that they tend to hear 'style,' which forms only a part of the discipline, and actually had a greatly reduced role in the preaching arts in Milton's day" (3). Yet Lares maintains that "in the preaching manuals that most greatly influenced Milton's thinking, i.e., those written in the sixteenth and earlier seventeenth centuries, the heaviest focus is placed on *inventio* and *disposition*" (4). The first two chapters detail how strongly Milton was influenced by English Reformation homiletics. In particular, Lares focuses on Andreas Gerhard Hyperius, a now-obscure figure whose work had "staggering implications for English homiletics" (12). The remaining three chapters detail the influence of rhetoric and homiletics in Milton's role in the Smectymnuan controversy, and in *Paradise Lost* and *Paradise Regained*.

The influence of rhetoric on Ignacio Loyola is detailed by Marjorie O'Rourke Boyle in *Loyola's Acts: The Rhetoric of the Self* (1997). Boyle demonstrates that

Loyola's account of his life was deeply influenced by the traditions and techniques of classical rhetoric. In doing so, she challenges "the premise of modern interpretation" that regards Loyola's "life" as "an autobiographical narrative" which is "a factually historical document" (2). In Boyle's view, Loyola's *Acts* (*Acta patris Ignatii*) is far from an autobiography in the twentieth-century sense of that term. The work is, rather, an example of what Boyle calls "the rhetoric of the self," a variation of the classical genre of epideictic oratory. The epideictic character of the *Acts* determines the text: "Although epideictic rhetoric assumed the matters for praise or blame to be true, it could by the rules exploit the techniques of fiction, so that every detail was not necessarily factual" (3). So it is with Loyola's life, a narrative that is morally true, but not necessarily empirically accurate. As epideictic rhetoric, rather than autobiography, the *Acts* is an exercise in praise and blame: praise of God's glory and condemnation of Loyola's vainglory.

Although the title suggests that *Loyola's Acts* is about Loyola's life, Boyle's book is more properly about Renaissance rhetoric broadly conceived. Boyle shows how Loyola's narrative is dependent upon the writings of Cicero, Quintilian, Augustine, Petrarch, Erasmus, and the many other authorities of the rhetorical culture of early-modern Europe. So great is this dependence that Boyle maintains "Loyola's piety is established in the renaissance revival of that rhetorical culture" (9).

John W. O'Malley's *Religious Culture in the Sixteenth Century: Preaching, Rhetoric, Spirituality, and Reform* (1993) is a wide-ranging collection of essays written over a period of more than a decade by O'Malley, an exceptional scholar of Renaissance preaching. Essays assembled here include examinations of Aquinas, Luther, Erasmus, and Charles Borromeo, as well as several essays about one of O'Malley's particular concerns, the early Jesuits.

The challenges and strategies of Catholic preaching from the middle sixteenth century to the early seventeenth centuries are examined in Frederick J. McGuiness, *Right Thinking and Sacred Oratory in Counter-Reformation Rome* (1995). McGuiness shows how the clerical elite in Rome formulated a response to Protestant reformers that required highly persuasive sacred oratory. To achieve the necessary persuasiveness, the elite turned to classical rhetoric to reinvigorate Catholic preaching.

Rhetoric and Education

Key Texts from the Revised Edition:
- T. W. Baldwin, *William Shakspere's Small Latine and Lesse Greek* (1944)
- Donald Lemen Clark, *John Milton at St. Paul's School* (1948)
- Anthony Grafton and Lisa Jardine, *From Humanism to the Humanities* (1986)

- Foster Watson, *The English Grammar Schools to 1660* (1908; reprint, 1968)
- William H. Woodward, *Studies in Education during the Age of the Renaissance, 1400–1600* (1906; reprint, 1924)

The importance of rhetoric to Renaissance education has been long a central concern of James J. Murphy, a preeminent scholar and teacher of rhetoric. Many of his essays on this subject are assembled in *Latin Education in the Middle Ages and Renaissance* (2005). About half of the essays in this volume address questions of Renaissance (rather than medieval) education. The range of these essays very nearly constitutes a history of rhetorical pedagogy in the fifteenth and sixteenth centuries. Murphy examines such figures as Caxton, Traversagni, Raffaele Regio, Antonio de Nebrija, Omer Talon, and Peter Ramus. An obvious companion to *Latin Rhetoric and Education* is *Rhetoric and Pedagogy: Its History, Philosophy, and Practice: Essays in Honor of James J. Murphy*, edited by Winifred Horner and Michael C. Leff (1995). This *festschrift* reflects Murphy's broad interest in the history of rhetoric. Part 2 is devoted to "Renaissance Textbooks and Rhetorical Education" and features essays by John Ward on Guarino de Verona, Jean Moss on Ludovico Carbone, and William Wallace on Antonio Riccobono. *Rhetoric and Pedagogy* also includes an essay by Beth Bennett and Michael Leff entitled "James J. Murphy and the Rhetorical Tradition," which neatly summarizes Murphy's contribution to advancing, by his example and his encouragement, the historical study of rhetoric.

Rhetoric figures importantly in Paul F. Grendler's *Schooling in Renaissance Italy: Literacy and Learning, 1300–1600* (1989). This is a massive study based on textbooks, teachers' records, and archival material about all of Italian education. In chapter 8, "Rhetoric," Grendler describes an ambitious curriculum that called for students to learn—by heart—vast amounts of Latin literature. In practice, however, teachers expected their charges to know a few essential texts very, very well. Based on the records of over two hundred teachers, Grendler documents the extent of Cicero's dominance of sixteenth-century curriculum. While it is not surprising that Cicero dominated Renaissance pedagogy, it is perhaps unexpected that "pride of place" for the principal textbook went to the *Epistulae ad familiares*. Renaissance masters extolled the virtues of the civic oration, but they also recognized that their students were more likely to write letters and documents than to give important public speeches. This decidedly dictaminal approach differed from medieval models of education both by being less technical about structure and form and by keeping the link between rhetoric and civic life at the forefront of education. Grendler concedes that this education was "built on a utopian dream" that improbably projected that students would become Ciceronian orators exercising wisdom and eloquence.

Perhaps, says Grendler, but education always involves "lofty assumptions that students will step from the classroom into an orderly world that can be comprehended and managed to some degree by one's learning" (234).

The role of rhetoric in the teaching of writing is explored in my "Rhetoric and Writing in the Renaissance," in *A Short History of Writing Instruction from Ancient Greece to Modern America,* edited by James J. Murphy (2001). In this chapter, I look primarily at two institutions: the grammar schools of England and the Jesuit colleges of the Continent. Scrutiny of these institutions offers a number of advantages for an investigation of writing instruction in the Renaissance. First, it was in these schools that rhetoric was most often taught. Although rhetoric was also a university subject, philosophy and theology, broadly defined, frequently overshadowed rhetoric in higher education. Second, an examination of the grammar schools and the Jesuit colleges ensures an emphasis on the pedagogical rather than the theoretical issues. The schoolmasters were intensely interested in how their young students should be taught to write and, fortunately, left considerable testimony as to their methods. Third, an examination of these schools maintains an emphasis on the development of the system of writing instruction ultimately inherited by the public and parochial schools of the United States.

The grammar schools and the Jesuit schools provided boys with an intense education in rhetoric and writing. However, these institutions were not intended to offer instruction to girls. Renaissance schoolmasters saw rhetoric as a preparation for public life; because girls were not expected to participate in that life in adulthood, there was little reason to prepare them for it. The exclusion of women from rhetorical education is examined by Catherine R. Eskin in "The Rei(g)ning of Women's Tongues in English Books of Instruction and Rhetoric," in *Women's Education in Early Modern Europe: A History, 1500–1800* (1999). Eskin discovers that though many Elizabethan educators would restrict women's education, others would not. She concludes that there was a "range of attitudes toward female education and speech which makes it clear that "the Renaissance did accept this idea of the female voice and, by extension, of female agency" (124).

Rhetoric and Science

Key Texts from the Revised Edition:
- Morris W. Croll, *Style, Rhetoric, and Rhythm* (1966)
- Lisa Jardine, *Francis Bacon: Discovery and the Art of Discourse* (1974)
- Richard F. Jones, *The Triumph of the English Language* (1953)
- Brian Vickers, *Francis Bacon and Renaissance Prose* (1968)

- Karl R. Wallace, *Francis Bacon on Communication and Rhetoric* (1943)
- George Williamson, *The Senecan Amble* (1951; reprint, 1966)

The role of rhetoric in the development of modern science has received considerable attention since the previous edition. A convenient historical overview is presented by Heather Greaves in *Rhetoric in(to) Science: Style as Invention in Inquiry* (2005). The second chapter, "A History—How the Scientific Method Appropriated Rhetorical Invention during the Rise of Science," includes a brief statement about the early Renaissance as well as more detailed discussions about Francis Bacon and Robert Boyle. Two recent anthologies about science and rhetoric contain several studies of Renaissance inquiry. *Persuading Science: The Art of Scientific Rhetoric,* edited by Marcello Pera and William R. Shea (1991), includes several essays relevant to the Renaissance: Paolo Rossi, "Mnemonical Loci and Natural Loci"; "Galileo and Newton: Different Rhetorical Strategies"; William R. Shea, "Descartes and the Art of Persuasion"; Peter Machamer, "The Person-Centered Rhetoric of Seventeenth-Century Science"; and Maurizio Mamiani, "The Rhetoric of Certainty: Newton's Method in Science and the Interpretation of the Apocalypse." Another recent anthology, although containing fewer essays on the Renaissance, is *Science, Reason, and Rhetoric,* edited by Henry Krips, J. E. McGuire, and Trevor Melia (1995). Essays include Gerald J. Massey's "Rhetoric and Rationality in William Harvey's *De Motu Cordis,*" and R. Feldhay's "Producing Sunspots on an Iron Pan: Galileo's Scientific Discourse," which is accompanied by Peter Machamer's "Comment: A New Way of Seeing Galileo's Sunspots (and New Ways of Talking Too)."

In *Rhetoric and Dialectic in the Time of Galileo* (2003), Jean Dietz Moss and William A. Wallace consider both Galileo and his rhetorical milieu. The starting point of this work is Galileo's theological and astronomical conflict with the Church over the Copernican system. Moss and Wallace present Galileo as a skilled controversialist trained in humanistic rhetoric. Their work, then, aims to fully explain how Galileo and his opponents might have understood and employed the argumentative process. To understand the rhetorical context of this dispute requires an acquaintance with the argumentative processes of the time, and Moss and Wallace argue that it is just this aspect that has been overlooked in recent scholarship on Renaissance rhetoric. They maintain that the careful efforts in recent scholarship exploring *elocutio,* and especially the figures and tropes, have obscured *inventio,* the other dominant element of rhetoric.

While Moss and Wallace choose Galileo's conflict with the Church to commence their study, Galileo himself is soon relegated to the background as the two principal subjects of this study emerge: Ludovico Carbone (1545–1597) and Antonio Riccobono (1541–1599). The majority of *Rhetoric and Dialectic in the Time of Galileo* comprises translations of texts of these two humanists.

The texts by Carbone included in this volume are *Introduction to Logic, Tables of Soarez's Rhetoric, Art of Speaking, On Invention,* and *On Divine Rhetoric.* Only one text by Riccobono is included: *Essays on Aristotle's "Rhetoric."* Each translation is accompanied by a brief introduction explaining the context and significance of the work. Only one text is translated in its entirety: the *Tabulae rhetoricae,* Carbone's guide to the *De arte rhetorica* of Cypriano Soarez. Soarez's work, the principal rhetorical text of the Jesuit's *ratio studiorum,* remains one of the most popular and influential rhetorics in the history of this ancient art. As Moss and Wallace point out, summaries and epitomes of *De arte rhetorica* were virtually as popular as Soarez's original. The inclusion of a complete text of Carbone's *Tabulae* provides a reasonably concise way to see a complete rhetoric of Galileo's time. The appeal that the *Tabulae* must have had to Renaissance students is quite understandable: the ability to master a long and sometimes tedious work in a clear and concise format. The English translation of the *Tabulae* offers an excellent and concise introduction to humanistic rhetoric.

Francis Bacon has long been recognized as a key figure in the relationship between rhetoric and science. An important collection that explores various aspects of Bacon as a writer is *Francis Bacon's Legacy of Texts,* edited by William A. Sessions (1990). In it, Brian Vickers, long a leading scholar of Bacon's "truly imaginative approach to thought and language," explores "Bacon's Use of Theatrical Imagery" (171). Also of interest in the same volume is Michael Malherbe's "Bacon's Critique of Logic."

Robert M. Schuler, in *Francis Bacon and Scientific Poetry* (1992), examines Bacon's use of and attitudes toward "scientific poetry." That is, the genre of poetry Puttenham calls "the forme wherein honest and profitable arts and sciences were treated" (quoted in Schuler, 23). According to Schuler, Bacon's view of poetry of this kind reveals an unresolved tension in Baconian thought between science and poetry.

Women and Rhetoric

One of the most notable developments that has occurred since the previous edition of *The Present State* is the reappraisal of the place of women in the history of rhetoric generally and in Renaissance rhetoric particularly. That reappraisal might be said to have begun with *Reclaiming Rhetorica: Women in the Rhetorical Tradition,* edited by Andrea Lunsford (1995). Lunsford says the essays in *Reclaiming Rhetorica* "do not attempt to redefine a 'new' rhetoric but rather to interrupt the seamless narrative usually told about the rhetorical tradition and to open up the possibilities of multiple rhetorics, rhetorics that would not name and valorize one traditional, competitive, agonistic, and linear mode of rhetorical discourse" (6). The Renaissance is represented in this new narrative by Christine Mason Sutherland's "Mary Astell: Reclaiming Rhetorica in the

Seventeenth Century." Sutherland maintains that "it would be possible to claim a place for Mary Astell in the history of rhetoric solely on the grounds of her magnificent practice of it. In her own day she was renowned for her eloquence" (97). Astell was not only a gifted writer but also a student of the rhetorical tradition who was influenced by Descartes, Arnauld and Nichole, and Lamy. Although Astell was fully aware of rhetorical techniques and practices, Sutherland concludes that "she goes beyond her sources in extending such principles to include the discourse of women. She challenges women's exclusion from the rhetorical tradition, and thus contributes to that tradition" (112).

In *Rhetoric Retold: Regendering the Tradition from Antiquity through the Renaissance* (1997), Cheryl Glenn challenges "canonical rhetorical history," which "has represented the experience of males, powerful males, with no provision or allowance for females. In short, rhetorical history has replicated the power politics of gender, with men in the highest cultural role and social rank. And our view of rhetoric has remained one of a gendered landscape, with no female rhetorician (theoreticians) clearly in sight" (x). Her alternative to this approach is to provide "a fully gendered rather than only a women's history of rhetoric" (119). The Renaissance is presented in chapter 4: "Inscribed in the Margins: Renaissance Women and Rhetorical Culture." In this chapter, Glenn presents a brief overview of the Renaissance and women's place in it before surveying Renaissance rhetoric, "which flourished as a male-dominated practice that connected at various points with literature, education, religion, science, and politics" (119). Last, she recounts the rhetorical contributions of three women—Margaret More Roper, Anne Askew, and Elizabeth I. "These three women," says Glenn, "demonstrated their inimitable rhetorics and contributed to the multiple oratorical and literary discourses we call *rhetoric*, speaking across the centuries to the body of rhetorical tradition from their marginalized positions as women, even when the woman was king of England" (172).

Much like the two preceding books, *Listening to Their Voices: The Rhetorical Activities of Historical Women* (1997), edited by Molly Meijer Wertheimer, offers a broad historical scope tracing women's rhetoric from ancient Egypt to turn-of-the-century America. Students of the Renaissance will be particularly interested in part 4, "Women's Intellectual Desires," which includes studies of Margaret Cavendish, Bathsua Makin, and the *Querelle des Femmes*.

The Changing Tradition: Women in the History of Rhetoric (1999), edited by Christine Mason Sutherland and Rebecca Sutcliffe, also examines the role of women across the entirety of the rhetorical tradition. The essays in the collection are not arranged chronologically, but rather according to the relationship of the women studied to that tradition. The categories most relevant to the Renaissance are the ones in which women function "Alongside the Rhetorical Tradition," and those in which women are seen to be "Participating in the Rhetorical Tradition." This latter category is composed of "women who knew the rhetorical tradition and used it" (3). Among early modern women who did just that are Lady Mary Wroth and Mary Astell.

A useful supplement to the historical surveys noted above is *Available Means: An Anthology of Women's Rhetoric(s)* (2001), edited by Joy Ritchie and Kate Ronald. This collection includes some sixty-seven examples of women's speaking and writing, beginning with Aspasia and concluding with Gloria Steinem. Renaissance women include Elizabeth I, Jane Anger, Rachel Speght, Margaret Fell, Sor Juana Inés de la Cruz, and Mary Astell. *Available Means* concludes with "A Select Bibliography of Works on Women's Rhetorics." A similar collection is *Rhetorical Theory by Women before 1900: An Anthology* (2002), edited by Jane Donawerth. However, this anthology features theory, that is, preceptive texts about speaking and writing, and thus does not include examples of applied rhetoric such as speeches, poems, and letters. Renaissance theorists include Margaret Cavendish, Margaret Fell, Bathsua Makin, Madeline de Scudéry, and Mary Astell.

The works discussed thus far look at the place of women in the rhetorical tradition and include considerations of the Renaissance within the context of that larger tradition. Other studies, however, concentrate on the Renaissance itself. One such work is Carole Levin and Patricia A. Sullivan's *Political Rhetoric, Power, and Renaissance Women* (1995). This interdisciplinary collection examines "political rhetoric" in the broadest sense, looking at women who were both powerful and persuasive—some only fleetingly so. Thus, the powerful women include Anne Boleyn, Elizabeth I, Catherine de Médicis, Anne Askew, Elizabeth Cary, and Aphra Behn.

In *Women Writing of Divinest Things: Rhetoric and the Poetry of Pembroke, Wroth, and Lanyer* (2004), Lyn Bennett, in response to the works already noted above by Lunsford, Wertheimer, and Sutherland and Sutcliffe, expresses concern that these studies have focused almost "exclusively on prose. Perhaps because rhetoric has always been most readily associated with oratory, prose seems the most likely area to explore when writing about women in the history" (vii). Bennett regrets that these earlier works have not readily acknowledged that women wrote verse. Given the rhetorical nature of Renaissance poetry, an appreciation of women and rhetoric requires a full appreciation of women and poetry. Bennett corrects this omission by examining the poetry of Mary Sidney Herbert, Lady Mary Wroth, and Aemilia Lanyer. Bennett finds all three of these poets to be accomplished rhetors despite the fact that, as females, they were excluded from the rhetorical education accorded males. She argues that "to assume that women did not know rhetoric simply because they were not, like many of their male counterparts, also subject to endless drills in the classroom is not only naive, it also implies that early modern girls were not alert or perceptive enough to pick up the prevailing habits of a culture in which rhetoric was almost literally a part of the air they breathed" (10). Thus, "some girls not only learned the tropes, figures and conventions of rhetoric, but learned them so well they became second nature" (10). And so, she concludes, while historians may have excluded women from rhetoric's history, women included themselves, even though without invitation.

Rhetoric and New Worlds

The centrality of rhetoric in the Renaissance ensured that as European influence expanded, so too would the province of rhetoric. Yet the arrival of rhetoric in the Americas was long a neglected aspect of this ancient discipline's long history. I attempt to address this neglect in *Rhetoric in the New World: Rhetorical Theory and Practice in Colonial Spanish America* (1996). From the beginning of the Spanish expansion, rhetorical treatises were shipped to the Americas, rhetoric was taught in schools, and it was taught to the sons of Spaniards and, at times, to the sons of American Indians. In particular, the Spanish recognized that the ancient art of persuasion promised a program for accomplishing Spain's enormous colonial and evangelical endeavor in New Spain and Peru.

Spanish rhetoricians saw three very different, and competing, functions for rhetoric in the evangelization of the indigenous peoples of the New World: persuasion, conversion, and coercion. Some Spaniards argued simply that the principles of classical rhetoric were universal and therefore could be directly applied to persuade the newly encountered peoples. Other rhetoricians maintained that ancient rhetoric must be substantially altered in order to convert audiences unimagined by Aristotle and Cicero. And finally, still other writers maintained that only rudimentary aspects of rhetoric could be employed to augment the coercion required to Christianize recalcitrant natives who must not be fully human. I examine these various approaches as they are manifest in the works of such key figures as Luis de Granada, Bernardino de Sahagún, Diego Valadés, José de Acosta, Bartolomé de las Casas, and José de Arriaga.

One of the most extraordinary of these rhetoricians is Diego Valadés. In "Diego Valadés and the Origins of Rhetoric in the Americas," *Rhetoric and Pedagogy* (1995), I consider the singular career of Valadés, who was born in Mexico to a native mother and a Spanish father, educated there by the Franciscans, and wrote what can reasonably be called the first American rhetoric. His work, the *Rhetorica Christiana*, initiates the attempt to create a rhetoric that reflects both the Old World and the New.

For a more recent treatment of Valadés, see César Chaparro-Gómez's "Emblemática y memoria, política e historia en la *Rhetorica christiana* de Diego Valadés" (2005). Chaparro-Gómez explores the great importance Valadés assigns to memory and graphic imagery. In *Retórica, comunicación, y realidad: La construcción retórica de las batallas en la crónicas de la conquista* (2003), Alfonso

Mendiola considers the influence of rhetoric and *narratio* on the formation of the Spanish chronicles recounting the violent conquest of the New World.

The English, rather than the Spanish, colonial experience is examined by Andrew Fitzmaurice in "Classical Rhetoric and the Promotion of the New World" (1997). Fitzmaurice argues that the majority of Elizabethan and Jacobean writings about the New World were intended to promote the colonial enterprise. These promotional tracts were, of course, exercises in persuasion, and the writers' understanding of persuasion naturally derived from their familiarity with classical rhetoric. Fitzmaurice further develops the themes in an essay in *Humanism and America: An Intellectual History of English Colonization, 1500–1625* (2003). In that work, he reaches the interesting conclusion that humanism did more "to shape the English understanding of the New World than that of other Europeans" (7).

The Future of Renaissance Rhetoric

Future scholarship in any field must be built upon the foundation of the research that preceded it. The remarkable quantity and quality of scholarship undertaken at the end of the twentieth century and the beginning of the twenty-first points the way to a promising future for inquiry into Renaissance rhetoric. In particular, greatly improved bibliographic resources do much to enhance future research. James J. Murphy once called Renaissance rhetoric the discipline with "a thousand and one neglected authors" (*Rennaissane Eloquence,* 20). Even as the neglect of Renaissance authors has decreased, the number of rhetoricians about whom we have knowledge has increased. While I would not want to suggest there are now "1701 neglected authors" (Green and Murphy, xi), it remains the case that our understanding of Renaissance rhetoric is dependent on a limited number of authors.

Green and Murphy and Plett all conclude that the lack of comprehensive bibliographies has limited our interpretation of English, and indeed all, Renaissance rhetoric. Plett says the interest in Renaissance rhetoric "has been restricted to a relatively small corpus of texts which has continued to be reedited and reinterpreted throughout several generations of scholars" (1). Similarly, Green and Murphy argue that the significance of many treatises has been distorted by an absence of bibliographic investigation. They conclude, for example, that "the vaunted influence of Leonard Cox's *Arte or Crafte of Rhethoricke,* or Richard Sherry's *Treatise of Schemes and Tropes,* or even George Puttenham's *Arte of English Poesie,* will not survive scrutiny; these appeared in nearly solitary printings, and no publisher anticipated the cost of subsequent editions" (xiii).

Thus, additional scrutiny of "neglected authors" and of neglected treatises should yield new interpretations and new understanding of rhetoric in the

Renaissance. Indeed, many of the new areas of scholarship that have emerged since the previous edition of *The Present State* are the result of attending to formerly neglected sources. Searching for rhetoric where it was thought not to be found—in the hands of women and in the lands of New Spain and Peru—has expanded the boundaries of early-modern rhetorical studies.

The record of research since 1990, and it is a distinguished record to be sure, has by no means exhausted the subject. Indeed, this work points to what must be the inexhaustibility of rhetoric in the Renaissance. Rhetoric was so fundamental to so many aspects of Renaissance culture that it is sometimes difficult, in this postmodern world, to fully appreciate how pervasive the art of persuasion was to an earlier age. Yet this very pervasiveness ensures that Renaissance rhetoric will continue to present almost inexhaustible resources for future scholarly enterprise. In their *Renaissance Rhetoric Short-Title Catalogue,* Green and Murphy reach a conclusion that is at once daunting and encouraging to scholars of Renaissance rhetoric: they declare that "despite all the research that has been done in the last five decades, there is still everything to do" (xii).

BIBLIOGRAPHY

This bibliography includes all the works cited in this chapter. The "Key Texts from the Revised Edition" are cited first, followed by citations to the works discussed in this chapter. Articles that are mentioned in this chapter but not discussed fully are not cited individually. The work in which the article can be found is, of course, cited fully. A small number of works are included in the bibliography that are not discussed above. For the most part, these are materials that became available to me too late in the revision process to be treated in detail. Common sources of facsimile reprints are abbreviated as follows:

SFR: Scholars' Facsimiles and Reprints. Gainesville, FL.
EngLing: English Linguistics, 1500–1800: A Collection of Facsimile Reprints. Ed. R. C. Alston. Menston, U.K.: Scholar Press.
EngEx: The English Experience: Its Record in Early Printed Books. Published in Facsimile. New York: Da Capo Press.

Bibliographies and Other Reference Works

Alston, R. C. *A Bibliography of the English Language from the Invention of Printing to the Year 1800.* 20 vols. Vol. 6, *Rhetoric, Style, Elocution, Prosody, Rhyme, Pronunciation, Spelling Reform.* Ilkley, Yorkshire, U.K.: Janus Press, 1974.
Enos, Theresa, ed. *The Encyclopedia of Rhetoric and Composition: Communication from Ancient Times to the Information Age.* New York: Garland, 1996.

Green, Lawrence D., and James J. Murphy. *Renaissance Rhetoric Short-Title Catalogue, 1460–1700.* Aldershot, U.K.: Ashgate, 2006.

Lausberg, Heinrich. *Handbook of Literary Rhetoric: A Foundation for Literary Study.* Trans. Matthew T. Bliss, Annemiek Jansen, and Davis E. Orton; ed. Davis E. Orton and R. Dean Anderson. Leiden, Netherlands: Brill, 1998.

Murphy, James J. *Renaissance Rhetoric: A Short Title Catalogue of Works on Rhetorical Theory from the Beginning of Printing to A.D. 1700, with Special Attention to the Holdings of the Bodleian Library, Oxford. With Select Basic Bibliography of Secondary Works on Renaissance Rhetoric.* New York: Garland, 1981.

Plett, Heinrich F. *English Renaissance Rhetoric and Poetics: A Systematic Bibliography of Primary and Secondary Sources.* Leiden, Netherlands: Brill, 1995.

Sloane, Thomas, ed. *The Encyclopedia of Rhetoric.* Oxford: Oxford University Press, 2001.

Old Texts and New Databases

Artaza, Elena, ed. *Antología de textos retóricos españoles del siglo XVI.* Bilbao, Spain: Universidad de Duesto, 1997.

Bizzell, Patricia, and Bruce Herzberg, eds. *The Rhetorical Tradition: Readings from Classical Times to the Present.* 2nd ed. Boston: Bedford/St. Martin's, 2001.

British and Continental Rhetoric and Elocution. Sixteen microfilm reels. Ann Arbor: University Microfilms, 1953.

Cox, Leonard. *The Arte or Craft of Rhetorike* (1530?). Ed. Frederic Ives Carpenter. 1899. Reprint, Folcroft, PA: Folcroft Press, 1969; Norwood, PA: Norwood Editions, 1975.

——. *The Arte or Craft of Rhetorike* (1530?). *EngEx,* no. 862, 1977.

Early English Books Online. http://eebo.chadwyck.com/home.

Fraunce, Abraham. *The Arcadian Rhetorike* (1588). Ed. Ethel Seaton. Oxford: Blackwell, 1950.

Garrido Gallardo, Miguel Ángel ed. *Retóricas españolas del siglo xvi escritas en latín, edición digital.* Madrid: DIGIBUS, 2004.

Lipsius, Justus. *Principles of Letter-Writing: A Bilingual Text of "Justi Lipsi Epistolica Institutio."* Ed. and trans. R. V. Young and M. Thomas Hester. Carbondale: Southern Illinois University Press, 1999.

Medine, Peter E., ed. *Thomas Wilson: The Art of Rhetoric.* University Park: Pennsylvania State University Press, 1994.

Murphy, James J., ed. *Renaissance Rhetoric: A Microfiche Collection of Key Texts, A.D. 1472–1602.* Elmsford, NY: Microforms International, 1987.

Puttenham, George. *The Art of English Poesie* (1589). Ed. Gladys Doidge Willcock and Alice Walker. Cambridge: Cambridge University Press, 1936.

——. *The Art of English Poesie* (1589). *EngLing,* no. 110, 1968.

Ramus, Peter. *Peter Ramus's Attack on Cicero: Text and Translation of Ramus's "Brutinae Quaestiones."* Ed. James J. Murphy; trans. Carole Newlands. Davis, CA: Hermagoras Press, 1992.

Rebhorn, Wayne, ed and trans. *Renaissance Debates on Rhetoric.* Ithaca: Cornell University Press, 2000.

Renascence Editions. http://www.uoregon.edu/~rbear/ren.htm.

Scott, Izora. *Controversies over the Imitation of Cicero in the Renaissance. With Translations of Letters between Pietro Bembo and Gianfrancesco Pico "On Imitation" and a Translation of Desiderius Erasmus, "The Ciceronian (Ciceronianus)."* Davis, CA: Hermagoras Press, 1991.

Sherry, Richard. *A Treatise of Schemes and Tropes* (1550). Ed. Herbert W. Hildebrandt. *SFR*, 1961.

Swynnerton, Thomas. *A Reformation Rhetoric: Thomas Swynnerton's "The Tropes and Figures."* Ed. Richard Rex. London: Thoemmes Continuum, 1996.

Vickers, Brian, ed. *English Literary Criticism in the Renaissance.* Oxford: Oxford University Press, 1999.

Wilson, Thomas. *The Arte of Rhetorique* (1553). Ed. G. H. Mair. Oxford: Clarendon Press, 1909.

———. *The Arte of Rhetorique* (1553). Ed. Robert Hood Bowers. *SFR*, 1962.

———. *The Arte of Rhetorique* (1553). *EngEx,* no. 206, 1969.

Comprehensive Studies

Fumaroli, Marc. *L'âge de l'éloquence: Rhétorique et "res literaria" de la Renaissance au seuil de l'époque classique.* Geneva: Librairie Droz, 1980.

Fumaroli, Marc, ed. *Histoire de la rhétorique dans l'Europe moderne, 1450–1950.* Paris: Presses Universitaires de France, 2002.

Howell, Wilbur S. *Logic and Rhetoric in England, 1500–1700.* Princeton: Princeton University Press, 1956.

Mack, Peter. *Elizabethan Rhetoric: Theory and Practice.* Cambridge: Cambridge University Press, 2002.

Murphy, James J., ed. *Renaissance Eloquence: Studies in the Theory and Practice of Renaissance Rhetoric.* Berkeley: University of California Press, 1983.

Plett, Heinrich F. *Rhetoric and Renaissance Culture.* Berlin: de Gruyter, 2004.

Rebhorn, Wayne. *The Emperor of Men's Minds: Literature and the Renaissance Discourse of Rhetoric.* Ithaca: Cornell University Press, 1995.

Vickers, Brian. *In Defence of Rhetoric.* Oxford: Clarendon Press, 1988.

Rhetoric and Humanism

Armstrong, Edward. *Ciceronian Sunburn: A Tudor Dialogue on Rhetoric and Civic Poetics.* Columbia: University of South Carolina Press, 2006.

Gray, Hanna H. "Renaissance Humanism: The Pursuit of Eloquence." In *Renaissance Essays from the Journal of the History of Ideas,* ed. Paul O. Kristellar and Philip P. Wiener, 192–218. New York: Harper and Row, 1968.

Hankins, James. *Renaissance Civic Humanism: Reappraisals and Reflections.* Cambridge: Cambridge University Press, 2000.

Kahn, Victoria. *Machiavellian Rhetoric from the Counter-Reformation to Milton.* Princeton: Princeton University Press, 1994.

———. *Rhetoric, Prudence, and Skepticism in the Renaissance.* Ithaca: Cornell University Press, 1985.

Kristeller, Paul Oskar. *Renaissance Thought and Its Sources.* Ed. Michael Mooney. New York: Columbia University Press, 1979.

Mack, Peter. "Humanist Rhetoric and Dialectic." In *The Cambridge Companion to Renaissance Humanism,* ed. Jill Kray, 82–99. Cambridge: Cambridge University Press, 1996.

———. *Renaissance Argument: Valla and Agricola in the Traditions of Rhetoric and Dialectic.* Leiden, Netherlands: Brill, 1993.

Monfasani, John. "Humanism and Rhetoric." In *Renaissance Humanism: Foundations, Forms, and Legacy.* Vol. 3, *Humanism and the Disciplines,* ed. Albert Rabil Jr., 171–235. Philadelphia: University of Pennsylvania Press, 1988

Poster, Carol, and Linda C. Mitchell, eds. *Letter-Writing Manuals and Instruction from Antiquity to the Present: Historical and Bibliographical Studies.* Columbia: University of South Carolina Press, 2007.

Remer, Gary. *Humanism and the Rhetoric of Toleration.* University Park: Pennsylvania State University Press, 1996.

Sloane, Thomas O. *On the Contrary: The Protocol of Traditional Rhetoric.* Washington, D.C.: Catholic University of America Press, 1997.

Witt, Ronald G. *In the Footsteps of the Ancients: The Origins of Humanism from Lovato to Bruni.* Leiden, Netherlands: Brill, 2000.

Rhetoric, Logic, and Philosophy

Carr, Thomas M., Jr. *Descartes and the Resilience of Rhetoric: Varieties of Cartesian Rhetorical Theory.* Carbondale: Southern Illinois University Press, 1990.

Cogan, Marc. "Rodolphus Agricola and the Semantic Revolutions of the History of Invention." *Rhetorica* 2 (1984): 163–94.

Garsten, Bryan. *Saving Persuasion: A Defense of Rhetoric and Judgment.* Cambridge: Harvard University Press, 2006.

Lechner, Sister Joan Marie, O.S.U. *Renaissance Concepts of the Commonplaces: An Historical Investigation of the General and Universal Ideas Used in All Argumentation and Persuasion with Special Emphasis on the Educational and Literary Tradition of the Sixteenth and Seventeenth Centuries.* New York: Pageant Press, 1962.

Meerhof, Kees. *Rhétorique et poétique au XVIe siècle en France: Du Bellay, Ramus et les autres.* Leiden, Netherlands: Brill, 1986.

Ong, Walter, S.J. *Ramus, Method, and the Decay of Dialogue: From the Art of Discourse to the Art of Reason.* Cambridge: Harvard University Press, 1958.

Skinner, Quentin. *Rhetoric and Reason in the Philosophy of Hobbes.* Cambridge: Cambridge University Press, 1996.

Rhetoric and Literature

Altman, Joel B. *The Tudor Play of the Mind: Rhetorical Inquiry and the Development of Elizabethan Drama.* Berkeley: University of California Press, 1978.

Beister, James. *Lyric Wonder: Rhetoric and Wit in English Renaissance Poetry.* Ithaca: Cornell University Press, 1997.

Donker, Marjorie. *Shakespeare's Proverbial Themes: A Rhetorical Context for the "Sententia" as "Res."* Westport, CT: Greenwood, 1992.

Green, Lawrence D. "Aristotelian *Lexis* and Renaissance *Elocutio.*" In *Rereading Aristotle's Rhetoric,* ed. Alan G. Gross and Arthur E. Walzer, 149–65. Carbondale: Southern Illinois University Press, 2000.

Hardison, O. B. Jr. *The Enduring Monument: A Study of the Idea of Praise in Renaissance Literary Theory and Practice.* Chapel Hill: University of North Carolina Press, 1962.

Joseph, Sister Miriam, C.S.C. *Rhetoric in Shakespeare's Time: Literary Theory of Renaissance Europe.* 1947. Reprint, New York: Harcourt, Brace and World, 1962.

McNeely, Trevor. *Proteus Unmasked: Sixteenth-Century Rhetoric and the Art of Shakespeare.* Bethlehem, PA: Lehigh University Press, 2004.

Olmstead, Wendy. *The Imperfect Friend: Emotion and Rhetoric in Sidney, Milton, and Their Contexts.* Toronto: University of Toronto Press, 2008.

Sell, Jonathan P. A. *Rhetoric and Wonder in English Travel Writing, 1560–1613.* Aldershot, U.K.: Ashgate, 2006.

Trimpi, Wesley. *Ben Jonson's Poems: A Study of the Plain Style.* Palo Alto: Stanford University Press, 1962.

Trousdale, Marion. "Rhetoric." In *A Companion to English Renaissance Literature and Culture,* ed. Michael Hattaway, 623–33. Oxford: Blackwell, 2000.

———. *Shakespeare and the Rhetoricians.* Chapel Hill: University of North Carolina Press, 1982.

Tuve, Rosemond. *Elizabethan and Metaphysical Imagery: Renaissance Poetic and Twentieth-Century Critics.* Chicago: University of Chicago Press, 1947.

Vickers, Brian. "Rhetoric." In *The Cambridge Companion to English Poetry—Donne to Marvel,* ed. Thomas N. Corns, 101–20. Cambridge: Cambridge University Press, 1993.

Rhetoric and Preaching

Blench, J. W. *Preaching in England in the Late Fifteenth and Sixteenth Centuries: A Study of English Sermons, 1450–c. 1600.* Oxford: Blackwell, 1964.

Boyle, Marjorie O'Rourke. *Loyola's Acts: The Rhetoric of the Self.* Berkeley: University of California Press, 1997.

Edwards, O. C., Jr. *A History of Preaching.* Nashville: Abington, 2004.

Herr, Alan F. *The Elizabethan Sermon: A Survey and a Bibliography.* New York: Octagon, 1969.

Lares, Jameela. *Milton and the Preaching Arts.* Pittsburg: Duquesne University Press, 2001.

McGuiness, Frederick J. *Right Thinking and Sacred Oratory in Counter-Reformation Rome.* Princeton: Princeton University Press, 1995.

Mitchell, W. Fraser. *English Pulpit Oratory from Andrewes to Tillotson: A Study of Its Literary Aspects.* 1932. Reprint, New York: Russell and Russell, 1962.

O'Malley, John W. *Religious Culture in the Sixteenth Century: Preaching, Rhetoric, Spirituality, and Reform.* Aldershot, U.K.: Ashgate, 1993.

Shuger, Debora K. *Sacred Rhetoric: The Christian Grand Style in the English Renaissance.* Princeton: Princeton University Press, 1988.

Rhetoric and Education

Abbott, Don Paul. "Rhetoric and Writing in the Renaissance." In *A Short History of Writing Instruction from Ancient Greece to Modern America,* ed. James J. Murphy, 145–172. Mahwah, NJ: Earlbaum, 2001.

Baldwin, T. W. *William Shakspere's Small Latine and Lesse Greek.* 2 vols. Urbana: University of Illinois Press, 1944.

Clark, Donald Lemen. *John Milton at St. Paul's School: A Study of Ancient Rhetoric in English Renaissance Education.* New York: Columbia University Press, 1948.

Eskin, Catherine R. "The Rei(g)ning of Women's Tongues in English Books of Instruction and Rhetoric." In *Women's Education in Early Modern Europe: A History, 1500–1800,* ed. Barbara J. Whitehead, 101–32. New York: Garland, 1999.

Grafton, Anthony, and Lisa Jardine. *From Humanism to the Humanities: Education and the Liberal Arts in Fifteenth- and Sixteenth-Century Europe.* Cambridge: Harvard University Press, 1986.

Grendler, Paul F. *Schooling in Renaissance Italy: Literacy and Learning, 1300–1600.* Baltimore: Johns Hopkins University Press, 1989.

Horner, Winifred, and Michael Leff, eds. *Rhetoric and Pedagogy: Its History, Philosophy, and Practice: Essays in Honor of James J. Murphy.* Mahwah, NJ: Earlbaum, 1995.

Murphy, James J., ed. *A Short History of Writing Instruction from Ancient Greece to Modern America*. Mahwah, NJ: Earlbaum, 2001.

Watson, Foster. *The English Grammar Schools to 1660: Their Curriculum and Practice*. 1908. Reprint, London: Frank Cass, 1968.

Whitehead, Barbara J., ed. *Women's Education in Early Modern Europe: A History, 1500–1800*. New York: Garland, 1999.

Rhetoric and Science

Croll, Morris W. *Style, Rhetoric, and Rhythm: Essays by Morris W. Croll*. Ed. J. Max Patrick and Robert O. Evans, with John M. Wallace and R. J. Schoeck. Princeton: Princeton University Press, 1966.

Greaves, Heather. *Rhetoric in(to) Science: Style as Invention in Inquiry*. Creskill, NJ: Hampton, 2005.

Jardine, Lisa. *Francis Bacon: Discovery and the Art of Discourse*. Cambridge: Cambridge University Press, 1974.

Jones, Richard F. *The Triumph of the English Language: A Survey of Opinions Concerning the Vernacular from the Introduction of Printing to the Restoration*. Palo Alto: Stanford University Press, 1953.

Krips, Henry, J. E. McGuire, and Trevor Melia, eds. *Science, Reason, and Rhetoric*. Pittsburgh: University of Pittsburgh Press, 1995.

Moss, Jean Dietz, and William A. Wallace. *Rhetoric and Dialectic in the Time of Galileo*. Washington, D.C.: Catholic University of America Press, 2003.

Pera, Marcello, and William R. Shea, eds. *Persuading Science: The Art of Scientific Rhetoric*. Canton, MA: Science History, 1991.

Schuler, Robert M. *Francis Bacon and Scientific Poetry*. Philadelphia: American Philosophical Society, 1992.

Sessions, William A., ed. *Francis Bacon's Legacy of Texts*. New York: AMS, 1990.

Vickers, Brian. *Francis Bacon and Renaissance Prose*. Cambridge: Cambridge University Press, 1968.

Wallace, Karl R. *Francis Bacon on Communication and Rhetoric, or The Art of Applying Reason to the Imagination for the Better Moving of the Will*. Chapel Hill: University of North Carolina Press, 1943.

Williamson, George. *The Senecan Amble: A Study in Prose Form from Bacon to Collier*. 1951. Reprint, Chicago: University of Chicago Press, 1966.

Women and Rhetoric

Bennett, Lyn. *Women Writing of Divinest Things: Rhetoric and the Poetry of Pembroke, Wroth, and Lanyer*. Pittsburgh: Duquesne University Press, 2004.

Donawerth, Jane. *Rhetorical Theory by Women before 1900: An Anthology*. Lanham, MD: Rowman and Littlefield, 2002.

Glenn, Cheryl. *Rhetoric Retold: Regendering the Tradition from Antiquity through the Renaissance.* Carbondale: Southern Illinois University Press, 1997.

Levin, Carole, and Patricia A. Sullivan, eds. *Political Rhetoric, Power, and Renaissance Women.* Albany: State University of New York Press, 1995.

Lunsford, Andrea. *Reclaiming Rhetorica: Women in the Rhetorical Tradition.* Pittsburgh: University of Pittsburgh Press, 1995.

Richards, Jennifer, and Alison Thorne, eds. *Rhetoric, Women, and Politics in Early Modern England.* London: Routledge, 2007.

Ritchie, Joy, and Kate Ronald, eds. *Available Means: An Anthology of Women's Rhetoric(s).* Pittsburgh: University of Pittsburgh Press, 2001.

Sutherland, Christine Mason, and Rebecca Sutcliffe, eds. *The Changing Tradition: Women in the History of Rhetoric.* Calgary: University of Calgary Press, 1999.

Wertheimer, Molly Meijer ed. *Listening to Their Voices: The Rhetorical Activities of Historical Women.* Columbia: University of South Carolina Press, 1997.

Rhetoric and New Worlds

Abbott, Don Paul. "Diego Valadés and the Origins of Rhetoric in the Americas." In *Rhetoric and Pedagogy: Its History, Philosophy, and Practice: Essays in Honor of James J. Murphy,* ed. Winifred Horner and Michael Leff, 227–242. Mahwah, NJ: Earlbaum, 1995.

———. *Rhetoric in the New World: Rhetorical Theory and Practice in Colonial Spanish America.* Columbia: University of South Carolina Press, 1996.

Chaparro-Gómez, César. "Emblemática y memoria, política e historia en la *Rhetorica christiana* de Diego Valadés." *Rhetorica* 22 (2005): 173–202.

Fitzmaurice, Andrew. "Classical Rhetoric and the Promotion of the New World." *Journal of the History of Ideas* 58 (1997): 221–43.

———. *Humanism and America: An Intellectual History of English Colonization, 1500–1625.* Cambridge: Cambridge University Press, 2003.

Mendiola, Alfonso. *Retórica, comunicación, y realidad: La construcción retórica de las batallas en la crónicas de la conquista.* Mexico City: Universidad Iberoamericana, 2003.

4

The Eighteenth Century

Linda Ferreira-Buckley

The long-held view that Western rhetoric atrophied in the eighteenth century has given way amid an abundance of new scholarship. Scholars of rhetoric, along with those working in such diverse fields as political theory, fine arts, and science, have reexamined the period's rhetorics and tracked their influences. What's more, these scholars have expanded their scope beyond that which was called "rhetoric" to include areas recognized today as well within the purview of rhetorical studies. Then as now, "rhetoric" is an expansive phenomenon and a slippery term. Understanding the eighteenth century requires looking beyond disciplinary boundaries that may have come to seem natural.

For these and other reasons, the last two decades have seen significant new scholarship in the eighteenth century. This scholarship crosses continents, expands what we know about gender and class, broadens earlier definitions of rhetoric, and deepens our understanding of established figures. Some of it uses traditional methodologies to mine archives previously unstudied by scholars, and some returns to well-known materials with fresh perspectives. Some of it focuses on one or more primary theorists; others on social and political movements or on institutions and groups. Two decades ago Winifred Bryan Horner and Kerri Morris Barton observed, "Scholarship in eighteenth-century historical rhetoric for the past six years is characterized by its paucity and its narrow approach" (138). Scholars have answered that call for more extensive study, and scholarship written in English on Great Britain and North America—the focus of this chapter—is flourishing. Following a brief historical overview, I will first discuss the state of primary texts, then review secondary scholarship, and conclude by considering future directions.

Overview

In the British Isles and North America, the eighteenth century was a time of colonial exploration, expansion, and rebellion; a time of rethinking and refiguring political arrangements by way of Acts of Union, the U.S. Constitution, and the Federalist Papers; of innovation and development of natural resources to aid industrialization; of the emergence of a middle class with a chance for mobility; of enslaving, selling, and purchasing some humans while freeing others from the impositions of class; of innovation in science, technology, and medicine; of competition between religious tolerance and intolerance; of wealth and poverty; of great or little opportunity to study—or none at all.

Given such diversity, what can be said about the century's rhetorical education and practice? Individual oral performances remained vital in many public forums, ensuring that boys and men of means continued to study political speeches, religious sermons, legal presentations, and the like. Ancient and modern oratory retained a secure place in the curriculum. With the advent of better and cheaper means of composing, printing, and distributing texts, writing became customary in business, government, and society. Concomitantly, attention to textual reception expanded, and theory and instruction paid growing attention to analysis and interpretation. As access to written texts broadened, Latin and Greek, long esteemed in the West as the languages of learning, loosened their stranglehold on curriculum (elite schools excepted), and English became an object of formal study. These changes both resulted *from* and resulted *in* shifts in economic, political, and societal power and, in turn, created sizeable markets for the study of rhetoric, leading to remarkable productivity in rhetorical theory and pedagogy. Because the goal of instruction was primarily proficiency in oral discourse, writing was practiced as scripting for speech.

Who studied rhetoric? As before, those who aspired to be political leaders, legal advocates, men of learning, and men of the cloth did, and they were joined by increasing numbers of gentlewomen and gentlemen, and, of course, the teachers, tutors, and governesses responsible for instructing them at home or at sundry educational institutions. Individuals—indeed whole factions—sought to improve themselves academically, culturally, and economically. Across Europe, interest in education, both formal and informal, swelled. Books and periodicals, schools and universities, clubs and societies, public lectures and personal correspondence flourished as means of national and self-improvement, and access to education expanded across class and gender, though not racial lines. However, democratization of opportunity left most of the poor untouched, a condition scholars of rhetoric have been slow to acknowledge.

In the latter half of the eighteenth century, Scotland, hailed as the Athens of the North for its role in the Enlightenment, was a site and stimulus for major shifts in Western epistemology, and hence of rhetorical theory. An effect of the Scientific Revolution, Enlightenment perspectives emphasized the rationality of a world in which people were endowed with the faculty of reason to study, understand, order, and improve their physical, political, cultural, and psychological universes. Careful observation and inductive reasoning were the order of the day. Political and economic theory, epistemology, pedagogy, communication—indeed the nature of language itself—became vital areas for rethinking rhetoric, the individual, and society.

A key figure was David Hume, who maintained that humans could know only what can be gathered from experience, itself limited by the capacity of the human mind. On one hand, basic institutions came under scrutiny; on the other, religious dictates still wielded power during this time of intellectual daring, and freethinkers sometimes paid a high price. Hume's skepticism so unsettled and outraged some of the devout, for example, that he was censored, condemned, and tried in court. Fellow Scotsman George Campbell corresponded with Hume in hope of proving the reasonableness of religious faith, and fellow Scotsman Hugh Blair rallied others to affirm Hume's right to free inquiry. Both Campbell and Blair, rhetoricians who will be discussed below, were respected clergy who stood for what was most admirable in the eighteenth century: spirited and open debate about fundamental issues.

Moral philosophers sought to construct theories of values or principles congruent with their new understandings and beliefs in order to guide people as individuals and as a collective to live ethical lives. In so doing, they explored, in both particular and general ways, the roles of knowledge, happiness, and wealth. Ethics is philosophy with practical implications, and in a period pushing the boundaries of the human and social sciences, it was manifestly interdisciplinary.

In the eighteenth century, aesthetics too was linked to cognition, though taste's precise relationship to emotion or reason varied. At the century's beginning, Joseph Addison popularized the belief that fine criticism (as well as fine arts and letters) inspired the pleasures of the human imagination. Even Hume affirmed a theory of taste whose rules are knowable: "Strong sense, united to delicate sentiment, improved by practice, perfected by comparison, and cleared of all prejudice" (147). Taste resides neither in the object perceived nor in the perceiver; rather it is the "impression" (Hume) or the "idea" (Francis Hutcheson) that results in the perceiver. For others like Blair, taste is a faculty inherent in all people. Taste is related to "sentiment" or "feeling," which in the view of many Enlightenment thinkers helps one to discriminate and motivate ethical behavior. The claim that all humans possess this inner sense in some fashion had startlingly democratic implications: judgments about matters of taste could be proven empirically over time and thus be studied. Although theories differed significantly in particulars, rather diverse thinkers concurred that rhetorical education must be reformed. Father of laissez-faire economics and author of *An Inquiry into the Nature and Causes of the Wealth of Nations* (1776), Adam Smith maintained that language must be understood and improved as a means of maintaining individual and societal well-being. By century's end, however, Immanuel Kant had severed aesthetic judgments from moral judgments.

These opening generalizations cannot convey the complex theories and diverse matters preoccupying the eighteenth century. They should, however, suggest why the period proved a climate rich for the study and practice of rhetoric.

The State of Primary Texts

Most canonical texts are available.* The unabridged edition of George Campbell's *Philosophy of Rhetoric,* edited by Lloyd Bitzer (1963), is a facsimile of the 1850 London edition, which is faithful to the 1776 first edition. Hugh Blair's *Lectures on Rhetoric and Belles Lettres,* edited by Linda Ferreira-Buckley and S. Michael Halloran (2005), uses the 1785 London edition, which includes corrections Blair made to the 1783 first edition. Adam Smith's *Lectures on Rhetoric and Belles Letters,* lost to scholars before John M. Lothian's 1958 discovery of student notes at an Aberdeen auction, is edited by J. C. Bryce (1983). Joseph Priestley's *A Course of Lectures on Oratory and Criticism* (1777) has been published recently in facsimile form (2007). Others have been out for decades, including John Lawson's *Lectures Concerning Oratory,* edited by E. Neal Claussen and Karl L. Wallace (1963), and *Thomas Sheridan: A Discourse, Being Introductory to His Course of Lectures on Elocution and the English Language* (1759), introduced by G. P. Mohrmann (1969). Most include helpful introductions and ancillary materials. These and many other rhetorics are often available from multiple publishers.

Some volumes comprise related texts from a single author. For example, Thomas P. Miller's *The Selected Writings of John Witherspoon* (1990) brings together eight selections from the 1802 American edition of Witherspoon's work, including his lectures on eloquence and on moral philosophy, which Witherspoon, a former classmate of Blair's at Edinburgh, delivered as president of Princeton. Read together, these lectures make plain the inextricable connection that the Scots drew between rhetoric and moral philosophy and should serve as a caution against reading rhetorics in isolation.

---

* The question of what is "in print"—once easily answered by checking *Books in Print*—is now vexed. Publishers occasionally choose to hold in reserve (and thus refrain from reporting) some books in their inventory. This practice may not be new, of course. What is new, however, is that books not officially "in print" (new *or* used) are easily located online from booksellers across the globe. In addition, many volumes are easily accessed online.

Histories of rhetoric must also take stock of the scores of works that apply "empirical" methods to the study of aesthetics. Texts critical to understanding the period's rhetoric include *Characteristics of Men, Manners, Opinions, Times* (1711) by Anthony Ashley Cooper, Lord Shaftesbury; *An Inquiry into the Original of Our Ideas of Beauty and Virtue* (1725) by Francis Hutcheson, a professor at the University of Glasgow who inspired such thinkers as Adam Smith and Thomas Reid; and the influential three-volume *Elements of Criticism* (1762) by Henry Holmes, Lord Kames, the influential Scottish judge who arranged for public lectures to be delivered by Smith and Blair. These and other texts are available in several editions, and many are excerpted in anthologies of rhetoric or aesthetics.

Two long volumes of several thousand pages warrant mention: John V. Price's *British Rhetoric in the Eighteenth Century* (2001) and Carol Poster's *The Elocutionary Movement* (2003). Both include an impressive number of works and authors, the latter in facsimile. Books of British and Continental rhetoric continue to be available on microfilm reels through University Microfilms International. James Irvine (1995) lists and locates the eighteenth-century British and Continental rhetoric and elocution books available in the microfilm collection prepared by the Speech Association of America, a service to scholars navigating the collection.

Primary texts written by women are more difficult to find. Jane Donawerth's 2002 *Rhetorical Theory by Women before 1900: An Anthology* includes excerpts from writing and rhetoric texts, conduct books, letter-writing manuals, and conversation guides, for example. General anthologies of rhetoric often include a few selections, often by Mary Astell and Mary Wollstonecraft. Recovering such work should be a clear priority in the years ahead.

The period's material artifacts, including books and manuscripts, deserve more attention. The tables in Ian Michael's *The Teaching of English: From the Sixteenth Century to 1870* (2005) locate at least one library holding original volumes, a help to scholars unable to track down a book, and many textbooks are readily available in libraries and secondhand bookshops. Scholars should now discriminate *between* and *within* schools of rhetoric. Comparing textbooks, for example, will reveal how theory is retained, reshaped, and deleted in introductions, ancillary materials, and main texts. Drawing such distinctions—as Ferreira-Buckley and Halloran have done with the many published versions of Blair's belletristic rhetoric, for instance—will sharpen our historical understanding of influential thinkers. Future scholarship should take up prepublication notes and materials, such as those listed in James Irvine and G. J. Gravelee's "Hugh Blair: A Select Bibliography of Manuscripts in Scottish Archives" (1983). To be sure, significant original materials available for examination in the manuscript collections of universities, libraries, and historical societies are underused and often unknown. Thomas P. Miller's "The Formation of College English: A Survey of the Archives of Eighteenth-Century Rhetorical Theory and Practice" (2000) and James Irvine's "Rhetoric and Moral Philosophy: A Selected Inventory of Student Notes and Dictates in Scottish Archives" (1983) point the way.

There is no systematic accounting of the period's speeches. Many anthologies include samplings of eighteenth-century rhetorical practices, often with brief introductions or commentary. Among the best is Barbara Alice Mann's *Native American Speakers of the Eastern Woodlands* (2001), which contains the words of male and female native speakers, preserved in or translated into English, accompanied by critical essays that historicize them. They should dispel lingering stereotypes of undeveloped civilizations. A few anthologies include texts still not widely known: for example, *The Wisdom of the Native Americans* (1999), edited by Kent Nerburn; *Indian Oratory: Famous Speeches by Noted Indian Chieftains* (1971), compiled by W. C. Vanderwerth; and *The Voice of Black America: Major Speeches by Negroes in the United States, 1797–1973* (1975), edited by Philip S. Foner. The speeches in Ronald F. Reid and James F. Klumpp's (2004) massive anthology *American Rhetorical Discourse,* now in its third edition, illustrate the role of public discourse, and a few focus on the eighteenth century. *Black Atlantic Writers of the Eighteenth Century: Living the New Exodus in England and the Americas* (1995), edited by Adam Potkay and Sandra Burr, presents facsimiles of a sermon and four narratives published in the last decades of the century by Ottobah Cugoano, Olaudah Equiano, Ukawsaw Gronniosaw, and John Marrant.

Research must continue to thrive at places like the U.S. National Archives (www.archives.gov) and the Schomburg Center for Research in Black Culture (including its strong eighteenth-century rare book collection), and also at countless smaller, out-of-the-way sites. Guides such as Dorothy B. Porter's "Early American Negro Writings: A Bibliographical Study" (1945) point scholars to less well-known locations. Online resources, such as americanrhetoric.com's Online Speech Bank, though not vetted by scholars, can be useful.

One final note. Editions of many texts can also be found online. For example, the Glasgow edition of the works of Adam Smith can be accessed in facsimile PDF, HTML, and in e-book PDF format at the Online Library of Liberty (search http://oll.libertyfund.org/index.php). Texts of rhetorics and rhetorical practices are increasingly posted online by researchers and programs whose work will surely broaden and deepen accounts of eighteenth-century rhetoric. A few cautions: Not all of these texts are reproduced accurately, and few specify their source. Finally, scholars should remain mindful of what can be learned from handling and studying the material artifacts themselves.

Additional sources, mentioned below, point scholars to other primary works. In short, archival tools are scattered, and there exists no systematic accounting.

Our histories will remain incomplete and, frankly, misleading, until we study the rhetorical practices of all those who have spoken and written in Great Britain and North America.

The Scholarship

The reach of eighteenth-century Scotland—home of the Scottish Enlightenment—extended over land and across oceans, influencing all aspects of society, including rhetorical practice and theory. The essays collected in Jennifer J. Carter and Joan H. Pittock's *Aberdeen and the Enlightenment* (1987) remain essential for their insight into the theoretical (for example, humor and linguistic theory) and the material (printing and the book trade). Richard B. Sher's *Church and University in the Scottish Enlightenment: The Moderate Literati of Edinburgh* (1985) offers a sophisticated account of the period's essential thinkers—"the moderate literati"—by viewing them "within an international framework of values and beliefs while still allowing for the uniqueness of the Scottish experience" (11).

The eighteenth century was an age of public lectures and private study societies. Peter Clark's *British Clubs and Societies, 1580–1800* (2000) chronicles and analyzes a broader range—from those for bird-watching to those for public speaking—of such institutions in England, Ireland, Scotland, and Wales, with some consideration of institutions in the British colonies. Davis Dunbar McElroy's well-known *Scotland's Age of Improvement: A Survey of Eighteenth-Century Literary Clubs and Societies* (1969) remains essential reading for historians of rhetoric. Other texts examine the transatlantic migration of these cultural practices. David S. Shield's *Civil Tongues and Polite Letters in British America* (1997), for example, establishes such private venues as clubs and coffeehouses, salons and societies, and taverns and tea tables as sites for practicing and studying civil discourse and refined manners. Unfortunately, the proceedings of nearly all of these nontraditional institutions remain unpublished and unexamined. A valuable exception is H. Lewis Ulman's edition (1990) of the rules, proposed questions, and minutes of the Aberdeen Philosophical Society from its founding in 1758 through 1773, which illustrates the critical significance of such forums. Its six founding and nine additional members typified well-rounded public intellectuals conversant across disciplines: They were professors of divinity, moral philosophy, philosophy, mathematics, oriental languages, humanity, Hebrew, logic, civil and natural history; they were also ministers, physicians, poets, and administrators. The society's minutes capture the conversation that gave rise to the period's signal works, among them Thomas Reid's *An Inquiry into the Human Mind, on the Principles of Common Sense* (1764), George Campbell's *Philosophy of Rhetoric* (1776), Alexander Gerard's

An Essay on Taste (1759) and *An Essay on Genius* (1774), and James Beattie's many essays.

Substantial foundational work still remains to make visible the contexts that shaped and were shaped by the period's rhetorics. Older works like Margaret Lee Wiley's *Gerard and the Scots Societies* (1940) and, more recently, Neil Campbell and his colleagues' *The Royal Society of Edinburgh* (1983) point out avenues for future study. So do current online resources such as the Scholarly Societies Project (www.scholarly-societies.org) sponsored by the University of Waterloo, from which charters, minutes, membership lists, and archives across the globe can be located.

Of the general histories of the period's rhetorics, only one is book length. Wilbur Samuel Howell's *Eighteenth-Century British Logic and Rhetoric,* first published by Princeton in 1971 and reissued by the Thoemmes Library in 2004, remains essential reading, in part because until recently its account was largely unchallenged. Howell notes the presence of classical rhetoric and deductive logic in the rhetorics of John Holmes, John Ward, and many others, but characterizes the "New Rhetoric" of (especially) Smith, Campbell, and Blair as breaking ties with the classical tradition. In Howell's view, the New Rhetoric's general theory of communication and its inductive approach to theory building, coupled with the elocutionary movement's diminution of rhetoric, caused the demise of rhetoric, a view that is now challenged. Articles like Douglas Ehninger's 1952 "Dominant Trends in English Rhetorical Thought, 1750–1800" offer helpful overviews, as do chapters in broader historical surveys such as Thomas M. Conley's *Rhetoric in the European Tradition* (1990). Two chapters from Renato Barilli's *Rhetoric* (1989)—"Early Modernity" (Descartes, Bacon, Vico) and "Modernity" (Kant, Hegel, Romanticism)—are especially helpful for understanding how eighteenth-century rhetoric emerged from philosophical concerns of the late seventeenth and eighteenth centuries.

Other work focuses on individuals. Michael G. Moran's edited collection *Eighteenth-Century British and American Rhetorics and Rhetoricians: Critical Studies and Sources* (1994) provides helpful chapters on key figures. Beth Innocenti Manolescu (2007) looks at Kames's criticism of Shakespeare as "rational science." Maintaining that scholars are inclined to a disciplinary myopia that predisposes them to misread eighteenth-century thinkers, Manolescu (2003) argues that *Elements of Criticism* is connected inextricably to Kames's legal training and practice, both arising from his views on humans and natural law. Stephen J. McKenna (2005) also examines Kames's legal career and writing as precedents to *Elements.*

Arguing that Adam Smith's approach to understanding society was essentially rhetorical, McKenna's book-length study *Adam Smith: The Rhetoric of Propriety* (2005) centers on the complex theory of propriety as both "the stylistic virtue that wins audience sympathy by communicating correctly, clearly, and appropriately," as manifest in Smith's *Lectures on Rhetoric* and "the mode of action that wins the approval of an internal audience—the 'impartial spectator' of conscience" in his *Theory of Moral Sentiments* (1759). Charles L. Griswold Jr. (1995) maintains that an abiding concern with rhetoric shaped Smith's economic and ethical theories. A. M. Endres (1991) argues that Smith's rhetoric lectures shaped the form and content of *Wealth of Nations*. Arthur M. Diamond Jr. and David M. Levy (1994) employ stylistic metrics derived from Smith to analyze ninety-seven American Economic Association keynote addresses. Srividhya Swaminathan (2007) argues that antiabolitionists, struck by the abolitionists' skillful use of Smith's economic and compositional theories, also turned to Smith to frame their message. Jack Russell Weinstein (2003) maintains that Smith's theory of argumentation, rhetorically based in human emotion and situational context, anticipates what is today studied as informal logic. William M. Purcell (1986) disagrees, however, maintaining that Smith's rhetoric is lodged in its time.

Arthur E. Walzer's *George Campbell: Rhetoric in the Age of Enlightenment* (2002) is the first book-length study of Campbell, one of the age's most complex and influential rhetorical theorists. It lays out a historical and philosophical framework to offer rich analyses of *Philosophy of Rhetoric* (1776), *Dissertation on Miracles* (1762), and *Lectures on Pulpit Eloquence* (1807). Lois Agnew's "The 'Perplexity' of George Campbell's Rhetoric: The Epistemic Function of Common Sense" (2000) examines Campbell's philosophical affinity with Aristotle and the Stoics as evidence of an epistemic function, rather than that of the strictly managerial function scholars have long claimed. Walzer, "On Reading George Campbell: 'Resemblance' and 'Vivacity' in the Philosophy of Rhetoric" (2000), illustrates how the treatise's terminology shifts meaning over the twenty-five years the text was composed.

Scientist and influential educator Joseph Priestly merits further scholarly attention. Ann L. George's 1998 examination of *A Course of Lectures on Oratory and Criticism* begins to redress the neglect by showing how Priestley's religious and philosophical foundations, developed during a particularly fraught time in English history, fueled a theory of rational argument quite distinct from the Scots' rhetorical thinking. Some of Priestly's other works, including *A Course of Lectures on the Theory of Language and Universal Grammar* (1762) and *Essay on a Course of Liberal Education for Civil and Active Life* (1765), offer historians insight into education at Warrington Academy. Carey McIntosh (2000) examines the rhetorical theory taught more broadly at dissenting academies.

Other scholars have studied non-British roots of modern rhetoric. Barbara Warnick's *The Sixth Canon: Belletristic Rhetorical Theory and Its French Antecedents* (1993) explores rhetoric's aesthetics roots in seventeenth- and eighteenth-century French belletristic theory, primarily those of Bernard Lamy, Charles Rollin, and François Fénelon. (Peter France's 1972 collection of essays, *Rhetoric and Truth in France: Descartes to Diderot*, had established the pervasiveness of the discipline there.) Catherine L. Hobbs (2002) looks to Scotland as well as to Italy and France to broaden eighteenth-century rhetorical materials. Her thoroughgoing analyses of the works of Giambattista Vico, Étienne de Condillac, and James Burnett, Lord Monboddo, make plain that understanding rhetoric requires examining all the communication arts, including accounts of the origins and development of language.

Recent work like Leo Catana's *Vico and Literary Mannerism: A Study in the Early Vico and His Idea of Rhetoric* (1999) establishes a critical place in rhetorical theory for Giambattista Vico. The essays in Ernesto Grassi's *Vico and Humanism: Essays on Vico, Heidegger, and Rhetoric* (1990) argue that Vico's theory of metaphor and imagination realigns the relationship between rhetoric and philosophy. John Schaeffer (1997) argues that Vico has been misinterpreted by scholars who maintain that he classifies primitive religious experience as either poetic or rhetoric. Michael Mooney's *Vico in the Tradition of Rhetoric* (1985) focuses on Vico's insistence in the *New Science* that language, mind, and society/culture are all forms of the same reality—the world of man or *monde civile*. Mooney focuses on rhetoric, pedagogy, and culture to make the case that Vico revitalized traditional theories, thus making possible nineteenth-century social theory. Nancy S. Struever challenges Mooney's interpretation, seeing Vico emerging instead from the Sophistic tradition. John Shaeffer (1990) shows how Vico works within the humanist rhetorical tradition to integrate Greek and Roman notions of *sensus communis* to fashion a complex theory of knowledge as both ethical judgment and linguistic consensus. Political theorist Carlo Bonura (2002) argues that Vico's and Aristotle's use of "location" in rhetoric offers profound insights into concepts of political community. Scholars will continue to reexamine Vico's corpus, especially to discern the role of rhetoric in formulating society's practical ethics.

Recent work debates Immanuel Kant's place in rhetorical history. Does Kant continue to deem rhetoric "a deceitful art," as he does in *Critique of the Power of Judgment* (1790)? Pat J. Gehrke (2002) faults communication scholars for failing to recognize the ethical role Kant attributes to rhetorical communities, but Scott R. Stroud (2006) in turn faults Gehrke for failing to account for Kant's corpus. Stroud (2005) traces Kant's initial account of ethical communities in *Groundwork for the Metaphysics of Morals* (1785) through his struggle to understand the formation of communities of self-governing moral agents in his late ethical, aesthetic, and political writings. In contrast, Don Paul Abbott (2007) argues that, taken as a whole, Kant's work subordinates rhetoric to poetry and philosophy and thus "prepares the way for the Romantic assault on rhetoric and the nineteenth-century fragmentation of the classical conception of rhetoric" (274). Abbott also recounts Protestant theologian Franz Theremin's sharp defense of rhetoric in the largely ignored *Eloquence a Virtue* (1814).

What was the relation among the terms *rhetoric, eloquence, belles lettres,* and *literature?* Were they competing? Complementary? Overlapping? Interchangeable? Answers differ by theorist (and occasionally within a theorist's corpus), but by midcentury some generalizations obtain; the following definitions come from the online edition of the second edition of the *OED Online,* beginning with the entry for *belles lettres:* "Elegant or polite literature or literary studies. A vaguely-used term, formerly taken sometimes in the wide sense of 'the humanities,' *literæ humaniores.*" The term *literature* was similarly vague: "'letters' or books; polite or humane learning." The term *rhetoric* was "Elegance or eloquence of language; eloquent speech or writing," and *eloquence* was "The action, practice, or art of expressing thought with fluency, force, and appropriateness, so as to appeal to the reason or move the feelings." These terms must be read as overlapping parts of a constellation.

Differences existed *among* the belles lettres, of course. Scholars continue to understand the shifting relationship between "rhetoric" and "poetry." Two classic studies—P. W. K. Stone, *The Art of Poetry, 1750–1820* (1967), and Meyer Howard Abrams, *The Mirror and the Lamp: Romantic Theory and the Critical Tradition* (1971)—remain a starting point for understanding the relationship. Until a few decades ago, scholars considered eighteenth-century rhetoric as moribund: stripped of invention and overly formulaic, it could not help but be scorned; its stranglehold on criticism was pernicious until rescued by the Romantics. (A complementary narrative also took hold: rhetoric's pronounced attention to analysis led to an impoverished pedagogy of composition.) Such accounts have proven overly simplistic. For example, Liam McIlvanney, in "Hugh Blair, Robert Burns, and the Invention of Scottish Literature" (2005), examines the commonplace book and letters of Burns to argue against David Daiches, Robert Crawford, and others who represent Burns's relationship with Blair "as the symbol of a literary culture dichotomized between vigorous vernacular poets and effete Anglicizing critics"—a relationship "emblematic of a radical and damaging fissure in eighteenth-century Scottish culture, a profound gulf between native and metropolitan trends, and between creative and critical endeavor" (26). Burns's private writing and correspondence make clear, however, that Burns respected Blair's judgment and appreciated his public support, despite Burns's frustration with the elder's class biases.

Scholars, following W. S. Howell, have generally passed over the implications of Herman Cohen's 1958 assertion that Blair is a Pre-Romantic who provides a critical segue between neoclassical and Romantic theories of composition and reception. Don H. Bialostosky and Lawrence D. Needham's 1995 collection,

Rhetorical Traditions and British Romantic Literature, is a welcome exception. By showing how rhetoric, especially classical and enlightenment rhetorics, influenced Romantic poetry, prose, and criticism, its essays disprove the claim that rhetoric and poetic were no longer linked at the end of the eighteenth and beginning of the nineteenth centuries. This book merits more attention than it has received. Lorna Clymer's "Graved in Tropes: The Figural Logic of Epitaphs and Elegies in Blair, Gray, Cowper, and Wordsworth" (1995) also analyzes the use of figural language—in this case to show how classical distinctions between *prosopopoeia* and *apostrophe* offer insight into Romantic composition.

What role did rhetoric, especially belletristic rhetoric, have in the formation of English studies? The essays in Robert Crawford's edited collection *The Scottish Invention of English Literature* (1998) establish Scottish institutions, practice, and theory as the provenance of the academic discipline of English literature. Neil Rhodes's "From Rhetoric to Criticism" offers an erudite account of the lineage of Scottish rhetoric, as well as of the subjects to which it gives rise, while Ian Duncan's "Adam Smith, Samuel Johnson, and the Institutions of English," looks closely at the period itself to see how the discipline forms. Paul Bator (1996, 1997) explains how the novel and romance come into the academy only after the discipline of rhetoric shifts attention from the production of oral argumentative discourse to the analysis of written texts. Scholars have also begun to explore how rhetoric has shaped fiction and poetry. Nancy Struever (1985) shows how eighteenth-century changes in rhetoric from public truth to private virtue are manifested in the novels of Jane Austen. Arthur E. Walzer (1995) reads Austen's *Persuasion* in light of contemporary rhetorical theory. By tracing how Hume's ideas register in the poetry of Thomas Gray, Alexander Pope, and James Macpherson and the novels of Stern, Adam Potkay's *The Fate of Eloquence in the Age of Hume* (1994) shows how a culture of politeness supplanted British dedication to political eloquence.

These rhetorics had special appeal in geographic, cultural, and institutional places outside sanctioned cultural authority. In *The Formation of College English: Rhetoric and Belles Lettres in the British Cultural Provinces* (1997), Thomas P. Miller argues that English studies evolved from professorships in rhetoric in dissenting academies and universities across the British cultural provinces, where the vernacular was valued and taught, in marked contrast to Oxbridge, which held on firmly to Latin and Greek and the trivium. Ferreira-Buckley (1998) makes the point that cultural outsiders included the new economic elite in London itself. The essays in Gaillet's 1998 collection, *Scottish Rhetoric and Its Influences*, establish the long reach of Enlightenment rhetorical theory and practice in Britain and America. (Indeed, this influence extends well beyond 1800, as works like Horner's *Nineteenth-Century Scottish Rhetoric: The American Connection* [1993] make clear.)

Education

Scholars continue to argue about whether and how the decline in classical rhetoric entailed a diminished engagement in civic issues. Did, as Neil Rhodes (1998) put it, the "art of speaking well" "dwindle . . . to the art of being well spoken" (32)? Michael Halloran (1983) discusses how the American desire for democratic participation led American colleges to train students to compose orations about matters of public concern and to do so in the vernacular rather than in the Greek and Latin required in British schools. Halloran bemoans the passing of this focus on classical rhetoric in favor of the nineteenth-century propensity for language study that favored professional advancement over public service. Mark Garrett Longaker, in *Rhetoric and the Republic: Politics, Civic Discourse, and Education in Early America* (2007), examines the economic, political, and religious views that sought to define citizenship and thus drove the formation of early American curriculums. Elizabethada A. Wright and S. Michael Halloran (2001) overview how rhetoric shaped writing instruction in America. E. Jennifer Monaghan's *Learning to Read and Write in Colonial America* (2005) offers a textured account of how children were taught to read and write, avoiding generalizations that ignore differences of race, ethnicity, class, locale, religion, and gender. Her analysis distinguishes among the educational experiences of the children of enslaved Africans, American Indians, and Europeans as well as between formal and informal schooling.

Ferreira-Buckley and Horner (2001) survey how rhetoric shaped writing instruction in Great Britain. Russell M. Wyland's "An Archival Study of Rhetoric Texts and Teaching at the University of Oxford, 1785–1820" (2003) offers a close examination of the teaching of rhetoric to young men at Oxford, where the study of classical rhetoric remained in place, even as new rhetorics took hold elsewhere. Thomas P. Miller (1997), mentioned earlier, analyzes how rhetoric developed in the cultural provinces. Far less is known about female education. Janet Carey Eldred and Peter Mortensen's *Imagining Rhetoric: Composing Women of the Early United States* (2002) examines women's writing pedagogy and practice, asserting that women considered literacy a means to civic engagement. Tania Sona Smith (2004) points out that early in the period, few books targeted females, and those that did prepared them for conventional female roles. The British *The Lady's Rhetorick* (1707) is a rare exception that draws on classical and French rhetorical traditions to promote women as effective rhetors by offering substantial instruction and daring examples of female practice.

Elocution

Attention to rhetoric's fifth canon was revived by the elocutionary movement. Books teaching the subject were published and reissued, pirated, and reprinted elsewhere in Great Britain and were eventually translated into local vernaculars in continental Europe, in South and North America, and beyond. These texts, which ranged from a few dozen pages to over five hundred, were variously substantial, thin, original, or derivative and treated one or more topics, including voice, posture, gesture, diction, reading, oral interpretation, preaching, acting, oratory, and linguistics. Some included an anthology of readings. A few of the titles of the scores of these texts suggest elocution's diversity and scope: J. Henley's *Oratory transactions; to be occasionally publish'd* (London, 1728); William Cockin's *The art of delivering written language; or, An essay on reading; in which the subject is treated philosophically as well as with a view to practice* (London, 1775); Richard Polwhele's *The English Orator: A Didactic Poem* (Exeter, 1785); James Burgh's *The Art of Speaking: containing I. An essay; in which are given rules for expressing properly the principal passions and humours which occur in reading or public speaking; and II. Lessons taken from the antients and moderns (with additions and alterations, where thought useful) exhibiting a variety of matter for practice; the emphatical words printed in italics; with notes of direction referring to the Essay . . .* (London, 1761); William Enfield's *The speaker: or, miscellaneous pieces, selected from the best English writers, and disposed under proper heads, with a view to facilitate the improvement of youth in reading and speaking. To which is prefixed an essay on elocution* (London, 1774). A few indigenous North American productions were published in the eighteenth century, among them Noah Webster's *An American selection of lessons in reading and speaking: Calculated to improve the minds and refine the taste of youth. And also to instruct them in the geography, history, and politics of the United States: To which are prefixed, rules in elocution, and directions for expressing the principal passions of the mind* (1792).

Scholars have paid scant attention to the movement, and much of that is dismissive. There are exceptions, however. William Benzie's (1972) *The Dublin Orator: Thomas Sheridan's Influence on Eighteenth Century Rhetoric and Belles Lettres* remains one of few books devoted to elocution. More recently, articles like Philippa M. Spoel's 2001 "Rereading the Elocutionists: The Rhetoric of Thomas Sheridan's *A Course of Lectures on Elocution* and John Walker's *Elements of Elocution*" reevaluate the movement. Madeleine Forell Marshall (2007) examines the Reverend W. Faulkner's *Sheridan's Strictures on Reading the Church-Service; with the notes, regularly annexed, and proper references,* a book that aims to improve the clergy's reading of the liturgy. Marshall maintains that Faulkner's work provides a rare record of "educated public speech as 'reading' in the late eighteenth century" (35). Paul C. Edwards investigates Shakespeare's dominance over the reading selections featured in eighteenth-century elocutionary texts to gauge the period's literary taste.

Benjamin Rush's medical teachings influenced American letters of the early Republic and antebellum periods, a time when, as Etta M. Madden (2006) explains, "the roles of author, physician, and man of science were merged" (242). She examines Rush's publications and accounts of delivering lectures and "performances" with patients to explain how Rush consciously marshaled rhetorical resources to establish and maintain his authority and how, in turn, these experiences shaped his scientific theories. Andrew McCann (2001) explores how political activist and orator John Thelwall helped to form a proletarian public sphere; in McCann's reading, the moral-aesthetic sensibility of Romanticism uses the "therapeutic practice" of elocution to "refashion" individuals for an engaged public life (215). As these articles suggest, research on elocution can move well beyond the realm of pedagogy to reveal other aspects of eighteenth-century life. Given the movement's variety, influence, and longevity, elocution deserves more scholarly attention.

Language

Understanding the nature, function, and use of a period's rhetorics requires understanding the period's linguistic attitudes. The age's penchant for observing, documenting, categorizing, understanding, and systematizing phenomena gave rise to grammars, dictionaries, and manuals of various sorts that often prescribed spelling, meaning, pronunciation, and usage. George Campbell understood that because language inevitably changes over time, so too must the rules that govern it; as he put it, usage must be national, reputable, and present. In this view, correctness was to be determined not by the elite few but by broader social use. Not surprisingly, most rhetorics proffered more conservative dictates, many professing the need to establish and propagate a national standard language across the British Isles or North America. In *Things, Thoughts, Words, and Actions: The Problem of Language in Late Eighteenth-Century British Rhetorical Theory* (1994), H. Lewis Ulman examines the role of language theory in the work of Campbell, Blair, and Sheridan, discussing its effects on their theories of grammar, rhetoric, style, criticism, and elocution. Ulman underscores how the problem of language emerges from particular epistemological challenges quite different from those of the twentieth century. Linda C. Mitchell's *Grammar Wars: Language as Cultural Battlefield in 17th and 18th Century England* (2002) provides a thoroughgoing examination of issues emerging from contemporary grammars.

Of course, many works discussed elsewhere in this chapter also take up issues of language, but scholars will also want to consult histories of language, many of which are written from a rhetorical perspective. Books by Tony Crowley (2003), Lynda Mugglestone (2007), and Ali Smith and Olivia Smith (1990), for example, explain how class politics motivated standardization, showing whose language served as the standard and whose was deemed inferior. Adam R. Beach (2001) reviews attempts to standardize language following the unsuccessful

Jacobite rebellion of 1745, after which the "Scottish" became "British" and both Highlanders and Lowlanders were encouraged to abandon Scots. Thomas Sheridan hoped that his manuals and lectures would, when paired with Samuel Johnson's *Dictionary,* help the Irish, Scots, and Welsh master the English many thought vital to national unity. Nicholas Hudson (1998) argues that current work oversimplifies the linguistic attitudes of Johnson and thus distorts historical understanding. Indeed, changes were not always decorous. Janet Sorensen (2004) follows the growing acceptance of cant and vulgar languages in Britain as they are recorded in canting dictionaries: At the beginning of the eighteenth century, using cant and slang marked the speaker as belonging to the criminal class; by the end, its use was hailed as a sign of freedom that created a rhetorical space for males of the lower classes.

Forms of Rhetoric

J. M. Bradbury (2003), in "New Science and the 'New Species of Writing': Eighteenth-Century Prose Genres," argues that the rhetorics of Campbell and Smith expanded prospects for classifying and explicating prose works. Conversely, Bruce G. Carruthers and Wendy Nelson Espeland (1991), drawing on sociological research on writing and literacy, maintain that in the eighteenth century, double-entry bookkeeping is itself a "new" rhetoric, conveying a sense of rationality as it functions to persuade others about business interests, thereby ushering in capitalism. Roger D. Lund (1998) argues for Daniel Defoe's place in the history of business communication. Darin Payne, in "Effacing Difference in the Royal Society: The Homogenizing Nature of Disciplinary Dialogue" (2001), studies *The Philosophical Transactions of the Royal Society* to ferret out how its discourse represents the construction and transmission of scientific knowledge in the seventeenth and eighteenth centuries.

But what of other forms of writing? The epistolary form flourished in the eighteenth-century. Bruce Redford, in *The Converse of the Pen: Acts of Intimacy in the Eighteenth-Century Familiar Letter* (1986), explores the "talking" letter as an artful form in which such writers as James Boswell, William Cowper, Thomas Gray, Samuel Johnson, Lady Mary Wortley Montagu, and Horace Walpole cultivated a performative act that seems to capture voice and movement. Letter-writing manuals, many of which were repeatedly reprinted in Great Britain and America during the eighteenth century, were major vehicles for instruction in rhetoric, schooling users in audience, occasion, purpose, style, voice, decorum, and conduct. Linda C. Mitchell (2007) investigates the instruction such manuals offer in rhetoric and grammar. Eve Tavor Bannet (2007) examines "what letter manuals can tell us about the dynamic interactions between manuscript and print, and on those aspects of these interactions which made manuscript and print cultures on both sides of the Atlantic collaborative, co-dependent and unexpectedly homologous effects of the same distinctive eighteenth-century practices of speaking, reading, collecting and inditing" (15). (Eighteenth-century letters collected in Linda C. Mitchell and Susan Green's anthology, *Studies in the Cultural History of Letter Writing* [2007], examine the forms and function of the art.)

Aesthetics

In 1976, Vincent M. Bevilacqua attributes the eighteenth-century unification of the fine arts to classical rhetorical theory's assumption that they share "common artistic means, precepts, and effects" (11). John Poulakas (2007) argues that classical rhetoric is a primary source in the formation of eighteenth-century aesthetics. Scholars in the fine arts have long, if not consistently, explored that relationship. Updating the still-helpful work of Paul Oskar Kristeller's "The Modern System of the Arts: A Study in the History of Aesthetics" (1951), H. James Jensen's *Signs and Meaning in Eighteenth-Century Art: Epistemology, Rhetoric, Painting, Poesy, Music, Dramatic Performance, and G. F. Handel* (1976) explains the rhetorical basis for art as understood by the era's artists and audiences. Jensen's discussion of Handel's oratorios illustrates how, grounded in common epistemological assumptions, they shared signs that allow meaning to be communicated. Marguerite Helmers (2004) maintains that today's visual rhetorical tradition has roots in the eighteenth-century aesthetic tradition, which posits a transactional relationship among viewer, art, and artist. In *Wordless Rhetoric: Musical Form and the Metaphor of the Oration* (1991), Mark Evans Bonds connects eighteenth-century music to theories of eloquence. G. G. Butler's "Fugue and Rhetoric" (2007) likewise explores the prevailing "musical-rhetorical concept of augmentation." H. F. Fullenwider (1989) shows how Hogarth used the language of elocution and rhetoric to describe instrumental music and the speaking voice in "The Rhetoric of Variety: Observations on a Rediscovered Hogarth Letter." Paul Goring's *The Rhetoric of Sensibility in Eighteenth-Century Culture* (2005) argues that British writers, actors, and orators, newly drawn to the human body, constructed a polite culture of the body to replace classical manners—what he calls the bourgeois ideals of sentimental eloquence. Goring's study maps out conventions of physical eloquence promoted in a number of genres, including elocutionary and acting manuals and novels. As Barbara Maria Stafford (1991) points out, the eighteenth century's unrelenting interdisciplinarity poses challenges, for scholars today work from different disciplinary paradigms and within institutional structures that can work against genuine historical understanding. Looked at another way, of course, these challenges suggest the intellectual rewards of collaboration across disciplines: a deeper understanding of the connectedness of rhetoric and her sister arts.

Oratory

Work in the interface of rhetoric and politics is thriving. Robert T. Oliver's *The Influence of Rhetoric in the Shaping of Great Britain: From the Roman Invasion to the Early Nineteenth Century* (1986) argues that oratory is central to the cultural formation of Britain. Christopher Reid (2004) studies the construction of ethos in Sir Henry Cavendish's parliamentary diary, which offers an unrivaled account of the period's political speech. Reid (2005) examines the various roles of "candour" in British speaking. Katherine O'Donnell (2002) sees the influence of the Gaelic poetry of Munster, the region in which he was raised, in Edmund Burke's passionate speeches asserting the abuses of the East India Company against India.

In *The Strategy of Rhetoric: Campaigning for the American Constitution* (1996),William H. Riker examines the persuasive techniques advocates employed in 1787 and 1788 that allowed the Constitution to be ratified despite substantial opposition. Sandra M. Gustafson's *Eloquence Is Power: Oratory and Performance in Early America* (2000) is the rare book that also examines the rhetorical performances of American Indians, African Americans, and women. Victoria Cliett overturns narratives of democracy in "The Rhetoric of Democracy: Contracts, Declarations, Bills of Sales" (2004). David C. Hoffman (2006) examines how Thomas Paine reframed his readers' attitudes about the British monarchy and constitution and about American independence, leading them to accept earlier views as unfortunate distortions of "habit and custom" (387). McCants's *Patrick Henry, the Orator* (1990) details the revolutionary's oratorical development and offers textual and contextual analyses of his speeches, maintaining that their deliberative and forensic functions must be read in religious evangelical terms. It includes the texts of Henry's major speeches. Stephen H. Browne's *Jefferson's Call for Nationhood: The First Inaugural Address* (2003) examines this forefather's strategically eloquent language.

Adam Potkay (2001) argues that *The Interesting Narrative of the Life of Olaudah Equiano, or Gustavus Vassa, the African. Written by Himself* must be read as emerging from an eighteenth-century oratorical culture, arguing against postcolonial and poststructuralist misreadings. Drawing on rhetorical and historical methodologies, V. Carretta's "Defining a Gentleman" (2000) argues that the strength of *The Interesting Narrative of the Life of Olaudah Equiano, or Gustavus Vassa, the African* lay in rhetorical construction rather than historical accuracy. Silvia Xavier (2005) looks at the rhetorical practices of two northern African Americans to show how they draw upon major theoretical and philosophical underpinnings of eighteenth-century rhetoric, especially George Campbell's theory of sympathy. Brycchan Carey's *British Abolitionism and the Rhetoric of Sensibility: Writing, Sentiment, and Slavery, 1760–1807* (2005) begins with an account of the "new rhetoric" that emerged in the mid-eighteenth century, which, following Hume, reclaims the emotions and establishes the role of sympathy. The book demonstrates how reformers, working in a range of oral and written genres in public debate and legislative intervention, "used the already available rhetoric of sensibility" (9). Clare Midgley's *Women against Slavery: The British Campaigns, 1780–1870* (2006) analyzes the means by which working- and middle-class women argued for abolition. Jeff D. Bass (1989) maintains that in the Parliamentary Debates of 1791–1792 abolitionists argued for ending the slave trade on fiscal grounds to counter the economic fears raised by its proponents. Susan Staves (1989) argues that Catharine Macaulay, whom Staves figures as the "Female Thucydides," builds upon the eighteenth-century satiric tradition to present a protofeminist critique of Edmund Burke's politics.

Religion

Much fine work has been done on the interface of religion and rhetoric. James A. Herrick's *The Radical Rhetoric of the English Deists: The Discourse of Skepticism, 1680–1750* (1997) looks at the battles between the Deists and the Church of England, which broadened from England to Europe and the American colonies. Sandra J. Sarkela (1997) argues that the eighteenth century's rhetorical embrace of moderation as a persuasive appeal derived from seventeenth-century interpretations of the New Testament. Vicki Tolar Burton's 2001 and 2008 examinations of John Wesley and Methodism demonstrate how religion served as both ground and vehicle for instruction in rhetoric, offering a rare and unexpected platform to women. Ann Matheson (1995) examines how Scottish theories of rhetoric and belles lettres shape sermon writing in Scotland.

In *Rhetoric and History in Revolutionary New England* (1988), Donald Weber focuses on the sermons, diaries, and letters of five ministers to show how religious and political discourses intermingled in colonial America in ways that helped congregants make their way through the trials of the independence movement. Christopher Grasso's *A Speaking Aristocracy: Transforming Public Discourse in Eighteenth-Century Connecticut* (1999) shows how Connecticut society moves from one dominated by the pulpit—in which the preacher as moral authority dominated—to one in which other citizens, inspired by the Enlightenment, education, growing availability of printed resources (newspapers, essays, books, and so forth), and libraries, broadened public discourse and the scope of public life and conferred legitimate authority upon lay leadership. The study of rhetoric flourished. According to Grasso, the century began with a moral authority—the preacher—speaking to a known audience—his congregation; by the end, however, the model had switched to writing and to an audience whose members were often unknown. These discursive practices both reflect and give rise to a changing society, one that is more democratic, more secular. Grasso maps out the increasing diversity of intellectual and public figures in Revolutionary America, among them clergy, lawyers, intellectuals, farmers, scientists, and public leaders. This book demonstrates the power of carefully researched local histories, providing deeper insight into language education at Yale College, for example, by contextualizing it within the surrounding community. Harry Stout (1988) studies thousands of sermons (including those available only in manuscript)—the well-known as well as the less known—throughout colonial/Puritan New England. He deftly analyzes how these sermons inscribe political as well as religious implications into the relationship between God and congregation.

Several works focus on the figure of the orator-preacher. Stephen R. Yarbrough and John C. Adams (1993) analyze Jonathan Edwards's rhetorical practices in their educational, historical, cultural, and theological contexts and explain his rhetorical legacy. The volume also includes key sermons. Jerome Dean Mahaffey (2007) presents and analyzes over a hundred sermons by prominent eighteenth-century itinerant evangelist George Whitefield to show how he shaped a rhetoric of community that blended religion and politics to forge an independent American political identity.

Women

Most acclaimed rhetors were men who, in or out of the religious domain, had public and professional forums in which to exercise their eloquence and who had benefited from formal training. True, few women had a European classical rhetorical education, but several works establish the importance of women in the rhetorical tradition. Jane Donawerth's "Poaching on Men's Philosophies of Rhetoric: Eighteenth- and Nineteenth-Century Rhetorical Theory by Women" (2000) argues that women have contributed to rhetorical theory, albeit in the domestic realm. Donawerth ferrets out the tactics that women, without benefit of instruction in the traditional forms of public rhetoric, appropriated from the men in their circles. Tania S. Smith (2004) maintains that late-seventeenth-century French author Madeleine de Scudéry served as a model for a small but significant subset of British women in the eighteenth century. De Scudéry's *Les Femmes Illustres,* published in English in 1756 and subsequently titled *Heroick Harangues of the Illustrious Women,* dared to figure women as orators.

Recognizing rhetoric's purview beyond the traditional public sphere opens vast areas for inquiry. Following the work of Jürgen Habermas and others, scholars have begun to examine these new public spheres. Salons, such as those hosted by "the Bluestockings," were vibrant rhetorical forums of cultural, social, and even political change. Pointing out that translations of Cicero's *De Officiis* reinforced the view that conversation was indeed a rhetorical art that could be taught and learned, Dieter Berger (1994) notes that hundreds of courtesy books featuring the art of conversation appeared between 1650 and 1800 (82). Tania S. Smith (2007) studies how Hester Thrale Piozzi—a principal of British salons—studied, practiced, and even theorized rhetoric. Under the mentorship of Arthur Collier and Samuel Johnson, she became expert in conversation as a rhetorical art in the semipublic parlor. In her handbook of English, *British Synonymy* (1794), she formulated her theory that conversation, a means of social and cultural influence, is rhetoric. Under Collier, Piozzi studied the trivium, perfecting speaking and writing, listening and reading. When Hester went on to campaign on behalf of her husband for Parliament, she was nonetheless ridiculed as a "very petticoated Demosthenes" in the *London Magazine.*

Future Directions

I will conclude by highlighting some areas especially in need of attention. Too little scholarship has been devoted to studying rhetoric in the first half of the eighteenth century. How was rhetoric taught in universities? How was it approached in the equivalent of secondary schools? What foundations were laid in early schooling? And how did all these differ by region and class? We still lack the sort of basic information that medieval and early modern scholars consider fundamental in their periods.

British and American rhetoric scholars have tended to focus on Western Europe (particularly Great Britain) and North America (though the far north regions—Canada today—are too rarely mentioned). This chapter's account of history and scholarship also reflects that limitation. The 1970 founding of the International Society for the History of Rhetoric (ISHR) "to promote the study of both the theory and practice of rhetoric in all periods and languages and the relationship of rhetoric to poetics, literary theory and criticism, philosophy, politics, religion, law, and other aspects of the cultural context" (Article II, Constitution), however, has helped scholars to broaden and deepen inquiries in part by recognizing scholarship from across the globe.

Donawerth's "An Annotated Bibliography of the History of Non-Western Rhetorical Theory before 1900" (1994) points to some of the figures and theories that deserve attention. New work by historians of rhetoric should complement scholarship such as that of Sara Suleri, whose *The Rhetoric of English India* (1992) complicates the claim that British and Indian colonizers communicated in mutually exclusive ways. It offers an astute analysis of British attempts to construct a rhetoric that captured the colonial encounter and Edmund Burke's attempts to impeach Warren Hastings for abusive practices on the Indian subcontinent that brought into question "the very nature of the legal discourse in which the trial was to be conducted" (49). Burke's attempts to bring justice were expressed in an excessive "surplus rhetoric," which the British "enjoyed, year after year, as rhetoric alone" (50).

As mentioned earlier, African American, African British, and African traditions are fertile ground for study. Ronald W. Walters and Cedric Johnson's *Bibliography of African American Leadership: An Annotated Guide* (2000) includes a section on colonial America that details key primary writings, as well as secondary scholarship, including dissertations and theses. The first section of Eileen Southern and Josephine Wright's *African-American Traditions in Song, Sermon, Tale, and Dance, 1600s–1920: An Annotated Bibliography of Literature, Collections, and Artworks* offers a rich, annotated account of primary source materials from the colonial and Federalist periods organized under four categories: "Social Activities," "Religious Experience," "The Song," and "The Tale." Western scholars are just beginning to explore the indigenous rhetorical traditions in the Americas.

Susan Romano (2007) characterizes the state of rhetoric in early eighteenth-century colonial Mexico as a disintegration of the imagined alignment between rhetoric as a course of university study and rhetoric as field practice. She examines *Farol Indiano,* a 1713 guide to staging rhetorical encounters between priests and native parishioners, which documents the means by which Nahua rhetorics confounded university-made knowledge about language and persuasion. According to Romano, author Manuel Pérez, an Augustian catechizer and professor of native languages at the Royal University, positions his own publicly defended thesis about language and truth as unworkable in practice, providing illustrations from his experiential repertoire. The rhetorical practices, pedagogies, and theories of other indigenous Americans, of the Irish, of the Welsh, among others living in the British Isles and the Americas, also have much to tell us. And what were the rhetorical practices, pedagogies, and theories in other lands that experienced British colonialism?

As scholars such as Keith Gilyard (2004) and Jacqueline Jones Royster (1999) suggest, however, such research entails more than simply expanding geographical and linguistic boundaries; in many cases, redefining rhetoric, correcting assumptions about where and why rhetoric flourished, and modifying research methodologies are vital parts of academic inquiry. How well do our current scholarly methodologies and vocabularies fit our future work? What might they obscure? The approaches taken by George A. Kennedy's *Comparative Rhetoric: An Historical and Cross-Cultural Introduction* (1997) provide a segue for new conceptions of scholarly inquiry.

To close, I will mention one more alternative direction: forms of expression not traditionally studied by historians of rhetoric that warrant study. Four very different studies suggest what might be gained. Maureen Daly Goggins's "An *Essamplaire Essai* on the Rhetoricity of Needlework Samplers: A Contribution to Theorizing and Historicizing Rhetorical Praxis" (2002) explains how samplers are "discursively circumscribed and imbued with meaning" (330), and Wendy Dasler Johnson's "Cultural Rhetorics of Women's Corsets" (2001) shows what debates about corsetry reveal about the period's attitudes about women. More unusual is Lester C. Olson's (2004) *Benjamin Franklin's Vision of American Community,* which argues persuasively for Franklin's acumen in visual rhetoric, studying how Franklin's iconography constructs images of America that reflect his political views towards Great Britain as they evolve from supporting a constitutional monarchy to advocating a republican government for an independent nation. Finally, Matthew Craske's *The Silent Rhetoric of the Body: A History of Monumental Sculpture and Commemorative Art in England, 1720–1770* (2008) analyzes the visual epideictic in cultural context.

Why has there been so little work in these areas? In some cases, archival evidence is scarce; in others, it has been passed over as inconsequential. In still others, linguistic barriers have inhibited cross-cultural study, or standing rhetorical paradigms have obscured our view. What is certain, however, is that the assiduous efforts of scholars will deepen and broaden our understanding of the period.

BIBLIOGRAPHY
Primary Works

Ashfield, Andrew, and Peter de Bolla, eds. *The Sublime: A Reader in British Eighteenth-Century Aesthetic Theory.* Cambridge: Cambridge University Press, 1996.

Astell, Mary. *A Serious Proposal to the Ladies, Parts I and II.* 1694, 1697. Reprint, ed. Patricia Springborg. London: Pickering and Chatto, 1997.

Burke, Edmund. *A Philosophical Enquiry into the Origin of Our Ideas of the Sublime and the Beautiful.* 1757. Reprint, ed. James T. Boulton. Notre Dame: University of Notre Dame Press, 1968.

Campbell, George. *The Philosophy of Rhetoric.* 1776. Reprint, ed. Lloyd Bitzer. Carbondale: Southern Illinois University Press, 1963.

Claussen, E. Neal, and Karl L. Wallace, eds. *John Lawson's Lectures Concerning Oratory.* Carbondale: Southern Illinois University Press, 1963.

Donawerth, Jane, ed. *Rhetorical Theory by Women before 1900: An Anthology.* Lanham, MD: Rowman and Littlefield, 2002.

Ferreira-Buckley, Linda, and S. Michael Halloran, eds. *Hugh Blair's Lectures on Rhetoric and Belles-Lettres.* Carbondale: Southern Illinois University Press, 2005.

Foner, Philip S., ed. *The Voice of Black America: Major Speeches by Negroes in the United States, 1797–1973.* New York: Capricorn Books, 1975.

Hume, David. *Selected Essays.* Ed. Stephen Copley and Andrew Edgar. Oxford World's Classics. New York: Oxford University Press, 2008.

Mann, Barbara Alice, ed. *Native American Speakers of the Eastern Woodlands: Selected Speeches and Critical Analyses.* Westport, CN: Greenwood Press, 2001.

Miller, Thomas, ed. *The Selected Writings of John Witherspoon.* 1810. Reprint, Carbondale: Southern Illinois University Press, 1990.

Moore, Alice Dunbar, ed. *Masterpieces of Negro Eloquence (The Best Speeches Delivered by the Negro from the Days of Slavery to the Present Time).* Mineola, NY: Dover, 2000.

Nerburn, Kent, ed. *The Wisdom of the Native Americans.* Novato, CA: New World Library, 1999.

Poster, Carol, compiler. *The Elocutionary Movement (British Rhetoric in the Eighteenth & Nineteenth Centuries).* Facsimile edition. London: Thoemmes Continuum, 2003.

Potkay, Adam, and Sandra Burr, eds. *Black Atlantic Writers of the Eighteenth Century: Living the New Exodus in England and the Americas.* Houndmills, Basingstoke, U.K.: Palgrave Macmillan, 1995.

Price, John V., ed. *British Rhetoric in the Eighteenth Century.* Facsimile edition. London: Thoemmes Continuum, 2001.

Priestley, Joseph. *A Course of Lectures on Oratory and Criticism.* 1777. Reprint, Whitefish, MT: Kessinger Publishing, 2007.

Reid, Ronald F., and James F. Klumpp, eds. *American Rhetorical Discourse.* 3rd ed. Prospect Heights, IL: Waveland Press, 2004.

Southern, Eileen, and Josephine Wright, compilers. *African-American Traditions in Song, Sermon, Tale, and Dance, 1600s–1920: An Annotated Bibliography of Literature, Collections, and Artworks.* Westport, CT: Greenwood Press, 1990.

Sheridan, Thomas. *Thomas Sheridan: A Discourse, Being Introductory to His Course of Lectures on Elocution and the English Language.* 1759. Reprint, with an introduction by G. P. Mohrmann. Imprint Los Angeles, William Andrews Clark Memorial Library, University of California, 1969. Augustan Reprint Society. Publication no. 136.

Smith, Adam. *An Inquiry into the Nature and Causes of the Wealth of Nations.* 1776. Reprint, Harvard Classics Series. New York: P.F. Collier and Sons, 1909.

———. *Lectures on Rhetoric and Belles Letters.* Ed. J. C. Bryce. Oxford: Oxford University Press, 1983.

Vanderwerth, W. C., compiler. *Indian Oratory: Famous Speeches by Noted Indian Chieftains.* Norman: University of Oklahoma Press, 1971.

Ward, John. *A System of Oratory.* Port Jervis, NY: Lubrecht and Cramer, 1969.

Whately, Richard. *Elements of Logic.* Facsimile reproduction, with introduction by Ray E. McKerrow. New York: Scholar's Facsimiles and Reprints, 1975.

———. *Elements of Rhetoric, Comprising an Analysis of the Laws of Moral Evidence and of Persuasion: With Rules for Argumentative Composition and Elocution.* Carbondale: Southern Illinois University Press, 1963.

Secondary Works

Abbott, Don Paul. "A Bibliography of Eighteenth- and Nineteenth-Century Spanish Treatises." *Rhetorica* 4, no. 3 (1986): 275–92.

———. "The Influence of Blair's Lectures in Spain." *Rhetorica* 7, no. 3 (1989): 275–89.

———. "Kant, Theremin, and the Morality of Rhetoric." *Philosophy and Rhetoric* 40, no. 3 (2007): 274–92.

———. "Mayans' Rhetórica and the Search for a Spanish Rhetoric." *Rhetorica* 11, no. 2 (1993): 157–79.

Abrams, Meyer Howard. *The Mirror and the Lamp: Romantic Theory and the Critical Tradition.* New York: Oxford University Press, 1971.

Agnew, Lois. *"Outward, Visible Propriety": Stoic Ethics and Eighteenth-Century British Rhetoric.* Columbia: University of South Carolina Press, 2008.

———. "The 'Perplexity' of George Campbell's Rhetoric: The Epistemic Function of Common Sense." *Rhetorica* 18, no. 1 (2000): 79–101.

Allen, Julia. "The Uses and Problems of a 'Manly' Rhetoric: Mary Wollstonecraft's Adaptation of Hugh Blair's *Lectures* in Her Two Vindications." In *Listening to Their Voices: The Rhetorical Activities of Historical Women,* ed. Molly Meijer Wertheimer, 320–26. Columbia: University of South Carolina Press, 1997.

Andrew, Donna T. "Popular Culture and Public Debate: London 1780." *Historical Journal* 39, no. 2 (1996): 405–23.

Bannet, Eve Tavor. "Printed Epistolary Manuals and the Transatlantic Rescripting of Manuscript Culture." *Studies in Eighteenth Century Culture* 36 (2007): 13–32.

Barilli, Renato. *Rhetoric.* Minneapolis: University of Minnesota Press, 1989.

Barlowe, Jamie. "Daring to Dialogue: Mary Wollstonecraft's Rhetoric of Feminist Dialogics." In *Reclaiming Rhetorica: Women in the Rhetorical Tradition,* ed. Andrea A. Lunsford, 117–36. Pittsburgh: University of Pittsburgh Press, 1995.

Barone, Dennis. "An Introduction to William Smith and Rhetoric at the College of Philadelphia." *Proceedings of the American Philosophical Society* 134, no. 2 (1990): 111–60.

Bass, Jeff D. "An Efficient Humanitarianism: The British Slave Trade Debates, 1791–1792." *Quarterly Journal of Speech* 75 (1989): 152–65.

Bator, Paul G. "The Formation of the Regius Chair of Rhetoric and Belles Lettres at the University of Edinburgh." *Quarterly Journal of Speech* 75 (1989): 40–64.

———. "Rhetoric and the Novel in the Eighteenth-Century British University Curriculum." *Eighteenth-Century Studies* 30, no. 2 (1996–1997): 173–95.

Beach, Adam R. "The Creation of a Classical Language in the Eighteenth Century: Standardizing English, Cultural Imperialism, and the Future of the

Literary Canon." *Texas Studies in Literature and Language* 43, no. 2 (2001): 117–41.

Benzie, William. *The Dublin Orator: Thomas Sheridan's Influence on Eighteenth Century Rhetoric and Belles Lettres.* Leeds, U.K.: University of Leeds School of English, 1972.

Berger, Dieter. "Maxims of Conduct into Literature: Jonathan Swift and Polite Conversation." In *The Crisis of Courtesy: Studies in the Conduct-Book in Britain, 1600–1900,* ed. Jacques Carré, 81–91. Brill's Studies in Intellectual History Series. New York: E. J. Brill, 1994.

Berry, Christopher J. "Adam Smith's Considerations on Language." *Journal of the History of Ideas* 35, no. 1 (1974): 130–38.

Bevilacqua, Vincent M. "Baconian Influences in the Development of Scottish Rhetorical Theory." *Proceedings of the American Philosophical Society* 111, no. 4 (1967): 212–18.

———. "Classical Rhetorical Influences in the Development of Eighteenth-Century British Aesthetic Criticism." *Transactions of the American Philological Association (1974)* 106 (1976): 11–28.

———. "Philosophical Influences in the Development of English Rhetorical Theory: 1748 to 1783." *Proceedings of the Leeds Philosophical and Literary Society, Literary and Historical Section* 12 (1968): 191–215.

———. "Two Newtonian Arguments Concerning 'Taste.'" *Philological Quarterly* 47 (1968): 585–90.

Bialostosky, Don H., and Lawrence D. Needham, eds. *Rhetorical Traditions and British Romantic Literature.* Bloomington: Indiana University Press, 1995.

Bitzer, Lloyd F. "Hume's Philosophy in George Campbell's Philosophy of Rhetoric." *Philosophy and Rhetoric* 2 (1969): 139–66.

Bitzer, Lloyd F., Don M. Burks, Herman Cohen, John Hagaman, and Howard L. Ulman. "The Most Significant Passage in George Campbell's Philosophy of Rhetoric." *Rhetoric Society Quarterly* 13 (1983): 13–27.

Bonds, Mark Evan. *Wordless Rhetoric: Musical Form and the Metaphor of the Oration.* Cambridge: Harvard University Press, 1991.

Bonura, Carlo. "Uncommon Topics: On the Topics of Location and Rhetoric in the Practice of Political Community." Paper presented at the Annual Meeting of the American Political Science Association, Boston Marriott Copley Place, Sheraton Boston and Hynes Convention Center, Boston, August 28, 2002. http://www .allacademic.com/meta/p64993_index.html.

Bormann, Dennis R. "George Campbell's Cura Prima on Eloquence, 1758." *Quarterly Journal of Speech* 74 (1988): 35–51.

———. "Some 'Common Sense' about Campbell, Hume, and Reid: The Extrinsic Evidence." *Quarterly Journal of Speech* 71 (1985): 395–421.

Bradbury, J. M. "New Science and the 'New Species of Writing': Eighteenth-Century Prose Genres." *Eighteenth-Century Life* 27 (2003): 28–51.

Bradley, Adelbert Edward, Jr. "The *Inventio* of John Ward." *Speech Monographs* 26 (1959): 56–63.

———. "John Ward's Concept of *Dispositio.*" *Rhetoric Society Quarterly* 24 (1957): 258–63.

Brekus, Catherine A. *Strangers and Pilgrims: Female Preaching in America, 1740–1845.* Chapel Hill: University of North Carolina Press, 1999.

Brown, Stuart C., and Thomas Willard. "George Campbell's Audience: Historical and Theoretical Considerations." In *A Sense of Audience in Written Communication,* ed. Gesa Kirsch and Duane Roen, 58–118. Beverly Hills, CA: Sage, 1990.

Browne, Stephen H. *Jefferson's Call for Nationhood: The First Inaugural Address.* College Station: Texas A&M University Press, 2003.

———. "Satirizing Women's Speech in Eighteenth-Century England." *Rhetoric Society Quarterly* 22, no. 3 (1992): 20–29.

Burton, Vicki Tolar. "John Wesley and the Liberty to Speak: The Rhetorical and Literacy Practices of Early Methodism." *College Composition and Communication* 53, no. 1 (2001): 65–91.

———. *Spiritual Literacy in John Wesley's Methodism.* Waco: Baylor University Press, 2008.

Butler, Gregory G. "Fugue and Rhetoric." *Journal of Music Theory* 21, no. 1 (1977): 49–109.

Campbell, Neil R., and Martin S. Smellie. *The Royal Society of Edinburgh, 1783–1983.* Edinburgh: The Society, 1983.

Carey, Brycchan. *British Abolitionism and the Rhetoric of Sensibility: Writing, Sentiment, and Slavery, 1760–1807.* Houndmills, Basingstoke, U.K.: Palgrave Macmillan, 2005.

Carretta, V. "Defining a Gentleman: The Status of Olaudah Equiano or Gustavus Vassa." *Language Sciences* 22, no. 3 (2000): 385–99.

Carruthers, Bruce G., and Wendy Nelson Espeland. "Accounting for Rationality: Double-Entry Bookkeeping and the Rhetoric of Economic Rationality." *American Journal of Sociology* 97, no. 1 (1991): 31–69.

Carter, Jennifer J., and Joan H. Pittock, eds. *Aberdeen and the Enlightenment.* Aberdeen: Aberdeen University Press, 1987.

Catana, Leo. *Vico and Literary Mannerism: A Study in the Early Vico and His Idea of Rhetoric and Ingenuity.* New York: Peter Lang, 1999.

Clark, Peter. *British Clubs and Societies, 1580–1800: The Origins of an Associational World.* New York: Oxford University Press, 2000.

Cliett, Victoria. "The Rhetoric of Democracy: Contracts, Declarations, Bills of Sales." In *African American Rhetoric(s): Interdisciplinary Perspectives,* ed. Elaine B. Richardson and Ronald L. Jackson, 170–86. Carbondale: Southern Illinois University Press, 2004, 2007.

Clymer, Lorna, "Graved in Tropes: The Figural Logic of Epitaphs and Elegies in Blair, Gray, Cowper, and Wordsworth." *ELH: A Journal of English Literary History* 62, no. 2 (1995): 347–86.

Cohen, Herman. "Hugh Blair's Theory of Taste." *Quarterly Journal of Speech* 44 (1958): 265–74. Reprinted in *Readings in Rhetoric*, ed. Lionel Crocker and Paul A. Carmack, 334–93. Springfield, IL: Charles C. Thomas, 1965.

Collins, Vicki Tolar. "The Speaker Respoken: Material Rhetoric as Feminist Methodology." *College English* 61, no. 5 (1999): 545–73.

Conley, Thomas M. *Rhetoric in the European Tradition.* Chicago: University of Chicago Press, 1990.

Craske, Matthew. *The Silent Rhetoric of the Body: A History of Monumental Sculpture and Commemorative Art in England, 1720–1770.* New Haven: Yale University Press, 2008.

Crawford, Robert, ed. *The Scottish Invention of English Literature.* Cambridge: Cambridge University Press, 1998.

Crowley, Tony. *Standard English and the Politics of Language.* Rev. ed. Basingstoke U.K.: Palgrave Macmillan, 2003.

Diamond, Arthur M., Jr., and David M. Levy. "The Metrics of Style: Adam Smith Teaches Efficient Rhetoric." *Economic Inquiry* 32, no. 1 (1994): 38–45.

Donawerth, Jane. "'As Becomes a Rational Woman to Speak': Madeleine de Scudéry's Rhetoric of Conversation." In *Listening to Their Voices: The Rhetorical Activities of Historical Women,* ed. Molly Meijer Wertheimer, 305–19. Columbia: University of South Carolina Press, 1997.

———. "Hannah More, Lydia Sigourney, and the Creation of a Women's Tradition of Rhetoric." In *Rhetoric, the Polis, and the Global Village: Selected Papers from the 1998 Thirtieth Anniversary Rhetoric Society of America Conference,* ed. C. Jan Swearingen and Dave Pruett, 155–62. Mahwah, NJ: Lawrence Erlbaum Associates, 1999.

———. "Poaching on Men's Philosophies of Rhetoric: Eighteenth- and Nineteenth-Century Rhetorical Theory by Women." *Philosophy and Rhetoric* 33, no. 3 (2000): 243–58.

Donawerth, Jane, and Julie Strongson. "Volume Editors' Introduction." In *Madeleine de Scudéry: Selected Letters, Orations, and Rhetorical Dialogues,* ed. Jane Donawerth and Julie Strongson, 1–38. Chicago: University of Chicago Press, 2004.

Donawerth, Jane, Michele L. Alvarez, Aubrey G. Baden, Joe Caulfield, Grace Coleman, Linda Dove, Audrey Kerr, W. Mark Lynch, Elaine Mack, Michele Mason, Denise D. Meringolo, Karen Nelson, Melissa Hope Peller, Patricia Porcarelli, Carla Porter, Rebecca Randall, Michael Schoop, Anne Sheehan, Synthia Shilling, and Melinda Schwenk. "An Annotated Bibliography of the History of Non-Western Rhetorical Theory before 1900." *Rhetoric Society Quarterly* 24, no. 3/4 (1994): 167–80.

Edwards, Paul C. "Elocution and Shakespeare: An Episode in the History of Literary Taste." *Shakespeare Quarterly* 35, no. 3 (1984): 305–14.

Ehninger, Douglas. "Dominant Trends in English Rhetorical Thought, 1750–1800." *Southern Speech Journal* 78 (1952): 3–12.

Eldred, Janet Carey, and Peter Mortensen. *Imagining Rhetoric: Composing Women of the Early United States.* Pittsburgh: Pittsburgh University Press, 2002.

——. "'Persuasion Dwelt on Her Tongue': Female Civic Rhetoric in Early America." *College English* 60, no. 2 (1998): 173–88.

Endres, A. M. "Adam Smith's Rhetoric of Economics: An Illustration Using 'Smithian' Compositional Rules." *Scottish Journal of Political Economy* 38, no. 1 (1991): 76–95.

Ferguson, Moira. "The Discovery of Mary Wollstonecraft's 'The Female Reader.'" *Signs* 3, no. 4 (1978): 945–57.

Ferreira-Buckley, Linda, and Winifred Bryan Horner. "Writing Instruction in Great Britain: Eighteenth and Nineteenth Centuries." In *A Short History of Writing Instruction from Ancient Greece to Twentieth Century America,* ed. James J. Murphy, 173–212. Davis, CA: Hermagoras Press, 2001.

France, Peter. *Rhetoric and Truth in France: Descartes to Diderot.* Oxford: Clarendon Press, 1972.

Fullenwider, H. F. "The Rhetoric of Variety: Observations on a Rediscovered Hogarth Letter." *Burlington Magazine* 131, no. 1040 (1989): 769–70.

Gaillet, Lynée Lewis. "George Jardine: Champion of the Scottish Philosophy of Democratic Intellect." *Rhetoric Society Quarterly* 28, no. 2 (1998): 37–53.

Gaillet, Lynée Lewis, ed. *Scottish Rhetoric and Its Influences.* Mahwah, NJ: Lawrence Erlbaum, 1998.

Gehrke, Pat J. "Turning Kant against the Priority of Autonomy: Communication Ethics and the Duty to Community." *Philosophy and Rhetoric* 35, no. 1 (2002): 1–21.

George, Ann L. "Grounds of Assent in Joseph Priestley's *Lectures on Oratory and Criticism.*" *Rhetorica* 16, no. 1 (1998): 81–109.

Gilyard, Keith. Introduction to *African American Rhetoric(s): Interdisciplinary Perspectives,* ed. Elaine Richardson and Ronald L. Jackson II, 1–18. Carbondale: University of Southern Illinois University Press, 2004.

Goggin, Maureen Daly. "Arguing in 'Pen of Steele and Silken Inke': Theorizing a Broader Material Base for Argumentation." In *Proceedings of the Fifth Conference of the International Society for the Study of Argumentation,* ed. Frans H. van Eemeren, J. Anthony Blair, Charles A. Willard, and A. Francisca Snoeck, 383–89. Amsterdam: Sic Sat International Center for the Study of Argumentation, 2003.

——. "An *Essamplaire Essai* on the Rhetoricity of Needlework Samplers: A Contribution to Theorizing and Historicizing Rhetorical Praxis." *Rhetoric Review* 21 (2002): 309–38.

——. "Visual Rhetoric in Pens of Steel and Inks of Silk: Challenging the Great Visual/Verbal Divide." In *Defining Visual Rhetoric*, ed. Charles Hill and Marguerite Helmers, 87–110. Mahwah, NJ : Lawrence Erlbaum, 2004.

Goring, Paul. *The Rhetoric of Sensibility in Eighteenth-Century Culture.* Cambridge: Cambridge University Press, 2005.

Graff, Harvey J. *The Labyrinths of Literacy: Reflections on Literacy Past and Present.* Rev. ed. Pittsburgh: University of Pittsburgh Press, 1995.

Grassi, Ernesto. *Vico and Humanism. Essays on Vico, Heidegger, and Rhetoric.* New York: Peter Lang, 1990.

Grasso, Christopher. *A Speaking Aristocracy: Transforming Public Discourse in Eighteenth-Century Connecticut.* Published for the Omohundro Institute of Early American History and Culture. Chapel Hill: University of North Carolina Press, 1999.

Griswold, Charles L., Jr. "Rhetoric and Ethics: Adam Smith and Theorizing about the Moral Sentiments." In *Science, Politics, and Social Practice: Essays on Marxism and Science, Philosophy of Culture, and the Social Sciences*, ed. K. Gavroglu, J. Stachel, and Marx W. Wartofsky, 295–320. Dordrecht, Netherlands: Kluwer Academic Publishers, 1995.

Gustafson, Sandra M. *Eloquence Is Power: Oratory and Performance in Early America.* Chapel Hill: University of North Carolina Press, 2000.

Habermas, Jurgen. *The Structural Transformation of the Public Sphere: An Inquiry into a Category of Bourgeois Society.* Trans. Thomas Burger. Cambridge, MA: MIT Press, 1991.

Halloran, S. Michael, "Rhetoric in the American College Curriculum: The Decline of Public Discourse." *Pre-Text* 3 (1982): 245–69. Reprinted in *Pre-Text: The First Decade*, ed. Victor Vitanza, 93–116. Pittsburgh: Pittsburgh University Press, 1994.

Hatch, Gary. "Student Notes of Hugh Blair's Lecture on Rhetoric." In *Scottish Rhetoric and Its Influences*, ed. Lynée Lewis Gaillet, 79–94. Mahwah, NJ: Lawrence Erlbaum, 1998.

Heller, Deborah. "Bluestocking Salons and the Public Sphere." *Eighteenth-Century Life* 22, no. 2 (1998): 59–82.

Helmers, Marguerite. "Framing the Fine Arts through Rhetoric." In *Defining Visual Rhetorics*, ed. Charles A. Hill and Marguerite Helmers, 63–86. Mahwah, NJ: Lawrence Erlbaum Associates, 2004.

Herrick, James A. *The Radical Rhetoric of the English Deists: The Discourse of Skepticism, 1680–1750.* Columbia: University of South Carolina Press, 1997.

Hoffman, David C. "Paine and Prejudice: Rhetorical Leadership through Perceptual Framing in Common Sense." *Rhetoric and Public Affairs* 9, no. 3 (2006): 373–410.

Horner, Winifred Bryan., ed. *Historical Rhetoric: An Annotated Bibliography of Selected Sources in English.* Boston: G. K. Hall, 1980.

——. *Nineteenth-Century Scottish Rhetoric: The American Connection.* Carbondale: Southern Illinois University Press, 1993.

——. "The Roots of Modern Writing Instruction: Eighteenth- and Nineteenth-Century Britain." *Rhetoric Review* 8, no. 2 (1990): 322–45.

Hudson, Nicholas. "Johnson's 'Dictionary' and the Politics of 'Standard English.'" *Yearbook of English Studies* 28 Eighteenth-Century Lexis and Lexicography (1998): 77–93.

Irvine, James. "British and Continental Rhetoric and Elocution: The Eighteenth Century Collection." *Rhetoric Society Quarterly* 25 (1995): 214–16.

——. "Lord Monboddo's 'Letter on Rhetorick': Defense of Aristotle." *Rhetoric Society Quarterly* 21, no. 4 (1991): 26–31.

——. "Rhetoric and Moral Philosophy: A Selected Inventory of Student Notes and Dictates in Scottish Archives." *Rhetoric Society Quarterly* 13 (1983): 159–64.

Irvine, James, and G. J. Gravelee. "Hugh Blair: A Select Bibliography of Manuscripts in Scottish Archives." *Rhetoric Society Quarterly* 13 (1983): 75–77.

Jackson, Ronald L., II., and Elaine B. Richardson, eds. *Understanding African American Rhetoric: Classical Origins to Contemporary Innovations.* New York: Routledge, 2003.

Jensen, H. James. *Signs and Meaning in Eighteenth-Century Art: Epistemology, Rhetoric, Painting, Poesy, Music, Dramatic Performance, and G. F. Handel.* Oxford: Peter Lang Publishing, 1997.

Johnson, Nan C. "Rhetoric and Belles Lettres in the Canadian Academy: An Historical Analysis." *College English* 50, no. 8 (1988): 861–73.

Johnson, Wendy Dasler. "Cultural Rhetorics of Women's Corsets." *Rhetoric Review* 20, no. 3/4 (2001): 203–33.

Kallich, Martin. *The Association of Ideas and Critical Theory in Eighteenth-Century England: A History of Psychological Method in English Criticism.* The Hague: Mouton, 1970.

Kaufman, Paul. "A Bookseller's Record of Eighteenth-Century Book Clubs." *The Library: The Transactions of the Bibliographic Society.* 15, no. 4 (1960): 278–87.

Kelly, Gary. "Bluestocking Feminism." In *Women, Writing, and the Public Sphere, 1700–1830,* ed. Elizabeth Eger, Charlotte Grant, Clíona Ó Gallchoir, and Penny Warburton, 163–80. Cambridge: Cambridge University Press, 2001.

Kennedy, George A. *Comparative Rhetoric: An Historical and Cross-Cultural Introduction.* New York: Oxford University Press, 1997.

Klein, Lawrence E. "Gender, Conversation, and the Public Sphere in Early Eighteenth-Century England." In *Textuality and Sexuality: Reading Theories and Practices,* ed. Judith Still and Michael Worton. 100–115. Manchester, U.K.: Manchester University Press, 1993.

Kristeller, Paul Oskar. "The Modern System of the Arts: A Study in the History of Aesthetics Part I." *Journal of the History of Ideas* 12, no. 4 (1951): 496–527.

Lessenich, Rolph P. *Elements of Pulpit Oratory in Eighteenth-Century England, 1660–1800.* Cologne: Bohlau Verlag, 1972.

Longaker, Mark Garrett. *Rhetoric and the Republic: Politics, Civic Discourse, and Education in Early America.* Tuscaloosa: University of Alabama Press, 2007.

Looby, Christopher. *Voicing America: Language, Literary Form, and the Origins of the United States.* Chicago: University of Chicago Press, 1996.

Madden, Etta M. "'To Make a Figure': Benjamin Rush's Rhetorical Self-Construction and Scientific Authorship." *Early American Literature* 41, no. 2 (2006): 241–72.

Mahaffey, Jerome Dean. *Preaching Politics: The Religious Rhetoric of George Whitefield and the Founding of a New Nation.* Waco, TX: Baylor University Press, 2007.

Manning, Susan. "Scottish Style and American Romantic Idiom." *Language Sciences* 22, no. 3 (2000): 265–83.

Manolescu, Beth Innocenti. "Clerics Competing for and against 'Eloquence' in Mid-Eighteenth-Century Britain." *Rhetoric Society Quarterly* 30, no. 1 (2000): 47–67.

———. "Motives for Practicing Shakespeare Criticism as a 'Rational Science' in Lord Kames's *Elements of Criticism.*" In *Advances in the History of Rhetoric: The First Six Years,* ed. Richard Leo Enos and David E. Beard, with Sarah L. Yoder and Amy K. Hermanson, 296–307. West Lafayette, IN: Parlor Press, 2007.

———. "Traditions of Rhetoric, Criticism, and Argument in Kames's *Elements of Criticism.*" *Rhetoric Review* 22, no. 3 (2003): 225–43.

Marshall, Madeleine Forell. "Late Eighteenth-Century Public Reading, with Particular Attention to Sheridan's Strictures on Reading the Church Service (1789)." *Studies in Eighteenth Century Culture* 36 (2007): 35–54.

Matheson, Anne, *Theories of Rhetoric in the 18th-Century Scottish Sermon.* Lewiston, NY: Edwin Mellen Press, 1995.

McCann, Andrew. "Romantic Self-Fashioning: John Thelwall and the Science of Elocution." *Studies in Romanticism* 40, no. 2 (2001): 215–32.

McCants, David A. *Patrick Henry, the Orator.* Westport, CT: Greenwood Press, 1990.

McElroy, Davis Dunbar. *Scotland's Age of Improvement: A Survey of Eighteenth-Century Literary Clubs and Societies.* Pullman: Washington State University Press, 1969.

McIlvanney, Liam. "Hugh Blair, Robert Burns, and the Invention of Scottish Literature." *Eighteenth-Century Life* 29, no. 2 (2005): 25–46.

McIntosh, Carey. "Elementary Rhetorical Ideas and Eighteenth-Century English." *Language Sciences* 22, no. 3 (2000): 231–49.

———. *The Evolution of English Prose, 1700–1800: Style, Politeness, and Print Culture.* Cambridge: Cambridge University Press, 1998.

McKenna, Stephen J. *Adam Smith: The Rhetoric of Propriety.* Albany: State University of New York Press, 2005.

———. "Kames's Legal Career and Writings as Precedents for *Elements of Criticism.*" *Rhetorica* 23, no. 3 (2005): 239–59.

Michael, Ian. *The Teaching of English: From the Sixteenth Century to 1870.* Cambridge: Cambridge University Press, 2005.

Michaelson, Patricia. *Speaking Volumes: Women, Reading, and Speech in the Age of Austen.* Stanford: Stanford University Press, 2002.

Midgley, Clare. *Women against Slavery: The British Campaigns, 1780–1870.* Montreal: McGill-Queen's University Press, 2006.

Miller, Thomas P. "The Formation of College English: A Survey of the Archives of Eighteenth-Century Rhetorical Theory and Practice." *Rhetoric Society Quarterly* 20, no. 3 (1990): 261–86.

———. *The Formation of College English: Rhetoric and Belles Lettres in the British Cultural Provinces.* Pittsburgh: University of Pittsburgh Press, 1997.

———. "The Rhetoric of Belles Lettres: The Political Context of the Eighteenth-Century Transition from Classical to Modern Cultural Studies." *Rhetoric Society Quarterly* 23, no. 2 (1993): 1–19.

Mitchell, Linda C. *Grammar Wars: Language as Cultural Battlefield in 17th and 18th Century England.* Aldershot, U.K.: Ashgate, 2002.

———. "Letter-Writing Instruction Manuals in Seventeenth- and Eighteenth-Century England." In *Letter-Writing Instruction Manuals and Instruction from Antiquity to the Present: Historical and Bibliographic Studies,* ed. Carol Poster and Linda C. Mitchell, 178–99. Studies in Rhetoric/Communication. Columbia: University of South Carolina Press, 2007.

Mitchell, Linda C., and Susan Green, eds. *Studies in the Cultural History of Letter Writing.* San Marino, CA: Huntington Library Press, 2007.

Monaghan, E. Jennifer. *Learning to Read and Write in Colonial America.* Amherst: University of Massachusetts Press, 2005.

Mooney, Michael. *Vico in the Tradition of Rhetoric.* Princeton: Princeton University Press, 1985.

Moran, Michael G., ed. *Eighteenth-Century British and American Rhetorics and Rhetoricians: Critical Studies and Sources.* Westport, CT: Greenwood Press, 1994.

Mugglestone, Lynda. *Talking Proper: The Rise of Accent as Social Symbol.* 2nd ed. New York: University of Oxford Press, 2007.

Mulvihill, James. *Upstart Talents: Rhetoric and the Career of Reason in English Romantic Discourse, 1790–1820.* Newark: University of Delaware Press, 2004.

O'Donnell, Katherine. "'Whether the white people like it or not': Edmund Burke's Speeches on India—Caoineadh's Cainte." *Eire-Ireland: Journal of Irish*

Studies Fall–Winter 2002. FindArticles.com. 03 Mar. 2008. http://findarticles. com/p/articles/mi_m0FKX/ is_2002_Fall-Winter/ai_95598127.

Oliver, Robert T. *The Influence of Rhetoric in the Shaping of Great Britain: From the Roman Invasion to the Early Nineteenth Century.* Newark: University of Delaware Press, 1986.

Olson, Lester C. *Benjamin Franklin's Vision of American Community: A Study in Rhetorical Iconology.* Columbia: University of South Carolina Press, 2004.

O'Rourke, Sean Patrick. "'Danced through Every Labyrinth of the Law': Benjamin Austin on Rhetoric as Virtue and Vice in Early American Legal Practice." In *Advances in the History of Rhetoric: The First Six Years,* ed. Richard Leo Enos and David E. Beard, with Sarah L. Yoder and Amy K. Hermanson, 98–111. West Lafayette, IN: Parlor Press, 2007.

———. "Sentimental Journey: The Place and Status of the Emotions in Hugh Blair's Rhetoric." In *Advances in the History of Rhetoric: The First Six Years,* ed. Richard Leo Enos and David E. Beard, with Sarah L. Yoder and Amy K. Hermanson, 308–25. West Lafayette, IN: Parlor Press, 2007.

Payne, Darin. "Effacing Difference in the Royal Society: The Homogenizing Nature of Disciplinary Dialogue." *Rhetoric Review* 20, no. 1/2 (2001): 94–112.

Perkins, David. "How the Romantics Recited Poetry." *Studies in English Literature, 1500–1900* 31, no. 4 (1991): 655–71.

Porter, Dorothy B. "Early American Negro Writings: A Bibliographical Study." *Papers of the Bibliographical Society of America* 39 (1945): 192–268.

Potkay, Adam. *The Fate of Eloquence in the Age of Hume.* Ithaca: Cornell University Press, 1994.

———. "History, Oratory, and God in Equiano's Interesting Narrative." *Eighteenth-Century Studies* 34, no. 4 (2001): 601–14.

Poulakos, John. "From the Depths of Rhetoric: The Emergence of Aesthetics as a Discipline." *Philosophy and Rhetoric* 40, no. 4 (2007): 335–52.

Purcell, William M. "Rhetorical Studies: A Reassessment of Adam Smith's Lectures on Rhetoric and Belles Lettres." *Central States Speech Journal* 37, no. 1 (1986): 45–54.

Read, Allen Walker. "The Speech of Negroes in Colonial America." *Journal of Negro History* 24, no. 3 (1939): 247–58.

Redford, Bruce. *The Converse of the Pen: Acts of Intimacy in the Eighteenth-Century Familiar Letter.* Chicago: University of Chicago Press, 1986.

Reid, Christopher. "Character Construction in the Eighteenth-Century House of Commons: Evidence from the Cavendish Diary (1768–74)." *Rhetorica* 22, no. 4 (2004): 375–99.

———. "Speaking Candidly: Rhetoric, Politics, and the Meanings of Candour in the Later Eighteenth Century." *British Journal for Eighteenth-Century Studies* 28 (2005): 67–82.

Reid, Ronald F. *American Revolution and the Rhetoric of History.* N.p.: National Speech Communication Association, 1978.

Rhodes, Neil. "From Rhetoric to Criticism." In *The Scottish Invention of English Literature,* ed. Robert Crawford, 22–36. Cambridge: Cambridge University Press, 1998.

Riker, William H. *The Strategy of Rhetoric: Campaigning for the American Constitution.* New Haven: Yale University Press, 1996.

Romano, Susan. "Rhetorics of Colonial Encounter: Nahua Moral Agency in Farol Indiano." Paper presented at the International Society of the History of Rhetoric, Strasbourg, France, July 2007.

Royster, Jacqueline Jones. "Sarah's Story: Making a Place for Historical Ethnography in Rhetorical Studies." In *Rhetoric, the Polis, and the Global Village: Selected Papers from the 1998 Thirtieth Anniversary Rhetoric Society of America Conference,* ed. C. Jan Swearingen and Dave Pruett, 39–51. Mahwah, NJ: Lawrence Erlbaum Associates, 1999.

Sarkela, Sandra J. "Moderation, Religion, and Public Discourse: The Rhetoric of Occasional Conformity in England, 1697–1711." *Rhetorica* 15, no. 1 (1997): 53–79.

Schaeffer, John. "From Natural Religion to Natural Law in Vico: Rhetoric, Poetic, and Vico's Imaginative Universals." *Rhetorica* 15, no. 1 (1997): 41–52.

———. *Sensus Communis: Vico, Rhetoric, and the Limits of Relativism.* Durham, NC: Duke University Press, 1990.

Schomburg, Arthur, ed. *The Negro: A Selected Bibliography.* Whitefish, MT: Kessinger Publishing, 2006.

Sher, Richard B. *Church and University in the Scottish Enlightenment: The Moderate Literati of Edinburgh.* Princeton: Princeton University Press, 1985.

Sherzer, Joel, and Anthony C. Woodbury, eds. *Native American Discourse: Poetics and Rhetoric.* Cambridge: Cambridge University Press, 1987.

Shield, David S. *Civil Tongues and Polite Letters in British America.* Chapel Hill: University of North Carolina Press, 1997.

Short, Bryan C. "Figurative Language in the Scottish New Rhetoric." *Language Sciences* 22, no. 3 (2000): 251–64.

Smith, Ali, and Olivia Smith. *Politics of Language: 1790–1819.* Oxford: Oxford University Press, 1990.

Smith, Tania Sona. "The Lady's Rhetorick (1707): The Tip of the Iceberg of Women's Rhetorical Education in Enlightenment France and Britain." *Rhetorica* 22, no. 4 (2004): 349–73.

———. "Learning Conversational Rhetoric in Eighteenth-Century Britain: Hester Thrale Piozzi and Her Mentors Collier and Johnson." *Rhetor: Journal of the Canadian Society for the Study of Rhetoric* 2 (2007). March 1, 2008. www. cssr-scer.ca/rhetor.

Sorensen, Janet. "Vulgar Tongues: Canting Dictionaries and the Language of the People in Eighteenth-Century Britain." *Eighteenth-Century Studies* 37, no. 3 (2004): 435–54.

Spoel, Philippa M. "Rereading the Elocutionists: The Rhetoric of Thomas Sheridan's *A Course of Lectures on Elocution* and John Walker's *Elements of Elocution.*" *Rhetorica* 19, no. 1 (2001): 49–91.

Stafford, Barbara Maria. *Body Criticism: Imaging the Unseen in Enlightenment Art and Medicine.* Cambridge, MA: MIT Press, 1991.

Stafford, Fiona. "Hugh Blair's Ossian, Romanticism and the Teaching of Literature." In *The Scottish Invention of English Literature,* ed. Robert Crawford, 68–88. New York: Cambridge University Press, 1998.

Staves, Susan. "'The Liberty of a She-Subject of England': Rights Rhetoric and the Female Thucydides." *Cardozo Studies in Law and Literature* 1, no. 2 (1989): 161–83.

Stone, P. W. K. *The Art of Poetry, 1750–1820.* New York: Barnes and Noble, 1967.

Stout, Harry. *The New England Soul: Preaching and Religious Culture in Colonial New England.* New York: Oxford University Press, 1988.

Stroud, Scott R., "Kant on Community: A Reply to Gehrke." *Philosophy and Rhetoric* 39, no. 2 (2006): 157–65.

———. "Rhetoric and Moral Progress in Kant's Ethical Community." *Philosophy and Rhetoric* 38, no. 4 (2005): 328–54.

Struever, Nancy S. "The Conversable World: Eighteenth-Century Transformations of the Relation of Rhetoric and Truth." In *Rhetoric and the Pursuit of Truth: Language Change in the Seventeenth and Eighteenth Centuries,* ed. Brian Vickers and Nancy S. Struever, 77–119. Los Angeles: William Andrews Clark Memorial Library, University of California Press, 1985.

———. "Rhetoric and Philosophy in Vichian Inquiry." *New Vico Studies* 3 (1985): 131–45.

Suleri, Sara. *The Rhetoric of English India.* Chicago: University of Chicago Press, 1992.

Swaminathan, Srividhya. "Adam Smith's Moral Economy and the Debate to Abolish the Slave Trade." *Rhetoric Society Quarterly* 37, no. 4 (2007): 481–507.

Sypher, Wylie. "Hutcheson and the 'Classical' Theory of Slavery." *Journal of Negro History* 24 (1939): 263–80.

Thale, Mary. "The Case of the British Inquisition: Money and Women in Mid-Eighteenth-Century London Debating Societies." *Albion: A Quarterly Journal Concerned with British Studies* 31, no. 1 (1999): 31–48.

Ulman, H. Lewis, ed. *Minutes of the Aberdeen Philosophical Society, 1758–1773.* MacMillan, 1990.

———. *Things, Thoughts, Words, and Actions: The Problem of Language in Late*

Eighteenth-Century British Rhetorical Theory. Carbondale: Southern Illinois University Press, 1994.

Vickers, Brian. *Rhetoric and the Pursuit of Truth: Language Change in the Seventeenth and Eighteenth Centuries.* Los Angeles: William Andrews Clark, 1985.

Walmsley, Peter. *Locke's Essay and the Rhetoric of Science.* Lewisburg, PA: Bucknell University Press, 2003.

Walters, Ronald W., and Cedric Johnson. *Bibliography of African American Leadership: An Annotated Guide.* Bibliographies and Indexes in Afro-American and African Studies. Westport, CT: Greenwood Press, 2000.

Walzer, Arthur E. "Campbell on the Passions: A Rereading of the 'Philosophy of Rhetoric.'" *Quarterly Journal of Speech* 85, no. 1 (1999): 72–85.

———. *George Campbell: Rhetoric in the Age of Enlightenment.* Albany: State University of New York Press, 2002.

———. "On Reading George Campbell: 'Resemblance' and 'Vivacity' in the Philosophy of Rhetoric." *Rhetorica* 18, no. 3 (2000): 321–42.

———. "Rhetoric and Gender in Jane Austen's Persuasion." *College English* 57, no. 6 (1995): 688–707.

Warner, Michael. *The Letters of the Republic: Publication and the Public Sphere in Eighteenth-Century America.* Boston: Harvard University Press, 1990.

Warnick, Barbara. *The Sixth Canon: Belletristic Rhetorical Theory and Its French Antecedents.* Columbia: University of South Carolina Press, 1993.

Weber, Donald. *Rhetoric and History in Revolutionary New England.* New York: Oxford University Press, 1988.

Weinsheimer, Joel C. "The Philosophy of Rhetoric in George Campbell's Philosophy of Rhetoric." In *Companion to Rhetoric and Rhetorical Criticism,* ed. Walter Jost and Wendy Olmsted, 141–51. Blackwell, 2004.

Weinstein, Jack Russell. "Emotion, Context and Rhetoric: Adam Smith's Informal Argumentation." In *Proceedings of the Fifth Conference of the International Society for the Study of Argumentation,* 1065–70. Amsterdam: Sic Sat, 2003.

White, Phillip M. *American Indian and African American People, Communities, and Interactions: An Annotated Bibliography.* Westport, CT: Praeger, 2004.

Wiley, Margaret Lee. *Gerard and the Scots Societies.* Austin: University of Texas Press, 1940.

Woodard, Helena. *African-British Writings in the Eighteenth Century.* Westport, CT: Greenwood Press, 1999.

Wright, Elizabethada A., and S. Michael Halloran. "From Rhetoric to Composition: The Teaching of Writing in America to 1900." In *A Short History of Writing Instruction from Ancient Greece to Twentieth Century America,* ed. James J. Murphy, 213–46. Davis, CA: Hermagoras Press, 2001.

Wyland, Russell M. "An Archival Study of Rhetoric Texts and Teaching at the University of Oxford, 1785–1820." *Rhetorica* 21, no. 3 (2003): 175–95.

Xavier, Silvia. "Engaging George Campbell's Sympathy in the Rhetoric of Charlotte Forten and Ann Plato, African-American Women of the Antebellum
North." *Rhetoric Review* 24, no. 4 (2005): 438–56.

Yarbrough, Stephen R., and John C. Adams. *Delightful Conviction: Jonathan
Edwards and the Rhetoric of Conversion.* Westport, CT: Greenwood Press,
1993.

5

The Nineteenth Century

Lynée Lewis Gaillet

In the 1990 edition of *The Present State of Scholarship*, Donald C. Stewart explains that the greatest difficulties in describing and categorizing nineteenth-century rhetoric stem from the period's apparent lack of an "intellectual, philosophical, or theoretical center" (151). Routinely, until the late twentieth century, histories of rhetoric either collapsed discussions of the eighteenth and nineteenth centuries, characterized the nineteenth century as a stagnant era of imitation, or dismissed the period as vacuous. However, Stewart argues that nineteenth-century rhetoric takes on shape and form when viewed in terms of the classical canon—invention, arrangement, style, memory, and delivery— and he delineates the following "strands" of nineteenth-century rhetoric: classical, elocutionary, psychological-epistemological, belletristic, and practical (composition). Stewart's divisions provided a useful rubric for codifying (both primary and secondary) nineteenth-century works and for understanding the implications of rhetorical theory and practice in Great Britain and the United States during the century. In 1990, Stewart summed up the present state of nineteenth-century rhetoric thus: "[W]e may say that while a few useful and valuable studies that attempt to generalize about the period of movements within it exist, they represent only the vanguard of work which is yet to come" (172).

Stewart called for an expansion of nineteenth-century studies to include "a body of scholarship to develop around figures," including minor rhetoricians (172); a reexamination of historiography characterizing the period in order to define rhetorical parameters of the field; and a modification of curriculum within English departments to reflect the growing interest in the history of nineteenth-century rhetoric (173). Professor Stewart died in 1992 and did not see his prophetic hopes for the field come to fruition. The late 1990s witnessed a watershed moment, however, particularly in American rhetoric, as revision and recovery research methods resurrected primary works and yielded secondary information about specific figures; the publication of anthologies led to the subsequent expansion of curricula to include both "recovered" rhetors and new "strands" of rhetorical practice. Pondering definitions and scope of nineteenth-century rhetoric, Stewart in 1990 asked how inclusive the term *rhetoric* should be:

> Broad enough to include not only the preceptive tradition but also the rhetorics of science, the feminist movement, abolition, and political and social rhetoric, both pre– and post–Civil War? Or should one narrow the definition to the preceptive tradition, as I have essentially done here, and then study the ways in which the other "rhetorics" of the period appropriated segments of the preceptive tradition? Or should one take a completely different approach, as James Berlin has done, and define the rhetoric of this or any other period in terms of its epistemological assumptions? (173)

A review of recent scholarship concerning the period attests that although each of Stewart's suggestions has merit (and followers), the tide has turned overwhelmingly in favor of a broadened and inclusive canon. How, then, do we now approach study of the era's rhetorical history when the period is no longer considered a void, a century of study contained within the traditional "strands," or a codified "preceptive" tradition? As I seek to describe the landscape of the current state of nineteenth-century scholarship, it becomes apparent that we are still standing in the stream when it comes to redefining and reinterpreting the period's traditional history; recent scholarship addressing the nineteenth century no longer neatly fits into Stewart's five strands or James Berlin's three systems of American rhetoric (classical, psychological-epistemological, and romantic). Cumulatively, the surveys, introductions, and detailed overviews of the period (discussed below) paint a vivid picture of the status of nineteenth-century rhetorical scholarship through the end of the twentieth century. I refer readers interested in this period to these widely accessible and foundational bibliographical works—and in this chapter, I will not reexamine the primary materials carefully examined therein. Instead, given the recent shifts in historiographical methods and methodologies, redefinitions of the scope of nineteenth-century rhetoric, the volume of scholarship concerning historically marginalized rhetors, and the (albeit limited) emergence of works addressing non-Western rhetorical traditions, I wish to survey primary materials, secondary sources, and new "strands" of rhetorical thought and practice that have come to light since the publication of the 1990 edition of *The Present State*. Traces of Stewart's "strands" are represented in the following pages, embedded within current contexts for examining the era's rhetorical histories but expanded, given the emergence of primary materials and new venues of study. These emerging materials, historiographical methodologies, and reclaimed rhetors and venues for rhetorical engagement complicate existing portraits of nineteenth-century rhetoric. This chapter, then, neither restates nor eclipses Stewart's chapter, but rather extends and updates the information found there.

The field as yet has not fully recodified nineteenth-century rhetoric to take into account the explosion of divergent scholarship spanning the last twenty years. I do not attempt to do so in this chapter but instead offer snapshots of the existing terrain. The photo is still blurry; the images are still materializing. Therefore, the following categories are messy; they overlap, twist back upon themselves, and are rather arbitrary. Stewart was right: there is no one "intellectual, philosophical, or theoretical center" for the period. Instead, we are finding multiple pulse points and nuanced avenues for discovering an expanded scope of rhetorical theory. Embedded within this chapter's subdivisions are discussions of literacy studies, elocution/oratory, religion, science, education, technology, literature, rhetoric and public affairs, race, and gender. The focus is heavily American, reflecting an abundance of scholarship that counters previous characterizations of the period as uninteresting and uneventful, and the bibliography includes considerable scholarship produced by scholars in English studies, who since the publication of the last edition of *The Present State* have joined their colleagues in communications in seeking layered, coexisting histories of the field. The following broad categories and discussions of rhetorical development, then, represent the protean ground from which future ways of understanding nineteenth-century rhetorical theory and practice might emerge.

Overviews and Bibliographies

Arguing that two prevailing conceptions of American rhetoric—viewing rhetoric as writing instruction (English departments) or oratory/elocution (speech departments)—present reductive views of nineteenth-century rhetorical theory and practice, Linda Ferreira-Buckley, in the "Nineteenth-Century Rhetoric" entry published in Enos's *Encyclopedia of Composition and Rhetoric* (1996), reminds us that "rhetorics of the period focused variously on the public (civic life), the professional (individual expertise), or the private (individual self-improvement)" (468). Likewise, describing "nineteenth-century rhetoric" in T. O. Sloane's *The Encyclopedia of Rhetoric* (2001), leading nineteenth-century scholar Nan Johnson extends and redefines Stewart's categories based on the classical five-part canon to make room for other emerging American rhetorics. Explaining that during the nineteenth century "the study of rhetoric was constructed as an opportunity that any literate American could take up, and because rhetorical skills were defined as universally applicable to all communicative occasions, the discipline of rhetoric defined itself as both accessible and indispensable" (518), Johnson's discussion of the period—divided into sections addressing "adaptation," "epistemology," "delivery/elocution," "arrangement," "style," "genres," and "invention"—modifies previous categories and occasions for studying the period's history to reflect notions of "access" and "utility." These two fine encyclopedia entries illustrate possible trajectories for refiguring discussions about nineteenth-century rhetorical theory and practice in North America, and for viewing the period's significance within the development of intellectual histories.

Enos's *Encyclopedia of Rhetoric and Composition: Communication from Ancient Times to the Information Age* (1996) and Sloane's *Encyclopedia of Rhetoric* (2001) serve as comprehensive sourcebooks and guides to rhetorical theory and practice, offering numerous specific entries pertinent to the period and focused essays detailing historical movements, trends, and figures. Other rich surveys of nineteenth-century rhetoric include Patricia Bizzell and Bruce Herzberg's introduction to the century found in the anthology *The Rhetorical Tradition: Readings from Classical Times to the Present* (2001); Gregory Clark and S. Michael Halloran's *Oratorical Culture in Nineteenth-Century America* (1993); Mark Longaker's recent *Rhetoric and the Republic: Politics, Civic Discourse, and Education in Early America* (2007); Ferreira-Buckley and Winifred Bryan Horner's chapter "Writing Instruction in Great Britain: The Eighteenth and Nineteenth Centuries" and Elizabethada Wright and Michael Halloran's "From Rhetoric to Composition: The Teaching of Writing in America to 1900," both in James Murphy's *A Short History of Writing Instruction: From Ancient Greece to Modern America* (2001); and Nan Johnson's important full-length work *Nineteenth-Century Rhetoric in North America* (1991). Foundational examinations of nineteenth-century American education include Warren Guthrie's oft-cited "The Development of Rhetorical Theory in America, 1635–1850," published serially in *Speech Monographs* between 1946 and 1951, Karl Wallace's *A History of Speech Education in America: Background Studies* (1954), Alfred Kitzhaber's *Rhetoric in American Colleges, 1850–1900* (1990), and James Berlin's *Writing Instruction in Nineteenth-Century American Colleges* (1984).

For general bibliographies useful for researching works from and about the period, see Forrest Houlette's acclaimed *Nineteenth-Century Rhetoric: An Enumerative Bibliography* (1989), along with many digital resources: the *CCC Online Archive* (http://www.inventio. us/ccc/), *CCCC Bibliography of Composition and Rhetoric* (http://www.ibiblio.org/cccc/), *ERIC* (http://www.eric. ed.gov/), Rich Haswell and Glenn Blalock's *CompPile* (http://comppile. tamucc. edu/), Rebecca Moore Howard's incredibly helpful and diverse *Bibliographies for Composition and Rhetoric* (http://wrt-howard.syr.edu/bibs.html), and print/ online indexes to journals routinely publishing scholarship about the period, such as *College Composition and Communication, College English, Journal of Scottish Philosophy, Peitho, Philosophy and Rhetoric, Quarterly Journal of Speech,*

Rhetorica, Rhetoric Review, Rhetoric Society Quarterly, and others. Specialized bibliographies have emerged in the wake of prolific scholarship addressing recovered venues of nineteenth-century rhetorical practice, and many of these sources not only recount existing work from and about the period but also provide maps to navigate new terrain and ways of interpreting nineteenth-century rhetoric. Bibliographical tools and guides addressing specific areas of nineteenth-century historical research are listed in the following subheadings, where appropriate.

Writing Instruction

The nineteenth-century origins of North American writing instruction have received considerable scholarly attention during the last two decades. Donald Stewart labeled this section "Practical Rhetoric" in his 1990 essay, and in those pages, he enumerated the texts (both British and American) associated with what has become known as current-traditional composition instruction. Nan Johnson's groundbreaking *Nineteenth-Century Rhetoric in North America* (1990) added considerably to the body of knowledge concerning American composition theorists and answered charges that the nineteenth century represented a period of decline within intellectual histories. Johnson, along with Gregory Clark and S. Michael Halloran in *Oratorical Culture in Nineteenth-Century America* (1993), convincingly argues that nineteenth-century education responded to rhetorical exigencies, dominated by the preparation of students and citizens to speak and write eloquently. No longer is this century viewed merely as an extension of eighteenth-century rhetoric or as an arhetorical age infamous for the origins and institutionalization of utilitarian writing instruction. The period's educational curricula and pedagogies are now studied against specific historical, political, and social localities— resulting in the emergence of complex and layered, coexisting histories of the discipline. As Robert Connors so aptly reminds us, "history is not, and never has been, systematic or scientific" ("Dreams and Play," 31).

As scholars of nineteenth-century American writing instruction challenged assumptions about the period and began to examine relationships between culture and writing instruction, conceptions of the nineteenth century as a time characterized only by borrowings and misappropriations of British rhetorical theory fell away, making space for new discoveries and analyses of writing instruction. For example, Keith Gilyard, in "African American Contributions to Composition Studies" (1999), argues that African American intellectual and rhetorical traditions of the nineteenth century made highly influential contributions to writing instruction. John Brereton's *Origins of Composition Studies in the American College, 1875–1925: A Documentary History* (1995) makes available a broad collection of archival materials, thereby opening avenues of instructional research. In *Historical Studies of Writing Program Administration: Individuals, Communities, and the Formation of a Discipline* (2004), Barb L'Eplattenier and Lisa Mastrangelo weave an extensive account of the development of writing program administration, an area often glossed over in traditional histories of nineteenth-century composition instruction. Other scholars of composition pedagogy have begun to question common assumptions surrounding writing instruction's role in the academy. Sharon Crowley's *Composition in the University: Historical and Polemical Essays* (1998) takes to task the primacy that has historically been given to first-year composition courses, and Mariolina Rizzi Salvatore, in *Pedagogy: Disturbing History, 1819–1929* (1996), presents an archival account of teaching in which she speculates why and how academics and administrators came to devalue pedagogy, seeing teaching as a skill secondary to research.

As this broadened conception of educational history led scholars to examine historical and institutional contexts for writing instruction, important archival materials concerning student writing (inside and outside the classroom) emerged. Lucille Schultz's *The Young Composers: Composition's Beginnings in Nineteenth-Century Schools* (1999), along with Carr, Carr, and Shultz's *Archives of Instruction* (2005), gave primacy to student essays, textbooks, journals, letters, and published articles. Archival collections addressing student writing, such as Erika Lindemann's "True and Candid Compositions: The Lives and Writings of Antebellum Students at the University of North Carolina" (2002)—a collection of 121 archival documents (including 108 student writings) from 1795–1869—provide rare glimpses into town-and-gown relationships. And Susan Miller's *Assuming the Positions: Cultural Pedagogy and the Politics of Commonplace Writing* (1998) analyzes nonacademic, everyday written accounts produced in Virginia from 1650 to 1880. She argues that historians of composition pedagogy must consider writings produced outside the classroom in order to paint a realistic picture of the history of composition.

Another emerging area of archival research concerns the reexamination of both major and minor figures associated with the birth of composition studies. Stewart urged us to complicate our notions of nineteenth-century figures and move away from characterizing our predecessors as either "villains" or "heroes." Charles Paine, in *Rhetoric as Immunity, 1850 to the Present* (1999), revisits the educational theories and practices of famous educators Edward T. Channing and Adams Sherman Hill in an effort to read these figures' contributions in light of their own times and cultural exigencies. The work of Gertrude Buck has been revisited by JoAnn Campbell in *Toward a Feminist Rhetoric: The Writing of Gertrude Buck* (1996) and by Suzanne Bordelon in *Feminist Legacy: The Rhetoric and Pedagogy of Gertrude Buck* (2007), which examines Buck's rhetorical theory as a genesis of feminist theories of argumentation and pedagogy. Donald and Patricia Stewart's biography of Fred Newton Scott (1997) and Susan Thomas's dissertation, "'Part of a Larger Whole': Fred Newton Scott and the Progressive Education Movement" (2002), present two divergent understandings of this heralded American compositionist. Thomas finds Scott's administrative style to be responsible in part for the subsequent erosion of the rhetoric program at the University of Michigan.

This "revision" of accepted notions of nineteenth-century American composition instruction is echoed in (re)examinations of nineteenth-century British university curriculum as well. Russell M. Wyland's "An Archival Study of Rhetoric Texts and Teaching at the University of Oxford, 1785–1820" (2003) analyzes public and personal documents in his study of curricular and pedagogical reform at elite institutions, while Thomas Miller's *The Formation of College English: Rhetoric and Belles Lettres in the British Cultural Provinces* (1997) looks to political and civic concerns associated with the adoption of rhetoric and belles lettres at institutions falling outside the Oxbridge collegiate system. See also Sherry Booth's "A Moment for Reform: Rhetoric and Literature at the University of Glasgow, 1862–1877" (2003) and Linda Ferreira-Buckley's "'Scotch' Knowledge and the Formation of Rhetorical Studies" (1997).

The study and critique of the unfolding history of nineteenth-century composition theories and practices is an important area for future research. In particular, the field needs additional contextualized archival resources from the period—including institutional data (such as John C. Gerber's description of "English at Iowa in the Nineteenth Century"), cataloged professors' lecture notes and course materials, nuanced student writings like the collection compiled by Lindemann, committee reports, society minutes, local school legislation and school-reform reports, teachers' and administrators' published and private thoughts, and transcriptions of commencement addresses.

Scottish Influences

Discussing eighteenth-century higher education, Douglas Sloan, in *The Scottish Enlightenment and the American College Ideal* (1971), convincingly outlines the "appeal" of the Scottish educational system for early American colleges, the influence of individual Scottish educators upon American curricula, and the role the Presbyterian Church played in eighteenth-century American higher education (ix). More recently, Thomas Miller's *The Formation of College English: Rhetoric and Belles Lettres in the British Cultural Provinces* (1997), an important examination of the civic and political role of rhetoric, reinforces many of Sloan's arguments. Scottish enlightenment rhetoric ideally suited a new nation determined to break from colonial rule and committed to educational and religious freedom. Winifred Bryan Horner's *Nineteenth-Century Scottish Rhetoric: The American Connection* (1993) explains how many Scottish immigrants, such as John Witherspoon, Benjamin Rush, James Madison, and James Wilson, made their marks in early American educational and political arenas. Additionally, historical records show that Scottish influence in American education extends well into the first half of the nineteenth century; as Horner explains, "it is during the nineteenth century in Scottish universities that English literature became an academic subject, that psychology evolved as a legitimate discipline, and that criticism developed out of the ancient study of rhetoric" (vii). Although the presence of Scottish commonsense philosophies within eighteenth-century American college curricula is widely documented (see works by Horner, Sloan, Miller, Sher and Smitten, and Ferreira-Buckley in the appended bibliography), the full extent of Scottish influence upon nineteenth-century American education, particularly in institutions falling outside the "Harvard tradition," is only now coming to light.

Scottish-based educational philosophy, often labeled the "Princeton School" —an alternative to Harvard's dominance over university curricula—echoes the philosophical theories of Scottish rhetoricians. John Witherspoon and John McCosh are recognized as the primary expounders of the Scottish tradition to America, and intellectual histories of the United States use the phrase "the Princeton School" to refer to the powerful point of view espoused by these two Scots. Scott Philip Segrest's 2005 dissertation, "Common Sense Philosophy and Politics in America: John Witherspoon, James McCosh, and William James," explains how Scottish educators "offer a vision of man and society that avoids the rigidity of dogmatic foundationalism, on the one hand, and the slackness of foundationless ethics and politics, on the other" (iv), and Mark Longaker, in *Rhetoric and the Republic* (2007), delves into the lasting effects of Witherspoon's reign at the College of New Jersey. Interdisciplinary scholarship, such as Thomas Olbricht and Hans Rollman's collection, *The Quest for Christian Unity, Peace, and Purity in Thomas Campbell's Declaration and Address: Text and Studies* (2000), and Carisse Berryhill's *Sense, Expression, and Purpose: Alexander Campbell's Natural Philosophy of Rhetoric* (1982) expand that limited conception of "the Princeton School" beyond the material walls of the College of New Jersey to include other early American colleges committed to the tenets of commonsense philosophy, Baconian scientific induction, and religious evangelism.

Textbook adoption records indicate that works by Scottish rhetors such as Hugh Blair, George Campbell, Henry Home (Lord Kames), Alexander Jamieson, and Alexander Bain were widely adopted in nineteenth-century American colleges, and students of the period are well aware of the current-traditional methods of writing instruction (mis)appropriated from Bain at the University of Aberdeen. For further elucidation, see Shelley Aley's "The Impact of Science on Rhetoric through the Contributions of the University of Aberdeen's Alexander Bain" (1998) and two articles by Andrea Lunsford: "Alexander

Bain's Contributions to Discourse Theory" (1990) and "Alexander Bain and the Teaching of Composition in North America" (1998). However, larger pedagogical issues and concerns—ones with far-reaching implications—were dictated by the Scots as well. For example, Winifred Horner explains how William Aytoun at Edinburgh introduced the study of English literature into university curricula forty years ahead of Oxford or Cambridge ("Aytoun," 58). Similar records are still surfacing in many cases because archives are scattered and interdisciplinary. One example, "The Campbell Collection" housed in the T. W. Phillips Memorial Library at Bethany College, West Virginia, along with holdings at the Disciples of Christ Historical Society in Nashville, Tennessee, details the magnitude and significance of Scottish influence upon the curricula of religious colleges founded by Scottish immigrants. How many other influences and voices are yet to be recovered through interdisciplinary, archival research?

To continue expanding our understanding of the century's rhetorical significance, the field needs interdisciplinary organizations, journals, and book series devoted to multifaceted study of the period. The Center for the Study of Scottish Philosophy (CSSP)—which takes as its mission (1) to raise interest in Scottish philosophy beyond the Scottish Enlightenment, (2) to explore the influence of Scottish philosophy upon liberal arts and theological education in North America, and (3) to recover philosophical and theological resources —serves as a worthy model. The CSSP publishes the international *Journal of Scottish Philosophy* (published for the center by Edinburgh University Press and incorporating the earlier publication *Reid Studies*), sponsors numerous conventions and annual meetings, and publishes inexpensive scholarly editions of works by both major and lesser-known Scottish philosophers. Interdisciplinary initiatives like the CSSP hold the most promise for continued expansion of our understanding of nineteenth-century rhetoric.

Elocution/Delivery

In addition to rigorous vocal training, elocutionary texts from the period detail (1) analysis of human anatomy and the "science" of speech production, (2) correlations between elocution manuals' instruction in the techniques of delivery and audience analysis, and (3) instruction in speaking and reading aloud. Both Johnson and Ferreira-Buckley's "Nineteenth Century" encyclopedia entries provide concise information concerning the century's elocution manuals. Other recent scholarship moves beyond discussions of elocutionary texts and education and instead attempts to put delivery into historical context by focusing on occasions, venues, and platforms for speaking; cultural discussions of speaking and silence; delivery and religion; the relationship between elocutionary and belletristic rhetoric; and gendered delivery and issues of class, race, and education. One of the most important recent areas of research on delivery addresses the recovery and analysis of women's oratorical education and practices; I discuss this scholarship in the "Women and Rhetoric" section below.

Ben McCorkle, in "Harbingers of the Printed Page: Nineteenth-Century Theories of Delivery as Remediation" (2005), argues against the established belief that belletristic and elocutionary traditions of the nineteenth century were at odds. He suggests that the two traditions shared a joint purpose: to naturalize print media and bring the attributes of print culture to handwriting and oratorical practice as "natural elements." Similarly, Susan Miller's *Trust in Texts: A Different History of Rhetoric* (2008) challenges the accepted idea of a singular rhetorical tradition, calling into question the centrality of logos to rhetoric. Miller argues that oratorical rhetoric is one (among many other) codes that guide the production of texts. Scholarship examining delivery practices and religion include Vicki Tolar Burton's "John Wesley and the Liberty to Speak: The Rhetorical and Literacy Practices of Early Methodism" (2001), which explains how this Protestant denomination, under the leadership of Wesley, empowered women and the working classes to read, write, and speak in public. Brian Fehler, in *Calvinist Rhetoric in Nineteenth-Century America: The Bartlet Professors of Sacred Rhetoric of Andover Seminary* (2007), a work based on examination of primary documents composed by prominent members of the Calvinist clergy, argues that the democratizing forces of U.S. oratorical culture greatly influenced Calvinist sermons and teachings. Many of the works discussed in the "Women and Rhetoric" and "African American Rhetoric" sections of this chapter concern delivery and religion; see those subheadings for details.

Other scholarship addressing delivery reexamines and reconsiders the work of orators and teachers of oratory in an effort to view these figures within their own historical milieu. Craig R. Smith's *Daniel Webster and the Oratory of Civil Religion* (2005), an "oratorical biography," depicts Webster's public (speaking) life; Philippa M. Spoel's "Rereading the Elocutionists: The Rhetoric of Thomas Sheridan's *A Course of Lectures on Elocution* and John Walker's *Elements of Elocution*" (2001) defend often-maligned elocutionary instruction by examining practitioners within their own sociohistorical context; and W. Stuart Towns collects eighty years' worth of Southern speeches justifying the region's way of life to those living outside the culture in *Oratory and Rhetoric in the Nineteenth-Century South: A Rhetoric of Defense* (1998).

Finally, elocution scholarship addressing the nineteenth century needs additional comparative views of elocutionary instruction in other cultures, such as Massimiliano Tomasi's *Rhetoric in Modern Japan: Western Influences on the Development of Narrative and Oratorical Style* (2004), and "The Impact of Western Rhetoric on the East: The Case of Japan" (1990), in which Roichi Okabe explains that despite the introduction of elocutionary texts to Japanese culture during the Meiji era (1868–1912), Western elocutionary rhetoric made no lasting changes in the Japanese rhetorical tradition because of elocutionary instruction's excessive artificiality.

Women and Rhetoric

One of the most prolific areas of recent scholarship on nineteenth-century rhetoric addresses feminist readings of the period and the recovery of female orators and writers. The traditional "strands" of nineteenth-century rhetoric identified by Donald Stewart—classical, elocutionary, psychological-epistemological, belletristic, and practical (composition)—are embedded in the following works, but scholars listed in this section expand the traditional canon of nineteenth-century scholarship not only to write women into existing histories of rhetoric, but also to address issues of culture, race, class, education, venues for rhetorical engagement, and nineteenth-century "women's ways of knowing" and participation.

Elizabeth Tasker has spearheaded two important collaborative bibliographical projects in this area: "A Brief Summary of Feminist Research Methodologies in Historic Rhetoric and Composition from the 1970s to the Present" (2006), sponsored by the Coalition of Women Scholars in the History of Rhetoric and published in *Peitho*, and "Feminist Research Methodologies in Historic Rhetoric and Composition: An Overview of Scholarship from the 1970s to the Present" (2008). Excellent collections of essays that regender the canon of nineteenth-century rhetorical theory include Andrea Lunsford's *Reclaiming Rhetorica: Women in the Rhetorical Tradition* (1995), Molly Meijer Wertheimer's *Listening to Their Voices: The Rhetorical Activities of Historical Women* (1997), and Christine Sutherland and Rebecca Sutcliffe's *The Changing Tradition: Women in the History of Rhetoric* (1999). These works explore a wide range of issues, strategies, and venues associated with female rhetoric.

Three important anthologies of women's rhetoric expand the rhetorical tradition to include female voices: Shirley Wilson Logan's *With Pen and Voice: A Critical Anthology of Nineteenth-Century African-American Women* (1995), Joy Ritchie and Kate Ronald's ambitious *Available Means: An Anthology of Women's Rhetoric(s)* (2001), and Jane Donawerth's *Rhetorical Theory by Women before 1900* (2002). In addition, the appended bibliography lists an impressive number of scholarly investigations of individual female rhetors' lives and work. Perhaps most encouraging, nineteenth-century women are now appearing not only in gendered collections of primary documents, but also in general anthologies of historical rhetoric. Bizzell and Herzberg's second edition of *The Rhetorical Tradition* includes works by Maria Stewart, Sarah Grimké, Phoebe Palmer, and Frances Willard—representing nearly half of the nineteenth-century featured figures in that volume.

The recent "remapping" of nineteenth-century rhetorical spaces and current avenues of feminist research is summarized in Nan Johnson's introduction, "The Feminist Analysis of Rhetoric as a Cultural Site," to her groundbreaking *Gender and Rhetorical Space in American Life, 1866–1910* (2002). In a related work, Lindal Buchanan's *Regendering Delivery: The Fifth Canon and Antebellum Women Rhetors* (2005) moors delivery to local exigencies and cultural and rhetorical contexts in her discussion of the public performances and private lives of antebellum female rhetors (both former slaves and privileged women, Northerners and Southerners, religious and secular figures).

In rescuing the voices of nineteenth-century women activists, feminist scholars illustrate the range of venues and occasions for speaking that prompted women's communicative discourse—despite their being barred from public rhetorical spaces. Works examining a wide range of women's religious roles in society (as preachers and activists) include Catherine Brekus's *Strangers and Pilgrims: Female Preaching in America* (1998); Vicki Tolar Collins's "Walking in Light, Walking in Darkness: The Story of Women's Changing Rhetorical Space in Early Methodism" (1996); Bettye Collier-Thomas's collection of primary documents *Daughters of Thunder: Black Women Preachers and Their Sermons, 1850–1979* (1998); Daphne Desser's "Fraught Literacy: American Missionary Women in Nineteenth-Century Hawai'i" (2007); Chanta Haywood's *Prophesying Daughters: Black Women Preachers and the Word, 1823–1913* (2003); and Roxanne Mountford's *The Gendered Pulpit: Preaching in American Protestant Spaces* (2003).

Suffragette rhetoric is the focus of works such as Katherine H. Adams and Michael L. Keene's *Alice Paul and the American Suffrage Campaign* (2008), Kathryn M. Conway's "Woman Suffrage and the History of Rhetoric at the Seven Sisters Colleges, 1865–1919" (1995), and Susan Zaeske's "'The Promiscuous Audience' Controversy and Emergence of the Early Woman's Rights Movement" (1995). Carolyn Skinner's "'The Purity of Truth': Nineteenth-Century American Women Physicians Write about Delicate Topics" (2007) and Susan Wells's *Out of the Dead House: Nineteenth-Century Women Physicians and the Writing of Medicine* (2001) explore female physicians' medical writings. And investigations of female education can be found in Katherine Adams's *A Group of Their Own: College Writing Courses and American Women Writers, 1880–1940* (2001), Catherine Hobbs's *Nineteenth-Century Women Learn to Write* (1995), and Susan Kates's *Activist Rhetorics and American Higher Education, 1885–1937* (2001).

The rhetorical activity of social reformers pervades many of the categories of women's rhetoric from the period and characterizes the studies of individual figures' writings and speeches. Two such works by Carol Mattingly analyze the work of women's temperance leagues: *Water Drops from Women Writers: A Temperance Reader* (2001) and *Well-Tempered Women: Nineteenth-Century*

Temperance Rhetoric (1998), along with Ann Ruggles Gere's *Intimate Practices: Literacy and Cultural Work in U.S. Women's Clubs, 1880–1920* (1992). The next section of this chapter discusses the writing and speeches of abolitionists, but particularly noteworthy (and award-winning) treatises addressing nineteenth-century women's underrepresented political rhetoric include Shirley Wilson Logan's important *"We Are Coming": The Persuasive Discourse of Nineteenth-Century Black Women* (1999), Jaqueline Bacon's *The Humblest May Stand Forth: Rhetoric, Empowerment, and Abolition* (2002), and Jackie Jones Royster's two recent texts, *Southern Horrors and Other Writings: The Anti-Lynching Campaign of Ida B. Wells, 1892–1900* (1997) and *Traces of a Stream: Literacy and Social Change among African-American Women* (2000).

Areas for future research within nineteenth-century feminist studies include the examination of student commencement addresses at women's colleges, comparative studies of male/female education, increased investigation into women's use of nontraditional rhetorical forms, analysis of feminist rhetoric outside the United States, and production of critical editions of rhetors' works. The breadth of recently recovered figures is impressive, but we now need a depth of scholarship addressing individual female figures from the period. (Note: Krista Ratcliffe's chapter in this collection outlines recent trends and debates regarding methods and methodologies characterizing feminist research.)

African American Rhetoric

Historiographical methodologies of regendering the canon and recovering lost voices define the recent flurry of scholarship within nineteenth-century studies. Specifically, research efforts concentrate on both gathering primary documents and analyzing rhetorical strategies of those working outside the dominant tradition (nonwhites and women). In the case of nineteenth-century African American scholarship, researchers look to speeches and writings of historical rhetors to ground current theories of African American communication, to understand connections between language use and rhetorical performance, and to establish correlations among the personal, the political, and rhetorical culture. Critical anthologies of nineteenth-century African American rhetoric include Philip S. Foner and Robert James Branham's *Lift Every Voice: African American Oratory, 1787–1900* (1998) and *Early Negro Writing, 1760–1837*, edited by Dorothy Porter (1971)—in addition to the two anthologies of works by African American women rhetors mentioned in the section above (see Logan and Collier-Thomas). These anthologies give voice to often unheard or ignored conversations and raise awareness of venues for African American rhetorical engagement from the period. Also worth noting are Elaine B. Richardson and Ronald Jackson's *African American Rhetoric(s): Interdisciplinary Perspectives* (2004), which makes available historical African American documents found in literature and popular culture, and *Understanding African American Rhetoric* (2003), a collection of eighteen essays examining the history of contemporary African American linguistic practices.

Other scholars look closely at the rhetorical performance of individual rhetors in order to make broader claims about identity, "racialized" writing, and the notion that "the personal is political": In *Black Identity: Rhetoric, Ideology, and Nineteenth-Century Black Nationalism* (2003), Dexter Gordon studies the speeches and writings of nineteenth-century abolitionists Maria Stewart, David Walker, and Henry Garnet to support claims of reconciliation among rhetorical theory, race, alienation, and the role of public memory in identity formation. David G. Holmes, in *Revisiting Racialized Voice: African American Ethos in Language and Literature* (2004), looks to the works of Frederick Douglass, Charles Chesnutt, W. E. B. Du Bois, Zora Neale Hurston, and others to suggest that turn-of-the-century misconceptions concerning black identity and voice inform current assumptions about African American authorship. In *The Afro-American Jeremiad: Appeals for Justice in America* (2005), David Howard-Pitney examines the speeches and writings of nineteenth- and twentieth-century leaders to demonstrate how these figures employed the rhetoric of social prophecy and criticism to create a distinctive African American rhetorical performance, and Glen McLish, in "William G. Allen's 'Orators and Oratory': Inventional Amalgamation, Pathos, and the Characterization of Violence in African-American Abolitionist Rhetoric" (2005), analyzes how Allen used audience appeals to enlist students in the cause of abolition.

Research examining literacy practices, language use, and African American literary societies includes Timothy Barnett's "Politicizing the Personal: Frederick Douglass, Richard Wright, and Some Thoughts on the Limits of Critical Literacy" (2006), Jaqueline Bacon and Glen McClish's "Reinventing the Master's Tools: Nineteenth-Century African-American Literary Societies of Philadelphia and Rhetorical Education" (2000), Bacon's "Do You Understand Your Own Language? Revolutionary Topoi in the Rhetoric of African-American Abolitionists" (1998), and Elizabeth McHenry's *Forgotten Readers: Rediscovering the Lost History of African American Literary Societies* (2002). For scholarship specifically concerned with the African American press and literary traditions, see Bacon's *Freedom's Journal: The First African-American Newspaper* (2007) and Joy Rouse's "'We Can Never Remain Silent': The Public Discourse of the Nineteenth-Century African-American Press" (2001).

We need to continue recovering African American voices from the period, remembering to examine these rhetors' words and practices within the contexts and venues in which they were delivered. Further research is also needed into the education and rhetorical training of African American speakers and writers from the period. As discussed in the next chapter, scholars must broaden their perspectives in studying this period, viewing nineteenth-century figures and actions from a variety of research stances. For information specifically concerning African American women's rhetoric, see the preceding heading.

Asian Rhetoric

A key bibliographical source for studying Chinese rhetoric is pioneer Vernon Jensen's important "Bibliography of East Asian Rhetoric" (1987). In addition, Joseph Adler's Web site for a course in Chinese rhetoric and religious studies at Kenyon College provides a rich storehouse of information on Chinese religion and culture from every historical period. He includes hundreds of links to general histories, maps, religions, texts, art, languages and translations, women, science, philosophy, medicine, politics, news pages, and government-sponsored sites; a wealth of information concerning nineteenth-century Chinese rhetorical history is cataloged on this site. Sources examining changes in nineteenth-century research methodologies include Sucheng Chan's "The Changing Contours of Asian-American Historiography" (2007), which traces alterations in the landscape of Asian American historiography practices from the 1850s to the present. Chan discusses more than a hundred major books published in the last fifteen years in areas of trauma, Asian diasporas, and the social dynamics of Asian culture. In *Rescuing History from the Nation: Questioning Narratives of Modern China* (1995), Prasenjit Duara offers an account of the relationship between nationalism and the concept of linear history. Focusing primarily on China, but also including discussions of India, Duara argues that historians of postcolonial nation-states who adopt linear, evolutionary (and invented) histories have written repressive, exclusionary, and incomplete accounts. Bo Wang, in "Survey of Research in Asian Rhetoric" (2004), calls for research in Eastern rhetoric that "is mindful of the logic of Orientalism, that studies Asian rhetoric in its own cultural and political contexts, that appropriates Asian rhetoric for Western contexts, and that applies Asian rhetorical traditions to the study of pedagogical issues" (173). Other historical periods boast the emergence of contextualized scholarship fitting this description, but nineteenth-century studies in this area are still negligible.

Hui Wu, a leading scholar of Chinese rhetoric, explains that comparative rhetoric as a subfield in the West did not emerge until the 1970s following the 1971 publication of Robert Oliver's *Communication and Culture in Ancient India and China* (e-mail to author). For a fuller discussion of comparative rhetorics, see Krista Ratcliffe's chapter on twentieth-century rhetoric in this collection. Comparative rhetorical scholarship addressing the nineteenth century includes Xiaosui Xiao's "From the Hierarchical 'Ren' to Egalitarianism: A Case of Cross-Cultural Rhetorical Mediation" (1996), which examines rhetorical relationships through the writing of Tan Sitong. Contextualizing situation, Xiao suggests the possible effects of "rhetorical mediation" between Western and Chinese cultures. Mary Garrett and Xiao, in the "The Rhetorical Situation Revisited" (1993), look at the Chinese response to the West during the Opium Wars as an example of how "the discourse tradition is both a source and a limiting horizon for the rhetor and for the audience of the rhetorical situation" (38). Emerging scholarship also addresses Chinese racial stereotypes. Erin Murphy, in "'Prelude to Imperialism': Whiteness and Chinese Exclusion in the Reimagining of the United States" (2005), analyzes "racial reimagining" of the United States after the Civil War. She argues that U.S. stereotypes of Chinese, such as "coolie" and "celestial," serve as a "prelude to imperialism" and downplay the more paternalistic "civilized" stereotypes of Chinese as the "model minority." Frank Dikötter, in *The Discourse of Race in Modern China* (1992), also examines the emergence of racial stereotypes in late nineteenth-century China, and Charles J. MacClain's *In Search of Equality: The Chinese Struggle against Discrimination in Nineteenth-Century America* (1994) studies Chinese efforts to battle discrimination on multiple fronts. Challenging the stereotypical image of a passive, insular group, McClain draws on English- and Chinese-language documents to chronicle the ways in which the Chinese sought redress and change within the American courts. Figure studies from the period include Norman J. Girardot's *The Victorian Translation of China: James Legge's Oriental Pilgrimage* (2002), an examination of a nineteenth-century translator in the cultural exchange between China and the West. Girardot's work adds to the intellectual history of two major aspects of the emergent "human sciences" at the end of the nineteenth century: sinology and comparative religions.

Although recent rhetorical study has taken a keen interest in non-Western rhetorical practices, Japanese rhetorical engagement in general has received little scholarly attention—until recently. Comparative studies, such as Roichi Okabe's "The Impact of Western Elocutionary Rhetoric on the East: The Case of Japan" (2005) and Massimiliano Tomasi's *Rhetoric in Modern Japan: Western Influences on the Development of Narrative and Oratorical Style* (2004), suggest avenues for examining nineteenth-century Japanese rhetorical history and oratorical practices. Studies of continental Indian rhetoric from the period are scant. The nineteenth century is only briefly noted in N. Krishnaswamy's entry for "Indian Rhetoric" in the *Encyclopedia of Rhetoric* (2001), although during this period the Indian continent was introduced to Western rhetoric by travelers, missionaries, British colonial rule, the introduction of science and technologies, and the adoption of English as India's language of commerce and education. Research delving into the results of this meeting of rhetorical styles or India's responses to Western rhetoric is scarce.

According to Wang, future scholarship should revisit the Western rhetorical tradition from non-Western perspectives, encourage dialogue between East and West, and refrain from imposing Western models upon investigations of Eastern traditions and practices. Although the scope of scholarship addressing

Asian rhetoric is expanding in general, scholarship specifically addressing nine-teenth-century developments in this area lags behind other historical periods.

American Indian Rhetoric

The examination of the rhetorical uses of language by American Indians is an important area of nineteenth-century scholarship. Although the field has witnessed emerging research addressing what Rebecca Moore Howard has col-lected and labeled "Native American Languages, Discourses, and Rhetorics" (http://wrthoward.syr.edu/Bibs/NativeAm.htm), historical/archival projects ad-dressing society, education, language use, and rhetorical engagement have just begun to scratch the surface of work to be done in this area. Analysis of primary texts of nineteenth-century rhetors include Siobhan Senier's *Voices of American Assimilation and Resistance* (2003), in which the author examines the writings and oratory of three women—white novelist Helen Hunt Jackson, Paiute au-tobiographer and performer Sarah Winnemucca, and Clackamas Chinook sto-ryteller Victoria Howard—who resisted the federal government's assimilation of American Indians. Ernest Stromberg's groundbreaking collection *American Indian Rhetorics of Survivance: Word Medicine, Word Magic* (2006) presents thirteen multifaceted readings of American Indian rhetoric through the lens of autobiographies, memoirs, prophecies, and storytelling traditions. Daniel Justice's *Our Fire Survives the Storm* (2006) addresses imagery associated with the *Cherokee Phoenix,* a newspaper of the Cherokee nation first published in 1828; Deborah Miranda's examination of composition pedagogy in "Indian" boarding schools (2000) offers a new historical perspective on the development of writing instruction; and Maureen Konkle's *Writing Indian Nations* (2004) provides a close reading of the work of American Indian activists during mid century.

Malea Powell's numerous and important contributions to American Indian rhetoric include "Rhetorics of Survivance" (2002), an examination of rhetors Sarah Winnemucca Hopkins and Charles Alexander Eastman's late-century discourse; "Extending the Hand of Empire: American Indians and the Indian Reform Movement, a Beginning" (2004); and "Down by the River, or How Susan La Flesche Picotte Can Teach Us about Alliance as a Practice of Surviv-ance" (2004). In these works, Powell recovers the voices and literary practices of nineteenth-century American Indian intellectuals. We must continue re-covering voices from this critical period and then study these figures' rhetori-cal practices within their own cultures, educational practices, languages, and motivations for rhetorical action.

Future Directions

I have suggested possible directions for study in the categories above, but other areas certainly remain unexplored. Stewart predicted that the next edition of *The Present State* would include works by and about Continental European rhetoricians. Despite the headway made by scholars in other rhetorical periods, the nineteenth century has not made great strides toward this goal. Both Stewart and Linda Ferreira-Buckley cite scholarship on German rhetoricians of the period; *The Rhetorical Tradition* (second edition) includes one work by Nietzsche; and the programs of the biennial meetings of the International Society of the History of Rhetoric (ISHR), while including scattered presentations regarding nineteenth-century Continental and non-Western rhetoric, reveals a preponderance of papers addressing British and American rhetorical theory from the century. The far-reaching influence of Blair, Campbell, and Whately continues to be a predominant topic, and discussions of other rhetorical traditions/comparative rhetorics are sometimes embedded within scholarship addressing the big three. A perusal of back issues of *Rhetorica*, the publication of the International Society of the History of Rhetoric, despite a diversified table of contents for other periods of study, echoes this trend with a few notable exceptions, such as Don Paul Abbott's "A Bibliography of Eighteenth- and Nineteenth-Century Spanish Treatises" (1986) and his "Mayans' *Rhetórica* and the Search for a Spanish Rhetoric" (1993). These examples are limited but indicate the need for closer examination of nineteenth-century continental rhetoric.

The publication of recent anthologies of nineteenth-century primary works is of the utmost importance, and the promise of a forthcoming *Norton Anthology of Rhetoric and Composition* (edited by Andrea Lunsford, Robert Hariman, Susan Jarratt, Lu Ming Mao, and Jackie Jones Royster) will revitalize (and further justify to some teachers and scholars outside the field) the importance of studying rhetors and their works. I hope that new collections of primary works and scholarship will continue to address underexplored areas of nineteenth-century rhetorical engagement, including Latino and Latina rhetors, political discourse accompanying statehood and the annexation of land purchases, studies of isolation and exclusion—to name but a few. However, we must acknowledge that the field is in sore need of full-length, scholarly editions of (well-known) nineteenth-century rhetors' works as well. Finally and lamentably, we have yet to see the publication of *Nineteenth-Century Rhetorics and Rhetoricians,* the obvious companion text to Michael Moran's *Eighteenth-Century British and American Rhetorics and Rhetoricians* (1994) and *Twentieth-Century Rhetorics and Rhetoricians* (2000).

BIBLIOGRAPHY
Primary Works

Adams, John Quincy. *Lectures on Rhetoric and Oratory, Delivered to the Classes of Senior and Junior Sophisters in Harvard University.* 2 vols. Cambridge:, Hilliard and Metcalf, 1810. Reprint, ed. Jeffrey Auer and Jerald L. Banninga. New York: Russell and Russell, 1962.

Austin, Gilbert. *Chironomia, or a Treatise on Rhetorical Delivery.* London: T. Cadell and W. Davies, 1806. Facsimile reprint, ed. Mary Margaret Robb and Lester Thonssen. Carbondale: Southern Illinois University Press, 1966.

Aytoun, William Edmondstoune. Manuscripts 4895–4914, 4925, 4928. National Library of Scotland. 1845–1865.

Bain, Alexander. *The Emotions and the Will.* London: Longmans, Green, 1875.

——. *English Composition and Rhetoric: A Manual.* London: Longmans, Green, 1866.

——. *On Teaching English.* London: Longmans, Green, 1887.

Beecher, Catherine. *An Essay on Slavery and Abolition, with Reference to the Duty of American Females.* Philadelphia: Perkins, 1837.

Bizzell, Patricia, and Bruce Herzberg, eds. *The Rhetorical Tradition: Readings from Classical Times to the Present.* 2nd ed. Boston: Bedford/St. Martin's, 2001.

Brereton, John C., ed. *The Origins of Composition Studies in the American College, 1875–1925: A Documentary History.* Pittsburgh: University of Pittsburgh Press, 1995.

Buck, Gertrude. *The Metaphor: A Study in the Psychology of Rhetoric.* Ann Arbor, MI: Inland, 1899.

Campbell, Joanne. *Toward a Feminist Rhetoric: The Writing of Gertrude Buck.* Pittsburgh: University of Pittsburgh Press. 1996.

Campbell, Karlyn Kohrs. *Man Cannot Speak for Her: Key Texts of the Early Feminists.* New York: Praeger, 1989.

Ceplair, Larry, ed. *The Public Years of Sarah and Angelina Grimké, Selected Writings, 1835–39.* New York: Columbia University Press, 1989.

Channing, Edward T. *Lectures Read to the Seniors at Harvard College.* Boston: Ticknor and Fields, 1856. Reprint, ed. Dorothy Anderson and Waldo Braden. Carbondale: Southern Illinois University Press, 1968.

Day, Henry N. *The Art of Discourse.* New York: Charles Scribner, 1867.

——. *Elements of Art of Rhetoric* New York: A. S. Barnes, 1850.

De Quincy, Thomas. *The Collected Writings of Thomas De Quincey.* Ed. David Masson. 14 vols. Edinburgh: Black, 1889–1890.

——. *De Quincey's Essays on Style, Rhetoric, and Language.* Ed. Fred Newton Scott. Boston: Allyn and Bacon, 1893.

——. *De Quincey's Literary Criticism.* Ed. Helen Darbishire. London: Henry Frowde, 1909.

———. *Essays on Rhetoric.* Ed. Frederick Burwick. Southern Illinois University Press. Landmarks in Public Address, ed. David Potter. Carbondale: Southern Illinois University Press, 1967.

Donawerth, Jane, ed. *Rhetorical Theory by Women before 1900.* New York: Rowman and Littlefield, 2002.

Foner, Philip S., and Robert James Branham, eds. *Lift Every Voice: African American Oratory, 1787–1900.* Tuscaloosa: University of Alabama Press, 1998.

Genung, John Franklin. *The Practical Elements of Rhetoric.* 2nd ed. Boston: Ginn, 1886.

Golden, James, and Edward P. J. Corbett. *The Rhetoric of Blair, Campbell, and Whately.* Carbondale: Southern Illinois University Press, 1990.

Goodrich, Chauncey Allen. *Select British Eloquence.* New York: Harper and Brothers, 1852.

Goodsell, Willystine, ed. *Pioneers of Women's Education in the United States.* New York: McGraw, 1931.

Hallowell, Anna, ed. *James and Lucretia Mott: Life and Letters.* New York: Houghton, 1884.

Hill, Adams Sherman. *The Principles of Rhetoric and Their Application.* 2nd ed. New York: American Book, 1895.

Hill, David J. *The Science of Rhetoric.* New York: Sheldon, 1877.

Holland, Patricia, and Ann Gordon, eds. *The Papers of Elizabeth Cady Stanton and Susan B. Anthony.* Wilmington, DE: Scholarly, 1991.

Hope, Matthew B. *The Princeton Text-Book in Rhetoric.* Princeton: John T. Robinson, 1859.

Jamieson, Alexander. *A Grammar of Rhetoric and Polite Literature.* First American from last London edition. New Haven: A. H. Maltby, 1820.

Jardine, George. "Correspondence of Professor Jardine with Baron Mure." *Selections from the Mure Family Papers Preserved at Caldwell.* Ed. William Mure. Glasgow: A. Gardner, 1883.

———. *Outlines of Philosophical Education, Illustrated by the Method of Teaching the Logic; or, First Class of Philosophy in the University of Glasgow.* Edinburgh: Oliver and Boyd, 1825.

Lindemann, Erika. "True and Candid Compositions: The Lives and Writings of Antebellum Students at the University of North Carolina." *Documenting the American South.* 2002. University of North Carolina at Chapel Hill. http://docsouth.unc.edu/true/intro/ overview.html.

Logan, Shirley Wilson, ed. *With Pen and Voice: A Critical Anthology of Nineteenth-Century African-American Women.* Carbondale: Southern Illinois University Press, 1995.

Lunsford, Andrea, Robert Hariman, Susan Jarratt, Lu Ming Mao, and Jackie Jones Royster, eds. *Norton Anthology of Rhetoric and Composition.* Norton: Forthcoming.

Mandeville, Henry. *The Elements of Reading and Oratory.* New York: Appleton, 1851.

Matthews, William. *Oratory and Orators.* Chicago: S. C. Griggs, 1878.

Mattingly, Carol, ed. *Water Drops from Women Writers: A Temperance Reader.* Carbondale: Southern Illinois University Press, 2001.

Newman, Samuel P. *A Practical System of Rhetoric.* Portland: Shirley and Hyde, 1827.

Nietzsche, Friedrich. *Beyond Good and Evil: Prelude to a Philosophy of the Future.* 1886. Reprint, trans. Judith Norman; ed. Rolf-Peter Horstmann and Judith Norman. New York: Cambridge University Press, 2002.

Pearson, Henry G. *The Principles of Composition, with an Introduction by Arlo Bates.* Boston: D. C. Heath, 1897.

Peirce, Charles Sanders. *Complete Published Works Including Selected Secondary Material.* Ed. Kenneth L. Ketner et al. Greenwich, CT: Johnson, 1977.

Plumptre, Charles John. *King's College Lectures on Elocution.* London: Kegan Paul, 1895.

Porter, Dorothy, ed. *Early Negro Writing, 1760–1837.* Boston: Beacon, 1971.

Porter, Ebenezer. *Analysis of the Principles of Rhetorical Delivery as Applied in Reading and Speaking.* Andover, MA: Newman, 1827.

Ritchie, Joy, and Kate Ronald, eds. *Available Means: An Anthology of Women's Rhetoric(s).* Pittsburgh: University of Pittsburgh Press, 2001.

Rush, James. *The Philosophy of the Human Voice.* Philadelphia: J. Maxwell, 1827. Reprint, Philadephia: Lippincott, 1867.

Russell, David R. *Writing in the Academic Disciplines: A Curricular History.* 2nd ed. Carbondale: Southern Illinois University Press, 2002.

Russell, William, and Anna Russell. *The Young Ladies' Elocutionary Reader; Containing a Selection of Reading Lessons, with Introductory Rules and Exercises in Elocution, Adapted to Female Readers.* Boston: Munroe, 1846.

Scott, Fred Newton, and Joseph Villiers Denney. *Composition-Rhetoric, Designed for Use in Secondary Schools.* Boston: Allyn and Bacon, 1897.

———. *Paragraph-Writing.* Boston: Allyn and Bacon, 1897.

Shoemaker, J. W. *Practical Elocution: For Use in Colleges and Schools and by Private Students.* Philadelphia: Penn, 1886.

Sigourney, Lydia. *The Girl's Reading-Book: In Prose and Poetry, for Schools.* New York: Taylor, 1838. Nietz Old Textbook Collection. Digital Research Library, University of Pittsburgh. 22 March 2008. http://digital.library.pitt.edu/nietz/.

[Spencer, Herbert]. "The Philosophy of Style." *Westminster Review* 114 (October 1852): 234–47.

Wendell, Barrett. *English Composition: Eight Lectures Given at the Lowell Institute.* New York: Charles Scribners' Sons, 1891.

Whately, Richard. *Elements of Rhetoric.* London, Oxford: John Murray and J. F. Parker, 1828. Reprint, ed. Douglas Ehninger. Carbondale: Southern Illinois University Press, 1963.

Secondary Works

Bibliographies and Overviews

Abbott, Don Paul. "A Bibliography of Eighteenth- and Nineteenth-Century Spanish Treatises." *Rhetorica* 4 (1986): 275–92.

Applebee, Arthur. *Tradition and Reform in the Teaching of English: A History.* Urbana: NCTE, 1974.

CCCC Bibliography of Composition and Rhetoric. Carbondale: Southern Illinois University Press, 1987–1995. 10 June 2007. http://www.ibiblio.org/cccc/.

CCC Online Archive. Urbana, IL: NCTE. 10 June 2007. http://www.inventio. us/ccc/.

Clark, Gregory, and S. Michael Halloran. *Oratorical Culture in Nineteenth-Century America.* Carbondale: Southern Illinois University Press, 1993.

ERIC (19). Washington, D.C.: U.S. Department of Education. http://www.eric. ed.gov/.

Ferreira-Buckley, Linda. "Nineteenth-Century Rhetoric." In *Encyclopedia of Rhetoric and Composition: Communication from Ancient Times to the Information Age,* ed. Theresa Enos, 468–73. New York: Garland, 1996.

Guthrie, Warren. "The Development of Rhetorical Theory in America, 1635–1850." *Speech Monographs* 13 (1946), 14–22; 14 (1947), 28–54; 15 (1948), 61–71; 16 (1949), 98–113; 18 (1951), 17–30.

Haswell, Rich, and Glenn Blalock. *CompPile.* Texas A&M University. http:// comppile. tamucc.edu/.

Herrick, James *The History and Theory of Rhetoric.* 3rd ed. Boston: Allyn and Bacon, 2005.

Horner, Winifred Bryan. *The Present State of Scholarship in Historical and Contemporary Rhetoric.* Rev. ed. Columbia: University of Missouri Press, 1990.

Houlette, Forrest. *Nineteenth-Century Rhetoric: An Enumerative Bibliography.* New York: Garland, 1989.

Howard, Rebecca Moore. *Bibliographies for Composition and Rhetoric.* http:// wrt-howard.syr.edu/bibs.html.

Johnson, Nan. "Nineteenth-Century Rhetoric." In *Encyclopedia of Rhetoric,* ed. T. O. Sloane, 518–27. Oxford: Oxford University Press, 2001.

———. *Nineteenth-Century Rhetoric in North America.* Carbondale: Southern Illinois University Press, 1991.

Kennedy, George A. *Classical Rhetoric and Its Christian and Secular Tradition from Ancient to Modern Times.* 2nd ed. Chapel Hill: University of North Carolina Press, 1999.

Kitzhaber, Albert R. *Rhetoric in American Colleges, 1850–1900.* Dallas: Southern Methodist University Press, 1990.

Longaker, Mark Garrett. *Rhetoric and the Republic: Politics, Civic Discourse, and Education in Early America.* Tuscaloosa: University of Alabama Press, 2007.

Stewart, Donald C. "The Nineteenth Century." In *The Present State of Scholarship in Historical and Contemporary Rhetoric,* 2nd ed., ed. Winifred Bryan Horner, 151–85. Columbia: University of Missouri Press, 1990.

Wallace, Karl R., ed. *A History of Speech Education in America: Background Studies.* Prepared by the Speech Association of America. New York: Appleton-Century-Crofts, 1954.

Writing Instruction

Berlin, James A. *Writing Instruction in Nineteenth-Century American Colleges.* Carbondale: Southern Illinois University Press, 1984.

Carr, Jean Ferguson, Stephen L. Carr, and Lucille M. Schultz. *Archives of Instruction: Nineteenth-Century Rhetorics, Readers, and Composition Books in the United States.* Carbondale: Southern Illinois University Press, 2005.

Carr, Thomas M. *Descartes and the Resilience of Rhetoric: Varieties of Cartesian Rhetorical Theory.* Carbondale: Southern Illinois University Press, 1990.

Connors, Robert J. *Composition-Rhetoric: Backgrounds, Theory, and Pedagogy.* Pittsburgh: University of Pittsburgh Press, 1997.

——. "Dreams and Play: Historical Method and Methodology." *Methods and Methodology in Composition Research.* Ed. Gesa Kirsch and Patricia Sullivan. Carbondale: Southern Illinois University Press, 1992.

——. "Overwork/Underpay: Labor and Status of Composition Teachers since 1880." *Rhetoric Review* 9, no. 1 (Fall 1990): 108–25.

——. "The Rise and Fall of the Modes of Discourse." *College Composition and Communication* 32 (1981): 444–55.

Crowley, Sharon. *Composition in the University: Historical and Polemical Essays.* Pittsburgh: University of Pittsburgh Press, 1997.

Ferreira-Buckley, Linda, and Winifred B. Horner. "Writing Instruction in Great Britain: The Eighteenth and Nineteenth Centuries." In *A Short History of Writing Instruction: From Ancient Greece to Modern America,* 2nd ed., ed. James J. Murphy, 173–212. Mahwah, NJ: Lawrence Erlbaum, 2001.

Fitzgerald, Kathryn. "A Rediscovered Tradition: European Pedagogy and Composition in Nineteenth-Century Normal Schools." *College Composition and Communication* 3 (2002): 224–50.

Gerber, John C. "English at Iowa in the Nineteenth Century." *Books at Iowa* 51 (1989). http://www.lib.uiowa.edu/spec-coll/Bai/gerber.htm.

Gilyard, Keith. "African American Contributions to Composition Studies." *College Composition and Communication* 50, no. 4 (1999): 626–44.

L'Eplattenier, Barbara, and Lisa Mastrangelo, eds. *Historical Studies of Writing Program Administration: Individuals, Communities, and the Formation of a Discipline.* West Lafayette, IN: Parlor Press, 2004.

Miller, Susan. *Assuming the Positions: Cultural Pedagogy and the Politics of Commonplace Writing.* Pittsburgh: University of Pittsburgh Press, 1998.

Paine, Charles. *The Resistant Writer: Rhetoric as Immunity, 1850 to the Present.* Albany: State University of New York Press, 1999.

Parker, William Riley. "Where Do English Departments Come From?" In *Essays on the Rhetoric of the Western World,* ed. Edward P. J. Corbett et al., 1–15. Dubuque: Kendall/Hunt, 1990.

Reid, Ronald F. "The Boylston Professorship of Rhetoric and Oratory, 1806–1904: A Case Study of Changing Concepts of Rhetoric and Pedagogy." In *Essays on the Rhetoric of the Western World,* ed. Edward P. J. Corbett et al., 261–82. Dubuque: Kendall/Hunt, 1990.

Roberts-Miller, Patricia. "Agonism, Wrangling, and John Quincy Adams." *Rhetoric Review* 25 (2006): 141–61.

Russell, David R. *Writing in the Academic Disciplines: A Curricular History.* 2nd ed. Carbondale: Southern Illinois University Press, 2002.

Salvatore, Mariolina. R., ed. *Pedagogy: Disturbing History, 1819–1929.* Pittsburgh: University of Pittsburgh Press, 1996.

Schultz, Lucille M. "Elaborating Our History: A Look at Mid-19th-Century First Books of Composition." *College Composition and Communication* 45, no. 1 (February 1994): 10–29.

———. *The Young Composers: Composition's Beginnings in Nineteenth-Century Schools.* Carbondale: Southern Illinois University Press, 1999.

Schultz, Lucille M., Jean Ferguson Carr, and Stephen Carr. *Archives of Instruction: Nineteenth-Century Rhetorics, Readers, and Composition Books in the United States.* Carbondale: Southern Illinois University Press, 2005.

Stewart, Donald C. "Two Model Teachers and the Harvardization of English Departments." In *The Rhetorical Tradition and Modern Writing,* ed. James J. Murphy, 118–29. New York: Modern Library Association, 1982.

Stewart, Donald, and Patricia L. Scott. *The Life and Legacy of Fred Newton Scott.* Pittsburgh: University of Pittsburgh Press, 1997.

Thomas, Susan Elizabeth. "'Part of a Larger Whole': Fred Newton Scott and the Progressive Education Movement." Ph.D. diss., Georgia State University, 2002.

Wiley, Mark. "Reading and Writing in an American Grain." *Rhetoric Review* 2 (Fall 1992): 133–45.

Winterowd, Ross W., and Vincent Gellespie, eds. *Composition in Context: Essays in Honor of Donald C. Stewart.* Carbondale: Southern Illinois University Press, 1994.

Wright, Elizabetha A., and S. Michael Halloran. "From Rhetoric to Composition: The Teaching of Writing in America to 1900." In *A Short History of Writing Instruction: From Ancient Greece to Modern America,* 2nd ed., ed. James J. Murphy, 213–46. Mahwah, NJ: Lawrence Erlbaum, 2001.

Scottish Influences

Agnew, Lois. *Outward, Visible Propriety: Stoic Philosophy and Eighteenth-Century British Rhetorics.* Columbia: University of South Carolina Press, 2009.

Aley, Shelley. "The Impact of Science on Rhetoric through the Contributions of the University of Aberdeen's Alexander Bain." In *Scottish Rhetoric and Its Influences,* ed. Lynée Lewis Gaillet, 209–17. Mahwah, NJ: Lawrence Erlbaum, 1998.

Anderson, Robert David. *Education and the Scottish People, 1750–1918.* Oxford: Oxford University Press, 1995.

Aspinwall, Bernard. *Portable Utopia: Glasgow and the United States, 1820–1920.* Aberdeen: Aberdeen University Press, 1984.

Berryhill, Carisse. "British Enlightenment Backgrounds for Thomas Campbell's Declaration and Address." Stone-Campbell Archives. http://www.bible.acu.edu/s-c/Default.asp?Bookmark=17651.

———. "A Descriptive Guide to Eight Early Alexander Campbell Manuscripts." December 2000. www.mun.ca/rels/restmov/texts/acampbell/acm/ACM00A.htm.

———. "Sense, Expression, and Purpose: Alexander Campbell's Natural Philosophy of Rhetoric." Ph.D. diss. Florida State University, 1982.

Bird, Barbara. "George Jardine's Investigative Rhetoric and Epistemic Writing Theory." Ph.D. diss. Ball State University, 2005.

Booth, Sherry. "A Moment for Reform: Rhetoric and Literature at the University of Glasgow, 1862–1877." *Rhetoric Review* 22 (2003): 374–95.

Chitnis, Anand C. *The Scottish Enlightenment and Early Victorian English Society.* London: Croom Helm, 1986.

Court, Franklin E. *The Scottish Connection: The Rise of English Literary Study in Early America.* Syracuse: Syracuse University Press, 2001.

Davie, George. *The Democratic Intellect.* Edinburgh: Edinburgh University Press, 1982.

Eble, Michelle F. "W. E. Aytoun, First Regius Professor of Rhetoric and English Literature: Contributions to the Discipline of English Studies." Ph.D. diss. Georgia State University, 2002.

Eble, Michelle, and Lynée Lewis Gaillet. "Informing the Discipline of Technical and Professional Communication: Rhetoric, Moral Philosophy, and Civic Engagement." *Technical Society Quarterly* 13, no. 3 (2004): 341–54.

Ferreira-Buckley, Linda. "'Scotch' Knowledge and the Formation of Rhetorical Studies." In *Scottish Rhetoric and Its Influence,* ed. Lynée Lewis Gaillet, 163–75. Mahwah, NJ: Lawrence Erlbaum Associates, 1997.

Frykman, Erik. *W. E. Aytoun, Pioneer Professor of English at Edinburgh.* Gothenburg Studies in English 17. Göteborg, Sweden: Acta Universitatis Gothoburgensis, 1963.

Gaillet, Lynée Lewis. "George Jardine: The Champion of the Scottish Commonsense School of Philosophy." *Rhetoric Society Quarterly* 28, no. 2 (1998): 37–53.

———. "George Jardine's *Outlines of Philosophical Education:* Prefiguring Twentieth-Century Composition Theory and Practice." In *Scottish Rhetoric and Its Influences,* ed. Lynée Lewis Gaillet, 193–208. Mahwah, NJ: Lawrence Erlbaum, 1998.

Gaillet, Lynée Lewis, ed. *Scottish Rhetoric and Its Influences.* Mahwah, NJ: Lawrence Erlbaum, 1998.

Hewett, Beth. "Samuel P. Newman's *A Practical System of Rhetoric:* An American Cousin of Scottish Rhetoric." In *Scottish Rhetoric and Its Influences,* ed. Lynée Lewis Gaillet, 179–92. Mahwah, NJ: Lawrence Erlbaum, 1998.

Hook, Andrew. *From Goosecreek to Gandercleugh: Studies in Scottish-American Literary and Cultural History.* East Lothian, Scotland: Tuckwell, 1999.

———. *Scotland and America: A Study in Cultural Relations, 1750–1835.* Edinburgh: Blackie, 1975.

Horner, Winifred Bryan. "Aytoun, William Edmondstoune." In *Encyclopedia of Rhetoric and Composition,* ed. Theresa Enos, 58–59. New York: Garland, 1996.

———. *Nineteenth-Century Scottish Rhetoric: The American Connection.* Carbondale: Southern Illinois University Press, 1993.

Lunsford, Andrea A. "Alexander Bain and the Teaching of Composition in North America." In *Scottish Rhetoric and Its Influences,* ed. Lynée Lewis Gaillet, 219–27. Mahwah, NJ: Lawrence Erlbaum, 1998.

———. "Alexander Bain's Contributions to Discourse Theory." In *Essays on the Rhetoric of the Western World,* ed. Edward P. J. Corbett et al., 283–93. Dubuque, IA: Kendall/Hunt, 1990.

Miller, Thomas P. *The Formation of College English: Rhetoric and Belles Lettres in the British Cultural Provinces.* Pittsburgh: University of Pittsburgh Press, 1997.

Olbricht, Thomas H., and Hans Rollman, eds. *The Quest for Christian Unity, Peace, and Purity in Thomas Campbell's Declaration and Address: Text and Studies.* ATLA Monograph Ser., 46. Lanham, MD: Scarecrow Press, 2000.

Segrest, Scott Philip. "Common Sense Philosophy and Politics in America: John Witherspoon, James McCosh, and William James." Ph.D. diss. Louisiana State University, 2005.

Sher, Richard, and Jeffrey R. Smitten, eds. *Scotland and America in the Age of the Enlightenment.* Princeton: Princeton University Press, 1990.

Sloan, Douglas. *The Scottish Enlightenment and the American College Ideal.* New York: Teachers College, 1971.

Wyland, Russell M. "An Archival Study of Rhetoric Texts and Teaching at the University of Oxford, 1785–1820." *Rhetorica* 21 (2003): 175–95.

Elocution/Delivery
(The numerous recent works addressing women and delivery are listed under "Women and Rhetoric.")

Burton, Vicki Tolar. "John Wesley and the Liberty to Speak: The Rhetorical and Literacy Practices of Early Methodism." *College Composition and Communication* 53 (2001): 65–91.

———. *Spiritual Literacy in John Wesley's Methodism: Reading, Writing, and Speaking to Believe.* Waco, TX: Baylor University Press, 2008.

Fehler, Brian. *Calvinist Rhetoric in Nineteenth-Century America: The Bartlet Professors of Sacred Rhetoric of Andover Seminary.* Lewiston, NY: Edwin Mellen, 2007.

McCorkle, Ben. "Harbingers of the Printed Page: Nineteenth-Century Theories of Delivery as Remediation." *Rhetoric Society Quarterly* 35, no. 4 (2005): 25–49.

Miller, Susan. *Trust in Texts: A Different History of Rhetoric.* Carbondale: Southern Illinois University Press, 2008.

Okabe, Roichi. "The Impact of Western Rhetoric on the East: The Case of Japan." *Rhetorica* (1990): 371–88.

Smith, Craig R. *Daniel Webster and the Oratory of Civil Religion.* Columbia: University of Missouri Press, 2005.

Spoel, Philippa M. "Rereading the Elocutionists: The Rhetoric of Thomas Sheridan's *A Course of Lectures on Elocution* and John Walker's *Elements of Elocution.*" *Rhetorica* 19 (2001): 49–91.

Towns, Stuart. *Oratory and Rhetoric in the Nineteenth-Century South: A Rhetoric of Defense.* New York: Greenwood, 2000.

Women and Rhetoric
(Anthologies of women's rhetoric are listed with primary sources.)

Adams, Katherine H. *A Group of Their Own: College Writing Courses and American Women Writers, 1880–1940.* Albany: State University of New York Press, 2001.

Adams, Katherine H., and Michael L. Keene. *Alice Paul and the American Suffrage Campaign.* Carbondale: Southern Illinois University Press, 2008.

Bacon, Jaqueline. *The Humblest May Stand Forth: Rhetoric, Empowerment, and Abolition.* Columbia: University of South Carolina Press, 2002.

Biesecker, Barbara. "Coming to Terms with Recent Attempts to Write Women into the History of Rhetoric." *Philosophy and Rhetoric* 25 (1992): 140–61.

Bizzell, Patricia. "Frances Willard, Phoebe Palmer, and the Ethos of the Methodist Woman Preacher." *Rhetoric Society Quarterly* 36, no. 4 (2006): 337–98.

Bordelon, Suzanne. "Challenging Nineteenth-Century Feminization Narratives: Mary Yost of Vassar College." *Peitho* 6, no. 1 (2002): 2–5.

——. *A Feminist Legacy: The Rhetoric and Pedagogy of Gertrude Buck.* Carbondale: Southern Illinois University Press, 2007.

Brekus, Catherine A. *Strangers and Pilgrims: Female Preaching in America, 1740–1845.* Chapel Hill: University of North Carolina Press, 1998.

Broaddus, Dorothy C. *Genteel Rhetoric: Writing High Culture in Nineteenth-Century Boston.* Columbia: University of South Carolina Press, 1999.

Browne, Stephen H. *Angelina Grimke: Rhetoric, Identity, and the Radical Imagination.* East Lansing: Michigan State University Press, 1999.

Buchanan, Lindal. *Regendering Delivery: The Fifth Canon and Antebellum Women Rhetors.* Carbondale: Southern Illinois University Press, 2005.

Collier-Thomas, Bettye, ed. *Daughters of Thunder: Black Women Preachers and Their Sermons, 1850–1979.* San Francisco: Jossey-Bass, 1998.

Collins, Vicki Tolar. "Walking in Light, Walking in Darkness: The Story of Women's Changing Rhetorical Space in Early Methodism." *Rhetoric Review* 14 (1996): 336–54.

——. "Women's Voices and Women's Silence in the Tradition of Early Methodism." In *Listening to Their Voices: The Rhetorical Activities of Historical Women,* ed. Molly Meijer Wertheimer, 233–54. Columbia: University of South Carolina Press, 1997.

Connors, Robert J. "Frances Wright: First Female Civic Rhetor." *College English* 62 (1999): 30–57.

Conway, Kathryn. M. "Woman Suffrage and the History of Rhetoric at the Seven Sisters Colleges, 1865–1919." In *Reclaiming Rhetorica: Women in the Rhetorical Tradition,* ed. Andrea Lunsford, 203–26. Pittsburgh: Pittsburgh University Press, 1995.

Desser, Daphne. "Fraught Literacy: American Missionary Women in Nineteenth-Century Hawai'i." *College English* 69 (2007): 443–69.

Donawerth, Jane. "Hannah More, Lydia Sigourney, and the Creation of Woman's Tradition of Rhetoric." In *Rhetoric, the Polis, and the Global Village,* eds. C. Jan Swearingin and D. Pruett, 155–61. Mahwah, NJ: Erlbaum, 1999.

——. "Nineteenth-Century United States Conduct Book Rhetoric by Women." *Rhetoric Review* 21 (2002): 5–21.

——. "Poaching on Men's Philosophies of Rhetoric: Eighteenth- and Nineteenth-Century Rhetorical Theory by Women." *Philosophy and Rhetoric* 33 (2000): 243–58.

Eldred, Janet Carey, and Peter Mortensen. *Imagining Rhetoric: Composing Women of the Early United States.* Pittsburgh: University of Pittsburgh Press, 2002.

Gaillet, Lynée Lewis, and Thomas P. Miller. "Making Use of the Nineteenth Century: The Writings of Robert Connors and Recent Histories of Rhetoric and Composition." *Rhetoric Review* 31 (2001): 147–57.

Gere, Anne R. *Intimate Practices: Literacy and Cultural Work in U.S. Women's Clubs, 1880–1920.* Carbondale, Southern Illinois University Press, 1992.

Gifford, Carolyn DeSwarte. "Frances Willard and the Woman's Christian Temperance Union's Conversion to Woman Suffrage." In *One Woman, One Vote: Rediscovering the Woman's Suffrage Movement,* ed. Marjorie S. Wheeler, 117–33. Troutdale, OR: New Sage, 1995.

Gring-Premble, Lisa M. "Writing Themselves into Consciousness: Creating a Rhetorical Bridge between the Public and Private Spheres." *Quarterly Journal of Speech* 84 (1998): 41–61.

Harris, Sharon, ed. *Blue Pencils and Hidden Hands: Women Editing Periodicals, 1830–1910.* Boston: Northeastern University Press, 2004.

Haywood, Chanta M. *Prophesying Daughters: Black Women Preachers and the Word, 1823–1913.* Columbia: University of Missouri Press, 2003.

Hobbs, Catherine, ed. *Nineteenth-Century Women Learn to Write.* Charlottesville: University of Virginia Press, 1995.

Hobbs, June H. *"I Sing for I Cannot Be Silent": The Feminization of American Hymnody, 1870–1920.* Pittsburgh: University of Pittsburgh Press, 1997.

Johnson, Nan. *Gender and Rhetorical Space in American Life, 1866–1910.* Carbondale: Southern Illinois University Press, 2002.

Kates, Susan. *Activist Rhetorics and American Higher Education, 1885–1937.* Carbondale: Southern Illinois University Press, 2001.

——. "The Embodied Rhetoric of Hallie Quinn Brown." *College English* 59, no. 1 (1997): 59–71.

——. "Subversive Feminism: The Politics of Correctness in Mary Augusta Jordan's *Correct Writing and Speaking* (1904)." *College Composition and Communication* 48, no. 4 (1997): 501–17.

Knight, Louise W. "An Authoritative Voice: Jane Addams and the Oratorical Tradition." *Gender and History* 10 (1998): 217.

Logan, Shirley Wilson. *"We Are Coming": The Persuasive Discourse of Nineteenth-Century Black Women.* Carbondale: Southern Illinois University Press, 1999.

Lunsford, Andrea A., ed. *Reclaiming Rhetorica: Women in the Rhetorical Tradition.* Pittsburgh: University of Pittsburgh Press, 1995.

Mattingly, Carol. *Appropriate[ing] Dress: Women's Rhetorical Style in Nineteenth-Century America.* Carbondale: Southern Illinois University Press, 2002.

——. *Well-Tempered Women: Nineteenth-Century Temperance Rhetoric.* Carbondale: Southern Illinois University Press, 1998.

Mountford, Roxanne. *The Gendered Pulpit: Preaching in American Protestant Spaces.* Carbondale: Southern Illinois University Press, 2003.

O'Connor, Lillian. *Pioneer Women Orators.* New York: Columbia University Press, 1954.

Royster, Jackie Jones, ed. *Southern Horrors and Other Writings: The Anti-Lynching Campaign of Ida B. Wells, 1892–1900.* Boston: Bedford Books, 1997.

——. *Traces of a Stream: Literacy and Social Change among African-American Women.* Pittsburgh: University of Pittsburgh Press, 2000.

Skinner, Carolyn. "'The Purity of Truth': Nineteenth-Century American Women Physicians Write about Delicate Topics." *Rhetoric Review* 26 (2007): 103–19.

Sutherland, Christine Mason, and Rebecca Sutcliffe, eds. *The Changing Tradition: Women in the History of Rhetoric.* Calgary: University of Calgary Press, 1999.

Tasker, Elizabeth, Frances Holt-Underwood, Cantice Green, Letizia Guglielmo, Gina Henderson, Xiumei Pu, and Alexis Bender. "A Brief Summary of Feminist Research Methodologies in Historic Rhetoric and Composition from the 1970s to the Present." *Peitho* (Spring 2006): 1–7.

Tasker, Elizabeth, and Frances Holt-Underwood. Contributions by Cantice Green, Letizia Guglielmo, Gina Henderson, Xiumei Pu, and Alexis Bender. "Feminist Research Methodologies in Historic Rhetoric and Composition: An Overview of Scholarship from the 1970s to the Present." *Rhetoric Review.* 27, no. 1 (2008): 54–71.

Tonn, Mari Boor. "Militant Motherhood: Labor's Mary Harris 'Mother' Jones." *Quarterly Journal of Speech* 82 (1996): 1–21.

Watson, Martha, ed. *Lives of Their Own: Rhetorical Dimensions in Autobiographies of Women Activists.* Columbia: University of South Carolina Press, 1999.

Wells, Susan. *Out of the Dead House: Nineteenth-Century Women Physicians and the Writing of Medicine.* Madison: University of Wisconsin Press, 2001.

——. "Women Write Science: The Case of Hannah Longshore." *College English* 58, no. 2 (1996): 176–91.

Wertheimer, Molly Meijer, ed. *Listening to Their Voices: The Rhetorical Activities of Historical Women.* Columbia: University of South Carolina Press, 1997.

Zaeske, Susan "'The Promiscuous Audience' Controversy and Emergence of the Early Woman's Rights Movement." *Quarterly Journal of Speech* 81 (1995): 191–207.

African American Rhetoric

(Anthologies of African American rhetoric are listed under primary sources.)

Bacon, Jaqueline. "Do You Understand Your Own Language? Revolutionary Topoi in the Rhetoric of African-American Abolitionists." *Rhetoric Society Quarterly* 28, no. 2 (1998): 55–76.

——. *Freedom's Journal: The First African-American Newspaper.* Lanham, MD: Lexington Books, 2007.

Bacon, Jaqueline, and Glen McClish. "Reinventing the Master's Tools: Nineteenth-Century African-American Literary Societies of Philadelphia and Rhetorical Education." *Rhetoric Society Quarterly* 30, no. 4 (2000): 19–48.

Barnett, Timothy. "Politicizing the Personal: Frederick Douglass, Richard Wright, and Some Thoughts on the Limits of Critical Literacy." *College English* 68, no. 4 (March 2006): 356–81.

Gordon, Dexter B. *Black Identity: Rhetoric, Ideology, and Nineteenth-Century Black Nationalism.* Carbondale: Southern Illinois University Press, 2003.

Holmes, David G. *Revisiting Racialized Voice: African American Ethos in Language and Literature.* Carbondale: Southern Illinois University Press, 2004.

Howard-Pitney, David. *The Afro-American Jeremiad: Appeals for Justice in America.* Rev. ed. Philadelphia: Temple University Press, 2005.

Jackson, Ronald, II, and Elaine B. Richardson, eds. *Understanding African American Rhetoric: Classical Origins to Contemporary Innovations.* New York: Taylor and Francis, 2003.

McHenry, Elizabeth. *Forgotten Readers: Rediscovering the Lost History of African American Literary Societies.* Durham: Duke University Press, 2002.

McLish, Glen. "William G. Allen's 'Orators and Oratory': Inventional Amalgamation, Pathos, and the Characterization of Violence in African-American Abolitionist Rhetoric." *Rhetoric Society Quarterly* 35, no. 1 (Winter 2005): 47–85.

Richardson, Elaine B., and Ronald Jackson II, eds. *African American Rhetoric(s): Interdisciplinary Perspectives.* Carbondale: Southern Illinois University Press, 2004.

Rouse, Joy P. "'We Can Never Remain Silent': The Public Discourse of the Nineteenth-Century African-American Press." In *Popular Literacy: Studies in Cultural Practices and Poetics,* ed. John Trimbur, 128–42. Pittsburgh: University of Pittsburgh Press, 2001.

Asian Rhetoric

Adler, Joseph. *Religious Studies 270: Chinese Religions.* Kenyon College. 15 July 2007. http://www2.kenyon.edu/Depts/Religion/Fac/Adler/Reln270/Syl270.htm.

Beamer, Linda. "Directness in Chinese Business Correspondence of the Nineteenth Century." *Journal of Business and Technical Communication* 17 (2003): 201–37.

Chan, Sucheng. "The Changing Contours of Asian-American Historiography." *Rethinking History* 11 (2007): 125–47.

Dikötter, Frank. *The Discourse of Race in Modern China.* London: Hurst, 1992.

Duara, Prasenjit. *Rescuing History from the Nation: Questioning Narratives of Modern China.* Chicago: University of Chicago Press, 1995.

Elman, Benjamin. *Classical Historiography for Chinese History.* http://www.sscnet.ucla.edu/history/elman/ClassBib/.

Garrett, Mary. "Chinese Rhetoric." In *Encyclopedia of Rhetoric,* ed. Thomas. O. Sloane, 89–92. Oxford: Oxford University Press, 2001.

——. "Some Elementary Methodological Reflections on the Study of the Chinese Rhetorical Tradition." *International and Intercultural Communication Annual* 22 (1999): 53–63.

Garrett, Mary, and Xiaosui Xiao. "The Rhetorical Situation Revisited." *Rhetoric Society Quarterly* 23, no. 2 (1993): 30–40.

Girardot, Norman J. *The Victorian Translation of China: James Legge's Oriental Pilgrimage.* Berkeley: University of California Press, 2002.

Jensen, J. Vernon. "Bibliography of East Asian Rhetoric." *Rhetoric Society Quarterly* 17, no. 2 (1987): 213–31.

Krishnaswamy, N. "Indian Rhetoric." In *Encyclopedia of Rhetoric,* ed. Thomas O. Sloane, 384–87. Oxford: Oxford University Press, 2001.

Liu, Yameng. "To Capture the Essence of Chinese Rhetoric: An Anatomy of a Paradigm in Comparative Rhetoric." *Rhetoric Review* 14 (1996): 318–35.

MacClain, Charles J. *In Search of Equality: The Chinese Struggle against Discrimination in Nineteenth-Century America.* Berkeley: University of California Press, 1994.

Murphy, Erin L. "Prelude to Imperialism: Whiteness and Chinese Exclusion in the Reimagining of the United States." *Journal of Historical Sociology* 18 (2005): 457–90.

Okabe, Roichi. "The Impact of Western Rhetoric on the East: The Case of Japan." *Rhetorica* (1990): 371–88.

Oliver, Robert. *Communication and Culture in Ancient India and China.* Syracuse: Syracuse University Press, 1971.

Ono, Kazuko. *Chinese Women in a Century of Revolution, 1850–1950.* Stanford: Stanford University Press, 1988.

Suleri, Sara. *The Rhetoric of English India.* Chicago: University of Chicago Press, 1992.

Tomasi, Massimiliano. *Rhetoric in Modern Japan: Western Influences on the Development of Narrative and Oratorical Style.* Honolulu: University of Hawai'i Press, 2004.

Wang, Bo. "A Survey of Research in Asian Rhetoric." *Rhetoric Review* 23 (2004): 171–81.

Xiao, Xiaosui. "From the Hierarchical *Ren* to Egalitarianism: A Case of Cross-Cultural Rhetorical Mediation." *Quarterly Journal of Speech* 82 (1996): 38–54.

American Indian Rhetoric

Cobb, Amanda. *Listening to Our Grandmothers' Stories: The Bloomfield Academy for Chickasaw Females, 1852–1949.* Lincoln: Bison Books, University of Nebraska Press. 2007.

Cox, James H. *Muting White Noise: Native American and European American Novel Traditions.* Norman: University of Oklahoma Press, 2006.

Howard, Rebecca Moore. *Native American Languages, Discourses, and Rheto-rics.* 15 June 2007. http://wrt-howard.syr.edu/Bibs/NativeAm.htm.

Jaimes, M. Annette, ed. *The State of Native America: Genocide, Colonization, and Resistance.* Boston: South End, 1992.

Justice, Daniel Heath. *Our Fire Survives the Storm: A Cherokee Literary History.* Minneapolis: University of Minnesota Press, 2006.

Konkle, Maureen. *Writing Indian Nations: Native Intellectuals and the Politics of Historiography, 1827–1863.* Chapel Hill: University of North Carolina Press, 2004.

Maddox, Lucy. *Citizen Indians: Native American Intellectuals, Race, and Reform.* Ithaca: Cornell University Press, 2005.

Miranda, Deborah A. "Down by the River, or How Susan La Flesche Picotte Can Teach Us about Alliance as a Practice of Survivance." *College English* 67, no. 1 (Sept. 2004): 38–60.

———. "Extending the Hand of Empire: American Indians and the Indian Re-form Movement, a Beginning." In *Rhetoric and Ethnicity,* ed. Keith Gilyard and V. Nunley, 37–45. Portsmouth, NH: Boynton/Cook, 2004.

———. "Rhetorics of Survivance: How American Indians Use Writing." *College Composition and Communication* 53 (2002): 396–434.

———. "'A String of Textbooks': Artifacts of Composition Pedagogy in Indian Boarding Schools." *Journal of Teaching Writing* 16, no. 2 (2000): 213–32.

Senier, Siobhan. *Voices of American Indian Assimilation and Resistance: Helen Hunt Jackson, Sarah Winnemucca, and Victoria Howard.* Norman: University of Oklahoma Press, 2003.

Stromberg, Ernest. *American Indian Rhetorics of Survivance: Word Medicine, Word Magic.* Pittsburgh: University of Pittsburgh Press, 2006.

Warrior, Robert Allen. *Tribal Secrets: Recovering American Indian Intellectual Traditions.* Minneapolis: University of Minnesota Press, 1995.

Williams, Robert, Jr. *Linking Arms Together: American Indian Treaty Visions of Law and Peace, 1600–1800.* New York: Routledge, 1999.

Womack, Craig S. *Red on Red.* Minneapolis: University of Minnesota Press, 1995.

Additional Sources from Conclusion

Abbott, Don Paul. "The Influence of Blair's *Lectures* in Spain." *Rhetorica* 7 (1989): 275–89.

———. "Mayans' *Rhetórica* and the Search for a Spanish Rhetoric." *Rhetorica* 11 (1993): 157–79.

Gilman, Sander L., Carole Blair, and David J. Parent, eds. *Friedrich Nietzsche on Rhetoric and Language.* New York: Oxford University Press, 1989.

6

The Twentieth and Twenty-First Centuries

Krista Ratcliffe

The present state of scholarship in twentieth- and twenty-first-century rhetoric studies is diverse. Rhetoric, in multiple guises, has permeated a variety of academic disciplines, such as advertising, anthropology, classics, communication, critical theory, economics, ethnic studies, law, literary studies, management, marketing, medicine, natural sciences, philosophy, psychology, rhetoric and composition, theater, theology, transnational politics, and women's and gender studies. Because tracing scholarship in all these disciplines is beyond the scope of this book, this chapter focuses on the diversity of the twentieth- and twenty-first-century scholarship that informs rhetoric and composition studies.

Thanks in part to this field's emergence in the mid-1960s,* rhetoric scholarship exploded during the 1970s and dispersed during the 1980s, 1990s, and

---

* Rhetorical studies traditionally focused on the integrated arts of speaking, reading, writing, and listening. But in 1914, speaking and listening split from reading and writing when public speaking professionals (influenced by a German model of the university that favored disciplinary departments) seceded from NCTE. Consequently, rhetorical studies split into two departments: speech (focusing primarily on speaking) and English (focusing primarily on reading), with listening and writing relegated to secondary status, respectively. During two world wars and the 1950s boom, this split became institutionalized within U.S. universities. English professors taught great literature, simply assuming students could write, but the increased enrollments in the 1960s exposed the myth of this assumption. Consequently, scholars and teachers organized to seek theories and methods for training writing teachers and for teaching students to write. Because rhetorical studies was one site where such theories and methods were rediscovered, rhetorical studies was revived as rhetoric and composition studies in English departments by scholars such as Edward P. J. Corbett, James Kinneavy, and Winifred Bryan Horner—all of whom are now heralded as pioneers of rhetoric and composition—primarily to ground composition pedagogy. Since the mid-1960s, however, rhetoric and composition studies have greatly diversified.

2000s. To map this dispersion, this chapter offers a 2009 snapshot of scholarship that both updates existing research areas from previous editions of this book and also identifies new research areas. As with all snapshots, this one leaves some scholarly landscape hovering outside the frame of this chapter. For example, research areas (such as rhetoric and disability studies) do not have separate sections here. Other research areas (such as rhetoric and hermeneutics) do not have separate sections here but are present in earlier editions of this book (1983 and 1990), which readers are encouraged to consult.

The value of this 2009 snapshot lies not simply in the nineteen updated or newly identified research areas but especially in the generous contributions of noted scholars in each research area. Given the diversity of rhetoric scholarship, no one scholar possesses expertise in all research areas (or at least I do not). Consequently, I invited the following scholars to contribute their expertise to this chapter: Michelle Ballif and Diane Davis, Patricia Bizzell, Richard Enos, Theresa Enos, Cheryl Glenn and Shirley Logan, Marguerite Helmers, Joyce Irene Middleton, Roxanne Mountford, Beverly Moss, Malea Powell, Kate Ronald and Hephzibah Roskelly, Jacqueline Jones Royster and Anne Mitchell, Rebecca Rickly, Duane Roen, John Schilb, Victor Villanueva, Hui Wu, and Morris Young.

These contributing scholars responded to the following requests: (1) list twenty sources that anyone new to a research area must read; and (2) identify five topics for future scholarship within that research area. Although each scholar was assigned only one research area, his or her work may inhabit more than one area; for example, note the multiple mentions of Villanueva's *Bootstraps*. Conversely, more than one research area may define a contributor's scholarly identity; note Villanueva's expertise in Latino/a studies, rhetorical theory, and composition pedagogy. Notably, these scholars accepted this invitation not only because of their interest in defining their research areas but also because of their respect and affection for Winifred Horner. Whatever their motivations, I am very grateful for their contributions, which helped frame each research area. And as is conventional in any acknowledgment, I claim any errors as my own.

"Traditional" Contemporary Rhetoric Theories

In 1984, Edward P. J. Corbett assigned the theories listed in this section's bibliography as required readings in a graduate seminar at the Ohio State University. These theories—written by Wayne Booth, Kenneth Burke, Chaim Perelman, I. A. Richards, and Stephen Toulmin—were presented along with theories from previous centuries as *the* foundations of rhetoric and composition studies. These theories are included here *not* as foundational but, rather, as evidence of a twentieth-century historical moment when rhetoric scholarship worked alongside expressivist process approaches, cognitive science, and critical theory to institutionalize the field of rhetoric and composition. In that moment, these "traditional" rhetoric theories appeared to be composed by theorists (read *white men*) educated at universities (read *privileged*) and interested in men's public rhetorical performances (read *rhetorical performances of power*). As such, these theories were, and are, undoubtedly important; as such, they also inspired searches for alternative theories and traditions.

During the late twentieth and early twenty-first centuries, these theories have been studied in ways that have remapped rhetoric studies. This remapping embraces different methods:** (1) rereading traditional rhetoric theories, as in Ann George and Jack Selzer's *Kenneth Burke in the 1930s* (2007); (2) recovering rhetoric theories and practices not included or preserved within traditional academic memory, as in Karen Foss, Sonja Foss, and Cindy Griffin's *Readings in Feminist Rhetorical Theory* (2006); (3) extrapolating theories from texts and practices not traditionally deemed rhetorical, as in my *Anglo-American Feminist Challenges to the Rhetorical Tradition* (1996); and (4) writing new theories, reflective of the times, such as John Schilb's *Rhetorical Refusals* (2008). Such remapping seeks not to negate traditional theories but, rather, to demonstrate that there is always more to the story. Indeed, remapping pushes these theories from the center of rhetoric studies while calling into question the very idea of a center. Though dethroned from a place of privilege, these rhetoric theories still prove valuable because their rhetorical wisdom informs current scholarship, such as Wayne Booth's *The Rhetoric of RHETORIC* (2004) or my *Rhetorical Listening* (2006), even as such current scholarship questions the limits of traditional rhetorical wisdom.

Topics for future research include: (1) historicizing claims and identifications that haunt traditional theories; (2) rereading traditional theories for heretofore unacknowledged traces of gender, nationality, race, and so on; (3) rereading theories from postcolonial and/or global lenses; (4) analyzing audience as fictionalized dis/identifications; and (5) rereading theories and cultures to identify silence and listening as rhetorical arts.

Contemporary Receptions of Histories of Rhetoric

History is not simply the past. History is a compilation of stories that we tell ourselves, at particular moments, about the past. As stories, histories of rhetoric are rife with characters, plots, settings, and narrative points of views. They differ depending on their sources, purposes, and authors' cultural locations. Yet they all represent their historical moments of production, which is why

---

** These four methods are the same four that I argue feminists have used to articulate feminist theories of rhetoric (Ratcliffe [1996], 2–6).

histories of rhetoric written in the twentieth and twenty-first centuries deserve a place within this chapter even if their topics are receptions of non-twentieth-century rhetoric.

Contemporary histories of rhetoric are as diverse as the discipline itself. They include not only traditional histories, as in Ed Corbett's heavily Aristotelian *Classical Rhetoric for the Modern Student* (1965), but also challenges to such histories, as in Susan Jarratt's *Rereading the Sophists* (1991); Kathleen Welch's *The Contemporary Reception of Classical Rhetoric* (1991); and Richard Enos's *Greek Rhetoric before Aristotle* (1993). These challenges reflect differences in both topic and historiography, which is the study of how histories are constructed. As a hallmark of twentieth- and twenty-first-century rhetoric scholarship, historiography invites these questions: What method of writing history is employed? Who is writing? How is the writer positioned historically and culturally? What authority does such positioning give—or not give—the writer? What is included; what is omitted? What sources are available for writing the history? What sources are employed? What other sources might be employed? How reliable and representative are such sources? What use might such histories serve, and for whom? And always, Why?

Contemporary histories of rhetoric vary not only in historiographical methods but also in focus and historical ranges. Some histories focus on a particular period, for example, the contemporary period, as in Lynn Bloom, Donald Daiker, and Edward White's *Composition in the New Millennium* (2003) and Steven Mailloux's *Disciplinary Identities* (2006). Other histories employ contemporary lenses with which to review 2,500 years of rhetoric theories and praxes, as in George Kennedy's *Classical Rhetoric and Its Christian and Secular Tradition from Ancient to Modern Times* (1999) and Patricia Bizzell and Bruce Herzberg's *The Rhetorical Tradition to the Present* (2001). Still other histories use contemporary lenses (such as ethnic studies and feminist studies) to map multiple histories, as in Jacqueline Jones Royster's *Southern Horrors and Other Writings* (1997), Cheryl Glenn's *Rhetoric Retold* (1997), and Molly Meijer Wertheimer's *Listening to Their Voices* (1997). And still other "histories" engage contemporary lenses (such as poststructuralist theories) to reimagine the functions of history altogether, as in Victor Vitanza's *Negation, Subjectivity, and the History of Rhetoric* (1997), Mailloux's *Reception Histories* (1998), and Susan Miller's *Trust in Texts* (2007). Regardless of theoretical orientation, the above scholarship proves that, in contemporary rhetoric studies, history matters.

One topic for future research is to explore histories of all the categories in this chapter. Rich Enos, who compiled the bibliography for this research area, identifies other topics: (1) women in the history of rhetoric; (2) orality and literacy—historical perspectives; (3) developing new research methods for the history of rhetoric; (4) rhetoric and religion; and (5) historical issues in comparative and contrastive rhetorics.

Rhetoric Reference Works

Rhetoric reference works have greatly increased in number since earlier editions of this book were published. This increase may be attributed to the growth of rhetoric and composition studies as a scholarly discipline and also to the expanding Internet, where search engines and library databases provide immediate access to online texts of rhetoric theories and rhetorical performances as well as to bibliographies, scholarly journals, encyclopedias, indices, dictionaries, disciplinary blogs, podcasts, listservs, and more.

Bibliographies provide ready access to rhetoric research. The online *Bedford Bibliography for Teachers of Writing* links users to "History and Theory," "The Rhetorical Tradition," "History of Rhetoric and Education," and "Rhetoric and Composition Theory" as well as to other bibliographies. Other online resources include the *CCCC Bibliography of Composition and Rhetoric,* which offers links to pre-2002 sources; Rich Haswell and Glenn Blalock's *CompPile,* which provides links to sources from 1939 to the present; and Rebecca Moore Howard's *Bibliographies for Composition and Rhetoric,* which provides invaluable links in a variety of categories, such as African American rhetoric, contrastive rhetoric, and visual rhetoric. In addition to online sources, useful rhetoric bibliographies may be found in books, such as James Murphy and Richard Katula's *Synoptic History of Classical Rhetoric* (2003), Murphy's *Short History of Writing Instruction* (2001), and Pat Bizzell and Bruce Herzberg's *The Rhetorical Tradition* (2nd ed., 2001). Nonrhetoric and composition bibliographies (whether online or not) may also serve as a resource for rhetoric scholarship. The *MLA International Bibliography* (accessible through most university libraries) includes a database of many rhetoric and language articles; in addition, Gregory Ward's Web site *Studies on LGBTQ Language* provides a bibliography for research in rhetoric and queer studies, and the online *Disability Studies Bibliography* enables users to search using "rhetoric" as an option.

Journals may also be studied to trace patterns in contemporary rhetoric scholarship. Online archives for *College Composition and Communication, JAC, Rhetoric Review,* and *Peitho* allow users to review tables of content and to download articles and book reviews that are associated mostly with rhetoric and composition studies. Journals that merge rhetoric and composition studies with communication, literary studies, and philosophy include *Rhetoric Society Quarterly (RSQ)* (the journal of the Rhetoric Society of America), *Rhetorica* (the journal of the International Society for the History of Rhetoric), *Quarterly Journal of Speech, College English, Philosophy and Rhetoric,* and *Hypatia.* Because its first volume was published in 1928, *RSQ* remains a valuable resource for tracing patterns in twentieth- and twenty-first-century scholarship.

Reference books and articles are valuable resources, too. Andrea Lunsford, Kirt Wilson, and Rosa Eberly's *The SAGE Handbook of Rhetorical Studies*

(2009) traces rhetorical studies in terms of four areas: history, academic disciplines, pedagogy, and public discourses. Michael Moran and Michelle Ballif's *Twentieth-Century Rhetorics and Rhetoricians* (2005) presents articles on influential rhetoricians. Two important encyclopedias for defining influential rhetoricians, theories, and concepts are Theresa Enos's *Encyclopedia of Rhetoric and Composition* (1996) and Thomas Sloane's *Encyclopedia of Rhetoric* (2001). Earlier versions of Winifred Horner's *The Present State of Scholarship in Historical and Contemporary Rhetoric* provide 1983 and 1990 snapshots of rhetoric scholarship. Victor Villanueva, C. Jan Swearingen, and Susan McDowell offer a 2005 snapshot of "Research in Rhetoric" in Peter Smagorinsky's *Research on Composition*. And the *Online Communication Studies Resources* Web site at the University of Iowa offers critical summaries of major rhetoric texts in a variety of categories, such as "Rhetorical and Cultural Studies: Critical Theory," "Rhetorical Studies, Theory, and Philosophy," and "Visual Rhetorics"—all of which evidence a continuing though tenuous link between rhetoric and composition studies and communication studies. But even given this recent explosion of reference materials, more work remains to be done.

Patricia Bizzell, who compiled the bibliography for this section, identifies the following topics for future research: (1) anthologies (comprehensive or special area) of rhetorics in different countries; (2) anthologies (comprehensive or special area) of rhetorics in different academic disciplines; (3) annotated bibliographies for English speakers of rhetorical work done in other languages; (4) annotated bibliographies for scholars in English, composition, and communication of rhetorical work done in other disciplines, such as classics, philosophy, political science, history; and (5) more "synoptic" histories of rhetoric that link traditional and revisionist works.

Rhetorical Criticism

Rhetorical criticism is a difficult term to discuss because it signifies myriad ways of reading, writing, speaking, and listening. Traditionally, it refers to methods of analyses grounded in rhetoric theories and used to analyze public discourses in terms of author (intent), audience (effect), textual strategies (content/form), and rhetorical situation (historical/cultural context). Early twentieth-century rhetorical analyses were written mostly within speech departments, resulting in oft-cited scholarship written by Thomas Benson, Lloyd Bitzer, Edwin Black, and Marie Hochmuth Nichols. As speech and public speaking gave way to communication studies, rhetorical analyses were expanded in terms of topics and methods, such as in Karlyn Kohrs Campbell's *Man Cannot Speak for Her* (1989), a groundbreaking work in women's rhetoric. As rhetoric and composition studies emerged in the second half of the twentieth century, rhetorical analyses tended initially to be grounded in Aristotelian theory. For example, Kenneth Burke's theories echo Aristotelian concepts even as they blend rhetoric and philosophy, Freud and Marx, literary analyses and cultural critiques, structuralist moves and poststructuralist leanings. And the Chicago school of narrative theory—Wayne Booth's *A Rhetoric of Fiction* (1961, 1983) and James Phelan and Peter Rabinowitz's *Narrative as Rhetoric* (1996)—forward neo-Aristotelian concepts of the rhetorical triangle (such as multiple levels of speakers and audiences) as strategies for reading narrative.

As the field of rhetoric and composition grew, there emerged a broader conception of rhetorical analyses than had dominated Western university curricula until the nineteenth century. Grounded in rhetorical elements of poststructuralist, feminist, psychoanalytic, and cultural theories, these twentieth-century analyses have been published by various journals, such as *JAC, College English,* and *Rhetoric Review.* Even more broadly, traces of rhetorical criticism haunt contemporary literary/cultural analyses in different disciplines, such as English studies, history, anthropology, and religion. For example, feminist critics analyze bodies of *authors* performing *textual strategies* at particular *cultural sites* in the presence of particular *audiences* for particular *purposes* at particular *historical moments.* New historicist critics analyze textual strategies and historical/cultural contexts; poststructuralist critics engage textual tactics of language play and tropes; and new formalist critics are currently reengaging style and so forth. Though evident in the journals mentioned above and in scholarly books, such as John Schilb's *Between the Lines* (1996), these traces of rhetorical criticism remain an area for future research.

Theresa Enos, who compiled the bibliography for this section, identifies the following topics for future research: (1) social-movement rhetorics; (2) political rhetorics; (3) religious rhetorics; (4) rhetorics of technologies and multimedia; and (5) global community rhetorics.

Rhetoric and Poststructuralism

In the 1970s, when the field of rhetoric and composition invited more questions than classical rhetoric theory, expressivist process theory, cognitive science, or structuralism could answer, poststructuralism emerged within the discipline's scholarly conversations. The juxtaposition of rhetoric studies and poststructuralism gave rise to a ludic scholarship that is sometimes called the Third Sophistic and is associated with the scholarship of Victor Vitanza and his colleagues, for example, Michelle Ballif's *Seduction, Sophistry, and the Woman with the Rhetorical Figure* (2000) and Diane Davis's *Breaking Up (at) Totality* (2000). Indebted to Friedrich Nietzsche, Jacques Derrida and others, this scholarship plays the deadly serious game-that-is-language as it informs subjectivity and culture, inviting us all along for the quest(ioning)-that-never-ends. But not everyone has come along willingly. Some Aristotelian/Ciceronian scholars denigrate poststructuralist theory for its traces of sophistic language theory. Other cultural studies scholars worry that poststructuralism's free play of the signifier might lend itself to ahistorical and, particularly, apolitical thought and action. But in the best scholarly intersections of rhetoric studies and poststructuralism, these fears prove groundless.

The metonymic juxtaposition of rhetoric and poststructuralism introduces myriad opportunities for questioning *the* rhetorical tradition, *the* methods of historiography, and *the* "methods" of rhetorical criticism. This juxtaposition enables rhetoric scholars to remap rhetoric studies, as in Cheryl Glenn's "Remapping Rhetorical Territory" (1995), Steven Mailloux's *Rhetorical Power* (1989), and Vitanza's "Seeing in Third Sophistic Ways" (2002). This juxtaposition enables historians of rhetoric to identify gaps in traditional histories and fill these gaps with their own musings, again in different ways, thus rethinking rhetorical history, as in Jaspar Neel's *Plato, Derrida, and Writing* (1988) and Susan Jarratt's *Rereading the Sophists* (1991). This juxtaposition also enables rhetoric scholars to identify functions of in/visible cultural categories, such as whiteness, in different ways, as in Lynn Worsham's "After Words" (1998) and Joyce Irene Middleton's "Toni Morrison and 'Race Matters' Rhetoric" (2005).

Michelle Ballif and Diane Davis, who compiled the bibliography for this section, cite texts from outside the field that have influenced rhetoric and composition scholarship. For this reason, they identify below not just the following five topics for future research but also some rhetoric and composition scholars working within these areas: (1) relationship between rhetoric, hermeneutics, and ethics (Davis, Michael Bernard-Donals, Mailloux); (2) relationship between rhetoric and subjectivity/agency (Ballif, Pat Bizzell, Davis, Vitanza); (3) relationship between rhetoric and body studies, affect, and/or desire (Jenny Edbauer, Debbie Hawhee, Byron Hawk, T. J. Johnson, Thomas Rickert, Daniel Smith, Worsham); (4) nonfoundational approaches to the histories of rhetoric and/or composition (Ballif, Sharon Crowley, Cheryl Glenn, Jarratt, Vitanza); and (5) nonfoundational approaches to the canons of rhetoric and to the teaching of writing (Lester Faigley, Thomas Kent, John Muckelbauer, Neel).

Rhetoric and Cultural Studies

Cultural studies heavily influenced rhetoric studies in the 1980s and 1990s. Early cultural studies scholarship emphasized class issues, but its male bias prompted Nedra Reynolds to echo feminists in other disciplines and write "Interrupting Our Way to Agency" (1998), a call for feminist interruption of cultural studies topics and methods that ignore or downplay the role of women. More recently, rhetoric and cultural studies scholars interrogate cultural discourses, such as gender, race, class, sexual orientation, age, region, nationality, religion, and so on. Wedding rhetoric and cultural studies enables scholars to take "high" and "low" cultures as their subject matters and use rhetorical analyses as methods. The results are critiques not just of culture but of rhetoric theory. For example, Jacqueline Jones Royster's CCCC's chair address, "When the First Voice You Hear Is Not Your Own" (1996), astutely reconceptualizes interlocutors by arguing that it is important to distinguish between subject position (one's identity) and cultural positions (one's multiple locations within cultures). For while cultural positions inform one's identity, one's identity can never be reduced to a single cultural position; thus, Royster theorizes a way to invoke the importance of cultural groups in rhetorical exchanges while resisting stereotypes.

The intersection of rhetoric studies with cultural studies is associated with the scholarship of James Berlin, Patty Harkin, John Schilb, John Trimbur, and Christine Farris—scholarship that engages cultural theories, analyzes cultural practices, and designs cultural studies pedagogies. As evidenced in *Cultural Studies in the English Classroom* (1992) and *Rhetorics, Poetics, and Cultures* (1993), Berlin is particularly adept at connecting rhetoric and cultural studies theories and discussing pedagogical implications. And as evidenced by the Indiana University composition program, Farris is particularly adept at designing theoretically grounded cultural studies composition pedagogy. While some traditional scholars worry that cultural studies is overshadowing rhetoric, some poststructuralist scholars worry that cultural studies analyses are too ploddingly Marxist to be productive. But the best scholarly intersections of rhetoric and cultural studies are finely attuned to the rhetoricity of discourse (as in Joyce Irene Middleton's studies of *whiteness*), to the constructedness of culture and subjectivity (as in Lester Faigley's and Victor Villanueva's studies of how culture informs the subject of composition as well as the composing subject), and to their material/ideological groundings and implications (as in John Trimbur's, Bruce Horner's, and Min Zhan Lu's studies of composition programs and pedagogy).

John Schilb, who compiled the bibliography for this section, identifies the following topics for future research: (1) rhetorics of visual culture; (2) the relationship of contemporary rhetorics to late capitalism, including globalization; (3) the role of popular culture, including popular new media, in rhetoric and composition classrooms; (4) the relationship between culture and agency; and (5) rhetorics of past and present social movements.

Rhetoric and Literacy Studies

Literacy is a term almost as slippery as *rhetoric*. In popular usage, *literacy* signifies the ability to read, but, in actuality, it encompasses all the rhetorical arts of reading, writing, speaking, and listening. Even more, literacy entails knowing how and when to employ these arts so as to navigate social and cultural systems, whether these systems be schools, workplaces, social networks, or bus routes. Consequently, literacy influences the way one thinks, the way one imagines oneself in the world, and the way one acts (or not). Because literacy studies explores how language fosters socialization, critical thinking, and communication, it intersects easily with rhetoric studies.

Literacy scholarship has evolved into two strands that have influenced rhetoric studies. One strand theorizes about minds of individuals, with a bias toward how literate minds produce more sophisticated thinking. Noted examples are Walter Ong's *Orality and Literacy* (1982) and Eric Havelock's *The Muse Learns to Write* (1986). To counter this bias toward literate minds, a second strand theorizes social/historical dimensions of literacy. This second strand employs empirical research methods, usually ethnography, to test traditional assumptions about literacy and to posit new ones. Harvey Graff's *The Literacy Myth* (1979) uses both quantitative and qualitative methods to challenge traditional apolitical assumptions about the places and practices of literacy in nineteenth-century North America; Sylvia Scribner and Michael Cole's *The Psychology of Literacy* (1981) models an ethnographic method much emulated; and Paulo Freire's *Pedagogy of the Oppressed* (1981) further politicizes this method and, along with Shirley Brice Heath's *Ways with Words* (1983), popularizes it within U.S. scholarship and classrooms.

Some traditional scholars worry that a focus on literacy ignores rhetoric as subject matter and reduces it to an unspoken/untheorized method for analyzing ethnographic data. Some poststructuralist scholars worry about naive objectivism and static identity politics. But again, in the best scholarly intersections of rhetoric and literacy studies, these fears prove groundless, as evidenced by the first-rate studies of Deborah Brandt, Ralph Cintron, Ellen Cushman, Marcia Farr, Ann Gere, Beverly Moss, Catherine Prendergast, Elaine Richardson, Jacqueline Jones Royster, Robert Yagelski, and Morris Young. Together, this research (much of it award-winning) not only exposes the constructedness of cultural categories, cultural assumptions, and cultural knowledge but also articulates how social/economic power differentials affect what counts as literacy, what affords one access to literacy, what may be achieved via literacy, and what results from a lack of literacy.

Beverly Moss, who compiled the bibliography for this section, identifies the following topics for future research: (1) language and literacy practices of non-academic communities, demonstrating their commonalities and differences with academic literacy practices; (2) changing natures of digital literacies and digital rhetorics, in concert with visual literacies and rhetorics; (3) relationships between religion(s), rhetoric, and literacies, particularly in understanding how religion impacts literate and rhetorical practices of recent immigrant populations; (4) gendered literacy and rhetorical practices; (5) literacy and rhetorical practices emerging from popular culture (such as hip-hop and other forms of music and culture, popular fiction, community and/or underground publications); and (6) defining *literacy*—that is, What does it mean to label someone "literate" in the twenty-first century, given the increasing globalization and digitization of the societies in which we use language? Is *literacy* even going to be the right term? Is it already being overused?

Rhetoric and Feminist Studies

In the 1980s, feminist rhetoric scholars began making three moves: writing women into the history of rhetoric, writing feminist issues into theories of rhetoric, and writing feminist perspectives into rhetorical criticism. Initially, these scholars drew on feminist scholarship from other disciplines, for example, African American studies (Barbara Christian's 1985 *Black Feminist Criticism* and bell hooks' 1981 *Ain't I a Woman*); Chicana studies (Gloria Anzaldua's 1981 *This Bridge Called My Back* and Cherrie Moraga's 1981 "Theories in the Flesh"); communication studies (Karlyn Kohrs Campbell's 1989 *Man Cannot Speak for Her*); linguistic studies (Dale Spender's 1980 *Man Made Language* and Deborah Cameron's 1985 *Feminism and Linguistic Theory*); and psychoanalytic studies (Helene Cixous's 1975 "The Laugh of the Medusa" and Julia Kristeva's 1974 *Revolution in Poetic Language*, both of which were translated into English in the 1980s). Once inspired, however, feminist rhetoric scholars began writing scholarship from the site of rhetoric and composition. By 1992, scholarship critiquing methods for writing women into the history of rhetoric emerged in Barbara Biesecker's "Coming to Terms with Recent Attempts to Write Women into the History of Rhetoric," Pat Bizzell's "Opportunities for Feminist Research in the History of Rhetoric," and Susan Jarratt's *RSQ Special Issue: Feminist Rereadings in the History of Rhetoric*. Scholarship that writes twentieth- and twenty-first-century women into histories of rhetoric include Andrea Lunsford's *Reclaiming Rhetorica* (1995), my *Anglo-American Feminist Challenges* (1996), and Joy Ritchie and Kate Ronald's *Available Means* (2001).

In the midst of this scholarly activity, intersections of rhetoric and feminist studies have been institutionalized within rhetoric and composition studies, thanks largely to the work of the Coalition of Women Scholars in the History of Rhetoric and Composition, which was organized by Winifred Horner, Jan Swearingen, Nan Johnson, Marjorie Curry Woods, and Kathleen Welch in 1988–1989 and was carried on by scholars such as Andrea Lunsford, Jackie Royster, Cheryl Glenn, and Shirley Logan. In 1996, the first edition of the coalition's newsletter, *Peitho*, was published by Jarratt. And two past presidents, Glenn and Logan, created and now coedit SIUP's Rhetorics and Feminisms series, which has published Elizabeth Flynn's *Feminism beyond Modernism* (2002), Nan Johnson's *Gender and Rhetorical Spaces in American Life, 1866–1910* (2002), Carol Mattingly's *Appropriate[ing] Dress* (2002), Roxanne Mountford's *The Gendered*

Pulpit (2003), my *Rhetorical Listening* (2006), and *Vote and Voice: Women's Organizations and Political Literacy, 1915–1930* (2007), among others.

Cheryl Glenn and Shirley Logan, who compiled the bibliography for this section, identify eight topics for future research: (1) feminist deliberations and collaborations across race, class, and nationality; (2) marginalized women's ways of being heard; (3) invitational rhetorics for people not (self-)identified as "feminist"; (4) women's rhetorical prowess within traditionally feminized spaces; (5) women and religion, such as television preachers and church leaders; (6) women's practices not yet identified as rhetorical; (7) feminist-, racially, and/or ethnically marked styles; and (8) women, rhetoric, and technology. In addition, a wealth of contemporary research possibilities exist in countries other than the United States, such as analyzing rhetorics of activist groups, such as WOZA (Women of Zimbabwe Arise), whose members regularly protest for civil rights despite very real threats of arrests, jail terms, and beatings.

Rhetoric and Critical Race Studies

Critical race studies emerged in the late twentieth century as an antiracist project in legal studies, most notably in the work of Patricia Williams and Derrick Bell. It evolved into an interdisciplinary academic study, as surveyed in Richard Delgado and Jean Sefancic's *Critical Race Theory* (1995, 2000) and as represented in literary criticism by Toni Morrison's *Playing in the Dark* (1992) and in history by David Roediger's *Working toward Whiteness* (2005). It evolved, in part, to counter the failures of multiculturalism. When multiculturalism gained prominence in education in the 1980s and 1990s, its mission was to promote understanding of and tolerance among all U.S. ethnic groups by studying ethnicity. *Ethnicity* was often defined as cultural heritages that inform people's identities even as people's identities are constructed by more than just ethnicity. As a result, African American studies, American Indian studies, Asian American studies, Latino/a studies, and so on became academic sites of scholarship and pedagogy. Critics charged that such categories resulted in static identity politics; proponents, however, demonstrated the ongoing change, diversity, and intersections within and among such categories. In rhetoric and composition studies, these categories emerged as popular and important areas of rhetoric study, as evidenced by the sections immediately following this one.

But the failures of multiculturalism are more complex than a debate over identity politics. As Greg Jay and Sandra Jones (2005) note in "Whiteness in the Multicultural Literature Classroom," multiculturalism branched in two directions: (1) a celebratory multiculturalism that promotes a feel-good smorgasbord of ethnic differences but renders racial power differentials invisible and unquestioned; and (2) a critical multiculturalism that emphasizes how power and discrimination—racial, gender, class, sexual, and so on—inform ethnicity, not just in the United States but globally (100). Critical race studies emerged, in part, to challenge the former and advocate the latter. Because critical race studies posits "race" as a socially constructed category grounded in bad science but embodied in all people via socialization, critical race studies easily intersects with rhetoric studies.

Rhetoric scholarship engaging critical race studies includes Victor Villanueva's *Bootstraps* (1993), Jacqueline Jones Royster's "First Voice" (1996), Keith Gilyard's *Race, Rhetoric, and Composition* (1999), Lynn Worsham and Gary Olson's *Race, Rhetoric, and the Postcolonial* (1999), Malea Powell's "Rhetorics of Survivance" (2002), Shirley Logan's "Changing Missions" (2003), Catherine Prendergast's *Literacy and Racial Justice* (2003), Gwendolyn Pough's *Check It While I Wreck It* (2004), Gilyard and Vorris Nunley's *Rhetoric and Ethnicity* (2004), Joyce Irene Middleton's "Toni Morrison and 'Race Matters' Rhetoric" (2005), Kathleen Welch's "Who Made Aristotle White?" (2005), as well as my *Rhetorical Listening* (2006). To acknowledge the principle that all racial categories need to be identified before they can be negotiated, *Rhetoric Review* ran a special 2005 Symposium on Whiteness Studies, guest-edited by Tammie Kennedy, Middleton, and myself.

Joyce Irene Middleton, who compiled the bibliography for this section, identifies the following topics for future research: (1) whiteness and visuality (or ocularcentrism); (2) unpacking white privilege embedded in color-blind rhetoric; (3) the meaning(s) of race in the twenty-first century; (4) rhetorical listening as a global rhetoric; (5) reproducing whiteness in academics, science, and/or popular culture; (6) teaching rhetorical listening in film as a code of cross-cultural conduct; (7) critical race studies and the rhetoric of science and/or medical practices; (8) critical race studies, rhetoric, and democracy; (9) critical race studies, assimilation, and immigration in the United States; and (10) critical race studies and definitions of cultural rhetorics.

Rhetoric and African American Studies

African American rhetoric has been present within U.S. culture since its beginnings (indeed, since before the nation was founded), but this rhetoric has not always been the subject of study within the academy. Within the past few decades, however, an explosion of research has emerged on intersections of rhetoric studies and African American studies. Jacqueline Jones Royster and Anne M. Mitchell, who compiled the bibliography for this section, divided their top twenty texts into three categories: (1) critical anthologies of rhetorical performances; (2) rhetorical history, theory, and criticism; and (3) language culture and rhetorical performances. These categories not only provide an apt framework for this particular discussion but also suggest the kinds of work needed for any emerging research area in rhetoric.

Critical anthologies serve several purposes: they recover rhetorical performances omitted from dominant histories; their critical glosses offer historical and theoretical interpretive frames; and their contents provide grounds for further research, whether rhetorical analyses of specific performances or extrapolations of rhetoric theories from such performances. For example, Gerald Early compiles African American essays by writers such as W. E. B. Du Bois and Alice Walker in a two-volume collection, *Speech and Power* (1992 and 1993), and Bettye Collier-Thomas compiles the sermons of black women preachers in *Daughters of Thunder* (1998).

Articulating African American rhetorical history, theory, and criticism is an important and complex enterprise. First, African American rhetorical history makes visible cultural conversations that have not always been present in the academy. Histories, such as the African American feminist thinking collected in Beverly Guy-Sheftall's *Words of Fire* (1995), remap disciplinary boundaries and challenge traditional criteria for inclusion in rhetorical history. Second, African American rhetoric theory provides a lexicon of principles and strategies for producing and analyzing texts, as in Royster's introduction to *Traces in a Stream* (2000), which calls for a new way of reading. Such theories, like the ones offered in Ronald Jackson and Elaine B. Richardson's collection *Understanding African American Rhetoric* (2003), supply interpretive frames for analyzing African American texts in terms of their own cultural traditions. And third, African American rhetorical criticism provides a scholarly and cultural forum for such analyses, enabling multiple arguments among and about African American texts, both written and oral, to be identified, debated, and judged, as in Carole K. Doreski and Albert Delpi's *Writing America Black* (1998), which rhetorically analyzes black journalism and literary works to make claims about how race informs concepts of history, literature, kinship, and nationhood. But perhaps the most important point about studying African American history, theory, and rhetorical criticism is that these three categories intersect in powerful ways: African American theories and rhetorical analyses are historically grounded; histories and rhetorical analyses merge to build theories; theories and rhetorical analyses emerge from and thus represent cultural moments.

Scholarship in rhetoric and African American studies that emphasizes connections among language, culture, and rhetorical performance is important, too. One strand identifies African American language use in order to challenge traditional (read: *white*) definitions of language competence and, more importantly, to offer definitions grounded in African American culture. Noted examples are Geneva Smitherman's *Talkin' and Testifyin'* (1977, 2000) and Keith Gilyard's *Voices of the Self* (1991). Another strand of scholarship highlights African American cultural contributions. In the realm of music, intersecting performances of culture, gender, and hip-hop are explored in Gwendolyn Pough's *Check It While I Wreck It* (2004) and Elaine Richardson's *Hip Hop*

Literacies (2006). In the realm of preaching, the power of words in relating the Word and in reimagining the world is evidenced in Beverly Moss's *Community Text Arises* (2003), Chanta Haywood's *Prophesying Daughters* (2003), Melissa Victoria Harris-Lacewell's *Barbershops, Bibles, and BET* (2004), and Davis W. Houck and David W. Dixon's collection, *Rhetoric, Religion, and the Civil Rights Movement* (2006). Running throughout these texts is an emphasis on how languages, cultures, and rhetorical performances intersect to inform and revise both personal and cultural identities.

Jackie Royster and Anne Mitchell, who composed the bibliography for this section, identify the following topics for future research: (1) how peoples of African descent engage in rhetorical practices in various sites and contexts; (2) how contemporary rhetorical practices within African diasporic communities in the United States and beyond show evidence of continuity and change over time and, especially in light of new media, in global contexts, and other distinctions that now exist in our contemporary world; (3) how using various types of analytical lenses (race, class, gender, sexuality, region, power, privilege, authority, and so forth) or various combinations of them enrich our capacity to interpret rhetorical behavior; (4) how theoretical frames have the interpretive power to enhance our understanding of particular rhetorical sites and practices and to clarify how such sites and practices connect with or diverge from others synchronically and diachronically; (5) what remains underinterrogated and undertheorized when we view rhetorical action from a more expansive perspective; and (6) implications of what we have come to understand about rhetorics in general and the rhetorical practices of peoples of African descent in particular regarding both formal and informal opportunities for rhetorical training and rhetorical performance.

Rhetoric and American Indian Studies

Studying intersections of rhetoric and American Indian studies requires a working knowledge of both fields. Many books in this bibliography engage American Indian histories and cultures, perhaps the most famous being the late Vine Deloria Jr.'s *Custer Died for Your Sins* (1969), *Red Earth, White Lies* (1995), *Evolution, Creationism, and Other Modern Myths* (2002), and *The World We Used to Live In* (2006)—all of which explain the world from a Native perspective. A work theorizing methods for employing Native perspectives as scholarly lenses is Linda Tuhiwai Smith's *Decolonizing Methodologies* (1999). Theorizing such research methods is important because scholars in this area are especially attuned to the following questions: Who is speaking? For whom? About what? And with what authority or vision? Important to scholars in this area are not just an attentiveness to method but also a lived engagement with American Indian issues and a willingness to immerse oneself in the study of these issues.

Although American Indian ancestry need not be a litmus test for scholarly authority, care should be taken when pursuing such research, not as a means for meeting some arbitrary notion of political correctness but, rather, as a means for showing respect because, far too often in the past five hundred years, respect for the reality of American Indian cultures has been missing in the dominant U.S. culture. Instead, there exists a history of romanticizing anything associated with American Indians, relegating such associations to the past, and collapsing myriad cultures into one. And in white academe, there exists a history of relegating American Indians to the status of objects of study rather than as subjects of their own scholarship and of defining Native concepts in terms of non-Native ones. Such history haunts scholarly research in this area. And it is precisely this concern with history, story, rhetorical situation, the positioning of interlocutors, the analyses of rhetorics in different types of texts, and a consideration of audience that foster productive intersections of rhetoric studies and American Indian studies.

In rhetoric and composition scholarship, Malea Powell brings American Indian lenses into rhetoric studies with "Blood and Scholarship" (1999), which exposes how rhetoric studies often imposes a non-Native frame on Native rhetorics; with "Listening to Ghosts" (2002), which questions the dismissal of emotion from academic argument and offers an alternative rhetoric; and with "Down by the River," which posits alliance as a rhetorical tactic that, unlike inclusion, does not force American Indian rhetorics into a European American framework (2004). In addition, research on different functions of writing emerges in James Axtell's "The Power of Print in the Eastern Woodlands" (1987), Laura Donaldson's "Writing the Talking Stick: Alphabetic Literacy as Colonial Technology and Postcolonial Appropriation" (1998), and Scott Lyons's "Rhetorical Sovereignty: What Do American Indians Want from Writing?" (2000). Research that focuses on how American Indians find a place (or not) in rhetoric and composition studies may be found in Resa Crane Bizzaro's "A Captivity Narrative" (1998) and "Making Places as Teacher-Scholars in Composition Studies" (2002). And research on how white teachers in tribal schools might rethink their pedagogical positions and pedagogical narratives is discussed in Stephen Gilbert Brown's *Words in the Wilderness* (2000). Research on the rhetorical tactic of silence in multiple American Indian cultures is explored in a chapter of Cheryl Glenn's *Unspoken* (2004), and the idea of Powell's nineteenth-century research on survivance is continued in Ernest Stromberg's edited collection *American Indian Rhetorics of Survivance* (2006).

Malea Powell, who compiled the bibliography for this section, identifies the following topics for future research: (1) American Indians and the Web; (2) more historical recovery; (3) more bridging of the rhetoric-poetics divide; (4) material culture and nonalphabetic texts; and (5) popular culture in relation to American Indians.

Rhetoric and Asian American Studies

Rhetoric and composition scholars articulating intersections of rhetoric studies with Asian American studies must acquire an understanding of the latter, an interdisciplinary field that focuses not only on multiple ethnic cultures that fall under the category "Asian American" but also on the way race has informed receptions of these cultures in the United States. Kent Ono provides an introduction to this interdisciplinary field in his edited collection *Asian American Studies after Critical Mass* (2005), which addresses globalization, politics, gay issues, film, and a host of other issues facing Asian Americans; Eric Liu uses autobiography and cultural analyses in *The Accidental Asian* (1998) to critique the roles of Asian Americans in U.S. culture and to critique the influence of dominant culture's perceptions of *Asian* on public policy; and Frank Wu names and unpacks prejudicial constructs such as "model minority" and argues for coalitions across ethnic and racial boundaries in *Yellow* (2002). In literary studies, Frank Chin and his coeditors provide a compilation of Asian American literature in *Aiiieeeee! An Anthology of Asian American Writers* (1974); King-Kok Cheung analyzes silence as an Asian American strategy in *Articulate Silences* (1993); and Patti Duncan continues this analysis, arguing that contemporary U.S. feminism needs to engage Asian American women's issues in *Tell This Silence* (2004). In education, multidisciplinary theories and practices that benefit Asian American students are recounted in Don Nakanishi and Tina Yamamoto Nishida's collection, *The Asian American Educational Experience* (1995). And contextualized language issues emerge in sociolinguistics and popular writings; for example, Charlene Sato's academic "Sociolinguistic Variation and Language Attitudes in Hawai'i" (1991) traces the origins of Pidgin (Hawai'i Creole English) to the Hawaii plantation economy and discusses the functions of Pidgin in employment discrimination and identity-building; Lisa Linn Kanae's autobiographical *Sista Tongue* (2001) explores the effects of code-shifting between Pidgin and English for speaking and writing; and Lee Tonouchi's collection of essays and poems, *Living Pidgin* (2002), presents Pidgin as a legitimate language.

The rhetorical dimensions of the above scholarship offer fertile grounds for intersections with rhetoric studies. Some rhetorical dimensions include analyzing the dominant U.S. culture's tendency to define *Asian* as "exotic," articulating multiple cultures and myriad personal identities collapsed into the terms *Asian* and *Asian American,* negotiating troubled notions of citizenship, and critiquing reading/writing pedagogy.

These and other issues are addressed by rhetoric and composition scholars. Yuet-Sim Chiang charges, in "Insider/Outsider/Other?" (1998), that composition research is grounded in white, middle-class assumptions and argues for its engaging Asian American cultures. Gail Okawa continues this questioning of composition research and extends the questioning to composition pedagogy in "Coming (in)to Consciousness" (1998) and "Removing Masks" (1999). Morris Young grounds the discussion of Hawaiian language debates in a rhetorical frame of Hawaii's shifting cultural logics in "Native Claims" (2004). He also combines autobiography and textual/cultural analyses in his award-winning *Minor Re/Visions* (2004) to critique U.S. discourses of citizenship as they are informed by race and ethnicity. LuMing Mao, who also publishes in comparative rhetorics, explores the construction of Asian American rhetorics in "Uniqueness or Borderlands?" (2004) and in *Reading Chinese Fortune Cookie* (2006).

Morris Young, who compiled the bibliography for this research area, identifies the following topics for future research: (1) hybrid rhetorical and discourse practices and forms; (2) Asian American diasporic and transnational rhetorical and discourse practices; (3) recuperation of Asian and Asian American rhetoric prior to the early twentieth century; (4) Asian and Asian American digital rhetorics; and (5) intersections of identity and rhetorical practices—that is, Asian Americans and issues of ethnicity, gender, sexuality, dis/ability, region, mixed-race, and so on.

Rhetoric and Latino/a Studies

Language issues haunt and energize Latino/a studies. Naming haunts this interdisciplinary field in that it has been variously named: Hispanic studies, Puerto Rican studies, Chicano/a studies, Latino/a studies, and more. These terms signify differently over time and place, depending on the local politics of their institutional usage, but, in general, they are defined as follows. *Hispanic* is a term created by the U.S. census bureau that reflects only a European ancestry (Spain) and, thus, is often viewed as the most conservative term, especially as it collapses many cultural groups into one category. *Puerto Rican, Nyorican* (Puerto Ricans in New York), and *Chicano* (Mexican American) all specify narrower focuses, thus visibly acknowledging differences. Although *Latino* retains traces of a European ancestry, collapses many different cultures into one category, and codes masculine (hence the use of *Latino/a*), this term has emerged as the one more commonly used.

This naming issue affects not only programs but scholarship. Suzanne Oboler, editor of *Latino Studies,* claims on the journal's online editorial page that the term *Latino* creates a space of common ground for scholarly and activist work, that the term does not negate but rather assumes differences among national origins, and that both Latino/as and non-Latino/as can participate in this scholarly and activist work. And though written as critical legal theory, Berta Esperanza Hernández-Truyol's "Building Bridges—Latinas and Latinos at the Crossroads" (1994) explains how the terms *Latina* and *Latino* function as identity markers. But such scholarship does not focus on ethnicity alone; it draws on critical race studies to foreground how cultural constructs of race inform receptions of ethnicity by Latino/as and non-Latino/as alike, as evidenced by Villanueva's "On the Rhetoric and Precedents of Racism" (1999).

But naming is not the only language issue haunting Latino/a studies; so is language choice. Not only do choices exist (as they do for English-writing academics in all research areas) about what kinds of English to use, but choices also exist about what kinds of Spanish to use. And there are choices not merely between English or Spanish but also about whether and how English and Spanish should be combined. These issues and others are explored both in Richard Delgado and Jean Stefancic's *The Latino/a Condition* (1997), an edited collection that defines this interdisciplinary field with a particular emphasis on legal issues, and in Harold Augenbraum and Margarite Fernández Olmos's *The Latino Reader* (1997), an anthology of Latino/a writings that traces Latino/a cultural influences in North America back to before the United States was formed.

In rhetoric and composition studies, intersections with Latino/a studies have emerged via ethnographic studies, rhetorical analyses of political rhetoric, and rewriting rhetorical histories. First, Victor Villanueva's *Bootstraps* (1993) is an autoethnography that skillfully weaves autobiography with cultural critique and theory. Other ethnographic research includes Ralph Cintron's *Angels' Town* (1998), which analyzes a Mexican American community in terms of the geographies of false documentation, graffiti, street gangs, and a boys' room—this analysis not only articulates Latino/a rhetorical practices of the everyday but also models a first-rate ethnographic method. Second, two important rhetorical analyses of Latino/a political rhetorics are J. Delgado-Figueroa's *The Rhetoric of Change* (1994), which identifies elements of Puerto Rican rhetorics based on political oratory, and John C. Hammerback and Richard J. Jensen's *The Rhetorical Career of César Chávez* (2003), which identifies elements of Chávez's rhetoric based on a historically grounded rhetorical analysis of speeches and interviews. Third, other scholarship rethinks rhetorical history, pedagogy, and theory. To rethink history and pedagogy, Susan Romano's "Tlaltelolco" (2004) describes this sixteenth-century educational institution's curriculum of grammar, rhetoric, and composition and foregrounds how this curriculum is linked to cultural power and oppression. To rethink pedagogy, Michelle Hall Kells, Valerie Balester, and Villanueva's collection *Latino/a Discourses* (2004) includes a section about literacy education that rethinks rhetorical concepts; for example, Jaime Mejía's chapter, "Bridging Rhetoric and Composition Studies with Chicano and Chicana Studies," argues that this bridge may help teachers rethink traditional pedagogical practices, such as collaboration, so as to construct a critical pedagogy that can help Chicano/a students learn effective academic literacies. And to rethink rhetorical history and theory, Jessica Enoch's "Para la Mujer" (2004) defines an early twentieth-century Chicana feminist rhetoric.

Victor Villanueva, who compiled the bibliography for this section, claims there is a need for more work in this research area and identifies the following topics for future research: (1) rhetorics of Chicano/as within different historical contexts—for example, during the acquisition of the Texas Republic, World Wars I and II, the Zoot Suit era, and the creation of LULAC and other organizations of the 1950s and 1960s; (2) the rhetoric of Pedro Albizu Campos, perhaps the most outspoken advocate for Puerto Rican independence, who spent many years in prison, mainly for his speeches; (3) rhetorics of Puerto Ricans—among those seeking independence, those seeking U.S. statehood, and those wishing to continue with the current commonwealth relationship to the United States; (4) rhetorical history of Chicana and Latina women; (5) rhetorics of exclusions—such as rhetorics of wishing to remove the Latino/a from the United States in the nineteenth century, during the twentieth-century instances of the Great Depression and Operation Wetback, and during current debates about citizenship and immigration; (6) counterrhetorics to the rhetorics of exclusion; (7) masculine Latino or Chicano rhetorics in the post–Civil Rights era, plus their similarities with and differences from similarly situated Latina and Chicana rhetorics.

Comparative/Contrastive Rhetorics

In his 1966 article "Cultural Thought Patterns in Intercultural Education," applied linguist Robert Kaplan diagrams five cultural traditions and argues that each generated its own rhetoric—that is, its own way to choose topics, select evidence, organize arguments, and so on. Thus the study of contrastive rhetoric was born, spurring discussions in linguistics and English as a Second Language (ESL) and, more recently, in rhetoric and composition. Landmark rhetoric scholarship includes Robert Oliver's *Communication and Culture in Ancient India and China* (1971) and George Kennedy's *Comparative Rhetoric* (1997). With the publication of Kennedy's book, the term *comparative rhetoric* gained popularity; as Kennedy used the term, it signified his attempt to discover a universal "General Theory of Rhetoric" (1). In short, this shift in terms between *contrastive rhetoric* and *comparative rhetoric* reflects a difference in method.

According to Hui Wu, who compiled the bibliography for this section, two competing methods have dominated this research area. The first method celebrates a focus on commonality. This method is represented by Oliver and Kennedy, who ground their *comparative* definitions and methods in Western models, as does Xing Lu in *Rhetoric in Ancient China* (1998), which offers parallel terms between Western and Chinese rhetorics. Although noting commonalities among rhetorics can be interesting, a problem arises when non-Western rhetorics are forced to fit a Western model: that problem is cultural imperialism, which risks relegating the "excess" of non-Western rhetorics to the status of unimportant at best and invisible at worst. The second method celebrates a focus on difference. This method is represented by Kaplan in his seminal work as well as by Wu in "Historical Studies of Women" (2002) and Clayann Panetta's *Contrastive Rhetoric Revisited and Redefined* (2001), which contains articles exploring implications of *contrastive* rhetoric studies for understanding issues as far ranging as cultural differences, student resistance, business writing, and computer classrooms. This focus on difference resists a Westernizing impulse and attempts to articulate cultural rhetorics on their own terms.

But as with all binary oppositions, a both/and third term always exists when two terms are put into play, as Yameng Liu does in "Contrastive Rhetoric/ Comparative Rhetoric" (2000). The rise of globalism has brought increased attention to contrastive/comparative rhetoric in terms of defining the research area. LuMing Mao's "Reflective Encounters" (2003) introduces the area by offering definitions and a brief history, with a particular focus on the tropes of *deficiency* and *difference*. Xin Lu's "Studies and Development of Comparative Rhetoric in the U.S.A." (2006) traces four stages of this research area. And Arabella Lyon and Sue Hum's "Advances in Comparative Rhetoric" in *The SAGE Handbook of Rhetoric* discusses advances triggered by "globalization, transnational politics, and the American empire" (153).

In addition, increased attention to contrastive/comparative rhetoric has arisen via scholarly interests in women's contributions and in translations. Women's contributions to Chinese rhetorical traditions are explored in Wu, "The Feminist Rhetoric of Post-Mao Chinese Writers" (2001), in Garrett's "Women and the Rhetorical Tradition in Pre-modern China" (2002), and in Bo Wang's "Rhetoric and Resistance in Lu Yin's Feminist Essays" (2007) (Wu, personal e-mail). And finally, translation of rhetoric theories and performances is a vital concern, both in terms of quality and quantity. The quality of translations influences scholarship in English because English-speakers' understanding and uses of non-Western rhetorical concepts are only as strong as the translations. The quantity of translated sources also influences scholarship in English in terms of how representative (or not) scholarly claims about a rhetoric may be and in terms of how accurate a rhetorical analysis may be, two important issues discussed in Yameng Lui's *Rhetoric Review* article "To Capture the Essence of Chinese Rhetoric" (1996).

Hui Wu, who compiled the bibliography for this section, identifies the following topics for future research: (1) definitions of comparative rhetorics and their components on their own terms, instead of their being forced into a Western model; (2) definitions of research methods appropriate to different cultural contexts; (3) rhetorical criticism, based on concepts of comparative/contrastive rhetoric theories; (4) identification and definitions of women's rhetorics; (5)

formation of different rhetorical traditions; (6) more translations of primary sources; and (7) historical studies of comparative/contrastive rhetorics. In addition, this research area provides a site for investigating intersections of rhetoric and transnational politics.

Rhetoric and Religion

Ars praedicandi, or the art of preaching, holds a time-honored place within rhetoric studies. In the early to mid-twentieth century, however, the scholarship about this art thrived more in theology and, to a lesser extent, in public speaking. In theology, Harry Emerson Fosdick and Henry H. Mitchell wrote influential tracts about preaching in the United States. In public speaking, Harry Caplan and Henry King documented European preaching practices (1949–1954). By the time rhetoric and composition studies was being institutionalized in the 1960s and 1970s, two oft-cited rhetoric and religion texts were Kenneth Burke's *The Rhetoric of Religion* (1961) and Richard Weaver's *Language Is Sermonic* (1970). Yet neither text focuses on religion as a subject matter; rather, each employs religion as a metaphoric vehicle for explaining the functions of rhetoric.

The late twentieth and early twenty-first centuries, however, have seen increased scholarly attention to rhetoric and religion as a subject matter. This increased attention reflects the rise of religious influence in the U.S. public sphere as well as the rise of postmodern studies of discourses, including religion, in the academy. With this increased attention, the question that has emerged is not *if* religion plays a role in personal and public life but, rather, *how.* To address this question, scholars in multiple fields have engaged contemporary intersections of rhetoric and religion. In history, Bettye Collier-Thomas identifies previously undocumented preaching practices of African American women in *Daughters of Thunder* (1998). In rhetoric and composition studies, Amy Goodburn questions how the writing classroom is influenced by fundamentalism in "It's a Question of Faith" (1998); Keith Miller analyzes Martin Luther King Jr.'s civil rights rhetoric in *Voices of Deliverance* (1992); and Roxanne Mountford analyzes women ministers' performances in *The Gendered Pulpit* (2003). According to Mountford, during the late twentieth and early twenty-first centuries, "rhetoric theory and criticism have reinvigorated traditional religious studies, including homiletics and biblical hermeneutics" (personal e-mail). And Sharon Crowley astutely questions the role of religion, particularly fundamentalism, in *Toward a Civil Discourse* (2006).

Roxanne Mountford, who compiled the bibliography for this section, identifies the following topics for future research: (1) effects of early Judeo-Christian thought on modernity in the West; (2) interventions—theoretical, critical, pedagogical—into cultural rhetorics that perpetuate fundamentalist fervor and global backlashes against it; (3) distinctive forms of religious rhetoric in the United States and other countries (for example, their roots, their outlets, both secular and religious, and their import for contemporary rhetoric studies); (4) histories of preaching in the United States (specifically histories of twentieth-century homiletic theories) of the sermon as a genre, of the roles of preachers (including African Americans, women, and those without seminary training), of distinctive traits, of Jewish preaching, and of Islamic preaching; (5) religious influences of philosophies, practices, and organizations on the history of instruction in oral and written English as well as on the education of the poor in the United States and other countries; and (6) rhetoric theories and methods of criticism, whether traditional or new, that are particularly well suited to the study of rhetoric and religion.

Rhetoric, Technology, and Technical Writing

Rhetoric and technology have transformed each other, an idea posited in Christina Haas's *Writing Technology* (1996) and contextualized in Carolyn Miller's "Learning from History" (1998). On the one hand, technology has transformed rhetoric studies as well as composition pedagogy in terms of on-line databases and wireless classrooms, and in terms of the ways people think, analyze, research, and compose, as explained in S. C. Herring's "Computer-Mediated Discourse Analysis" (2004). Conversely, rhetoric has transformed technology, as argued by Charles Bazerman in *The Languages of Edison's Light* (1999). But in relation to the above claims, two corollary questions inform rhetoric scholarship: what is technology, and what is its value? Philosopher Andrew Feenberg engages these questions in *Questioning Technology* (1999), positing a nonessentialist theory of technology. He further engages these questions in *Transforming Technology* (2002), arguing two points: first, that technology constructs our ways of seeing the world—a claim argued earlier and differently by Donna Haraway in *Simians, Cyborgs, and Women* (1991)—and, second, that it has potential for fostering the continued evolution of democracy.

Although debates about the value of technology abound, technology has influenced contemporary rhetoric studies. For instance, it affects how composition pedagogies have been reimagined, as in Patricia Sullivan and James E. Porter's *Opening Spaces* (1997) and in Michelle Sidler, Richard Morris, and Elizabeth Overman Smith's *Computers in the Composition Classroom* (2007), thus affecting the ways students and teachers compose. Technology also affects the ways we read visual texts, as discussed in Carolyn Handa's *Visual Rhetoric in a Digital World* (2004); it affects the ways we read our bodies, as theorized in Mary Lay, Laura J. Gurak, Clare Gravon, and Cynthia Myntti's *Body*

Talk (2000); and it affects the ways we conceptualize literacy, as in Cindy Selfe's *Technology and Literacy in the 21st Century* (1999), Kathleen Welch's *Electric Rhetoric* (1999), and Stuart Selber's *Multiliteracies for a Digital Age* (2004).

Rebecca Rickly, who compiled the bibliography for this section, identifies the following topics for future research in rhetoric and technology: (1) defining *visual rhetoric* and incorporating it into our rhetorical sensibilities as well as teaching and assessing it; (2) defining, designing, and employing electronic portfolios in different contexts; (3) analyzing rhetoric, technology, and global access—that is, who has access to the technologies of rhetoric, particularly advanced digital technologies, who decides who gets access, and who decides what access is provided; (4) determining the responsibilities of technologically advanced/wealthy nations or entities toward nations or entities that lack these technologies.

The related, though not identical, field of technical communications has generated a wealth of scholarly intersections with rhetoric studies. Several overviews of these intersections exist. Tim Peeples's *Professional Writing and Rhetoric* (2002) includes readings from classical rhetoric to the present. Laura Gurak and Mary Lay's collection *Research in Technical Communication* (2002) examines how these intersections are informed by ethics, cultural studies, feminism, different research methods, and so on. Johndan Johnson-Eilola and Stuart Selber's *Central Works in Technical Communication* (2004) collects landmark essays. And for added context, Bazerman's *Handbook of Research on Writing* (2007) examines the history of writing, including how writing is used in different societal sites.

In technical communication, traditional rhetorical concepts have been redefined for new contexts. Invention strategies are posited for visual rhetorics in Sonja Foss's "A Rhetorical Schema for the Evaluation of Visual Imagery" (1994). Arrangement strategies are explored as they relate to illustrations in Sam Dragga and Dan Voss's "Cruel Pies" (2001) and as they relate to genre in Bazerman's *Shaping Written Knowledge* (1988), Carol Berkenkotter and Thomas N. Huckin's *Genre Knowledge in Disciplinary Communication* (1995), and Clay Spinuzzi's *Tracing Genres* (2003). Style is discussed in Carolyn Rude's *Technical Editing* (2002). And the interaction of author and rhetorical situation is reexamined in Jennifer Slack, Jennifer Daryl, David James Miller, and Jeffrey Doak's "The Technical Communicator as Author"; Anne Beaufort's *Writing in the Real World* (1999); and Geoff Cross's *Forming the Collective Mind* (2001). Finally, the pedagogical implications of this scholarship are examined in Selber's collection *Computers and Technical Communication* (1997).

According to Rickly, future research for rhetoric and technical writing includes: (1) types of writing that professionals do in various rhetorical settings; (2) types of information and other literacies that professionals need in various jobs; (3) best practices for the effective and ethical design of technical documents, including but not limited to user manuals and instructions, software user interfaces, presentation slides (as in PowerPoint), and risk communications; (4) functions of communication within large organizations; (5) sources of rhetoric in technical communication—that is, actual objects (which implies that nonliving things have rhetoric), the design (which implies that the object instantiates the design of the creator), or the responses to the object; and (6) pedagogical implications of all of the above.

Visual Rhetoric

The visual has always haunted rhetoric studies via the canon of delivery; that is, hearing audiences have long *watched* performances of speakers, and reading audiences have long *gazed* at layouts/designs of texts, whether those texts are sculptures, papyri, photos, or paper. But twentieth-century explosions of new media and theories of the gaze have triggered concurrent explosions of scholarly interest in visual rhetoric. Crossing several disciplines (anthropology, art studies, film studies, literary studies, media studies, and rhetoric and composition studies, to name only a few), this scholarly explosion focuses not on simple mimesis but, rather, on the complications of representations. Because scholarship on visual rhetoric intersects with scholarship on visual literacy, rhetoric scholars posit questions of definition: What is the *visual?* What is *visual rhetoric?* What is *visual literacy?* And what are the intersections of the latter two? Scholars also engage questions of function and effect: How may images be interpreted (Roland Barthes)? What do images mean, and what do they want (W. J. T. Mitchell)? How do images affect what we believe, and how does what we believe affect what we see (David Blakesley and Collin Brooke)?

Some scholarship offers methods of interpretations based on elements of the image itself. Roland Barthes's famous "The Rhetoric of the Image" (1977) argues that the image may be interpreted via three semiotic codes: the linguistic, the denoted, and the connoted. Some scholarship examines methods of interpretation based on genre conventions. In *Understanding Comics: An Invisible Art* (1994), Scott McCloud raises the comic, and by implication the graphic novel, to the level of art by positing (in comics form) a theory of visual interpretation based on a process of composing comics. Some scholarship maps new directions. David Blakesley and Collin Brooke's introduction to the Fall 2001 edition of the online journal *Enculturation* encourages scholars not just to interpret elements of images and genres but also to explore how images inform people's interpretations of the world, calling for a theory of the visual that explores intersections of words and images (2). And some scholarship provides definitions, overviews, and introductions to the field. For example, in an effort to foreground the persuasive dimension of the visual, Charles Hill and Marguerite Helmers's *Defining Visual Rhetoric* (2004) brings together rhetoric scholars in composition and communication to define and model different methods and theories for analyzing visual texts and theorizing about visual rhetoric.

Marguerite Helmers, who compiled the bibliography for this section, offers the following areas for future research: (1) the role of authorial intent and the creator's mediation in the creation, dissemination, and reception of images; (2) the history and reception of how the image changes across time and place; (3) the role of images in preserving collective and cultural memory; (4) audience formulations of resistant readings of iconic images; (5) new theories of reading images sequentially, reading the margins, and reading the frames, instead of simply analyzing images discretely; (6) the visual enactment of rhetorical figures of speech in print, electronic, and film media; and (7) the extent to which hyperbole, parody, caricature, and impersonation serve as visual shorthands for argumentation.

Rhetoric and Program Administration

Rhetoric informs rhetoric and composition program administration at many institutional sites: writing programs, writing centers, writing across the curriculum programs, undergraduate majors, graduate programs, and national organizations. Although not all such sites self-identify as rhetoric studies, they all require administrators skilled in rhetorical negotiation. Overtly or not, administrators may invoke rhetoric theory as grounds for various actions: designing programs, negotiating with upper administration, negotiating with other programs across campus, training teachers, dealing with student issues, and running national organizations. Some overt scholarly intersections of rhetoric with program administration may be found in Locke Carter's *Market Matters: Applied Rhetoric Studies and Free Market Competition* (2005), Duane Roen's *Views from the Center: The CCCCs Chairs' Addresses, 1977–2005* (2006), Kathleen Yancey's *Delivering College Composition* (2006), and Rebecca Rickly's and my forthcoming *Feminism and Administration in Rhetoric and Composition Studies* (2009). But because all scholarship that trains administrators is, by function, deeply rhetorical, more overt scholarly connections remain to be made.

Duane Roen, who compiled the bibliography for this section, identifies the following topics for future research: (1) writing program administration as scholarship; (2) mentoring faculty and teaching assistants in writing programs; (3) assessing writing programs; (4) the nature of writing programs in countries outside the United States; (5) portfolio assessment in writing programs; (6) applying the WPA Outcomes Statement; (7) relationships between writing programs and writing centers; (8) relationships between writing programs and WAC programs; (9) the status of independent writing programs; and (10) learner-centered writing programs.

Rhetoric and the Teaching of Composition

Rhetoric theory undergirds diverse scholarship about twentieth- and twenty-first-century composition pedagogies, from first-year English to business writing, to writing in the disciplines, to writing cross-culturally. Classic uses of traditional rhetorical theory to ground composition pedagogy may be seen in Ed Corbett and Bob Connor's updated version of *Classical Rhetoric for the Modern Student* (1998) and in Lisa Ede and Andrea Lunsford's "Audience Addressed/Audience Invoked" (1984). Kathleen Welch advocates and critiques rhetorical pedagogy in *The Contemporary Reception of Classical Rhetoric* (1990); William Covino provides both a definition and defense of it in Gary Tate's *A Guide to Composition Pedagogies* (2001); and Kathleen Blake Yancey provides a new take on the fifth canon in *Delivering Composition* (2006).

In addition to delivery, the other four canons of rhetoric continue to inform composition pedagogy. Invention exists within composition pedagogy in terms of teaching neoclassical strategies that offer students rational frameworks for thinking through topics; in terms of teaching neo-Romantic strategies that encourage personal expressions of students' journeys with/in language; and in terms of teaching poststructuralist and cultural studies strategies of analyzing discourses to find traces, gaps, and images that writers may engage from their various subject positions. Arrangement manifests itself in terms of teaching organization, logic, and revision: that is, organization is important for teaching students not to conform to formulaic templates but, rather, to construct logics through which audiences are introduced to ideas; revision is a key way to teaching changing ideas and the order of ideas to strengthen texts' logics. Style is taught as an intersection of personal signature, cultural convention, and politics, with different teachers giving different weight to each function. And memory is invoked pedagogically as a means of reflecting on research and the storage of knowledge, whether stored in the human mind or in mind-made technologies such as books, libraries, or computer chips.

When rhetoric and composition first emerged, rhetoric studies invoked classical theories to posit writing as a rhetorical act, one that entailed an interlocutor's writing with an audience in mind. As rhetoric and composition evolved, writing took a turn to personal expressions, then a turn to social/cultural acts, and then a turn to spatial acts, as can be seen in the progression from Donald Murray's classic "Teach Writing as a Process Not Product" (1972), Kenneth Bruffee's "Collaborative Learning and the 'Conversation of Mankind'" (1984),

Karen LeFevre's *Invention as a Social Act* (1986), Joe Harris's *A Teaching Subject* (1996), Lisa Ede's *Situating Composition* (2004), my pedagogy chapter in *Rhetorical Listening* (2006), and Nedra Reynolds's *Geographies of Writing* (2007).

In this evolution, writing pedagogy has emerged as the purview of more than just first-year composition programs that train students to write as college students; although that function still exists, critics continually wonder if it should, as Sharon Crowley does in *Composition in the University* (1998). Writing pedagogy has also been theorized as a means of producing and analyzing rhetorics in different disciplines, as traced in David Russell's *Writing in the Academic Disciplines, 1870–1990* (1991). Writing pedagogy has also been theorized as engaging the rhetorics of public sphere issues, as evidenced in scholarship by teachers who engage service learning (Paula Mathieu in *Tactics of Hope*, 2005), cultural studies (James Berlin, *Rhetorics, Poetics, and Cultures,* 1993), critical pedagogies (Paulo Freire, *Pedagogy of the Oppressed,* 1970, 2000), and feminism (Kate Ronald and Joy Ritchie, *Teaching Rhetorica,* 2006). With a current emphasis on public discourse, specifically on connecting academic and public realms, the teaching of writing circles back to its classical origins more than 2,500 years ago, but in new and interesting ways that deserve more study.

Kate Ronald and Hephzibah Roskelly, who compiled the bibliography for this section, identify the following topics for future research: (1) effects of reclaimed and emerging canons of women's, gender, and ethnic rhetorics on rhetoric and composition pedagogy; (2) effects of rhetoric and composition scholarly diversity on rhetoric and composition pedagogy; (3) roles of individual imaginations and cultural imaginations—in terms of invention, memory, and creativity—in research and pedagogy; (4) influences of rhetorics from other disciplines (including literatures in English) on the teaching of writing; (5) ways to make the teaching of writing the task of other disciplines as well as of our own; and (6) pedagogies of civil discourse, particularly connecting classroom discourses to civic action.

BIBLIOGRAPHY

"Traditional" Twentieth-Century Rhetoric Theories
By Ed Corbett (circa 1984)

Bitzer, Lloyd. "The Rhetorical Situation." *Philosophy and Rhetoric* 1 (1968): 1–14.

Booth, Wayne C. "The Rhetorical Stance." *College Composition and Communication* 14 (1963): 139–45.

———. *A Rhetoric of Fiction.* 2nd ed. Chicago: University of Chicago Press, 1982.

Burke, Kenneth. *Counter-Statement.* 2nd ed. Berkeley: University of California Press, 1968.

——. *A Grammar of Motives*. 1945. Reprint, Berkeley: University of California Press, 1969.

——. *Language as Symbolic Action: Essays on Life, Literature, and Method*. Berkeley: University of California Press, 1966.

——. *A Rhetoric of Motives*. 1950. Reprint, Berkeley: University of California Press, 1969.

Corbett, Edward P. J., and Robert Connors. *Classical Rhetoric for the Modern Student*. 4th ed. New York: Oxford University Press, 1999.

Kinneavy, James. *A Theory of Discourse: The Aims of Discourse*. 1971. Reprint, New York: W. W. Norton, 1980.

Ong, Walter, S.J. "The Writer's Audience Is Always a Fiction." *PMLA* 90 (1975): 9–21.

Perelman, Chaim. *The Realm of Rhetoric*. Trans. William Kluback. Notre Dame: Notre Dame University Press, 1982.

Richards, I. A. *The Philosophy of Rhetoric*. New York: Oxford University Press, 1936.

Toulmin, Stephen. *The Uses of Argument*. 1958. Reprint, New York: Cambridge University Press, 2003.

Vatz, Richard. "The Myth of the Rhetorical Situation." *Philosophy and Rhetoric* 6 (1972): 154–61.

Weaver, Richard. *Language Is Sermonic: Richard Weaver on the Nature of Rhetoric*. Ed. Richard L. Johannesen, Rennard Strickland, and Ralph T. Eubanks. Baton Rouge: Louisiana State University Press, 1970.

Contemporary Receptions of Histories of Rhetoric
By Richard Leo Enos

Berlin, James A. *Writing Instruction in Nineteenth-Century American Colleges*. Carbondale: Southern Illinois University Press, 1984.

Bizzell, Patricia, and Bruce Herzberg, eds. *The Rhetorical Tradition: Readings from Classical Times to the Present*. 2nd ed. Boston: Bedford/St. Martin's, 2001.

Conley, Thomas M. *Rhetoric in the European Tradition*. New York: Longman, 1990.

Enos, Richard Leo. *Greek Rhetoric before Aristotle*. Prospect Heights, IL: Waveland Press, 1993.

——. *Roman Rhetoric: Revolution and the Greek Influence*. Rev. and expanded ed. West Lafayette, IN: Parlor Press, 2008.

Glenn, Cheryl. *Rhetoric Retold: Regendering the Tradition from Antiquity through the Renaissance*. Carbondale: Southern Illinois University Press, 1997.

Golden, James L., and Edward P. J. Corbett. *The Rhetoric of Blair, Campbell, and Whately*. 1968. Reprint, Carbondale: Southern Illinois University Press, 1990.

Havelock, Eric A. *Preface to Plato.* Cambridge: Belknap Press, Harvard University Press, 1982.

Horner, Winifred Bryan. *Nineteenth-Century Scottish Rhetoric: The American Connection.* Carbondale: Southern Illinois University Press, 1993.

Howell, Wilbur Samuel. *Eighteenth-Century British Logic and Rhetoric.* Princeton: Princeton University Press, 1971.

——. *Logic and Rhetoric in England, 1500–1700.* New York: Russell and Russell, 1961.

Kennedy, George A. *Classical Rhetoric and Its Christian and Secular Tradition from Ancient to Modern Times.* 2nd rev. ed. Chapel Hill: University of North Carolina Press, 1999.

——. *Comparative Rhetoric: An Historical and Cross-Cultural Introduction.* New York: Oxford University Press, 1998.

——. *Greek Rhetoric under Christian Emperors.* Princeton: Princeton University Press, 1983.

Kustas, George L. *Studies in Byzantine Rhetoric.* Thessalonike, Greece: Patriarchion Idruma Paterikon Meleton, 1973.

Lipson, Carol S., and Roberta A. Binkley, eds. *Rhetoric before and beyond the Greeks.* Albany: State University of New York Press, 2004.

Lunsford, Andrea, ed. *Reclaiming Rhetorica: Women in the Rhetorical Tradition.* Pittsburgh: University of Pittsburgh Press, 1995.

Miller, Thomas P. *The Formation of College English: Rhetoric and Belles Lettres in the British Cultural Provinces.* Pittsburgh: University of Pittsburgh Press, 1997.

Murphy, James J. *Rhetoric in the Middle Ages: A History of Rhetorical Theory from St. Augustine to the Renaissance.* Berkeley: University of California Press, 1974.

Murphy, James J., and Richard A. Katula, eds. *Synoptic History of Classical Rhetoric.* 2nd ed. Davis, CA: Hermagoras Press, 2003.

Schiappa, Edward. *The Beginning of Rhetorical Theory in Classical Greece.* New Haven: Yale University Press, 1999.

Vickers, Brian. *In Defence of Rhetoric.* Oxford: Clarendon Press, 1988.

Walker, Jeffrey. *Rhetoric and Poetics in Antiquity.* New York: Oxford University Press, 2000.

Rhetoric Reference Works
By Patricia Bizzell

Arts and Humanities Citation Index (1980–). Philadelphia: Thomson Scientific.

Bizzell, Patricia, and Bruce Herzberg, eds. *The Rhetorical Tradition: Readings from Classical Times to the Present.* 2nd ed. Boston: Bedford/St. Martin's, 2001.

Conley, Thomas M. "Rhetoric after the Great War" and "Philosophers Turn to Rhetoric." In *Rhetoric in the European Tradition*, 260–311. Chicago: University of Chicago Press, 1990.

Department of Communication Studies. "Online Communication Studies Resources." University of Iowa. http://www.uiowa.edu/~commstud/resources/rhetorical.html.

Enos, Theresa, ed. *Encyclopedia of Rhetoric and Composition: Communication from Ancient Times to the Information Age.* New York: Routledge, 1996.

ERIC. Washington, D.C.: U.S. Department of Education. http://www.eric.ed.gov/.

Haswell, Rich, and Glenn Blalock. "CompPile." http://comppile.org/search/comppile_main_search.php.

Horner, Winifred, ed. *The Present State of Scholarship in Historical and Contemporary Rhetoric.* 1983. Rev. ed. Columbia: University of Missouri Press, 1990.

Howard, Rebecca Moore. "Bibliographies for Composition and Rhetoric." Syracuse University. http://wrt-howard.syr.edu/bibs.html.

Kennedy, Mary Lynch, ed. *Theorizing Composition: A Critical Sourcebook of Theory and Scholarship in Contemporary Composition Studies.* 1998. Reprint, Westport, CT: Greenwood Press, 2006.

Kirsch, Gesa, and Patricia Sullivan, eds. *Methods and Methodology in Composition Research.* Carbondale: Southern Illinois University Press, 1992.

Moran, Michael G., and Michelle Ballif, eds. *Twentieth-Century Rhetorics and Rhetoricians: Critical Studies and Sources.* Westport, CT: Greenwood Press, 2005.

Murphy, James, ed. "Bibliography." In *A Short History of Writing Instruction: From Ancient Greece to Modern America,* 2nd ed., 235–41. Mahwah, NY: Lawrence Erlbaum, 2001.

"On-line Resources." The International Society for the History of Rhetoric. http://ishr .cua.edu/resources.cfm.

Reynolds, Nedra, Patricia Bizzell, and Bruce Herzberg. *The Bedford Bibliography for Teachers of Writing.* 6th ed. Boston: Bedford/St. Martins Press, 2003. http://www .bedfordstmartins.com/bb/.

Ritchie, Joy, and Kate Ronald, eds., *Available Means: An Anthology of Women's Rhetorics.* Pittsburgh: University of Pittsburgh Press, 2001.

Sloane, Thomas O., ed. *Encyclopedia of Rhetoric.* New York: Oxford University Press, 2001.

Taylor, Todd, ed. "CCCC Bibliography of Composition and Rhetoric." Carbondale: Southern Illinois University Press, 1987–1995. http://www.ibiblio.org/cccc/.

Villanueva, Victor, ed. *Cross-Talk in Comp Theory.* 2nd ed. Urbana: National Council of Teachers of English, 2003.

Villanueva, Victor, C. Jan Swearingen, and Susan McDowell. "Research in Rhetoric." In *Research on Composition: Multiple Perspectives on Two Decades of Change,* ed. Peter Smagorinsky, 170–86. New York: Teachers College Press, 2005.

Rhetorical Criticism
By Theresa Enos

Benson, Thomas A., ed. *American Rhetoric: Context and Criticism.* Carbondale: Southern Illinois University Press, 1989.

——. *Landmark Essays on Rhetorical Criticism.* Davis, CA: Hermagoras Press, 1993.

Bitzer, Lloyd, and Edwin Black, eds. *The Prospect of Rhetoric: Report of the National Development Project.* Englewood Cliffs, NJ: Prentice-Hall, 1971.

Black, Edwin. *Rhetorical Criticism: A Study in Method.* 2nd ed. Madison: University of Wisconsin Press, 1978.

Brigance, William Norwood, and Marie Hochmuth (Nichols), eds. *A History and Criticism of American Public Address.* 3 vols. New York: Russell and Russell, 1943–1960.

Brockriede, Wayne. "Rhetorical Criticism as Argument." *Quarterly Journal of Speech* 60 (1974): 165–74.

Brummett, Barry. *Rhetorical Dimensions of Popular Culture.* Tuscaloosa: University of Alabama Press, 1991.

Burgchardt, Carl R., ed. *Readings in Rhetorical Criticism.* 3rd ed. State College, PA: Strata, 2005.

Campbell, John Angus, ed. *Special Issue on Rhetorical Criticism. Western Journal of Speech Communication* 54 (1990): 249–428.

Drummond, A. M. *Studies in Rhetoric and Public Speaking in Honor of James Albert Winans.* New York: Century, 1925.

Enos, Theresa, ed. *Making and Unmaking the Prospects for Rhetoric: Selected Papers from the 1996 Rhetoric Society of America Conference.* Mahwah, NJ: Lawrence Erlbaum, 1997.

Foss, Sonja K. *Rhetorical Criticism: Exploration and Practice.* 3rd ed. Long Grove, IL: Waveland Press, 2004.

Hasian, Marouf. "Silences and Articulations in Modern Rhetorical Criticism." *Western Journal of Communication* 65 (2001): 295–313.

Howell, Wilbur Samuel. *Poetics, Rhetoric, and Logic: Studies in the Basic Discipline of Criticism.* Ithaca: Cornell University Press, 1975.

Jamieson, Kathleen M. "The Cunning Rhetor, the Complicitous Audience, the Conned Censor, and the Critic." *Communication Monographs* 57 (1990): 73–78.

Jasinski, James. "The Status of Theory and Method in Rhetorical Criticism." *Western Journal of Communication* 65 (2001): 249–70.

McKeon, Zahava Karl. *Novels and Arguments: Inventing Rhetorical Criticism.* Chicago: University of Chicago Press, 1982.

Mohrmann, G. P., Charles J. Stewart, and Donovan J. Ochs. *Explorations in Rhetorical Criticism.* University Park: Pennsylvania State University Press, 1973.

Nichols, Marie Hochmuth. *Rhetoric and Criticism.* Baton Rouge: Louisiana State University Press, 1963.

Nothstine, William L., Carol Blair, and Gary A. Copeland, eds. *Critical Questions: Invention, Creativity, and the Criticism of Discourse and Media.* New York: St. Martin's, 1994.

Rhetoric and Poststructuralist Studies
By Michelle Ballif and Diane Davis

Austin, J. L. *How to Do Things with Words.* 2nd ed. Ed. J. O. Urmson and Marina Sbisa. Cambridge: Harvard University Press, 1975.

Bakhtin, M. M. *The Dialogic Imagination.* Ed. Michael Holquist; trans. Vadim Liapunov and Kenneth Brostrom. Austin: University of Texas Press, 1982.

Barthes, Roland. *Writing Degree Zero.* Trans. Annette Lavers and Colin Smith. New York: Hill and Wang, 1968.

Baudrillard, Jean. *Simulacra and Simulation.* Trans. Sheila Faria Glaser. Ann Arbor: University of Michigan Press, 1994.

Butler, Judith. *Gender Trouble: Feminism and the Subversion of Identity.* New York: Routledge, 1999.

Cixous, Hélène, and Catherine Clément. *The Newly Born Woman.* Trans. Betsy Wing. Minneapolis: University of Minnesota Press, 1986.

Deleuze, Gilles, and Felix Guattari. *Anti-Oedipus: Capitalism and Schizophrenia.* Trans. Robert Hurley, Mark Seem, and Helen R. Lane. Minneapolis: University of Minnesota Press, 1983.

De Man, Paul. *Allegories of Reading: Figural Language in Rousseau, Nietzsche, Rilke, and Proust.* New Haven: Yale University Press, 1979.

Derrida, Jacques. *Limited Inc.* Trans. Samuel Weber and Jeffery Mehlman. Evanston, IL: Northwestern University Press, 1988.

——. *Of Grammatology.* Trans. Gayatri Chakravorty Spivak. Baltimore: Johns Hopkins University Press, 1976.

Foucault, Michel. *The Archaeology of Knowledge and the Discourse on Language.* 1972. Reprint, trans. A. M. Sheridan Smith. New York: Routledge, 2002.

——. *The Order of Things: An Archaeology of the Human Sciences.* 1971. Reprint, New York: Routledge, 2002.

Freud, Sigmund. *The Interpretation of Dreams.* 1923. Reprint, New York: Oxford University Press, 1999.

Heidegger, Martin. *Poetry, Language, Thought.* 1971. Reprint, trans. Albert Hofstadter. New York: Perennial, 1975.

Kristiva, Julia. *Desire in Language: A Semiotic Approach to Literature and Art.* Ed. Leon S. Roudiez; trans. Thomas Gora, Alice Jardine, and Leon S. Roudiez. New York: Columbia University Press, 1980.

Lacan, Jacques. *Écrits: A Selection.* Trans. Alan Sheridan. New York: Norton, 1977.

Levinas, Emmanuel. *Otherwise Than Being; or, Beyond Essence.* 1981. Reprint, trans. Alphonso Lingis. Pittsburgh, PA: Duquesne University Press, 1998.

Lyotard, Jean-François. *The Differend: Phrases in Dispute.* Trans. Georges Van Den Abbeele. Minneapolis: University of Minnesota Press, 1988.

Nancy, Jean-Luc. *The Inoperative Community.* Ed. Peter Connor; trans. Peter Connor, et al. Minneapolis: University of Minnesota Press, 1991.

Nietzsche, Friedrich. "On Truth and Lies in an Extra-Moral Sense." In *Friedrich Nietzsche on Rhetoric and Language,* ed. Sander L. Gilman, Carole Blair, and David J. Parent, 246–57. New York: Oxford University Press, 1989.

Ronell, Avital. *Stupidity.* Champaign: University of Illinois Press, 2002.

Spivak, Gayatri. *The Post-Colonial Critic: Interviews, Strategies, Dialogues.* Ed. Sarah Harasym. New York: Routledge, 1990.

Rhetoric and Cultural Studies
By John Schilb

Anderson, Benedict. *Imagined Communities: Reflections on the Origin and Spread of Nationalism.* Rev. ed. New York: Verso, 2006.

Barthes, Roland. *Mythologies.* 1957. Reprint, trans. Annette Lavers. New York: Hill and Wang, 1972.

Benjamin, Walter. "The Work of Art in the Age of Mechanical Reproduction." In *Illuminations: Essays and Reflections,* ed. Hannah Arendt; trans. Harry Zohn, 217–51. New York: Schocken Books, 1968.

Berger, John, *Ways of Seeing.* 1972. Reprint, New York: Penguin, 1990.

Berlin, James A. "Rhetoric and Ideology in the Writing Class." *College English* 50 (1988): 477–94.

———. *Rhetorics, Poetics, and Cultures: Refiguring College English Studies.* West Lafayette, IN: Parlor Press, 1993.

Bourdieu, Pierre. *Distinction: A Social Critique of the Judgment of Taste.* Trans. Richard Nice. Cambridge: Harvard University Press, 1984.

Butler, Judith. *Excitable Speech: A Politics of the Performative.* New York: Routledge, 1997.

Charland, Maurice. "Rehabilitating Rhetoric: Confronting Blindspots in Discourse and Social Theory." *Communication* 11 (1990): 253–64.

Faigley, Lester. *Fragments of Rationality: Postmodernity and the Subject of Composition.* Pittsburgh: University of Pittsburgh Press, 1993.

Foucault, Michel. "What Is an Author?" In *The Essential Foucault: Selections from Essential Works of Foucault, 1954–1984,* ed. Paul Rabinow and Nikolas Rose, 377–91. New York: New Press, 2003.

Geertz, Clifford. *The Interpretation of Cultures: Selected Essays.* New York: Basic Books, 1973.

Habermas, Jurgen. *The Structural Transformation of the Public Sphere: An Inquiry into a Category of Bourgeois Society.* Trans. Thomas Burger and Frederick Lawrence. Cambridge: Massachusetts Institute of Technology Press, 1989.

Hall, Stuart. "Encoding/Decoding." In *Culture, Media, Language: Working Papers in Cultural Studies,* ed. Stuart Hall, Dorothy Hobson, Andrew Lowe, and Paul Willis, 128–38. London: Hutchinson, 1980.

Jameson, Fredric. "The Cultural Logic of Late Capitalism." In *Postmodernism; or, The Cultural Logic of Late Capitalism,* 1–54. Durham: Duke University Press, 1991.

Lyotard, Jean-François. *The Postmodern Condition: A Report on Knowledge.* Trans. Geoff Bennington and Brian Massumi. Minneapolis: University of Minnesota Press, 1984.

Mailloux, Steven. *Rhetorical Power.* Ithaca: Cornell University Press, 1989.

McGee, Michael Calvin. "The 'Ideograph': A Link between Rhetoric and Ideology." *Quarterly Journal of Speech* 6 (1980): 1–16.

McKerrow, Raymie E. "Critical Rhetoric: Theory and Praxis." *Communication Monographs* 56 (1989): 91–111.

Miller, Susan. *Textual Carnivals: The Politics of Composition.* Carbondale: Southern Illinois University Press, 1991.

Reynolds, Nedra. "Interrupting Our Way to Agency: Feminist Cultural Studies and Composition." In *Feminism and Composition Studies: In Other Words,* ed. Susan C. Jarratt and Lynn Worsham, 58–73. New York: Modern Language Association, 1998.

Trimbur, John. "Composition and the Circulation of Writing." *College Composition and Communication* 52 (2000): 188–219.

Villanueva, Victor. *Bootstraps: From an Academic of Color.* Urbana, IL: National Council of Teachers of English, 1993.

Rhetoric and Literacy Studies
By Beverly Moss

Barton, David, Mary Hamilton, and Roz Ivanic, eds. *Situated Literacies: Reading and Writing in Context.* New York: Routledge, 2000.

Branch, Kirk. *Eyes on the Ought to Be: What We Teach When We Teach about Literacy.* Cresskill, NJ: Hampton Press, 2007.

Brandt, Deborah. *Literacy in American Lives.* New York: Cambridge University Press, 2001.

Cushman, Ellen. *The Struggles and the Tools: Oral and Literate Strategies in an Inner City School.* Albany: State University of New York Press, 1998.

Cushman, Ellen, Eugene R. Kintgen, Barry Kroll, and Mike Rose, eds. *Literacy: A Critical Sourcebook.* New York: Bedford/St. Martin's, 2001. [See essays by Scribner and Cole; Graff; Farr; and Peck, Flower, and Higgins.]

Daniell, Beth, and Peter Mortensen, eds. *Women and Literacy: Local and Global Inquiries for a New Century.* Urbana, IL: NCTE-LEA, 2007.

Eldred, Janet Carey, and Peterson Mortensen. "Reading Literacy Narratives." *College English* 54 (1992): 512–39.

Farr, Marcia. *Rancheros in Chicagoacán: Language and Identity in a Transnational Community.* Austin: University of Texas Press, 2006.

Freire, Paulo. *Pedagogy of the Oppressed.* 1970, 1981. Reprint, trans. Myra Bergman Ramos. New York: Continuum, 2000.

Gee, James. *Social Linguistics and Literacies: Ideology in Discourses.* 3rd ed. Bristol, PA: Taylor and Francis, 2007.

Gere, Anne. *Intimate Practices: Literacy and Cultural Work in U.S. Women's Clubs, 1880–1920.* Champaign: University of Illinois Press, 1997.

Heath, Shirley Brice. *Ways with Words: Language, Life and Work in Communities and Classrooms.* New York: Cambridge University Press, 1983.

Moss, Beverly J. *A Community Text Arises: A Literate Text and a Literacy Tradition in African-American Churches.* Cresskill, NJ: Hampton Press, 2003.

Prendergast, Catherine. *Literacy and Racial Justice: The Politics of Learning after "Brown v. Board of Education."* Carbondale: Southern Illinois University Press, 2003.

Richardson, Elaine. *African American Literacies.* New York: Routledge, 2003.

Rose, Mike. *Lives on the Boundary: A Moving Account of the Struggles and Achievements of America's Educational Underclass.* New York: Penguin, 1990.

Royster, Jacqueline Jones. *Traces of a Stream: Literacy and Social Change among African-American Women.* Pittsburgh: University of Pittsburgh Press, 2000.

Scribner, Sylvia. "Literacy in Three Metaphors." *American Journal of Education* 93 (1984): 6–21.

Selfe, Cynthia. *Technology and Literacy in the 21st Century: The Importance of Paying Attention.* Carbondale: Southern Illinois University Press, 1999.

Smitherman, Geneva. *Talkin' and Testifyin': The Language of Black America.* 1977. Reprint, Boston: Houghton Mifflin, 2000.

Street, Brian, ed. *Cross Approaches to Literacy.* New York: Cambridge University Press, 1993.

Tannen, Deborah, ed. *Spoken and Written Language: Exploring Orality and Literacy.* Norwood, NJ: Ablex, 1992.

Yagelski, Robert. *Literacy Matters: Writing and Reading the Social Self.* New York: Teachers College Press, 2000.

Young, Morris. *Minor Re/Visions: Asian American Literacy Narratives as a Rhetoric of Citizenship.* Carbondale: Southern Illinois University Press, 2004.

Rhetoric and Feminism Studies
By Cheryl Glenn and Shirley Wilson Logan

Biesecker, Barbara. "Coming to Terms with Recent Attempts to Write Women into the History of Rhetoric." *Philosophy and Rhetoric* 25 (1992): 140–61.

Bizzell, Patricia. "Opportunities for Feminist Research in the History of Rhetoric." *Rhetoric Review* 11 (1992): 50–58.

Campbell, Karlyn Kohrs, ed. *Man Cannot Speak for Her.* 2 vols. Westport, CT: Greenwood Press, 1989.

Campbell, Karlyn Kohrs, and Susan Zaeske, eds. *Rhetoric and Gender.* Thousand Oaks, CA: SAGE, 2006.

Foss, Karen, Sonia Foss, and Cindy L. Griffin. *Feminist Rhetorical Theories.* Thousand Oaks, CA: SAGE, 1999.

——. *Readings in Feminist Rhetorical Theory.* Prospect Heights, IL: Waveland Press, 2006

Glenn, Cheryl. *Rhetoric Retold: Regendering the Tradition from Antiquity through the Renaissance.* Carbondale: Southern Illinois University Press, 1997.

——. *Unspoken: A Rhetoric of Silence.* Carbondale: Southern Illinois University Press, 2004.

Jarratt, Susan, ed. *Special Issue: Feminist Rereadings in the History of Rhetoric. Rhetoric Society Quarterly* 22 (1992).

Johnson, Nan. *Gender and Rhetorical Spaces in American Life, 1866–1910.* Carbondale: Southern Illinois University Press, 2002.

Logan, Shirley Wilson. "Changing Missions, Shifting Positions, and Breaking Silences." *College Composition and Communication* 55 (2003): 330–42.

Lunsford, Andrea, ed. *Reclaiming Rhetorica: Women in the Rhetorical Tradition.* Pittsburgh: University of Pittsburgh Press, 1995.

Mountford, Roxanne. *The Gendered Pulpit: Preaching in American Protestant Spaces.* Carbondale: Southern Illinois University Press, 2005.

Ratcliffe, Krista. *Anglo-American Feminist Challenges to the Rhetorical Tradition: Virginia Woolf, Mary Daly, Adrienne Rich.* Carbondale: Southern Illinois University Press, 1996.

——. *Rhetorical Listening: Identification, Gender, Whiteness.* Carbondale: Southern Illinois University Press, 2006.

Rich, Adrienne. *On Lies, Secrets, and Silence.* New York: Norton, 1979.

Ritchie, Joy, and Kate Ronald, eds., *Available Means: An Anthology of Women's Rhetorics*. Pittsburgh: University of Pittsburgh Press, 2001.

Royster, Jacqueline Jones. *Southern Horrors and Other Writings: The Anti-Lynching Campaign of Ida B. Wells, 1892–1900*. Boston: Bedford Books, 1997.

Worsham, Lynn. "After Words: A Choice of Words Remains." In *Feminism and Composition Studies: In Other Words*, ed. Susan C. Jarratt and Lynn Worsham, 329–56. New York: Modern Language Association, 1998.

Rhetoric and Critical Race Studies
By Joyce Irene Middleton

Allen, Danielle. "Rhetoric: A Good Thing." In *Talking to Strangers: Anxieties of Citizenship since "Brown v. Board of Education,"* 140–60. Chicago: University of Chicago Press, 2004.

Delgado, Richard, and Jean Sefancic, eds. *Critical White Studies: Looking behind the Mirror*. Philadelphia: Temple University Press, 1997.

Fiskin, Shelley Fisher. *Was Huck Black? Mark Twain and African-American Voices*. New York: Oxford University Press, 1993.

Giroux, Henry. "Rewriting the Discourse of Racial Identity: Towards a Pedagogy and Politics of Whiteness." *Harvard Educational Review* 67 (1997): 285–320.

hooks, bell. *Black Looks: Race and Representation*. Cambridge, MA: South End Press, 1992.

Jay, Gregory, and Sandra Jones. "Whiteness in the Multicultural Literature Classroom." *MELUS* 30 (2005): 99–121.

Kennedy, Tammy, Joyce Irene Middleton, and Krista Ratcliffe, eds. "Symposium on Whiteness Studies." *Rhetoric Review* 24 (2005): 359–402.

Logan, Shirley Wilson. "Changing Missions, Shifting Positions, and Breaking Silences." *College Composition and Communication* 55 (2003): 330–42.

Middleton, Joyce Irene. "'Both Print and Oral' and 'Talking about Race': Transforming Toni Morrison's Language Issues into Teaching Issues." In *African American Rhetoric(s): Interdisciplinary Perspectives*, ed. Elaine Richardson and Ronald Jackson, 242–58. Carbondale: Southern Illinois University Press, 2004.

Morrison, Toni. *Playing in the Dark: Whiteness and the Literary Imagination*. Cambridge: Harvard University Press, 1992.

Pough, Gwendolyn. *Check It While I Wreck It: Black Womanhood, Hip-Hop Culture, and the Public Sphere*. Boston: Northeastern University Press, 2004.

Prendergast, Catherine. "Race: The Absent Presence in Composition Studies." *College Composition and Communication* 50 (1998): 36–53.

Ratcliffe, Krista. *Rhetorical Listening: Identification, Gender, Whiteness.* Carbondale: Southern Illinois University Press, 2006.

Richardson, Elaine, and Ronald Jackson, eds. *African American Rhetoric(s): Interdisciplinary Perspectives.* Carbondale: Southern Illinois University Press, 2004.

Roediger, David. *Working toward Whiteness: How America's Immigrants Became White: The Strange Journey from Ellis Island to the Suburbs.* Cambridge, MA: Basic Books, 2005.

Royster, Jacqueline Jones. "When the First Voice You Hear Is Not Your Own." *College Composition and Communication* 47 (1996): 29–40.

Royster, Jacqueline Jones, and Anna Marie Mann Simpkins, eds. *Calling Cards: Theory and Practice in the Study of Race, Gender, and Culture.* Albany: State University of New York Press, 2005.

Tatum, Beverly. *"Why Are All the Black Kids Sitting Together in the Cafeteria?": A Psychologist Explains the Development of Racial Identity.* Rev. ed. New York: Basic Books, 2003.

Villanueva, Victor. *Bootstraps: From an Academic of Color.* Urbana, IL: National Council of Teachers of English, 1993.

Welch, Kathleen. "Who Made Aristotle White?" *Rhetoric Review* 24 (2005): 373–77.

Williams, Patricia. *The Alchemy of Race and Rights.* Cambridge: Harvard University Press, 1991.

———. *Seeing a Color-Blind Future: The Paradox of Race.* 1997. Reprint, New York: Noonday Press, 2000.

Worsham, Lynn, and Gary Olson, eds. *Race, Rhetoric, and the Postcolonial.* Albany: State University of New York Press, 1999.

Rhetoric and African American Studies

By Jacqueline Jones Royster and Anne M. Mitchell

Anthologies of African American Rhetorical Performances

Collier-Thomas, Bettye, ed. *Daughters of Thunder: Black Women Preachers and Their Sermons, 1850–1979.* San Francisco: Jossey-Bass, 1998.

Early, Gerald, ed. *Speech and Power: The African American Essay and Its Cultural Content from Polemics to Pulpit.* 2 vols. Hopewell, NJ: Ecco Press, 1992, 1993.

Guy-Sheftall, Beverly, ed. *Words of Fire: An Anthology of African American Feminist Thought.* New York: New Press, 1995.

Meacham, Jon, ed. *Voices in Our Blood: America's Best on the Civil Rights Movement.* New York: Random House, 2001.

Rhetorical History, Theory, and Criticism

The Black Public Sphere Collective. *The Black Public Sphere: A Public Culture Book.* Chicago: University of Chicago Press, 1995.

Byrd, Rudolph P., and Beverly Guy-Sheftall, eds. *Traps: African American Men on Gender and Sexuality.* Bloomington: Indiana University Press, 2001.

Doreski, Carole K., and Albert Delpi. *Writing America Black: Race Rhetoric in the Public Sphere.* New York: Cambridge University Press, 1998.

Howard-Pitney, David. *The Afro-American Jeremiad: Appeals for Justice in America.* Rev. ed. Philadelphia: Temple University Press, 2005.

Jackson, Ronald, II, and Elaine B. Richardson. *Understanding African American Rhetoric: Classical Origins to Contemporary Innovations.* New York: Taylor and Francis, 2003.

Ogbar, Jeffrey O. G. *Black Power: Radical Politics and African American Identity.* Baltimore: Johns Hopkins University Press, 2004.

Royster, Jacqueline Jones. "Introduction: A Call for Other Ways of Reading." In *Traces of a Stream: Literacy and Social Change among African-American Women,* 3–16. Pittsburgh: University of Pittsburgh Press, 2000.

Language, Culture, and Rhetorical Performance

Davis, Angela Y. *Blues Legacies and Black Feminism: Gertrude "Ma" Rainey, Bessie Smith, and Billie Holiday.* New York: Pantheon Books, 1998.

Gilyard, Keith. *Voices of the Self: A Study of Language Competence.* Detroit: Wayne State University Press, 1991.

Harris-Lacewell, Melissa Victoria. *Barbershops, Bibles, and BET: Everyday Talk and Black Political Thought.* Princeton: Princeton University Press, 2004.

Haywood, Chanta M. *Prophesying Daughters: Black Women Preachers and the Word, 1823–1913.* Columbia: University of Missouri Press, 2003.

Houck, Davis W., and David W. Dixon, eds. *Rhetoric, Religion, and the Civil Rights Movement, 1954–1965.* Waco, TX: Baylor University Press, 2006.

Moss, Beverly J. *A Community Text Arises: A Literate Text and a Literacy Tradition in African-American Churches.* Cresskill, NJ: Hampton Press, 2003.

Pough, Gwendolyn. *Check It While I Wreck It: Black Womanhood, Hip-Hop Culture, and the Public Sphere.* Boston: Northeastern University Press, 2004.

Richardson, Elaine. *Hip Hop Literacies.* New York: Taylor and Francis, 2006.

Smitherman, Geneva. *Talkin' and Testifyin': The Language of Black America.* 1977. Reprint, Boston: Houghton Mifflin, 2000.

Rhetoric and American Indian Studies
By Malea Powell

Bizzaro, Resa Crane. "Making Places as Teacher-Scholars in Composition Studies: Comparing Transition Narratives." *College Composition and Communication* 53 (2002): 487–506.

——. "Shooting Our Last Arrow: Developing a Rhetoric of Identity for Unenrolled American Indians." *College English* 67 (2004): 61–74.

Carney, Virginia. *Eastern Band Cherokee Women: Cultural Persistence in Their Letters and Speeches.* Knoxville: University of Tennessee Press, 2005.

Cobb, Amanda. *Listening to Our Grandmothers' Stories: The Bloomfield Academy for Chickasaw Females, 1852–1949.* Lincoln: University of Nebraska Press, 2000.

Cruikshank, Julie. *Life Lived Like a Story: Life Stories of Three Yukon Native Elders.* Lincoln: University of Nebraska Press, 1991.

Deloria, Phillip J. *Indians in Unexpected Places.* Lawrence: University Press of Kansas, 2004.

Deloria, Vine, Jr. *Custer Died for Your Sins: An Indian Manifesto.* 1969. Reprint, Golden, CO: Fulcrum Press, 1988.

——. *Red Earth, White Lies: Native Americans and the Myth of Scientific Fact.* Golden, CO: Fulcrum Press, 1997.

Deloria, Vine, Jr., and Daniel Wildcat. *Power and Place: Indian Education in America.* Golden, CO: Fulcrum Press, 2001.

Donaldson, Laura E. "Writing the Talking Stick: Alphabetic Literacy as Colonial Technology and Postcolonial Appropriation." *American Indian Quarterly* 22 (1998): 46–63.

King, Thomas. *The Truth about Stories: A Native Narrative.* Toronto: Anansi Press, 2003.

LaDuke, Winona. *All Our Relations: Native Struggles for Land and Life.* Cambridge, MA: South End Press, 1999.

Lyons, Scott. "A Captivity Narrative: Indians, Mixedbloods, and 'White' Academy." In *Outbursts in Academe: Multiculturalism and Other Sources of Conflict,* ed. Kathleen Dixon, 87–108. Portsmouth, NH: Boynton/Cook, 1998.

——. "Rhetorical Sovereignty: What Do American Indians Want from Writing?" *College Composition and Communication* 51 (2000): 447–68.

Maddox, Lucy. *Citizen Indians: Native American Intellectuals, Race, and Reform.* Ithaca: Cornell University Press, 2005.

Powell, Malea. "Blood and Scholarship." In *Race, Rhetoric, and Composition,* ed. Keith Gilyard, 1–6. Ithaca, NY: Boynton/Cook, 1999.

——. "Down by the River, or How Susan La Flesche Picotte Can Teach Us about Alliance as a Practice of Survivance." *College English* 67 (2004): 38–60.

——. "Listening to Ghosts: An Alternative (Non)Argument." In *ALT DIS: Alternatives to Academic Discourse,* ed. Helen Fox and Christopher Schroeder, 11–22. Portsmouth, NH: Boynton/Cook-Heinemann, 2002.

Shoemaker, Nancy, ed. *Clearing a Path: Theorizing the Past in Native American Studies.* New York: Routledge, 2002.

Smith, Andrea. *Conquest: Sexual Violence and American Indian Genocide.* Cambridge, MA: South End Press, 2005.

Smith, Linda Tuhiwai. *Decolonizing Methodologies: Research and Indigenous Peoples.* New York: Palgrave Press, 1999.

Stromberg, Ernest. *American Indian Rhetorics of Survivance: Word Medicine, Word Magic.* Pittsburgh: University of Pittsburgh Press, 2006.

Vizenor, Gerald. *Manifest Manners.* Hanover, NH: University Press of New England, 1994.

Warrior, Robert Allen. *Tribal Secrets: Recovering American Indian Intellectual Traditions.* Minneapolis: University of Minnesota Press, 1995.

Rhetoric and Asian American Studies
By Morris Young

Ancheta, Angelo. *Race, Rights, and the Asian American Experience.* New Brunswick, NJ: Rutgers University Press, 1998.

Chang, Robert S. *Disoriented: Asian Americans, Law, and the Nation-State.* New York: New York University Press, 1999.

Cheung, King-Kok. *Articulate Silences: Hisaye Yamamoto, Maxine Hong Kingston, Joy Kogawa.* Ithaca: Cornell University Press, 1993.

Chiang, Yuet-Sim. "Insider/Outsider/Other? Confronting the Centeredness of Race, Class, Color and Ethnicity in Composition Research." In *Under Construction: Working at the Intersections of Composition Theory, Research, and Practice,* ed. Christine Farris and Chris M. Anson, 150–65. Logan: Utah State University Press, 1998.

Chin, Frank, Jeffrey Chan, Lawson Inada, and Shawn Wong, eds. *Aiiieeeee! An Anthology of Asian American Writers.* 1974. Reprint, New York: Mentor, 1991.

Chuh, Kandice. *Imagine Otherwise: On Asian Americanist Critique.* Durham: Duke University Press, 2003.

Duncan, Patti. *Tell This Silence: Asian American Women Writers and the Politics of Speech.* Iowa City: University of Iowa Press, 2004.

Kanae, Lisa Linn. *Sista Tongue.* Honolulu: Tinfish Press, 2001.

Lee, Rachel C., and Sau-ling Cynthia Wong, eds. *AsianAmerica.Net: Ethnicity, Nationalism, and Cyberspace.* New York: Routledge, 2003.

Liu, Eric. *The Accidental Asian: Notes of a Native Speaker.* New York: Vintage, 1998.

Lowe, Lisa. *Immigrant Acts: On Asian American Cultural Politics.* Durham: Duke University Press, 1996.

Mao, LuMing. *Reading Chinese Fortune Cookie: The Making of Chinese American Rhetoric.* Logan: Utah State University Press, 2006.

———. "Uniqueness or Borderlands? The Making of Asian American Rhetorics." In *Rhetoric and Ethnicity,* ed. Keith Gilyard and Vorris Nunley, 46–55. Portsmouth, NH: Boynton, 2004.

Matsuda, Mari J. *Where Is Your Body? And Other Essays on Race, Gender, and the Law.* Boston: Beacon Press, 1996.

Nakanishi, Don T., and Tina Yamamoto Nishida, eds. *The Asian American Educational Experience: A Source Book for Teachers and Students.* New York: Routledge, 1995.

Okawa, Gail. "Coming (in)to Consciousness: One Asian American Teacher's Journey into Activist Teaching and Research." In *Under Construction: Working at the Intersections of Composition Theory, Research, and Practice,* ed. Christine Farris and Chris M. Anson, 282–301. Logan: Utah State University Press, 1998.

———. "Removing Masks: Confronting Graceful Evasion and Bad Habits in a Graduate English Class." In *Race, Rhetoric, and Composition,* ed. Keith Gilyard, 124–43. Portsmouth, NH: Boynton/Cook, 1999.

Ono, Kent. *Asian American Studies after Critical Mass.* Malden, MA: Blackwell, 2005.

Palumbo-Liu, David. *Asian/American: Historical Crossings of a Racial Frontier.* Stanford: Stanford University Press, 1999.

Said, Edward. *Orientalism.* New York: Pantheon, 1978.

Sato, Charlene J. "Sociolinguistic Variation and Language Attitudes in Hawai'i." In *English around the World,* ed. Jenny Chesire, 647–63. New York: Cambridge University Press, 1991.

Tonouchi, Lee. *Living Pidgin: Contemplations on Pidgin Culture.* Honolulu: Tinfish Press, 2002.

Wu, Frank H. *Yellow: Race in America beyond Black and White.* New York: Basic Books, 2002.

Young, Morris. *Minor Re/Visions: Asian American Literacy Narratives as a Rhetoric of Citizenship.* Carbondale: Southern Illinois University Press, 2004.

———. "Native Claims: Cultural Citizenship, Ethnic Expressions, and the Rhetorics of 'Hawaiianness.'" *College English* 67 (2004): 83–101.

Rhetoric and Latino/a Studies
By Victor Villanueva

Anzaldúa, Gloria. *Borderlands*/La Frontera: *The New Mestiza.* 3rd ed. San Francisco: Aunt Lute Books, 2007.

Cintron, Ralph. *Angels' Town: Chero Ways, Gang Life, and the Rhetorics of the Everyday.* Ypsilanti, MI: Beacon Press, 1998.

Delgado, Richard, and Jean Stefancic, eds. *The Latino/a Condition: A Critical Reader.* New York: New York University Press, 1997.

Delgado-Figueroa, J. *The Rhetoric of Change: Metaphor and Politics in the Commonwealth of Puerto Rico.* Columbia, SC: Hispanic Caribbean Press, 1994.

Enoch, Jessica. "*Para la Mujer:* Defining a Chicana Feminist Rhetoric at the Turn of the Century." *College English* 67 (2004): 20–37.

Hammerback, John C., and Richard J. Jensen. *The Rhetorical Career of César Chávez.* College Station: Texas A&M University Press, 2003.

Hernández-Truyol, Berta Esperanza. "Building Bridges—Latinas and Latinos at the Crossroads: And the Reconstruction of Realities, Rhetoric, and Replacement." *Columbia Human Rights Law Review* 25 (1994): 369–433. Reprinted in *The Latino/a Condition: A Critical Reader,* ed. Richard Delgado and Jean Stefancic, 24–31. New York: New York University Press, 1997.

Iglesias, Elizabeth M. "Rape, Race, and Representation: The Power of Discourse, Discourses of Power, and the Reconstruction of Heterosexuality." *Vanderbilt Law Review* 49 (1996): 869–991. Reprinted in part as "Maternal Power and the Deconstruction of Male Supremacy," in *The Latino/a Condition: A Critical Reader,* ed. Richard Delgado and Jean Stefancic, 508–15. New York: New York University Press, 1997.

Kells, Michelle Hall, Valerie Balester, and Victor Villanueva. *Latino/a Discourses: On Language, Identity, and Literacy Education.* Portsmouth, NH: Boynton/Cook, 2004.

Romano, Susan "Tlaltelolco: The Grammatical-Rhetorical Indios of Colonial Mexico." *College English* 66 (2004): 257–77.

Villanueva, Victor. *Bootstraps: From an Academic of Color.* Urbana, IL: National Council of Teachers of English, 1993.

——. "On the Rhetoric and Precedents of Racism." *College Composition and Communication* 50 (1999): 645–61.

Comparative/Contrastive Rhetorics
By Hui Wu

Blinn, Sharon Bracci, and Mary Garrett. "Aristotelian Topoi as a Cross-cultural Analytical Tool." *Philosophy and Rhetoric* 26 (1993): 93–112.

Comb, Steve. *The Dao of Rhetoric*. Albany: State University of New York Press, 2005.

Garrett, Mary M., and Xiaosui Xiao. "The Rhetorical Situation Revisited." *Rhetoric Society Quarterly* 23 (1993): 30–40.

Heisey, D. Rey, ed. *Chinese Perspectives in Rhetoric and Communication*. Stamford, CT: Ablex, 2000.

Jia, Wenshen, Xing Lu, and D. Rey Heisey, eds. *Chinese Communication Theory and Research*. Westport, CT: Ablex, 2002.

Kennedy, George A. *Comparative Rhetoric: An Historical and Cross-Cultural Introduction*. New York: Oxford University Press, 1998.

Kirkpatrick, Andy. "The Arrangement of Letters: Hierarchy or Culture? From Cicero to China." *Journal of Asian Pacific Communication* 17 (2007): 245–58.

Liu, Yameng. "Contrastive Rhetoric/Comparative Rhetoric." In *Coming of Age: The Advanced Writing Curriculum*, ed. Linda K. Shamoon, Rebecca Moore Howard, Sandra Jamieson, and Robert A. Schwegler, 71–75. Portsmouth, NH: Heinemann Boynton/Cook, 2000.

———. "To Capture the Essence of Chinese Rhetoric: An Anatomy of a Paradigm in Comparative Rhetoric." *Rhetoric Review* 14 (1996): 318–35.

Lu, Xing. *Rhetoric of the Chinese Cultural Revolution: The Impact on Chinese Thought, Culture, and Communication*. Columbia: University of South Carolina Press, 2000.

———. "Studies and Development of Comparative Rhetoric in the U.S.A.: Chinese and Western Rhetoric in Focus." *China Media Research* 2 (2006): 112–16. http://www.chinamediaresearch.net/vol2no2/12_Lucy_Lu_done.pdf.

Mao, LuMing. "Reflective Encounters: Illustrating Comparative Rhetoric." *Style* 37 (2003): 401–25.

———. "Rhetorical Borderlands: Chinese American Rhetoric in the Making." *College Composition and Communication* 56 (2005): 422–65.

———. "Studying the Chinese Rhetorical Tradition in the Present: Re-presenting the Native's Point of View." *College English* 69 (2007): 216–37.

Tomasi, Massimiliano. *Rhetoric in Modern Japan: Western Influence on the Development of Narrative and Oratorical Style*. Honolulu: University of Hawai'i Press, 2004.

Wang, Bo. "A Survey of Research in Asian Rhetoric." *Rhetoric Review* 23 (2004): 171–81.

Wu, Hui. "The Feminist Rhetoric of Post-Mao Chinese Writers: A Perspective from the Rhetorical Situation." In *Alternative Rhetorics*, ed. Laura Gray-Rosendale and Sibylle Gruber, 219–34. Albany: State University of New York Press, 2001.

———. "Historical Studies of Rhetorical Women Here and There: Methodological Challenges to Dominant Interpretive Frameworks." *Rhetoric Society Quarterly* 32 (2002): 81–98.

Xiao, Xiaosui. "The 1923 Scientistic Campaign and Dao-Discourse: A Cross-Cultural Study of the Rhetoric of Science." *Quarterly Journal of Speech* 90 (2004): 469–94.

You, Xiaoye. "Conflation of Rhetorical Traditions: The Formation of Modern Chinese Writing Instruction." *Rhetoric Review* 24 (2005): 150–69.

Rhetoric and Religion
By Roxanne Mountford

Burke, Kenneth. *The Rhetoric of Religion: Studies in Logology.* Boston: Beacon, 1961.

Collier-Thomas, Bettye, ed. *Daughters of Thunder: Black Women Preachers and Their Sermons, 1850–1979.* San Francisco: Jossey-Bass, 1998.

Crowley, Sharon. *Toward a Civil Discourse: Rhetoric and Fundamentalism.* Pittsburgh: University of Pittsburgh Press, 2006.

Fish, Stanley. "One Nation, under God?" *Chronicle of Higher Education* 51 (2005): C1.

Fosdick, Harry Emerson. "What Is the Matter with Preaching?" In *Harry Emerson Fosdick's Art of Preaching: An Anthology,* ed. Lionel Crocker, 27–41. Springfield, IL: Charles C. Thomas, 1971.

Friedenberg, Robert V. *"Hear O Israel": The History of American Jewish Preaching, 1654–1970.* Tuscaloosa: University of Alabama Press, 1989.

Goodburn, Amy. "It's a Question of Faith: Discourses of Fundamentalism and Critical Pedagogy in the Writing Classroom." *JAC* 18 (1998): 333–52.

Griffith, R. Marie, and Barbara Dianne Savage, eds. *Women and Religion in the African Diaspora: Knowledge, Power, and Performance.* Baltimore: Johns Hopkins University Press, 2006.

Howard-Pitney, David. *The African American Jeremiad: Appeals for Justice in America.* 1990. Philadelphia: Temple University Press, 2005.

Jost, Walter, and Wendy Olmstead, eds. *Rhetorical Invention and Religious Inquiry: New Perspectives.* New Haven: Yale University Press, 2000. [See essays by Ong, Booth, Shuger, Jost, and Ricoeur.]

Katz, Stephen B. "The Epistemology of the Kabbalah: Toward a Jewish Philosophy of Rhetoric." *Rhetoric Society Quarterly* 25 (1995): 107–22.

Kennedy, George A. *New Testament Interpretation through Rhetorical Criticism.* Chapel Hill: University of North Carolina Press, 1984.

LaRue, Cleophus J. *The Heart of Black Preaching.* Louisville, KY: Westminster John Knox, 2000.

Lischer, Richard, ed. *Theories of Preaching: Selected Readings in the Homiletic Tradition.* Durham, NC: Labyrinth Press, 1987.

Lyotard, Jean-François. *The Differend: Phrases in Dispute.* Trans. Georges Van Den Abbeele. Minneapolis: University of Minnesota Press, 1988.

Mack, Burton L. *Rhetoric and the New Testament.* Minneapolis: Fortress, 1990.

Miller, Keith D. *Voices of Deliverance: The Language of Martin Luther King, Jr., and Its Sources.* New York: Free Press, 1992.

Mitchell, Henry H. *Black Preaching: The Recovery of a Powerful Art.* 1970. Reprint, Nashville: Abingdon, 1990.

Moore, MariJo, ed. *Eating Fire, Tasting Blood: Breaking the Great Silence of the American Indian Holocaust.* New York: Thunder's Mouth, 2006.

Mountford, Roxanne. *The Gendered Pulpit: Preaching in American Protestant Spaces.* Carbondale: Southern Illinois University Press, 2005.

Rosenberg, Bruce A. *The Art of the American Folk Preacher.* New York: Paulist Press, 1968.

Schüssler Fiorenza, Elizabeth. *Rhetoric and Ethic: The Politics of Biblical Interpretation.* Minneapolis: Fortress, 1999.

Warner, Michael. *American Sermons: The Pilgrims to Martin Luther King, Jr.* New York: Library of America, 1999.

White, James Boyd, ed. *How Should We Talk about Religion? Perspectives, Contexts, Particularities.* Notre Dame: University of Notre Dame Press, 2006.

Rhetoric, Technology, and Technical Writing
By Rebecca Rickly

Rhetoric and Technology

Bolter, Jay David. *Writing Space: Computers, Hypertext, and the Remediation of Print.* 2nd ed. Mahwah, NJ: Erlbaum, 2001.

Feenberg, Andrew. *Questioning Technology.* New York: Routledge, 1999.

Haraway, Donna J. *Simians, Cyborgs, and Women: The Reinvention of Nature.* New York: Routledge, 1991.

Lay, Mary M., Laura J. Gurak, Clare Gravon, and Cynthia Myntti. *Body Talk: Rhetoric, Technology, Reproduction.* Madison: University of Wisconsin Press, 2000.

Negroponte, Nicholas. *Being Digital.* New York: Vintage, 2000.

Scharff, Robert, and Val Dusek, eds. *Philosophy of Technology: The Technological Condition: An Anthology.* Malden, MA: Blackwell Publishers, 2003.

Selber, Stuart A. *Multiliteracies for a Digital Age.* Carbondale: Southern Illinois University Press, 2004.

Selfe, Cynthia. *Technology and Literacy in the 21st Century: The Importance of Paying Attention.* Carbondale: Southern Illinois University Press, 1999.

Sidler, Michelle, Richard Morris, and Elizabeth Overman Smith. *Computers in the Composition Classroom: A Critical Sourcebook.* Boston: Bedford/St. Martin's, 2007.

Sullivan, Patricia, and James E. Porter. *Opening Spaces: Writing Technologies and Critical Research Practices.* Greenwich, CT: Ablex, 1997.

Welch, Kathleen E. *Electric Rhetoric: Classical Rhetoric, Oralism, and a New Literacy.* Cambridge: Massachusetts Institute of Technology Press, 1999.

Rhetoric and Technical Writing

Bazerman, Charles. *Shaping Written Knowledge: The Genre and Activity of the Experimental Article in Science.* Madison: University of Wisconsin Press, 1988.

Cross, Geoffrey. *Forming the Collective Mind: A Contextual Exploration of Large-Scale Group Writing.* Cresskill, NJ: Hampton Press, 2001.

Gurak, Laura, and Mary Lay, eds. *Research in Technical Communication.* Westport, CT: Praeger Press, 2002.

Johnson, Robert R. *User-Centered Technology: A Rhetorical Theory for Computers and Other Mundane Artifacts.* Albany: State University of New York Press, 1998.

Johnson-Eilola, Johndan, and Stuart A. Selber. *Central Works in Technical Communication.* New York: Oxford University Press, 2004.

Kynell, Teresa C., and Michael G. Moran, eds. *Three Keys to the Past: The History of Technical Communication.* Stamford, CT: Ablex, 1999.

Longo, Bernadette. *Spurious Coin: A History of Science, Management, and Technical Writing.* Albany: State University of New York Press, 2000.

Peeples, Tim. *Professional Writing and Rhetoric: Readings from the Field.* New York: Longman, 2002.

Schriver, Karen A. *Dynamics in Document Design.* New York: John Wiley and Sons, 1997.

Selber, Stuart, ed. *Computers and Technical Communication: Pedagogical and Programmatic Perspectives.* Westport, CT: Greenwood Press, 1997.

Spinuzzi, Clay. *Tracing Genres through Organizations: A Sociocultural Approach to Information Design.* Cambridge: Massachusetts Institute of Technology Press, 2003.

Staples, Katherine, and Cezar Ornatowski, eds. *Foundations for Teaching Technical Communication: Theory, Practice, and Program Design.* Greenwich, CT: Ablex, 1998.

Visual Rhetoric
By Marguerite Helmers

Arnheim, Rudolf. *Visual Thinking.* 1969. Reprint, Berkeley: University of California Press, 2004.

Barthes, Roland. "The Rhetoric of the Image." In *Image, Music, Text,* trans. Stephen Heath, 32–51. New York: Hill and Wang, 1977. Reprinted in *Visual Rhetoric in a Digital World: A Critical Sourcebook,* ed. Carolyn Handa,152–163. Boston: Bedford, 2004.

Berger, John. *Ways of Seeing.* 1972. Reprint, New York: Penguin, 1990.

Blair, J. Anthony. "The Possibility and Actuality of Visual Arguments." *Argumentation and Advocacy* 33 (Summer 1996): 23–39.

Blakesley, David. *The Terministic Screen: Rhetorical Perspectives on Film.* Carbondale: Southern Illinois University Press, 2003.

Elkins, James. *Visual Studies: A Skeptical Introduction.* New York: Routledge, 2003.

Faigley, Lester. "Material Literacy and Visual Design." In *Rhetorical Bodies,* ed. Jack Selzer and Sharon Crowley, 171–201. Madison: University of Wisconsin Press, 1999.

Fleming, David. "Can Pictures Be Arguments?" *Argumentation and Advocacy* 33 (Summer 1996): 11–22.

Foss, Sonja K. "A Rhetorical Schema for the Evaluation of Visual Imagery." *Communication Studies* 45 (1994): 213–24.

Fox, Roy F. *Images in Language, Media, and Mind.* Urbana, Il.: National Council of Teachers of English, 1994.

Handa, Carolyn. *Visual Rhetoric in a Digital World: A Critical Sourcebook.* Boston: Bedford, 2004.

Hariman, Robert, and John Louis Lucaites. *No Caption Needed: Iconic Photographs, Public Culture, and Liberal Democracy.* Chicago: University of Chicago Press, 2007.

Heywood, Ian, and Barry Sandywell, eds. *Interpreting Visual Culture: Explorations in the Hermeneutics of the Vision.* New York: Routledge, 1998.

Hill, Charles, and Marguerite Helmers. *Defining Visual Rhetorics.* Mahwah, NJ: Erlbaum, 2004.

Kress, Gunther, and Theo Van Leeuwen. *Reading Images: The Grammar of Visual Design.* London: Routledge, 1996.

Kostelnick, Charles. *Shaping Information: The Rhetoric of Visual Conventions.* Carbondale: Southern Illinois University Press, 2003.

McCloud, Scott. *Understanding Comics: The Invisible Art.* 1993. Reprint, New York: Harper, 1994.

Mitchell, W. J. T. *Iconology: Image, Text, Ideology.* Chicago: University of Chicago Press, 1986.

Prelli, Lawrence J. *Rhetorics of Display.* Columbia: University of South Carolina Press, 2006.

Sontag, Susan. *On Photography.* 1977. Reprint, New York: Picador, 2001.

Rhetoric and Program Administration

By Duane Roen

Bazerman, Charles, Joseph Little, Lisa Bethel, Teri Chavkin, Danielle Fouquette, and Janet Garufis, eds. *Reference Guide to Writing across the Curriculum.* West Lafayette, IN: Parlor Press, 2005.

Bloom, Lynn Z., Donald A. Daiker, and Edward M. White, eds. *Composition in the Twenty-First Century: Crisis and Change.* Carbondale: Southern Illinois University Press, 1996.

Bousquet, Marc, Tony Scott, and Leo Parascondola, eds. *Writing Instruction in the Managed University: Tenured Bosses and Disposable Teachers.* Carbondale: Southern Illinois University Press, 2004.

Brown, Stuart C., and Theresa Enos, eds. *The Writing Program Administrator's Resource: A Guide to Reflective Institutional Practice.* Mahwah, NJ: Lawrence Erlbaum, 2002.

Carter, Locke, ed. *Market Matters: Applied Rhetoric Studies and Free Market Competition.* Cresskill, NJ: Hampton Press, 2005.

Gebhardt, Richard C., and Barbara Gebhardt, eds. *Scholarship, Promotion, and Tenure in Composition Studies.* Hillsdale, NJ: Lawrence Erlbaum, 1996.

George, Diana, ed. *Kitchen Cooks, Plate Twirlers, and Troubadours: Writing Program Administrators Tell Their Stories.* Portsmouth, NH: Boynton/Cook, 1999.

Harrington, Susanmarie, Keith Rhodes, Ruth Fischer, and Rita Malenczyk, eds. *The Outcomes Book: Debate and Consensus after the WPA Outcomes Statement.* Logan: Utah State University Press, 2005.

L'Eplattenier, Barbara, and Lisa Mastrangelo, eds. *Historical Studies of Writing Program Administration: Individuals, Communities, and the Formation of a Discipline.* West Lafayette, IN: Parlor Press, 2004.

McGee, Sharon James, and Carolyn Handa, eds. *Discord and Direction: The Postmodern Writing Program Administrator.* Logan: Utah State University Press, 2005.

McLeod, Susan H. *Writing Program Administration.* West Lafayette, IN: Parlor Press, 2007.

Murphy, Christina, and Byron L. Stay, eds. *The Writing Center Director's Resource Book.* Mahwah, NJ: Lawrence Erlbaum, 2006.

O'Neill, Peggy, Angela Crow, and Larry W. Burton, eds. *A Field of Dreams: Independent Writing Programs and the Future of Composition Studies.* Logan: Utah State University Press, 2002.

Pemberton, Michael A., and Joyce Kinkead, eds. *The Center Will Hold: Critical Perspectives in Writing Center Scholarship.* Logan: Utah State University Press, 2003.

Roen, Duane, Theresa Enos, and Stuart Brown, eds. *Composing Our Lives in Rhetoric and Composition: Stories about the Growth of a Discipline.* Mahwah, NJ: Lawrence Erlbaum, 1999.

Rose, Shirley, and Irwin Weiser, eds. *The Writing Program Administrator as Researcher: Inquiry in Action and Reflection.* Portsmouth, NH: Boynton/Cook-Heinemann, 1999.

——. *The Writing Program Administrator as Theorist.* Portsmouth, NH: Heinemann, 2002.

Russell, David. *Writing in the Academic Disciplines: A Curricular History.* 2nd ed. Carbondale: Southern Illinois University Press, 2002.

Shamoon, Linda K., Rebecca Moore Howard, Sandra Jamieson, and Robert A. Schwegler, eds. *Coming of Age: The Advanced Writing Curriculum.* Portsmouth, NH: Heinemann Boynton/Cook, 2000.

Stock, Patricia Lambert, and Eileen E. Schell, eds. *Moving a Mountain: Transforming the Role of Contingent Faculty in Composition Studies and Higher Education.* Urbana, IL: National Council of Teachers of English, 2000.

Ward, Irene, and William J. Carpenter, eds. *The Allyn and Bacon Sourcebook for Writing Program Administrators.* New York: Longman, 2002.

White, Edward M. *Developing Successful College Writing Programs.* Portland, ME: Calendar Island Publishers, 1998.

Writing Program Administration: Journal of the Council of Writing Program Administrators.

Yancey, Kathleen Blake, ed. *Delivering College Composition: The Fifth Canon.* Portsmouth, NH: Boynton/Cook, 2006.

Rhetoric and the Teaching of Composition
By Kate Ronald and Hephzibah Roskelly

Berlin, James. *Rhetorics, Poetics, and Cultures: Refiguring College English Studies.* West Lafayette, IN: Parlor Press, 1993.

Berthoff, Ann E. *The Sense of Learning.* Portsmouth, NH: Boynton/Cook, 1990.

Britton, James. "Spectator Role and the Beginnings of Writing." In *What Writers Know: The Language, Process, and Structure of Written Discourse,* ed. Martin Nystrand, 149–69. New York: Academic Press, 1982.

Christensen, Francis. *Notes toward a New Rhetoric: Six Essays for Teachers.* New York: Harper and Row, 1967.

Corbett, Edward P. J., and Robert Connors. *Classical Rhetoric for the Modern Student.* 4th ed. New York: Oxford University Press, 1999.

Covino, William. "Rhetorical Pedagogy." In *A Guide to Composition Pedagogies,* ed. Gary Tate, Amy Rupiper, and Kurt Schick, 36–53. New York: Oxford University Press, 2001.

Crowley, Sharon. *Composition in the University: Historical and Polemical Essays.* Pittsburgh: University of Pittsburgh Press,1998.

Ede, Lisa. *Situating Composition: Composition Studies and the Politics of Location.* Carbondale: Southern Illinois University Press, 2004.

Emig, Janet. *The Web of Meaning.* Portsmouth, NH: Boynton/Cook, 1983.

Flower, Linda, et al. "Detection, Diagnosis and the Strategies of Revision." *College Composition and Communication* 37 (1986): 16–55.

Freire, Paulo. *Letters to Cristina: Reflections on My Life and Work.* New York: Routledge, 1996.

Hairston, Maxine. "Diversity, Ideology, and Teaching Writing." *College Composition and Communication* 43 (1992): 179–95.

Harris, Joseph. *A Teaching Subject: Composition since 1966.* Upper Saddle River, NJ: Prentice Hall, 1996.

hooks, bell. *Teaching to Transgress: Education as the Practice of Freedom.* New York: Routledge, 1994.

LeFevre, Karen Burke. *Invention as a Social Act.* Carbondale: Southern Illinois University Press, 1986.

Murphy, James J., ed. *A Short History of Writing Instruction: From Ancient Greece to Modern America.* 2nd ed. Mahwah, NY: Lawrence Erlbaum, 2001.

Murray, Donald. "Teach Writing as a Process Not Product." 1972. Reprinted in *Cross-Talk in Comp Theory: A Reader,* ed. Victor Villanueva, 3–6. Urbana, IL: NCTE, 2003.

Reynolds, Nedra. *Geographies of Writing: Inhabiting Places and Encountering Difference.* Carbondale: Southern Illinois University Press, 2007.

Ronald, Kate, and Joy Ritchie, eds. *Teaching Rhetorica: Theory/Practice/Pedagogy.* New York: Heinemann, 2006.

Roskelly, Hephzibah, and Kate Ronald. *Reason to Believe: Romanticism, Pragmatism, and the Teaching of Writing.* State University of New York Press, 1998.

Russell, David. *Writing in the Academic Disciplines, 1870–1990: A Curricular History.* Carbondale: Southern Illinois University Press, 1991.

Welch, Kathleen. *The Contemporary Reception of Classical Rhetoric: Appropriations of Ancient Discourse.* Hillsdale, NJ: Lawrence Erlbaum, 1990.

Worsham, Lynn. "Writing against Writing: The Predicament of *Ecriture Féminine* in Composition Studies." In *Contending with Words: Composition and Rhetoric in a Postmodern Age,* ed. Patricia Harkin and John Schilb, 82–104. New York: Modern Language Association, 1991.

Yancey, Kathleen Blake, ed. *Delivering College Composition: The Fifth Canon.* Portsmouth, NH: Boynton/Cook, 2006.

Contributors

Don Paul Abbott is Professor of English at the University of California, Davis. He has written widely on the history of rhetoric and rhetoric in the Renaissance, including *Rhetoric in the New World: Rhetorical Theory and Practice in Colonial Spanish America* (1996). His most recent publications include "Splendor and Misery: Semiotics and the End of Rhetoric," in *Rhetorica* (2006), and "Kant, Theremin, and the Morality of Rhetoric," in *Philosophy and Rhetoric* (2007).

Lois Agnew is Associate Professor of Writing and Rhetoric at Syracuse University. She has published articles in journals including *Rhetorica, Rhetoric Society Quarterly*, and *Rhetoric Review* and has recently completed a manuscript that traces the influence of Stoic philosophy on eighteenth-century British rhetorical theories.

Linda Ferreira-Buckley is Chair of the Department of Rhetoric and Writing at the University of Texas at Austin. She is the coeditor of *Hugh Blair's Lectures on Rhetoric and Belles Lettres* and has published essays in many books and journals on eighteenth- and nineteenth-century rhetoric, historiography, and the history of English studies.

Lynée Lewis Gaillet is Associate Professor of English at Georgia State University, where she teaches undergraduate and graduate courses in writing theory and practice, history of rhetoric, and academic publishing. She has served as the Executive Director of the South Atlantic Modern Language Association and President of the Coalition of Women Scholars in the History of Rhetoric and Composition. She is the editor of *Scottish Rhetoric and Its Influences* (1998) and coeditor of *Stories of Mentoring: Theory and Praxis* (2009). She is author of numerous articles and book chapters addressing contemporary composition instruction and the history of rhetoric/writing practices.

Winifred Bryan Horner is University of Missouri Professor of English Emerita and Texas Christian University Radford Chair of Rhetoric Emerita. She has published twelve books on rhetoric and composition and has lectured widely both nationally and internationally. Her many students are well-known active scholars in the fields of Rhetoric and Composition.

Krista Ratcliffe is currently Professor and Chair of English at Marquette University in Milwaukee, Wisconsin, where she has served as Director of the First-Year Writing Program, which under her direction won a 2006 CCCC Certificate of Excellence Award for its emphasis on rhetoric, literacy, and diversity. She has served as President of NCTE's College Forum, and as President of CCCC's Coalition of Women Scholars in the History of Rhetoric and Composition. She teaches undergraduate and graduate courses in rhetoric and composition theory, writing, and women's literature for which she won a university teaching award. Her research focuses on the intersections of rhetoric and feminist theory. Her publications include *Anglo-American Feminist Challenges to the Rhetorical Tradition* (1996), *Who's Having This Baby?* (with Helen Sterk, Carla Hay, Alice Kehoe, and Leona VandeVusse) (2002), and *Rhetorical Listening: Identification, Gender, Whiteness* (2005—winner of the 2006 *JAC* Gary Olson Award and a 2007 CCCC Outstanding Book Award); her work has appeared in edited collections, as well as in *CCC, JAC, Rhetoric Review,* and *College English.*

Denise Stodola is Assistant Professor of Communication at Kettering University in Michigan. Her degree includes two areas of specialization—medieval literature and rhetoric/composition—and she has given presentations at various international conferences, including the Association Internationale de Linguistique Appliquée, the International Medieval Congress, and the New Chaucer Society. Teaching courses primarily in communication, she extends her research beyond that focus, venturing into medieval rhetoric and literature as well as modern-day rhetorical and stylistic analysis.

Author Index

Rhetor Index

Thematic Index

This index is designed to facilitate interdisciplinary or specialized study and scholarly research across the traditional historical periods. The themes are not mutually exclusive and unlike a subject index, this thematic guide references discussions about major topics rather than providing page references for specific terms. For titles and listings of secondary sources, see the bibliographical entries at the end of each chapter. A list of historical rhetors follows the author index.